VICIMUS

REGINALD BALIOL BRETT
ETON, 1868.

JOURNALS AND LETTERS

OF

Reginald
Viscount Esher

—◆—

EDITED BY

Maurice V. Brett

—◆—

"LOYAL JE SERAI"

VOL. 1
1870-1903

IVOR NICHOLSON & WATSON
LIMITED · · · LONDON
MCMXXXIV

FIRST EDITION . . *September* 1934
REPRINTED . . . *December* 1934

Printed in Great Britain by
Hazell, Watson & Viney, Ltd., London and Aylesbury.

I DEDICATE THIS BOOK

TO THE DEAR MEMORY OF

REGINALD, VISCOUNT ESHER,

AND TO

ELEANOR ESHER,

WHOSE LOVE AND THOUGHTS WERE WOVEN TOGETHER

DURING A CONSTANT COMPANIONSHIP

OF FIFTY YEARS

Ruskin, discoursing on the Stones of Venice, remarked that restored history is of little more value than restored painting or architecture, and that the only history worth reading was written at the time of which it treats. He excepted such volumes of biography as contained letters, memoranda, and journals which had escaped destruction, declaring them to be unrestored portions of the fabric of a man's life, indispensable to the psychologist and the student. . . .

Cloud-cap't Towers.

1852.   Born June 30th.

1863–65.   Cheam School.

1865–70.   Eton College.

1870–77.   Cambridge University.

1878–85.   Private Secretary to Lord Hartington.

1879.   Married Eleanor, daughter of M. Van de Weyer.

1880–85.   M.P. for Penryn and Falmouth.

1886.   Offered Editorship of *Daily News*.   (Refused.)

1891.   Offered Editorship of *New Review*.   (Refused.)

1895–1902.   Secretary to H.M. Office of Works.

1897.   C.B.

1898.   Asked to write Life of Disraeli.   (Refused.)

1899.   Offered Under-Secretaryship for the Colonies. (Refused.)

1900.   Offered Under-Secretaryship for War. (Refused.)
Offered Governorship of Cape Colony. (Refused.)
K.C.V.O.

1901.   Hon. Secretary to Committee for Queen Victoria's Memorial.
Lieutenant and Deputy-Governor of Windsor Castle.

1902.   K.C.B.
Member of Royal Commission on South African War.

1903.   Director of the Opera.
Co-Editor of *Queen Victoria's Letters*.
Offered Secretaryship of State for War. (Refused.)
Commissioner of the Exhibition of 1851.

1904.   Chairman of War Office Reconstitution Committee.

1905.   G.C.V.O.
Commander of the Legion of Honour.

1905.   Permanent Member of the Committee of Imperial
        Defence.
        Offered G.C.B.   (Refused.)
1906.   Royal Trustee to the British Museum.
        Chairman of Committee to organise Territorial Army.
1907.   Governor of the Imperial College of Science.
        Trustee of the Wallace Collection.
1908.   Offered Viceroyship of India.   (Refused.)
        G.C.B.
1909.   Chairman of the County of London Territorial Force
        Association.
1910.   Chairman of Board of Management of Exhibition of
        1851.
1911.   Trustee of London Museum.
1912.   President of the County of London Territorial
        Force Association.
        Chairman of Executive Committee of the British
        School at Rome.
1914.   LL.D. Cambridge.
1919.   D.L. St. Andrews.
        Chairman of Committee on Organisation of Indian
        Army.
1922.   Privy Councillor.
1928.   Governor of Windsor Castle.
1930.   Died January 22nd.

N.B.—He was also offered and refused an Earldom, but as
the date is uncertain it has been omitted.

LIST OF ILLUSTRATIONS

FOREWORD

NOTES ON THE YEARS 1852–1870

DESCENDED from William Brett of Brett's Hall in the county of Warwick (Henry III) and, on the female side through the Scotts of Scott's Hall, from the Baliols of Scotland, Reginald Baliol Brett, the eldest son of William Baliol Brett (Master of the Rolls and 1st Viscount Esher) and Eugenie, daughter of Louis Meyer, was born in London on June 30th, 1852.

The early years of his life were spent between London and Paris, and in his book, *Cloud-cap't Towers*, he writes:

"As a child, in a poplin frock, I had been seated on the lap of a little wizened old man who had once played the violin before Marie Antoinette. Later, in my great-aunt's house in Paris, I had been presented to a stout, dark-skinned man with masses of grizzled hair, an enormous hat held curiously between his knees. It was Alexandre Dumas. And again later, I had been treated with sympathetic kindness by a dignified, charming gentleman, perfectly dressed in what seemed to me the fashion of a pre-historic age. It was Lord Lansdowne's grandfather, the Comte de Flahault, who, as Napoleon's aide-de-camp, had accompanied the Emperor home from Moscow, and ridden that tragic ride alongside of his master away from the field of Waterloo."

From his childhood he was particularly fond of the study of history. In a précis of his early journals, written in 1877, he states:

"I had always been fond of this particular study. My favourite book as a very small boy was Southey's *Nelson*. I remember sleeping with the little brown volume under my pillow for many a night. Before I was twelve years old I had read Hume's *History of England*, getting through all the volumes; and every one of the Waverley novels with the exception of *Redgauntlet* which I never could persevere with in those days. On my tenth birthday I was given a Shakespeare and we used to act *Henry IV* in the nursery. But four years before that my father had given me a Goldsmith, and I read the 'Deserted Village' before I was seven years old."

In 1863 he went to a private school at Cheam, where he was ". . . loaded with easily won prizes for French, German and mathematics, having been well trained in these branches of learning," and in 1865 to Eton, where he boarded at Evans's. His tutor was Arthur Ainger, ". . . a true and good friend," but he very soon fell under the influence of that great Etonian and lover of youth William Johnson,[1] which soon developed into a lifelong friendship. Concerning him W. J. wrote in his journal:

"I have a new friend who plays tunes on my piano, with taste and nimbleness, learning my favourite bits for me; he is remarkably graceful and kindly, and I begin to see now shelling off conceit or egotism, thinking wisely about his friends."

By 1868 he was going regularly to W. J.'s two rooms (called the Trap and the Cabin) and writes: "Whatever I know, worth knowing; whatever I am worth being; whatever I am without which is unworthy; was learnt in those rooms." In that year, too, he got into the *Britannia*, although he did not really like rowing, and also was given his house-colours for football, which was a great joy to him, as ". . . that game is the only one to which I have always felt attached, and one of the saddest moments was the day when I ceased to take the same keen pleasure in it." But his happiest hours were spent with his

[1] William Johnson, the author of *Ionica*, changed his name to Cory, and was known among his friends as W. J.

friends in W. J.'s rooms or idling on the river or in the playing-fields. Under the date of June 26th, 1868, he writes:

"A day worth remembering. 'After twelve' Frank Thornhill and I went, specially invited, to the Trap. There we found three young men, Scott Holland,[1] Stephen Freemantle, and Frederick Wood,[2] better known as 'Mouse.' Chat [Williamson] had some time before wounded his foot while bathing. During several weeks he was lame, unable to move, and most of my spare time was spent in his room. On this day, Mouse and I carried him in a silk quilt from Vidal's to the Trap; and there we sang and played until dinner time. Frank and I later on, were commissioned to take a boat from the Brocas, down stream to the playing-fields. We picked up My Tutor and Mrs. Cornish (my excellent good friend Richmond Ritchie's sister). The others had gone on. My Tutor and I rowed, while Frank sat against Mrs. Cornish on the floor of the boat, with his head on her lap, while she decked his hat with vine leaves. At Ankerwick we met the other boat, and moored ours alongside it. I shifted my place, on request, to help the singing. And then we sang, Chat leading, with his sweet young voice, such glees as 'When first I saw your face,' 'See our oars with feathered spray,' and 'Blow, blow, thou winter wind.'"

A month previously, on the 28th of May, he had been up to London and ". . . in the afternoon went down to the House of Commons and for the first time heard Mr. Bright speak."

In the holidays William Johnson wrote continuously criticising, approving, or advising. "W. J. warned me against displaying myself as a linguist. Accomplished people, he said, are almost always shallow; and I ought to conquer some great difficulty like Greek or Trigonometry." And again, "Your life," he wrote, "is more like what the books tell us of a Provençal troubadour than anything I have seen; sweet and pretty as it is, I doubt whether there is enough back-bone to it. Try for concen-

[1] Afterwards Canon of St. Paul's.   [2] Younger son of Lord Halifax.

tration; see what W. Scott says at the beginning of *The Talisman* about splitting the diamond; it is but a metaphor, but it serves to remind one of the general true doctrine that multiplicity of sympathies, tastes, accomplishments and engagements is not very favourable to the making of *character*."

In the summer holidays ". . . I got my first lesson in politics. I was taken to Holland House and introduced to that Acropolis, that sacred shrine of Whiggery. Lady Holland, I remember, looked then a little quiet grey woman, dressed in an Indian shawl. I was most struck by Mrs. Norton who spoke to me for some time. I can remember nothing but one observation, which perhaps was not original; she said, and I recorded it in my journal, that poetical natures were never happy unless they were perfectly miserable. . . .

"I was taught at that time, and hold to it still, that there has been generally or universally a very great improvement in the *character* of our public men. I was taught at that time, and believe it still, that more than to any one man this improvement is owing to Mr. Pitt, who trained men to be honest, laborious, patriotic administrators. And I have endeavoured to forebear from railing at Ministers.

"W. J. used to warn us in politics, as well as in literature, and in the other ranges of human intercourse, 'to strive to be musical in the heart far below the reach of taste.' "

Every autumn he went to Lowther. In his journal he wrote:

"Early in the month of August we went, the whole family of us, to Lowther Castle, seat of the Earl of Lonsdale, the Lord Eskdale of Coningsby. It was a yearly visit paid with great regularity by me from the year of my birth to the death of the old lord in 1872. Lowther was a home to us. It was there that I learnt to ride and shoot. The society was not of a high degree of merit, but I have no doubt that occasionally I got the benefit of clever talk. Certainly our host's experiences were of a varied kind. Anyhow, it was there on several occasions I met Lord Brougham; at that time a wreck, but very grand in decay.

Other children were occasionally asked to keep us company.
We were all provided with ponies, and were constantly gallop-
ing over the park, and the distant fells."

And in *Cloud-cap't Towers* he writes:

". . . The Colonel's eldest son, Henry, afterwards fourth
Earl of Lonsdale, was the beau-ideal of us all. Every year we
awaited his arrival with eagerness. He was not young in years.
His sons were of much the same age as their cousin James
Lowther, now Lord Ullswater. But no one was in reality
younger than this florid M.F.H., this fine horseman with
'hands' of gossamer, who taught us to jump over a bar in the
riding school without stirrups on a 7-lb. saddle; who on autumn
afternoons would creep with us through fences, ford streams up
to our ponies' girths, and skylark back with us through the park
as the sun began to set over the hills above Patterdale. Or, on
Shap Fells, where in the primitive muzzle-loading fashion of
that ingenuous time his favourite companion—as I flattered
myself I was—would carry for him his powder flask as an
acolyte carries a censer. . . ."

In his *Journals* he continues:

"From Lowther I accompanied my relatives into Scotland. I
saw Edinburgh for the first time, and from a letter from W. J.
in answer to one of mine, apparently with great admiration.
We coasted along the west from Glasgow to Oban, where we
separated; my relatives going to stay with Sir Thomas Riddell,
and I continuing my journey to Inverness.

"I had been invited by a school friend, Murray Finch-Hatton,
to stay with him at Geddes House, near the little northern town
of Nairn. From him and from his brother Henry, who loved
me well at that time, I had received pressing letters and I was
allowed to leave my relatives, not without some heart-burning.

"Lady Winchilsea, their mother, I looked upon as the kindest
and most true hearted of women. Whether this were true or
not, she was brimful of sympathy, and of real affection and love

of youth. 'Go out for walks with your hostess,' wrote W. J. to me, 'and talk to her thoughtfully but freely; she will trim the luxuriance of your foliage and make garlands of the snippings just the same. She is like me, a true lover of beauty and youth, and thinks the sentimental part of life as real as the jolting in the ruts of business.'

"I spent some very happy days at Geddes. To W. J. my hostess wrote thus of my visit. 'So much mutual love and admiration, so much youth and beauty and music with so little that was otherwise than beautiful and sweet is rarely seen. To me it was a continual feast. I walked with the children in the lovely woods of pine, climbing mossy steeps covered with ferns and heather, and each looked more beautiful than the other. Henry had his gun, and Murray and Reginald hunted the dogs and found and carried his game. You should have seen them gathered round a poor fluttering pigeon and then sitting with the dogs on their knees and their arms linked round and round each other, with Evelyn in happy admiration, and the soft wind made the gentlest of rushing sounds in the pine-heads above.'

". . . I was glad to return to Eton in September. . . . Lady Winchilsea occasionally wrote to me, tender poetical letters asking for accounts of my friends and of the glorious autumn sunsets. To please her I used to go into Poet's walk and watch the red gables of College grow redder in the sunlight, and the river catching the colour as it rolled under the walls, die again into yellow and greys as it floated away past the elms of the playing-fields to the meadows beyond. Sometimes I was alone, sometimes accompanied by Arthur Lyttelton.[1]

"The autumn—of a general election and a resignation of Mr. Disraeli's government—made my father a Judge. He gave up his seat of Helstone and the Solicitor-Generalship, not seeing an opening for many years of a return to office. My Eton life was varied by the appearance at My Dame's of my young brother [2] . . . ."

[1] Afterwards Bishop of Southampton.   [2] Eugene Brett.

On October 5th "the new regulations came into force (Balston had been succeeded as H.M. by J. J. Hornby) and we were to have a morning chapel for the first time. The gas escaped and made chapel so unbearable that there was a general spontaneous move made to the open air"; on the 18th "a tiring game after 12 yesterday, though I got three rouges. My tutor, W. J. and I went for a walk in Windsor Park roaming through fern. This morning we had a long funeral oration from Wilder, who lauded old Carter for having turned a sonnet of Keats into elegiacs at 93. What would he say to Auber who is finishing an opera at 86 or Rossini who composes freely at 90?"; and on the 28th "a holiday. Chat [Williamson] brought a little lad called Freeland to breakfast, a contralto singer, and we had 'Greeting.' After chapel some of us rushed off to change, put on 4th of June shirts, ties, straw hats; then assembled at my tutor's. W. J. Tutor, Marindin, Dick Jones, John Savile Lumley, Herbert Griffiths, Willink, Alfred Lyttelton, Elliott[1] and Chat [Williamson] and Sidney Herbert.[2] We drove to Burnham Beeches singing 'When first I saw,' 'See our oars,' 'O who will o'er the downs,' 'Hardy Norsemen,' etc. I sat between Sid and Elliott, opposite Chat. Sid, Elliott, Chat and I roamed about among the fern and trees; glorious in autumn colours. Then we ran races, I carrying Chat on my shoulders against Elliott carrying Alfred. Presently we started again on our drive. Stopped outside Dropmore. Walked through the park under the cedars; and talked to the gardener about Bevil Fortescue. We drove on to Skindle's and dined. Afterwards we walked up to the weir, running races, and jumping stiles. Returning, Chat got into the box seat with me, and drove our speedy pair of grey horses, making me put my arm round him to keep him warm, and hold him on. When it got dark he went into the carriage to the rugs, leaving me to drive. At the Trap we found tea ready, and Chat sat with me on the green chair eating out of one plate, Elliott's honey brought from Hymettus. Then I played and Chat sang 'Colinette.'

[1] Afterwards Sir Francis Elliott, Minister at Athens.
[2] Afterwards Lord Pembroke.

The others played cards; W. J. playing piquet with Lumley, Tutor and Marindin went away to pupil room and at 8 I had to go to a 'private,' leaving the others playing a round game. After Greek history I returned to the Cabin. . . ."

Again on November 21st "W. J. gave a memorable concert in the mathematical school. Dannreuther, Blagrove and Booth played three trios, with incidental songs by amateurs for padding. I do not remember before this to have heard any good chamber music. On this occasion I heard the three greatest works of the kind ever written; Beethoven's trio in B flat, Schubert's in the same key, and Mendelssohn's trio in C minor."

Not long after, the last theatrical performance but one ever given at Eton took place, and in December "an Eton master preached for the first time in chapel; a wise innovation. E. Warre [1] gave us what I called in my journal 'a fine impetuous sermon'; telling the story of a man's fall; and I have added 'the world moralizes but does not change.' . . ."

In the early days of 1869 "for what immediate reason I forget —I passed through a phase of religious speculation. After much of the ordinary class of doubt, I find the following result: 'I cannot understand the doctrines we have flung at us on Sundays, and I am not sure that I wish to. I am content with the certainty that for happiness, it is sufficient to try to be kindly and humble and affectionate. The difficulty is to concentrate one's mind on attaining these things.' I cannot recollect that even by fits and starts I was influenced by religion; and about this time, owing to the influence of my friend Julian Sturgis, and with a view to remaining with Francis Elliott, I expressed a wish to go to Balliol College, Oxford. I rejoice to think that my wishes were not strong enough to overcome the opposition of my tutor, and the plan of my going to Trinity was adhered to." [2]

[1] Afterwards Head Master.
[2] His friend Julian Sturgis writes on December 29th:

DEAR REGGY,

I was much amused by your account of Cambridge, and by no means surprised that they spoilt you there as much as it is your lot to be spoilt every-

In the holidays he went to Hazels, "near Knowsley in Lancashire, a place belonging to an old-fashioned Whig, Sir Thomas Birch. I remember being struck by the old-fashioned house, with all the discomforts of the last century still about it, and the curious pews in the neighbouring church, out of which it is impossible to see, owing to the height of the wooden partitions. We had a large fireplace in our pew, and through the sermon Sir Thomas stoked the fire and snored loudly by turns."

In the summer he was promoted from the *Britannia* into the *Victory*, but by this time "I must say that I hated the hard rowing, and I avoided it as much as possible. Still I enjoyed many long hours on the river in the twilight with a good crew, or in a 'pair' with Elliott. He and I trained severely together, and started for the 'pulling.' We did pretty well but we were not strong enough to cope with the older and more powerful lads who in addition were more energetic than we were."

At Easter in 1870 he went to Paris, and in *Ionicus* he states:

"The Easter holidays of 1870 I spent in Paris with my French relatives, living in the rue Daru at the top of the Faubourg St. Honoré, opposite the Russian church. William Johnson was amused and interested by my crude letters. I returned to Eton full of rumours of war, which everyone in Paris—in spite of Lord Granville's optimistic blindness—believed to be imminent and inevitable. I had been taken to the last ball ever given by the Emperor at the Tuileries, and was introduced to Mme. de Pourtalés, then one of the reigning beauties among the friends of the Empress. It was a curious interlude in the life of an Eton boy.

"That summer, in the middle of the war,[1] so full of anxieties to my people, I left Eton.

where. You know that you are one of fortune's favourites, who gains a great deal of affection at the expense of going about with a pleasant smile and an engaging manner, receiving a great deal as your right, and giving very little. I suppose the organists and principals of Cambridge have quite persuaded you to go to that University. . . .

[1] The Franco-Prussian War.

"We spent the autumn as usual at Lowther Castle, and in October I went up to Trinity."

After going up to Trinity College, Cambridge, he spent his vacations either on circuit with his father, staying with Eton or Cambridge friends, or more usually at Halsdon, the house of his old friend, William Johnson, and his daily Journal begins.

Francis   Mr.   Lord   Violet Brett. Eugene Brett.   Sir William Lady Brett.
Lowther. Robinson. Malmesbury.   Reginald Brett.   Brett.
William,
3rd Lord Lonsdale.

FISHING AT ULLSWATER.

From a painting by Jacob Thompson, 1868.

xx]

JOURNALS AND LETTERS

[*To Lady Brett.*] TRINITY COLLEGE, CAMBRIDGE,
FEBRUARY 6TH, 1871.

'Tis not so easy, dear Mama, to write when one's head posi- *Cambridge.*
tively is swimming with the eternal aphorisms and quibbles
of Paley—an unelegant but necessary work, so say the authorities, to enable one to pass a trivial but tiresome exam., called
euphonically "Little Go."

My arm may not have taken for one of two reasons. Insufficient power of lymph; or no want of vaccination. I incline
to the former. Weather wet, warm, muggy. Temperature,
window-openy. Cambridge for the first time assumed a place
of interest in my mind yesterday. A bright moon-light night.
The place looked decently well—for two reasons. It was sufficiently light for you to see the tops of the colleges, glorious
works of men's hands—and dark enough to hide the inhabi-
tants thereof, but sorry specimens of God's creation.

Cynical, but true, as the court fool said when he was painted
in the robes of his master.

Very little news to-day. . . .

[*To Sir William Brett.*] TRINITY COLLEGE, CAMBRIDGE,
MARCH 2ND.

. . . Another agrarian murder! The more I think and see of *Current*
politics, the more tempted am I to be a governmentarian, i.e. a *Politics.*
supporter of whatever party is in power. . . .

. . . Law is no use in Ireland. It is an Englishman's bulwark;

his birthright. Dizzy's speeches have been brilliant enough; but not earnest; he never will frame a great opposition, for he fails to *convince*. He is a critic, and a capital one, of a bad government; but not the counter theorist who by dint of facts and perseverance can gain his end.

Why have the French by their love of bravado, by their delight to kick against the pricks, invited this triumphal entry? [1] How Thiers, if he is the man we think him, must rage at newspapers like the *Figaro*, and men like Félix Pyat. They make diplomacy impossible; by forcing upon the German Chancellor, the hopes and desires of the German people. How I hate newspapers and scoffers, and none worse than those who misrepresent, misstate and misrule. . . .

[*Journals.*]   HALSDON,
                                 MAY 14TH, 1872.

Eton.   . . . I heard from Alfred Lyttelton this morning. He writes freshly and cleverly, a very amusing account of Eton, of himself, and of his friends. A very precocious letter for a boy of his age. . . .

. . . Eugene [2] writes, too: tenderly of Eton, which seems to have power to give him a blunt eloquence when touching on that theme beloved by both of us. . . . At Eton all was bright and fair, a free outspoken truth-before-everything kind of life, with liberty carefully restricted, but encouraged. At Cambridge, less heartiness, less openness, although maybe a little more freedom of action. In the world you are your own master, free to go where you will, do what you will, but fettered with social chains heavy to bear, impossible to break. Later on professional chains bind you down more closely than ever school discipline did, intercourse is shallow and heartless between man and man, friendships rare, intimacy impossible. . . .

[1] By the Germans into Paris.
[2] Eugene Brett, his brother.

[*Journals.*]   HALSDON,
                                                      MAY 17TH.

. . . Rosebery writes that if Gladstone is turned out he, i.e.
Gladstone, retires from Parliament into private life.   It is hardly
conceivable that a man of such headstrong passions, uncontroll-
able temper, and patriotic zeal, should relinquish the idea of
dying in harness like the Homeric heroes of whom he is so fond.
Joab[1] also says that the King of the Belgians made one of the best
chairman's speeches ever known, the other day at the Literary
Fund dinner. . . .

. . . There is a good story of Lady Macclesfield the other
day when travelling to Sandringham with Major Teesdale,
an equerry, seeing him, as they approached their destination
pull out a comb and arrange his hair, said "Major Teesdale!
comb—coxcomb!" Upon which he replied instantly "Lady
Macclesfield! tortoiseshell—cat!"

[*Journals.*]   HALSDON,
                                                      MAY 20TH.

W. J. and I walked along the river: down stream to Wooley,
nearly six miles and back.   We found gorgeous bits of wood and
little rock ferns without end and some graceful columbine.

We were too tired to go to church and sat indoors reading
weekly papers.   In the evening I read *Notre Dame de Paris*, and
had an occasional tune on the piano. . . .

. . . I read an account of Raleigh's death.   It is curious, that *16th-century*
constant desire to kill, to force their opinions on everyone,   *Bigotry.*
noticeable in the upper classes during the sixteenth century;
they had no safety-valve to let off steam; no idea of making war
against the hills, the winds and the seas.   When we are making a
Suez Canal they would be executing bishops and persecuting
old women.   If only they had had the notion of emigrating, of

[1] Nickname given to Lord Rosebery at Eton.

colonising, of slaying wild beasts.   But I suppose a gentleman might have lived in 1520 in London and never heard of the desperate efforts of the Spaniards to conquer the New World. It would be interesting to read Erasmus and see if he ever alludes to the discoveries in foreign countries.   There was always a thirst for gold which prompted man later, to seek the New World, the Eldorado of Raleigh, but it does not appear that any interest was taken in clearing, in slaying wild beasts, or even savages, although there was a desire to force men to be Christians.

[*Journals.*]   DURHAM,
                                          JULY 8TH.

My London season is over. . . . Henry Manners is to get me a commission from his uncle the Duke of Rutland, in his regiment. I want to have experience of the technical side of the military profession. . . .

[*Journals.*]   DURHAM,
                                          JULY 29TH.

Charlotte Brontë.   It is mysterious how any woman's soul could have been moved to cry aloud in words such as those written in *Villette*. How anyone can think he can probe the depths of our literature or possess a clear insight into the mind of a woman! I have marvelled at the wonderful depth and versatility of the French writers. But great as Octave Feuillet and Hugo are, yet they are too exclusively the children of Voltaire.

Full of subtle passion, of noble feeling in its broadest sense, of ingenuous movements of the heart and mind, Charlotte Brontë's writing is at once manly and tender.   So tender, that none but a woman's hand could have traced the working of her women's hearts, and the patient love and suffering of one woman's soul. *Villette* is an incomparable work of art. A gem of priceless value. George Eliot, brilliant as she is, perfect master of expression and original of thought as she shows herself to be, has never succeeded more completely in delineating the patience and long-suffering of womanhood, the perverseness and goodness of an original mind tempered by the warmest of hearts, nor has she succeeded better in creating characters that haunt one with their reality and individuality.

[*Journals.*]   MANCHESTER,
                               AUGUST 4TH.

Before I was out of bed on Thursday morning I received a *A Friend's* letter from Chat [Williamson] at Baden, telling me of Bicker- *Death.* steth's illness, a slight fever. On going down to breakfast I got another dated Tuesday telling me of our dear boy's death. . . . I cannot think of that restless boy lying at peace for ever. I cannot write and I can think of nothing but him. A. T. L. [Lyttelton] writes me floods of thoughts and tender memories of our dear boy. But for me it is an impossibility. Shall we never see him again? I cannot think that. But I do look back into my past life with him only with few regrets. About those early days with him at My Dame's, memory throws a happy halo of remembrances. It may be pride, but I refuse to believe that he ever could have thought harshly of us, his friends. If we are to believe anything, let us believe that Love on earth is respected and cherished hereafter, if there is a hereafter.

But there is one thing I dare not contemplate. It is the death of the body in one so young; the perishing of one so beautiful. It is in thinking of this that one is in need of the faith that sustained the Christian martyrs. Whatever contempt for one's own death one may have in one's own mind, death in another, a beloved, a beautiful friend, has all the bitterness assigned to it by one who knew what friendship was!

Mode of
Travel.

On Tuesday I left Liverpool at half past eight. James [Lowther][1] was up to see me off and Papa and he sat with me during breakfast. At 7.30 I was at Perth, where I dined badly enough and slept till twelve o'clock. At one I left with Sir William Armstrong[2] for the north. At sunrise we were in the birch country, Drummochter, and at Garve Sir William got out. Not that Garve is near that country, inasmuch as we passed through Nairn and Inverness and Dingwall before we parted company. At about one we got to Strome Ferry, where we left the railway and steamed over to Portree, arriving at 7 or thereabouts. I found a decent fishing smack willing to take me over to Harris for £4 10s. It was an open boat of about thirty tons, with a one-armed Captain (John Robertson) and two sailors. We left Portree at eight expecting to be in Harris next morning. At sunrise it fell calm, and about Brother's Point we lay for many hours. Late on Thursday I insisted on getting out the sweeps, and we rowed by help of the tide past Trotternish Point and towards Table Island. I had nothing but a few biscuits to eat and they made me some tea. I had slept about four hours the night before. When the tide turned we found that all our rowing did not prevent us from drifting, but to my satisfaction we slowly passed into Tarbet.

[*Journals.*]   HALSDON,
                                            SEPTEMBER 29TH.

Gladstone.

. . . W. J. was telling us a story at breakfast of Gladstone's boyhood, characteristic of him. Keate[3] was threatening to whip him for having left out a name in his præpostor's book and flourish-

---

[1] Afterwards Speaker of the House of Commons.
[2] The late Lord Armstrong.
[3] Then Headmaster of Eton.

ing in his usual way said something about breach of trust. Upon which Gladstone, who until then had listened calmly, looked up and said, "I beg to differ with you sir, there is no breach of trust. There would have been had I accepted the office of præpostor voluntarily, but it was forced upon me." Keate thereupon was so astounded that he relinquished the notion of whipping. This is as prophetic as Metcalfe riding up High St. Eton on a menagerie camel!

I have read again George Eliot's *Spanish Gypsy*. A mental treat, yet which stirs no strong feeling. She spoils the effect of it by a compromise between narrative and drama. Sometimes giving mere stage directions spun out; at other times writing long bits of narrative. It is on the whole a failure as a drama. *George Eliot.*

[*Journals.*]　　　　　　　　LONDON,
　　　　　　　　　　　　DECEMBER 26TH.

Yesterday, Christmas Day, we kept in the morning at Wells Street, where they sang Gounod and Mozart to us. At half-past two I went to the Albert Hall, and heard the divine airs of the Messiah, and three glorious choruses. . . .

. . . I go into college next term, if I live. Vernon Harcourt[1] gives up his rooms. They are very ill-furnished and in a very mediocre condition, but are in Neville's Court close to Bertie[2] and A. T. L. [Lyttelton], and have the additional attraction of being panelled and having a large gyp-room. *College Rooms.*

I put most of my furniture in them of course, which will brighten them up a bit. . . .

. . . This year has nearly passed away, and with it the hopes and fears of one sweet life whose earthly future was the subject of constant thoughts of several who loved him truly and disinterestedly.

[1] Sir William Harcourt, afterwards Chancellor of the Exchequer. These rooms are now kept as the Guest Rooms at Trinity.

[2] Afterwards Earl Grey, Governor-General of Canada.

Tennyson.

. . . Tennyson has given us another Idyll, *Gareth and Lynette*, in language perhaps a little forced but in manner irresistibly taking, and worked into a most excellent story and admirable climax.

There are some truly touching and poetical descriptions, one or two glorious images and deep thoughts. . . .

[*Journals.*]   LONDON,
                                        JANUARY 14TH, 1873.

On the ninth of the month at Chiselhurst died Napoleon the Third, one of the most famous men of our time, regretted more by his hereditary foes than by his own countrymen.

[*Journals.*]   CAMBRIDGE.

This term has been very pleasant. My rooms in Neville's Court are very pretty and at night engaging for the sake of visitors like Henry Jackson[1] and Edmund Gurney.[2] Last night we talked over all our acquaintances. It is difficult to say that anyone will cut a great figure. Gerald Balfour is to my mind the most likely, or Maitland.[3]

*George
Eliot.*

Last week George Eliot and her husband, Lewes, came to stay with Myers. They brought with them a Miss Huth, a young girl, very clever and interesting, who took Gurney's heart by storm. George Eliot was more than an interesting visitor. Her presence has hallowed the place. Her low sweet voice thanked me for giving her tickets for the Choir Festival at King's, to which she, interested in every or any religious service, took her husband, who had not entered a church for years.

He told us how she had been into some Roman Catholic

---

[1] Regius Professor.   [2] Musical genius.
[3] Afterwards Professor of Law at Cambridge.

church abroad and sat there watching the women and children praying round her.

Her face reminds me of Savonarola's bust and pictures at San Marco, Florence. . . .

[*Journals.*]   LIVERPOOL,
                                               AUGUST 28TH.

Saturday evening we drove over to Knowsley. There was a large party to meet us. Lord Derby was pleasant. Sunday after church rain came down in torrents, so that I sat in the library all day, read MSS., James, Earl of Derby's *Devotions* written in the Isle of Man, and an account of his execution at Bolton, composed by his servant; also saw the late lord's MSS. of his Homer, very neatly written on slips of note paper. We inspected the stables and returned here on Monday morning. *Lord Derby.*

[*Journals.*]   -   KNOWSLEY,
                                               AUGUST 30TH.

. . . We found Lord and Lady Odo Russell,[1] and Lady Skelmersdale, Colonel and Mrs. Wilbraham with their daughter, a pretty girl of the Sir Joshua Reynolds' type. Lady Skelmersdale is without her husband, who is on the Atlantic on his way to America to buy shorthorn cattle. . . .

. . . We had a very pleasant party, everybody very kind. Lord Derby talked about George Eliot, in whose personality he is much interested, and of Froude; but he is a difficult man to talk to, pausing as he does for an answer and pausing himself before he answers a question, so fearful of not expressing exactly what he means. He has many peculiarities. One of them is his horror of seeing anyone touch anything. He thinks hands are dirty things. Probably an idea derived from his mother, who used to put on gloves to open the door. *Lord Derby.*

[1] Afterwards Lord Ampthill.

Germany.   Lord Odo talked a good deal. He is Minister at Berlin. He has been in Italy, at Vienna, at Constantinople. Of German literature, he says that now the Germans are a united people their prose will improve. Bismarck is a great purist; has all the despatches written in German; and by circular advises all his diplomatists to write carefully, only to put one idea in each sentence, and keep their sentences short. As yet he says there is no style. Since the consolidation of the Empire, invitation cards are written in German, which never could have happened formerly. He himself has seen the idea of "unity" in two people ripen and bear fruit under the hands of Bismarck and Cavour. Bismarck, he says, is the "biggest thing of the century." In his conversation there flash out sparks of genius and it is wonderful the gleam of light he throws upon every subject he handles. He was a lawyer once, and then a diplomatist. At Frankfurt he made the King's acquaintance, when Crown Prince and out of favour. There he studied the King and the wants of the German people. Then he went to Paris. When the King wanted to carry his Army Bill for four years' service, and dissolved four Parliaments running, he sent for Bismarck to help him, as a man willing to act against the constitution. He carried the Army Bill against the wishes of the nation. From that time he governed the King and the Conservative Party. He taught the Germans to look for unity. He planned the Danish campaign to try the strength of Austria. He forced on the Austrian war, by offering impossible terms: that Austria should retire from the Diet, abandon Vienna as a capital, and go somewhere further from Prussia. When in 1870 Benedetti had nearly arranged matters with the King, he sent the telegram "of the insult" flying over Europe and made war inevitable. The King of Prussia began the war with no thoughts of Empire; even now he is shy under the new dignity.

When the deputation was told by Bismarck to offer the crown to the King, he would not accept it; only said "Can the Crown be offered by the Sovereigns in whom the elective right is vested?" A courier was sent off to Bavaria. The King was found dressed for dinner. He asked what would happen if he did not sign. "Then," they said, "the King of Saxony will." So he signed, believing it to be an offer for life to the King of Prussia. When he found what he had done, he was furiously angry, and has refused to see the Emperor since. It was against the opinion of the Army that Paris was bombarded. Bismarck alone wanted it. "Starvation will act on their stomachs, bombardment on their nervous systems." It shortened the siege by two months.

Odo Russell says the balance of power is gone in Europe. The German Army is invincible. The organisation is so great. Every regiment has its commissariat. The letters are all written and stamped to call out 1,000,000 of men in 10 days. Every soldier carries a map of the country in his cap.

Odo Russell sends all this home to our Government, but *War of* nothing is done. Cavalry are now learning near Berlin to break 1870. up and mend railways. He made careful enquiries at Sedan and found that Napoleon was really under heavy fire for some hours. Prince Frederick Charles asks affectionately after his antagonist Bazaine, and hates the French for court-martialling him, and he offered to give evidence.

Odo Russell from Versailles went to see one of the villas which was much exposed. He found there an officer who had not had his boots off for two months, reading Darwin. One of the greatest horrors of the war was, to see the artillery take up a position and ride over their own men. The Germans objected to chloroform. The Crown Prince is a hero he says, and full of chivalrous feeling and detestation of war. . . .

. . . Odo Russell sang to us charmingly. We left Knowsley this morning. . . .

[*To Lady Brett.*]   HOWICK, NORTHUMBERLAND,
                                              DECEMBER 25TH.

We arrived quite safe. I met Albert [Grey] and the Lambtons at York, and we got here about seven. There is no one but the family; rather a comfort after the excitements of Knowsley.

Lady Grey is very good natured and the Earl kind and good tempered. There is an uncle and aunt and Albert's family. We have walked by the sea just now in a gale of wind, which prevents me writing steadily.

The House is very good. Externally plain. The interior very old-fashioned and handsome but not pretty. The grounds are beautiful. All wood and valley with burns running through them down to the sea which is magnificently wild; along a rocky coast stretching away towards Dunstanborough Castle, an old ruin on a headland, and Holy Island, famous in legend.

There is a fine library and two grand halls. The Earl himself is an interesting relic. We shall probably go over to Alnwick which is only 6 miles off.

[*Journals.*]   LONDON,
                                          JUNE 20TH, 1874.

Cambridge Friends.   Since the last scrap of an entry was made, I have been a term at Cambridge, the chief event of which was entertaining my father, who came as Judge to the Lodge, and Arthur Lyttelton as his marshal. In May I was with my Militia. In June I spent a happy fortnight at Cambridge. Read for six days and took my degree this morning. Myers,[1] Gurney and Buttons [Arthur Lyttelton] made the term very pleasant. S. H. Butcher,[2] Hallam Tennyson, his brother, and Macaulay have come much into my life: also Jebb,[3] the Public Orator, and Henry Jackson. . . .

[*Journals.*]   LONDON,
                                          JUNE 26TH.

The day before yesterday, my mother's birthday, I kept at the Crystal Palace, where the triennial Handel Festival had brought

---

[1] Poet and founder of the Society of Psychical Research.
[2] M.P. for Cambridge University.
[3] Sir Richard Jebb, afterwards Professor of Greek at Cambridge.

together twenty thousand people. Yesterday at Henley I saw our boys just beaten for the Grand Challenge, after a splendid race with a London crew. We came down from Henley to Windsor in a steam launch, a merry party including a daughter of Mario and Grisi, who, I believe sings, but not like her parents.

[*Journals.*]　　　　　　　　　　　　　　EXETER,
　　　　　　　　　　　　　　　　　　　JULY 28TH.

. . . Coleridge is the chief feature of interest on circuit. He is, *Lord*
I think it would be fair to him to say, a perfect picture of bland *Justice*
insincerity, but underneath I believe him to be capable of real *Coleridge.*
friendship. He is more than civil, he is very kind indeed to me,
and I do nothing to deserve it. He gave me very spontaneously a
very engaging book, Wordsworth's *Tour in Scotland*. Upon the
whole I should say he is not fitted for his position. He is too
critical to be plain, and so is misunderstood; he is too eloquent to
be to the point, and so wastes time; and he is too uncertain of the
law to be decisive and these are qualities and deficiencies which
will prevent him becoming a great judge.

[*Journals.*]　　　　　　　　　　　　　　BODMIN,
　　　　　　　　　　　　　　　　　　　JULY 30TH.

On Sunday we went over to Powderham, and spent a very *Lord*
quiet day among the pictures of the Courtenays, and the trees *Devon.*
under which generations of them have wandered. Lord Devon
bears up under his misfortunes in a manly, humble, and Christian
manner. It is very noble to see his earnestness to do good, to be
kind and just to all men. . . .
After dinner we had a short service in the private chapel which
is done up like a ritualist church. His servants are trained to sing,
and he makes it a *sine quâ non* for his gardener boys and men.
Gregorian chants were sung, of course, and three hymns, but

they stick to the old hymn-book, which would shock the St. Albans folk. Lord Devon officiated and read a chapter of the Corinthians, and some well chosen prayers, very earnestly and impressively; but he has a most distinct rolling of the r's and an accent which might well be French. This is a good fact for Darwin, inasmuch as he is a direct descendant of the Norman Courtenays; and his lineage is as spotless and pure as any in the English Peerage.

[*Journals.*] NEW INN, CLOVELLY,
AUGUST 2ND.

*Mode of
Travel*

Yesterday at midday the business was over at Bodmin, and at one we started, my Father and I, in a chaise and pair, and drove through driving mist, with no intervals of sunshine through Pencarron, over the Camel, which was swollen and yellow, between hedges where the spiders' webs hung like nets to catch dewdrops, past St. Jude, a village, like all Cornish villages with a square tower church, to Boscastle. We crossed a deep ravine called the Devil's Jump, because, said the driver, "he joomped from yon coombe, which yu see yonder, to this yeer. . . ."

At Boscastle, Mr. Scott keeps the Wellington Hotel, a very substantial inn for so small a village. He harnessed for us a good pair of horses that took us briskly up to Bude; while he was doing so I played the harmonium which probably for the only time in its existence awoke some chords of Spohr's *Faust*.

There were busts of Byron and Scott in the hall. In the visitors' book I found the names of Orlando and Ernest Bridgeman, who had been there a week before. The honeysuckle was in full bloom in the hedges, but the mist hung on thicker and thicker.

Before getting to Bude, you pass the canal from Bude to Launceston. It is on different levels, with tramways between, up which barges are drawn. They gave us there a wagonette drawn by Dartmoor ponies, and we dashed through the picturesque village just out of Bude, and on up the terrible hill into Kilkhampton in fine style. On our right lay Stamford Hill, where Hopton fought his battle. Kilkhampton possesses a shady churchyard, a fine church with two aisles and a nave, and a sixteenth-century porch, jasmine-covered and well shaped.

The road then became very dreary, owing to the mists and the coming darkness, and it was night when we pulled up at the top of the village, and I walked with my Father down the "pitch path" steps of the street to the inn. Our room is comfortable, filled with china, some very old and beautiful. The landlady had collected it from a child and they have the house full of it, in the rooms, in the store, and packed away under the garden bushes. . . .

[*Journals.*]   WELLS,
                                              AUGUST 8TH.

Thursday the Bar dined here, but I got leave, and had a very pleasant evening at the Palace,[1] where we were pressed into rowing the ladies round the moat. In the evening I played one of Bach's preludes, and the Louis the Thirteenth Gavotte, which was preferred to the Bach. Last night we dined here in state. I sat next Freeman,[2] who has adopted the manners of the Normans about whom he wrote. . . .

. . . I played some scraps including Bach's "My heart ever faithful." Basil played three of Mendelssohn's "Lieder," quite perfectly, and he and Ernlé [Johnson] sang "O wert thou in the cauld blast" and my accompaniment was full of tears. . . .

[*Journals.*]   LONGLEAT,
                                              AUGUST 9TH.

The party here consists of Lord and Lady Bath and their children: Weymouth, their eldest born, whose tutor turns out to be

---

[1] With the Bishop, Constantine Hervey's father.   [2] The historian.

young Frewer, son of an Eton usher, and John who is about eight. Mr. Disraeli,[1] Sir Augustus and Lady Paget,[2] Percy Wyndham and his wife, Lord Malmesbury,[3] and Lady Marion Alford and Mr. Chesney. We left Wells yesterday at five and got here about seven. Lord Bath was on the steps waiting for us. He walked us round the garden and talked commonplaces in a very pleasant way. He is very refined in appearance, not unlike Sidney Herbert to judge from the picture at Wilton. He is full of crotchets and whims on all political subjects, and they prevent him from holding office, for which his talents most certainly render him fit. Lady Bath is Eustace Vesey's sister, my old playmate. She is still a very lovely woman. . . .

Lord Bath.

Paget is a diplomatist, and is Minister at Rome. Very British in appearance, but chiefly remarkable for his wife, a very striking Austrian lady, fluent and fond of admiration, to the partial neglect of a fair-haired Eton boy who looks more her brother than her son. She is very intimate with Lord Malmesbury, who has pushed her husband a good deal. Lady Marion Alford is one of those ladies of whom it is said, "She is a very difficult person to know." She poses as a blue-stocking although she is a woman of some parts. Mrs. Wyndham is most engaging and decorates her fine person with gorgeous diamonds, which she carries off well, almost as well as a conversation on any literary, artistic or political subject. They make a bevy of very bright, handsome, and pleasant women. . . .

To Mr. Chesney I am grateful for having hoped, as we parted, that we should meet again. He is a very well informed man, who has lived much abroad, and in the houses of the most twinkling portion of the aristocracy. He has picked up much information, and he is a thorough master of the art of using it socially. Lord Malmesbury is kind and good natured. Dinner last night was not very lively. The party had not shaken itself into comfort. To-day we breakfasted in the hall, and after breakfast a very amusing scene occurred. Some little misunder-

---

[1] Then Prime Minister.   [2] Ambassador at Rome.
[3] Secretary of State for Foreign Affairs.

standing arose about the sending of despatches, and Lord Malmesbury had been guilty of the indiscretion of delivering a box to some unauthorised person. Dizzy, understanding this all of a sudden, burst out in half anger with "Run directly, Malmesbury, and get it back. Go immediately, go! else there will be some confusion or other!" His tone was quick and irritable. But Lord Malmesbury trotted out of the room as if he were a lower boy to obey his command.

We attended church in the private chapel in the house, and very handsome our ladies looked, standing in the front of the pew over the heads of the congregation, while we admiringly retired to the back of the room. . . .

. . . Late in the afternoon I went up to the school-room where we had a fine romp until dinner time, Weymouth and young Paget and I. The small boy, Lord John, came to tea. Asked as a great favour. He was subdued, but sharp as a needle. Weymouth was very jolly. He goes to Eton next year.

At dinner Dizzy talked a great deal. Of Dicky Doyle he said *Disraeli's* that grace and fancy—fancy, not imagination—were his char- *Conversa-* acteristics. His treatment of fairyland was full of genius, and that *tion.* he ought to be court painter to Queen Titania. . . .

. . . But for twenty minutes while telling a story quite inimitably, of his visit to Brighton and his three dinners with the Brunnows, the Gerard Sturts, and the Clanricardes, and the recognising of him when he wished to be incognito, by the Christy Minstrels, he kept us in roars of laughter and maintained his reputation for being, when he chooses, the best talker, the best mimic, the best actor, and the most agreeable companion it is possible to contemplate.

His silence, even, is unutterably droll. The evening was spent very pleasantly. The dinner excellent, the management perfect. We have rose-water provided in our bedrooms for washing purposes. Everything is done most nobly and becomingly.

Dizzy's account of his visit to Brighton at a time of year when he thought no one would be there . . . took the airs of a performance. He described how he wandered about the town, stopping to listen to bands, strolling into the Aquarium, and finally going to hear the Christy Minstrels, who all got up and made him a low and ceremonious bow. Directly he sat down he was recognised by the minstrels. Of course there was an end to his incognito. Then he went on to describe the three dinners. First, with the Brunnows (for she had seen him in the street), with the feast and gorgeous footmen; then the Sturts, with Lady A. insisting in the middle of dinner on having a special train to go up to town, and with difficulty dissuaded. Third with the Clanricardes, who gave him roast mutton, and dry sherry, "because," they said, "you said this morning that was what you liked!" "I had said so; one does say foolish things sometimes; but if there is one thing I never eat, it is roast mutton, and one thing I never drink, it is dry sherry; so I dined on Seltzer water."

[*Journals.*] LONDON,
NOVEMBER 8TH.

Irving's Hamlet.

... Last night we went to see Irving in *Hamlet*. He has read the play, as he is entitled to do, in his own way. It is not Goethe's conception of Hamlet, a man who is too weak to perform a great task put upon him. It is rather a feverish, cynical, passionate Hamlet with a discursive mind, which forbids him to follow to the end a purpose once formed, but rather tends to make him doubt himself, doubt the ghost, doubt immortality, ambition, and all things human and living. He plays best the scenes with Polonius, with Osric, with the courtiers, with Ophelia. The acting which leads up to the end of the play scene provokes genuine enthusiasm, but he gives a signal proof of his unwillingness to play the character as it is written, by leaving out the half wild, excited, madly-pleased snatch of song,

> Why, let the stricken deer go weep,
>   The hart ungalléd play;
> For some must watch while some must sleep,
>   So runs the world away.

... His perfect knowledge of the text enables him to give "O what a rogue and pleasant slave am I" as well as it could possibly be given; except the line "What's Hecuba to him or he to Hecuba?" which he intonates carelessly, not dreamily enough.

In his other great soliloquy he has not caught the manner of what Hazlitt called "thinking aloud," but still it is finely conceived and his attitude, the body thrown forward over the back of the chair, a stroke of genius.

... However, taken as a reading of the most curious psychological study ever put upon the stage, so curious that nearly everyone has his own theory of the character, it is truly admirable.

Irving has a right to read the part after his own fashion, and he does so, and does so carefully, with an ability which no one can deny him, and which with continued careful study may develop into real genius. After all Hamlet should be acted by angels.

[*Journals.*]   LONDON,
                                            NOVEMBER 17TH.

... On Monday at St. James' Hall, Joachim played a quartette *Music.* of Mendelssohn's with an andante too divinely constructed, and a Miss Sterling sang "Ich grolle nicht," one of Schumann's songs, which as Gurney says, simply "floors one." Bülow, the great pianist, whom people rave about, thumps out his slow movements too vilely, and his playing of quick things is quite good enough to make one hate him all the more for playing the softer things so badly. Another divine melody is in the few bars of introduction to the quartette in Mendelssohn's "Lauda Sion." It sends one of those cold thrills down one's back, which go some way towards relieving the intolerable tedium of existence. This is the kind of thing Gurney says of Nellie Farren. ...

[*Journals.*]   LONDON,
                                 NOVEMBER 26TH.

The music last week was extremely good. At the Crystal
Palace we had the "Ruy Blas" again, and a symphony of
Spohr's exquisitely played. On Monday Neruda played; the
quaint quartette of Haydn's so full of fun, and a rondeau of
Schubert's in B minor, were the best things. Hubert Parry,
whom I had not seen for some time, was there and Ivo Vesey and
his wife. Near me sat Norman Grosvenor and Spencer Lyttelton
and Arthur Balfour. Charlie Tytler, Cyril Oliphant,[1] the boys
of those old concerts at St. Mark's, now grown up into young
men, young still but not in the first blush of youth. And youth
is the one charming thing; youth that hopes, youth that listens,
youth that becomes fragrant in the "rapid germination and
decay of ideas and impressions, like the ash trees in Siberian
springs." Gurney writes sleepily rather from Harrow. On
Saturday I get away to Cambridge for a week.

[*Journals.*]   STAFFORD,
                                 DECEMBER 8TH.

On Saturday sennight I went to Cambridge. We have a very
pleasant A.D.C. week, playing *Heir at Law.* . . .
    . . . I got through a good deal of talk with Harding and
Butcher, mostly on the Contagious Diseases Act, and on subjects on which I had written to *The Times,* viz. the Brussels
Conference for re-arranging the rules of war.[2] (December
1st, 1874.)
    We had some music too, under the auspices of Gray, who takes

[1] Son of Mrs. Oliphant, the novelist.
[2] These talks with Harding and Butcher altered the trend of his life for a
time. Instead of leaving, he remained up at Cambridge for two years and
lectured for the University Extension Movement in the East End of
London.

Stanford's place for the nonce . . . Gladstone made £2,000 so far by his pamphlet,[1] and is writing another.

[*Journals.*]   WORCESTER,
                                    DECEMBER 15TH.

   This town was gaily decorated to-day, and I stood among the good-humoured and not very enthusiastic towns-folk and saw the Duke of Edinburgh and his wife drive through on their way to Witley. . . . It is pleasant to see the small and dirty boys reading the labels in the shop windows. It is one of the signs of *Education.* the happier future. Shall I live to see education of children forced upon parents? Why can it not be done? That great good which must come, but for which we have to linger and wait.

[*Journals.*]   HALSDON,
                                    JANUARY 4TH, 1875.

   On the 2nd I travelled here from town. Instead of coming from "Portsmouth Arms" it was necessary to go round by Torrington and then drive through snow, in parts piled up over the hedges. Paul is here and Harry Dean. . . .
   Stories told last night were these:

   " Seven Greek cities moaned for Homer dead
      Through which the living Homer begged his bread."

Lord Wensleydale met Sir David Dundas and asked him to dinner. "You are the seventh peer of the realm who has asked

   [1] *The Vatican decrees in their bearing on civil allegiance: a political expostula-
tion.* London. John Murray, 1874. The pamphlet was provoked by the decree of Papal Infallibility. It was published in New York, and translated into French, Spanish, Welsh and Danish. The second pamphlet was on the same subject.

me to dinner to-day," said D.   W. thought a moment, and then said,

> "Seven English peers have offered David bread,
> Who wouldn't care a damn were David dead."

Another good tale is of Peel staying at the Pavilion with George the Fourth. The King thought of some political thing after he had gone to bed, and sent for Peel. Peel thought the King was dying and came in a hurry in his bed-gown. When there he became very solemn and began to remonstrate, using quite the parliamentary action, until the exasperated King said, "Damn you, sir, don't stand there pawing the air, put your hands in your pockets." Peel nettled replied, "Damn you, sir, I have no pockets."

[*Journals.*]   HALSDON,
                                JANUARY 21ST

Two days ago the Army *Gazette* contained the list of direct commissions, and Eugene's name[1] appeared in the middle of it. He will be a very first rate soldier, as I think he has a decided turn for it, and he certainly has determination and plenty of moral courage.

[*Journals.*]   HALSDON,
                                JANUARY 24TH.

Maxims.   . . . Things worth remembering:
1. No English village obeys a foreign King.
2. The narrowest place is wide to the narrow-minded.
3. Death in the company of friends is a feast.
4. Age has for youth a natural priesthood.

A thought: To be a great statesman one must have a capacity for great friendships.

[1] His brother.

[*Journals.*]   LONDON,
                                          JANUARY 29TH.

. . . I have just dined very happily with Lord Derby, Lord *Inkerman.*
Coleridge, Lord Malmesbury. But after dinner Colonel Higginson, adjutant of the 3rd battalion of Grenadier Guards at Inkerman, talked to me about the battle. We went over the old ground. A great deal of what Hamilton states Higginson demurred to; and he says a great deal was omitted. Higginson happened to turn round hearing a cheery voice near him at the hottest moment in the sand-bag battery in time to see William Peel arrive with a boy on a pony, who was Evelyn Wood. Suddenly he felt a bullet in his bearskin *from behind*; and he said to Peel, "By God, our own men are firing at us!" But Peel after looking through his glasses found them to be Russians. He remembers very little about the battle. When they marched back and joined the detached companies, he remembers nothing but the men bursting into tears. They were hysterical all night. . . .

[*Journals.*]   LONDON,
                                          FEBRUARY 4TH.

The Whigs are vexed at reporters having been admitted yesterday into the Reform Club. However, as all the world must know that they chose Lord Hartington to be their leader, it does not matter much that they should know their reason for doing so.

[*Journals.*]   LONDON,
                                          FEBRUARY 6TH.

Yesterday Parliament was opened; not by the Queen, who has had too much anxiety and worry to come from Osborne.[1]

[1] Her youngest son, Prince Leopold, had been dangerously ill with typhoid fever.

In the morning Cross[1] sent home the new Bill[2] for my Father to look at. It extends flogging to all cases of violence. My Father wrote a long letter of disapproval, and is to draw up a new Bill by Monday.

In the evening Schouvaloff dined here, and a large party came later, including Capelli, a young Italian marchese of considerable grace and manner.

[*Journals.*]   HALSDON,
APRIL 12TH.

I found a comfortable bed and fire ready for me at Exeter on Friday (or rather Saturday morning, 3 a.m.). At half past 10 I was away again and arrived at one at Torrington. Griffiths was in front of the "Globe Inn," waiting to tell me that W. J. was busy with Petty Sessions, and that the Butlers had arrived unexpectedly. Montagu Butler (H.M. of Harrow) was in the sit-

*Butler of
Harrow.*

ting room into which I was shown for the purpose of lunch. We made acquaintance over chops, and settled to walk over together to Halsdon, and not wait for the carriage. We talked over all the usual subjects upon which men set to work on first meeting, and the ice was quickly broken.

. . . He said that Westminster Abbey has become under the Dean the "spiritual mouthpiece of the nation." The twelve persons who have had most influence on thought, English thought, are Carlyle, Tennyson, Arnold, George Eliot, J. S. Mill, Browning, Newman, F. D. Maurice, Jowett—I cannot recollect the other three; I know Darwin was not mentioned.

[1] The Home Secretary. "The Home Office went to an untried man in Richard Assheton Cross, the director of a Lancashire bank, and the appointment was an example of Disraeli's insight into character."—Low and Sanders, *Political History of England*, vol. xii, p. 272.

[2] The Bill was the Offences Against the Person Act, 1875. It was an amending act to the main bill of the same name in 1861, and has been largely superseded by the Criminal Law Amendment Act of 1885, so that it is no longer printed in Chitty's *Statutes of Practical Utility*.

W. J. said that he never knew a boy who before 14 cared for Mechanics who was a good scholar; or a boy who cared for Shakespeare who ever did anything.

[*Journals.*]   LONDON,
                                                APRIL 25TH.

Sir Charles Dilke asked Randolph Churchill and Gambetta to *Gambetta.* breakfast in Paris. Gambetta said the Orleanists were "Doctrinaires" and was not agreed with by R. C.

"Oui," said G. "Ils sont doctrinaires parce qu'ils n'ont pas de doctrines, de même qu'on dit 'poitrinaires' quand on n'a pas de poitrine."

[*Journals.*]   LONDON,
                                                APRIL 28TH.

. . . Afterwards I visited Albert Grey, whose aunt, Lady Caroline Barrington, died in the night. Mrs. Grey was gone to Kensington Palace, and met the Queen, who came up from Windsor with many beautiful flowers to see her dead waiting-woman. All the girls were at lunch, Louisa[1] looking very well. Albert and I went to the India Office to spy out the library and see Sir Bartle Frere[2]. . . .

[*To Lady Brett.*]   LONDON,
                                                MAY 10TH.

. . . As to Germany, of course she being strong, and not free, *Foreign* the love of having his own way, which is characteristic of *Politics.* Tyrants, influences Bismarck, unchecked by moral popular feel-

[1] Afterwards Countess of Antrim.
[2] Afterwards Governor of the Cape.

ing; and the result must inevitably be damaging to the dignity of any weak nation which thwarts what is called German policy.

In the interests of Europe and mankind I would prefer a revolution in Germany to a war, for in the ultimate pre-eminence of Teutonic races I have firm belief, and were Germany crippled 'twould be but to rise again, and freedom and peace be deferred perhaps a century beyond the time at which they may be hoped for.

I detest diplomacy. Men had better speak their minds at the risk of giving offence; it is a mean and short-sighted policy to be jealous of the power of other states. Meddlesome interference of the Palmerstonian kind all good men would wish to avoid. Of course there are some other things which must be done, such as sticking to treaties and defending Belgium. But France and Prussia can be well left to take care of themselves unless either of them do an act which threatens the independence of a neutral nation such as refusing to unarm when driven over a frontier, or attempting to bully Holland. For England should be ready always to defend the weak and unambitious people, who do not seek to be the "cock" countries. But it is ridiculous to suppose that France is weak, and were she to beat Germany, would be every bit as ready to bluster as her neighbour is now, and much more likely to act up to her threats, to judge from former experiences.

Now we have a guarantee of her good behaviour, for she is inferior to Germany in power, and a Republic. Imperialism and a victory like Jena would take us back to 1806. Germany will not go to war unless she is forced to it by the spirit of revenge in the French people; for she has nothing to gain and everything to lose by war.

But if Bismarck were to die and the republicans to make any way in Parliament, France would become a very uncomfortable neighbour and this is felt by all the German people who have the unity of their nation at heart.

Prussia is more likely to find trouble in the East and South than in the West, for the next ten years, and the meeting of these

Emperors shows it, for when perfect understandings exist, sovereigns and ministers don't find it necessary to meet and make a fuss before all Europe. Nicholas coming over here did not avert the Crimean war within six years, and Francis Joseph's trip to Berlin in 1863 did not prevent Sadowa.

All that is *diplomacy* again, promises given not to be performed, fair words with hidden meanings, and tacit reservations, and then we abuse the Greeks for deceitfulness, and despair of their future!

Patriotism is the noblest passion which can stir men's hearts, but then it must be a broad and true patriotism which admits of weaker and similar feeling for the welfare of all honourable and true countries. I do not call him a patriot who merely wishes for superiority of his own people. Napoleon was not a patriot. Cavour was and Johnny Russell is.

I am enjoying this month hugely owing to the young leaves and the beautiful country round Leicester. But I would much like to go to Madras with the new Governor. If he wants a secretary for a year you can offer my services. . . .

[*Journals.*]   STRAWBERRY HILL,
                                                    JUNE 13TH.

Last night we dined, and in the evening played "Poker," an American game of cards. So far as I have made out at present the party consists of Hochschild the Swede, Schenk the American, Rancés the Spaniard, Lord Dufferin, Lord Wolverton, Harcourt Johnston, and their respective female appendages; Lady Egerton of Tatton, Mrs. Glynn, William Harcourt, Hayward, and Courtenay Boyle.

Everything is managed with perfect smoothness. . . . There is more of the atmosphere of politics and less of literature about this than about Holland House. Although of course, here there is just a tinge of revivalism which is wanting at Lady Holland's.

The house has been much added to since Horace Walpole's

time, but the library and the picture gallery in the Tudor style are much as he left them. The gardens are beautiful, chiefly remarkable for an avenue of roses trained on wires about 200 yards long, and for some grand balsam poplars, planted by Horace Walpole 100 years ago. Nevertheless the place is not healthy. The atmosphere is too much that of the camp where intermediate issues, not ultimate results, are for ever under discussion. It is so evidently "parti avant patrie." Of course you must have a camp if you want to fight a battle.

. . . This afternoon came Musurus Pasha,[1] Sir George Bowen and a lovely Mrs. Sands, perfect in feature and in the contour of her head. She expresses "completeness." . . .

[*Journals.*]   STRAWBERRY HILL,
                                                              JUNE 26TH.

On Thursday we had a pleasant evening at Lady Ripon's. And yesterday I went to Lady Derby's to meet the Queen of Holland. She has grown very old since she nursed me on the Rhine steamer in 1860. . . .

[*Journal.*]   STRAWBERRY HILL,
                                                              MONDAY.

Yesterday we played lawn-tennis, Lord William Hay and I against Vernon Harcourt and Hervey. We beat them easily. After dinner I talked to Lady Waldegrave and Harcourt. They were abusing what they called "swelldom"; contrasting the days of their youth (the old story) when love of swells was not, with the snobbery of to-day, when literary society has passed from the patronage of aristocrats. For that is the explanation of the phenomenon of the non-appearance of literary men at Strawberry Hill and Holland House.

Harcourt told us a curious story about the French Empress.

[1] Turkish Ambassador.

She sold her jewels for £60,000; all except a pearl necklace worth £12,000. One day Clary went to Rothschild and told him that he had received a communication from a lady unknown, who said that on a certain day she would come to the Grosvenor Hotel closely veiled, look at the necklace, and if she liked it, would pay the money and carry it off. Clary asked for advice, for, as he said, there might be a man lurking behind who would play some trick and be off with the pearls. Rothschild said, "Well, if it comes to that I can lend you our big porter." So he did. And the lady came to time with three veils on, bought the necklace and went away. . . . It turned out a year afterwards that it was Madame P. who was living with a Prussian, whom she ruined of all his property save £12,000. When she heard of the pearls she asked him for the money, and he gave it to her. Then she said on her return that he had behaved so well and had trusted her that she would marry him, and she did so, and he got all his money back.

[*Journals.*]   LONDON,
                                                JULY 9TH.

On the 6th I enjoyed a charming evening at Grosvenor House. And yesterday I went at 11 to Lady Suffield's and saw the most poetic ball ever given in London. The Harbord girls and friends of theirs learn singing from Randegger. They sang trios and part songs, and ended by dancing to Farmer's Nursery Rhyme Quadrilles, and singing at the same time. The Princess of Wales stayed till three in the morning. I danced the cotillon with little Judy Harbord, aged 11, and came away quite at the end. To-day the Harrow match, but rain is falling gently.

[*Journals.*]   LONDON,
                                                SUNDAY.

The first sunny day for ten. We went to Eastbourne and enjoyed largely the sea and the children on the sands. It is quieter, prettier, and more attractive than Brighton for humble-minded people. . . . The Lord Chief Baron[1] told some of his remarkable fables fabulously well to-night. He was, as an octogenarian, much pleased at the tale my father told him of Lord Malmesbury, who asked his mother-in-law, Lady Tankerville, then considerably over eighty, when a woman ceased to feel *passion* and she answered him: "You must ask a woman older than I am, my dear Harris."

[*Journals.*]   LONDON,
                                                     JULY 21ST.

Last night I went to a Ball to meet the Prince and Princess of Wales at Stafford House. It was a fairy-like scene. Many celebrities were there; Irving, Patti, Nilsson, and Gustave Doré. Many beautiful women. . . .

[*Journals.*]   CROYDON,
                                                     JULY 28TH.

On Tuesday we drove in the morning from Maidstone to Chilston. The place, formerly my great-grandfather's, is now Mr. Douglas's,[2] who turned out to be Akers, once in my division, now married and a country gentleman. We next went to Lenham, my grandfather's vicarage, and saw the old rooms where my father and uncles lived. . . .

[*Journals.*]   KYLE AKIN,
                                                   ISLE OF SKYE,
                                                  AUGUST 22ND.

Political Theory.   . . . From de Tocqueville, whom I have been reading to-day I gather (and cases in point seem to verify it) that it is in com-

---

[1] Sir Fitzroy Kelly.   [2] Afterwards Lord Chilston.

promise that perfections, or as near to them as you can expect, are to be found. Democracies and Tyrannies have ineradicable vices. Monarchies and Republics are alike imperfect. It is probably in Democratic Monarchies or Aristocratic Republics that the true solution is to be found. . . .

[*Journals.*]　　　　　　　　　SKYE,
　　　　　　　　　　　　　　　AUGUST 29TH.

I have been writing on the organisation of our Army. The *The Army.* most perfect expression of our military wants is a small army in times of peace, a large army in times of war, and yet a larger army for purposes of defence; and yet what is wanted are not three armies, but one army.

. . . In these times the same old spirit remains. "We are not a military though we are a warlike nation," and we are quietly and undemonstratively a patriotic people, ready to make great sacrifices, ready to make the Thames and the Mersey and Cork and Falmouth as secure as Portsmouth and Dover, but not anxious to be forced to do what most of us are willing to do on our own accord.

[*Journals.*]　　　　　　　　COMRIE,
　　　　　　　　　　　　　　SEPTEMBER 5TH.

To-day we walked up Loch Earn and back again very slowly, *Sermon on* talking of many curious incidents and views of our youth. *Psalm* 103. This inn is kept by a steward of the late Breadalbane, who has known everyone in his time. To-night we had an impressive service in the hall from Mr. Whyte, minister of the Free Kirk, St. George's in Edinburgh, successor to Dr. Candlish.

He preached on the 103rd Psalm, the communion psalm of the Presbyterian Church. It had been chosen, he said, because it was the only psalm of thanksgiving free from any petition. It was written by David when he was an old man, in communing with his heart to which the psalm is addressed; he compared this kind of meditation in private with that which an ordinary man would use lying awake at night or walking on the hills or along the stream. Then he worked out very carefully the different terms of the thanksgiving. He dwelt especially on the verse in which David speaks of the Lord crowning the head of the sinner with tender mercies and loving kindness. Here his cultivation came out, and he was overcome by the beauty, the poetry of the expression. "If Shakespeare had written it you would never have heard the end of it," he burst out, "but the English in which it is put is lost in the meaning, the depth of truth in the fact." His distinction between the scholarly reading of the Bible and that of the women up in the glens, solitary and reft of their children, who had never been to school except the elementary class where they learnt their alphabet, who turn to it as their only book, was very elegant and touching. He told us about an old woman of ninety-eight, his parishioner, whose questions were always of her neighbour's children: "How about the schools, or the boys at sea, or the lad away in India"—never anxious about herself or grumbling. Then he turned to the last verse, the summing up of the Lord's benefits, his granting new life after sin just as an eagle renews her youth. This image, he said, David had borrowed from what he had seen on the hills, when the eagle after bringing up her young, and sending them away, retired with soiled plumes and torn wings, torn and soiled in the struggles for the food of her young, to a cleft in the rocks, and after moulting and being sick unto death, issued forth in full plumage and almost youthful beauty. Then he described what he imagined to have been the scene when David tottered up on to his palace wall to rest in the setting sun, leaving the manuscript wet on the table, and some servant passing looked at it, and then at his master and said:

"Look at him, the old man, he does not look as if youth is re-newed in him." And from this he drew distinction between the old and the youthful heart.

His peroration was an address on the peculiarity of the congregation, collected haphazard, never to meet again on this side of the grave. It was a striking discourse in the low dim-lighted room amid the weeping congregation. Sprung from the people, his use of the vernacular and of Scottish expressions, and local images of the moors and glens, made what he said very impressive and deeply touching.

[*Journals.*]　　　　　　　　　　VEVEY,
　　　　　　　　　　　　　　SEPTEMBER 20TH.

. . . About's book[1] has helped to weave the web of affection round my soul for Greece. . . . Some believe that the Latin nations are doomed to fade away before the northern brightness, and that any help given to non-Teutonic peoples is mere patchwork or bolstering. But who reads the noble quiet French writers and watches the splendid strivings of Italian patriots with any expectation of their not sustaining the life which seems bursting into fresh bloom every day? There does seem no rational hope that Turkey can survive her innate corruption and incapacity for modern institutions. She seems doomed to pass away from Europe, although the Mussulman spirit may find a useful field in Persia or Bokhara, where the contact with Europe is not so constant and irritating, and the necessity for modern forms of government not so strong. Then if Turkey in Europe is to fall a prey to division and spoliation, why should not Hellas arise out of her ruins? It seems possible that a capital of a Greek Republic could exist at Constantinople, a Republic not of Greece alone, but of Asia Minor and Rumania, and Montenegro and Albania; one people bound together by historic associations, blood, religion and glorious hope in the future. . . .

World Politics.

[1] Probably *La Grèce Contemporaine*, Paris, 1854, which appeared in English as *Greece and the Greeks of To-day*, Edinburgh, 1855. New editions of this book were still appearing up to this date.

[*Journals.*]   VEVEY,
                  SEPTEMBER 22ND.

Gortschakoff.   . . . I have listened to the Gortschakoffs[1] talking of some Poles who were in the house. The jealousy and dislike still rages. But I have seen his exquisite grandchildren fondled by him, the Chancellor, and his son kiss his hand humbly and lovingly, and cannot feel very ruthless. . . .

[*Journals.*]   VEVEY,
                  MONDAY.

Russia.   I sat next an intelligent Russian at dinner; he tried to persuade me that the tyranny of the Czar is both virtuous and necessary. There is a perfect little woman here, mother of a fair-haired child, niece of Gortschakoff. She smokes cigarettes, very small, very elegantly. She told me that Ignatieff never by any chance told the truth. It is a proverb in Russia: "Il ment comme Ignatieff."

Barbarism.   She was mentioning the overthrow of previous civilizations by barbaric forces; and we came to the conclusion that it was unlikely that the Tartars, who seem the only available barbarians, would stamp out the civilisation, extended as it is over the world. She expressed her belief that the dark force is developed with the brightness of prosperity all-pervading now; and then suggested that what could provide a force strong, ignorant, barbarian and widespread, is the lower populations of the various nations of Europe grouped in some such society as the International inbred with communistic and destructive notions. . . .

             [1] Chancellor of the Russian Empire.

[*Journals.*]   LONDON,
                              NOVEMBER 12TH.

I went to-night with Gurney to *Masks and Faces*, and saw
Ellen Terry play most gracefully and look most beautiful. My
days at Cambridge have been most pleasant, thanks to S. H.
[Butcher], Frank Balfour, and Alfred [Lyttelton].

[*Journals.*]   LONDON,
                              DECEMBER 2ND.

. . . Goschen[1] told Lady Ripon that both he and Bob Lowe[2]   *Suez*
think the Government stroke of policy [purchase of the Suez   *Canal*
Canal shares] wise and advantageous and that he would like to
have an opportunity of saying at once that he approves of the
step as a sound commercial and political transaction without
waiting until Parliament meets.

[*Journals.*]   LONDON,
                           JANUARY 22ND, 1876.

Yesterday afternoon I met Arthur Lyttelton, whom I had not
seen since last month, at the Gallery of Old Masters. In the
evening we saw *Masks and Faces*. I again got a sensation from
Ellen Terry's exquisite personality. Marie Wilton plays Peg
Woffington with much grace and spirit; and her dance in
Triplet's studio with Master Glover was charmingly executed. . . .

[1] G. J. Goschen, in opposition since February 1874, had been successively
President of the Poor Law Board and First Lord of the Admiralty in the
First Gladstone Cabinet.
[2] Robert Lowe, in opposition since February 1874, had been successively
Chancellor of the Exchequer and Home Secretary in the First Gladstone
Cabinet.

[Journals.]   LONDON,
                                                  AUGUST 21ST.

Disraeli.   Lady Derby writes to my father that Dizzy was only prevented from retiring by the "strongly expressed wishes of a
great lady."

Their difficulty is to know who is to go to the F.O. But, as
Dizzy says, they will be no nearer to a solution of it six months
or a year hence.

[Journals.]   LONDON,
                                                  AUGUST 23RD.

Foreign   If Dizzy goes and Lord D. [Derby] steps into his place, there
Policy.   will be very little chance for our Asians and Egyptians if they
wait for us to take the initiative. But that England will assure
the protectorate of Egypt; and that the Greeks in Asia Minor
will be rid of the Turks, I look upon as the inevitable result of all
the Eastern troubles of the last 40 years; and all that an English
Minister can do is to neglect it, for I don't believe he can delay
it a day. . . . .

[Journals.]   LONDON,
                                                  AUGUST 30TH.

Disraeli.   Speculation about the Buckinghamshire election has superseded chatter about Dizzy's earldom. The different analyses of
his motives in becoming a peer which we got in newspapers
from middle-aged scoffers, are entertaining and not confusing if
one rejects them all. A subtle correspondent suggests that it was
his desire to glorify the Hebrew race, by admitting one of the
chosen people to the hitherto untasted honours of the English
peerage.

I for my part think he was quite right from his point of view
in becoming a peer. Lemoine gives a good sketch of him in
the *Débats*, a paper that reflects England and Englishmen to
foreigners, but he misses the real point about D. which makes

him the unique P.M. His great merit is that he is a perfect captain of a side; that he has a true judgment about men's abilities, claims and propensities. He not only can choose his eleven correctly but he can keep them charging and backing each other up. No other Minister in recent times has had his knowledge of character and skill in dealing with various capabilities. His Ministry is the result of admirable skill and arranging. And on the whole they behave better than any set of Ministers ever known. . . .

[*Journals.*]   STUDLEY ROYAL,
                                                OCTOBER 8TH.

We had a glorious afternoon at Brimham, and clambered up and down rocks in a happy reckless manner, the bairns and I; her ladyship remaining calmly below, not fussing, nor making weak remarks. The spot was like fairy-land to me.

The Duke of Norfolk is an excellent fellow, with a strong will and a good head. . . . He possesses self-command to an extent not ordinary in a young man. . . .

The next arrival was Northcote;[1] the sort of politician *Politicians.* peculiar to Great Britain. A country gentleman with a fair education and all domestic virtues, simple and honourable, and continually rising to the occasion as demands are made upon him. There is no genius in him, but much capacity for sheer hard work, and some talent in arranging what he has to say. Added to this he has the necessary sense of humour.

After him came Harcourt[2] and James.[3] Harcourt has been

[1] Afterwards Lord Iddesleigh.

[2] Sir William Harcourt, having entered Parliament in 1868, at the age of 41, had held office only three months, as Solicitor-General in the First Gladstone Cabinet, and was now in opposition. His reputation already far exceeded his public position.

[3] Sir Henry James, afterwards Lord James of Hereford, had been successively Solicitor-General and Attorney-General in the First Gladstone Cabinet.

good to me for years. He is a man no one can be neutral about; either you like him or you hate him. I like him. I am grateful.

Read Forster's[1] speech. He is very sage; there is statesmanship and much of what Mat. Arnold would call "reasonableness" in every line of his speech. I like him for talking about Kossuth and the Hungarians. We may be proud of him and Hartington, who has also been prudent and wise. . . .

[*From Lord Ripon.*]   NOCTON HALL,
                                              NOVEMBER 13TH.

MY DEAR BRETT,

I have a favour to ask you, which I shall be much pleased if you can grant me. De Grey and I are resettling my estates and we are both equally anxious to induce you to let us appoint you as one of the Trustees of the settlement. The probabilities are that it will give you no trouble at all, as the settlement is of the simplest kind; but it would be a gratification to us to have your name connected with it, and to feel that, if there ever should, under possible contingencies of a minority or of any other kind, be anything of importance to be done by the Trustees we should have among them one in whose ability and judgment we both alike know that we can place implicit confidence.

Believe me, yours very sincerely,

RIPON.

[1] The Rt. Hon. W. E. Forster, Vice-President of the Council in the First Gladstone Cabinet.

Describing the reaction which set in after the wave of indignation raised against the Turks by the reported Bulgarian atrocities, the Annual Register says: "Mr. Forster, who had returned from a tour in the East, declared himself of opinion that autonomy of the revolted provinces would be impossible without occupation, even where the Mussulmans were in a decided minority."

[*Journals.*] LONDON,
ST. ANDREW'S DAY.

I came back here yesterday from Cambridge where I have been living happily for ten days. Beust, the Austrian Ambassador, dined here. He told me these stories:

A man asked an actress to supper, and signed the letter "Louis XIV." She understood him to mean that he would give her fourteen louis d'or. He did not ask her again, so she wrote and asked him to let her sup with him. He said yes, but he signed the letter "Napoleon III."

There were two restaurants in Paris; Riche and Hardy. At one you got a bad dinner cheap, at the other you got a good dinner dear. The wits used to say "Il faut être riche pour dîner chez Hardy, et il faut être hardi pour dîner chez Riche."

Musurus Pasha[1] has rented Combe Wood from Borthwick,[2] so Beust said to him "La Turquie a loué le Morning Post, et le Morning Post a loué la Turquie."

[*To Lady Brett.*] HALSDON,
JANUARY 9TH, 1877.

. . . Your letter coincided with one from another lady, and at the end of each was a recommendation to marry. I am afraid the advice, obviously so good, will have to be disregarded, unless I am positively provided with a wife, as I am with night shirts. My mind has never quite been made up, whether at the bottom of my heart, I am a gambler or not. Perhaps that part of me was left unfinished and the result is that I enjoy certain risks and dislike others.

On Marriage.

Taking a wife is among the latter. . . .

[1] Turkish Ambassador.
[2] Owned *Morning Post.*

*George
Eliot.*

I spent four hours this afternoon in the society of George Eliot. She talks like the best part of her books, the parts where she analyses without dissecting, the parts out of which compilers get her "wise, witty, and tender" sayings. She is wonderfully thoughtful even in trifles. She shut up George Lewes[1] when he tried to talk about her. She does not seem vain. She adores Charles Darwin, because of his humility. I suppose it is an event to have spent a day in her company.

[*To . . .*]   PARIS,
SEPTEMBER.

I was four and twenty, and no woman, save my mother, had kissed me, of her own accord. You know the story of my life. I have so often tried to tell it you. Besides, it is so commonplace, so very like the life of any other idle English boy. Before I saw your face I had not lived. One night—the night you kissed me, here, on my forehead—you gave me life. Since then you have given me my soul. Before my lips touched your hand the world was for me a story or a play. Among its great events, among its pleasures and its miseries, I passed, as men pass through a dream, happy or sad, and quickly forgotten. When your lips touched mine I awoke; and dream-life passed away. My love for you has taught me to love and bless the human race. . . .

While living for you alone I learnt to live for others. That lesson—the lesson that his life is not his to spend as he will—which every man must get for himself, by some sad or sweet experience, was taught me at your feet, and your fair haired head is the star to which I look for light.

Dear love, I am lonely in this gay, clever, beautiful Paris without you. I miss the meaning of things, and only see and hear them, while my thoughts carry me to your side. . . .

[1] Her husband.

Last night was a restless one for me, dearest, but the morning brought me a dream which made up for loss of sleep and gave me strength.

I was lying on the sloping grass under trees brown with autumn tints, while the red October sun set slowly over a low dark palace. White mist lay over the ornamental water, and I knew the air was cold though my head and hands were hot, and I did not care to move away. Before me lay a slip of paper, delicate and scented, with three words finely written across it, "Come to-night, late."

At last, after months of waiting. Do you remember that night? You wondered why my hair was wet with dew! I lay with your note close to my lips while the stars rose and sank in the heavens, until the old palace clock warned me that you were waiting. I stood for a moment in the dim rose light of the passage, with the intoxicating smell of flowers about me; and then lifted the curtain of your bright room. You were standing still in the white dress of Portia, with Bassanio's jewels on your neck, and your dear fair hair tossed into waves by the Venetian breezes. In a moment I was at your feet, and your cool white hand was on my forehead. Was it I who loosed the jewels from your neck, and then—O my darling—do you remember that night. . . .

[*Journals.*]   BRAYFIELD,
                                          SEPTEMBER 23RD.

I am alone here[1] revelling in autumnal quiet, in the calm, chill, mysterious days that precede the change of leaf and the dying of summer. I have plenty of books, and many pictures of beings I have loved and beings I have admired. Occasionally a few words come to me, scrawled by some one of them, unsuspecting of the pleasure to me, throwing light and giving life. . . .

[1] For the summer he and Julian Sturgis took a small house by the river at Bray, owned by Mme Van de Weyer, his future mother-in-law, who lived near by at New Lodge.

This day a year ago I walked with John Oswald through the dewy woods of Raith. There is no record in this volume of this summer. Many bright days were spent at Eton, with Claude, George Curzon, Gerald Portal and Wilfred Greenwood.

[*Journals.*]　　　　　　　　　　　　BRAYFIELD,
　　　　　　　　　　　　　　　　　　SEPTEMBER 25TH.

Political
Figures.　　Lord Hartington is too calm, too moderate, to have succeeded as an ordinary man. Such men usually become isolated. Political success, like popularity, belongs to extremes. The fault Lord H. picks in Mr. Gladstone has been picked before. It unfits him to be a trusted leader of educated men; but does not affect his power over the masses. In like manner his passions, which blind the perspective of his mind, do not stand in his way as a politician, although they stand between him and the highest statesmanship.

Dizzy, on the other hand, possesses self-control. He is without hatred, and never appears to bear malice. This together with his wit, and the air of mystery that is about him, captivates men who have a great deal of political ability with a small store of imagination. . . .

[*Journals.*]　　　　　　　　　　　　BRAYFIELD,
　　　　　　　　　　　　　　　　　　SEPTEMBER 30TH.

It is a very calm autumn afternoon. I am left quite alone for Julian [Sturgis] has gone over to the Van de Weyer's to play lawn tennis and dine. I had not the heart to go. Six days ago in India, dear Charlie Tytler died. He was to have been married next month. Christina Liddell, his sister, writes to me, and tells me the sad news because she knows how I loved him. A letter to me was full of joy, of the girl he was to have made happy. *Sic transit anima deorum hominumque dilecta.* . . .

Sir William Harcourt now recommended him to Lord Hartington as Private Secretary, and was trying to persuade him to accept the offer. Lord Ripon also recommended him, and had written to Lady Ripon on July 14th:

". . . I have written to H. [Hartington] by this post and when I had said what I really think of B. [Brett] and read it over I was almost afraid to send it lest it should sound like exaggeration. However, it will go as it was written off and you must get Wlm. H. [Harcourt] to assure H. that every word of it is the simple truth. . . ."

He ultimately accepted, and on his appointment he left Cambridge and his official life began.

[*Journals.*]   TRINITY COLLEGE,
OCTOBER 15TH.

Could I be of any use to Lord H. [Hartington]? That is the question. He has been compared with Lord Althorp. There are many points of resemblance between him and that "most true-hearted of God's creatures," as Jeffrey called him; but chiefly political and social resemblances, personally not much alike. Lord H. is much abler, better educated, and I should say, more gifted with political grasp and instinct. But he lacks the other's cheerfulness and benevolence, and although perfectly frank, the other's artlessness and although brave, his sweet-blooded courage.

Lord Hartington.

[*Journals.*]   TRINITY COLLEGE,
DECEMBER 30TH.

Harcourt writes that Hartington wants me as his private secretary. I am not elated.

[*Journals.*]   HALSDON,
                                        JANUARY 3RD, 1878.

On his   . . . After the long political training I have had, I am perhaps
Appoint- as well fitted to be Hartington's secretary as most of my con-
ment.   temporaries. . . . There are several people very anxious that the
thing should be; and as I am not unwilling I suppose it will be.
My feeling is, however, a mixed one, half gladness to possess the
power and knowledge which such a position brings, and half
regret at having to come out of my shell, to break some old
literary habits that are endeared to me. . . .

[*From Albert Grey.*]   WESTONBIRT, TETBURY,
                                            JANUARY 13TH.
DEAR REGGY,

That's grand.[1] I am really delighted it is settled. I am glad too
that the appointment comes when it does—for being in opposition the work will not be so great, and you will, I hope, be able to
go on with your own studies. You will learn, I fear, a great deal
that will disgust you in the way that National questions are regarded from Party rather than from "English" interests. But
you I know will use your influence in the other direction and
make Patriotism the acting, as it is the right Principle of Politics.
As my father was Private Secretary for a large part of his life,
I know pretty well what it means—and so you will allow me
to say this. You will have proportionally more work and less
thanks than any other official in the Kingdom—the advantage of
the position is this, that so long as you retain the confidence of
your Chief, you will be the possessor of a whole host of interesting secrets, but beyond this, you will obtain an influence—the
amount of which will be unsuspected from without, but still an
influence in promoting National Concerns. It is the consciousness of this unacknowledged influence in much that is of the
highest importance, that makes the chief and dearest reward of a
Private Secretary.

           [1] Written on hearing of the appointment.

[*From Alfred Lyttelton.*]   HAWARDEN CASTLE,
JANUARY 17TH.

MY DEAR REGGIE,

I must write to wish you with all cordiality good luck in your
new life. I had known of it for some little time but did not
write lest there might possibly be a slip twixt the cup and
the lip. . . .

You will now have a real opportunity of displaying what is
your peculiar genius (for no other word expresses it) the great
faculty you have for influencing people, upon a man who will
be worth influencing, and this too in matters about which you
have special knowledge. I can conceive no one more fitted for
the post or who will be more useful to a man like Hartington.
And it is because I feel this (and curiously enough have felt it for
long) that I can put aside my very great personal sorrow at losing
you, in the pleasure of seeing you in the place which above all
others you are qualified to fill.

Bless you old boy.

Yours affectionately,
ALFRED LYTTELTON.

[*Journals.*]   HALSDON,
JANUARY 9TH.

. . . Friendship is an art. A virtuoso would with the intellect
keep guard over the heart; or better, would to the mind give the
heart in guard.

A French lady observed to Valbert or Bastiat: "Nous aimons
nos amis autant qu'autrefois; mais autrefois nous les aimions en
gros, et maintenant nous les aimons en détail."

Bastiat broke with one friend "parce qu'il n'a jamais voulu
parler de moi," and with another "parce qu'il n'a jamais voulu
parler de lui." The difficulty in speaking of oneself is to know
when to stop. As Dumas observes, the best plan is never to say
more than half you mean.

[*Journals.*]   HALSDON,
                                                 JANUARY 12TH.

I heard from Harcourt this morning. Hartington will be in
town on Monday, and I leave this place to-day. I am once more
sorrowfully saying goodbye.

[*Journals.*]   LONDON,
                                        MONDAY, JANUARY 14TH.

I breakfasted this morning with Harcourt. Later I went to
Devonshire House, and was installed as Hartington's private
secretary. He was shy. . . .

Lord Granville wrote to the Duke of Sutherland asking him to
dinner on Wednesday. S. answered "Dear G. If you had asked
me a week ago I should have been delighted. But I have accepted
an invitation from Lord Beaconsfield. A poor devil must dine
somewhere you know."

[*Journals.*]   LONDON,
                                             FEBRUARY 19TH.

These two weeks have been anxious and troublesome ones;
especially for Lord Hartington. Not only has he had the usual
responsibility of an opposition leader, but the additional difficulty of managing a refractory, undisciplined party, and sooth-
ing the furious outbursts of Mr. Gladstone. A less calm, less
self-controlled, less patriotic, vainer man than he would have
given up long ago, and most assuredly last week. He sticks to
his guns with difficulty, grudgingly, but still valiantly.

[*Journals.*]   LONDON,
                                              MARCH 29TH.

On Saturday I went to Latimer and met Mr. Gladstone. . . .
Last night Lord Derby announced his resignation.[1] Very unexpectedly; it had been known by a few people since Wednesday morning, but the secret was wonderfully kept.

[*Journals.*]   LONDON,
                                               APRIL 4TH.

Gladstone says of Lord Derby, "He cannot do a difficult right,
and would not do a dangerous wrong." Of Lord Salisbury,
"He can do a difficult right, and may do a dangerous wrong."

[*Journals.*]   LONDON,
                                              JUNE 12TH.

C'est que j'ai rencontré des regards dont la flamme semble
avec mes regards, ou briller ou mourir. Et cette âme, sœur de
mon âme, hélas! que j'attendais pour aimer et souffrir.[2]

[*Journals.*]   DEVONSHIRE HO.,
                                              JULY 31ST.

The papers are full of our "success" at Berlin.[3] Dizzy is the
most popular statesman in Europe. The "breeze of popular
favour" seems to set steadily in his direction. It must veer in
time.

[1] On Lord Beaconsfield calling out the Reserve after the Treaty of San
Stefano.

[2] This was written after his first meeting with Miss Eleanor Van de
Weyer, then only just sixteen.

[3] The Congress of Berlin and "Peace with Honour."

There was an amusing passage of arms between him and Lord Granville last night on the subject of Mr. Gladstone, whom Dizzy had attacked rather sharply in an after dinner speech. The Lords cheered the old man with unusual lustiness for them. . . .

I am a Liberal on other grounds than differences of foreign policy. The "Tories of England are the Whigs of Europe" said Mme de Staël. . . .

The greatest sensation I have got this year has been from Ellen Terry's acting in *Olivia*. She is undoubtedly the best English actress in my recollection, and one of the most fascinating of personalities. . . .

Yesterday appeared the announcement that Lorne is to succeed Lord Dufferin in Canada. It is a good idea of Dizzy's. He is a bit of a poet. Rob. Lytton in India, Lorne in the Dominion. The world is then to be governed by poets.

[*Journals.*]   LONDON,
                                                  AUGUST 3RD.

The world came back from Goodwood last night, in time to divide on Lord Hartington's resolutions. The result was a large majority for the Government, and I cannot but think well deserved.[1]

The unbeaten Hungarian mare Kincsem won the Cup, being

[1] In the debate on the Congress and Treaty of Berlin the Marquis of Hartington, as Leader of the Opposition, put the following motion to the House:

"That, whilst the House has learned with satisfaction that the troubles which have arisen in the East of Europe have been terminated by the Treaty of Berlin without a further recourse to arms, and rejoices in the extension of the liberty and self-government of some of the populations of European Turkey, this House regrets that it has not been found practicable to deal in a satisfactory manner with the claims of the Kingdom of Greece and of the Greek subjects of the Porte; that by the assumption under the Anglo-Turkish Convention of a sole guarantee of the integrity of the remaining territories the thirty-seventh race she has secured. They call her Hungarian because she was bred and is owned by a Hungarian count, but her sire was Cambuscan and her dam Water Nymph.

[*Journals.*]　　　　　　　　　　　　　　　　　LONDON,
　　　　　　　　　　　　　　　　　　　　　　　AUGUST 4TH.

. . . This morning I heard from George Curzon[1] who last *On* Friday ceased to be one of the cleverest and most engaging of *Curzon.* Eton boys.

The previous letter Mr. Brett had received from Curzon, which was the last he received from him from Eton, was dated March 4th and reads:

MY DEAR BRETT,

I do not know if you authorise me to write to you by your Christian name yet. I hope the privilege may be granted in time. I have not written before, as I hoped to see you last Thursday when I was in town and when I went down to the House. Having your letter open before me I can thank you for it more satisfactorily than when I had not yet seen it.

I know what you say about flattery is quite true; I do not know myself that I have been spoilt by flattery or even that I have received it; but other people (Stanites) are so often telling me so and saying it of me, that I have arrived at the state of receiving it as a truth. I can safely say one thing, that if I am being flattered,

of Turkey in Asia, the military liabilities of this country have been unnecessarily extended; that the undefined engagements entered into by Her Majesty's Government in respect of the better administration of those provinces have imposed heavy responsibility upon the State whilst no sufficient means have been indicated for securing their fulfilment: and that such engagements have been entered into and responsibilities incurred without the previous knowledge of Parliament."

Pending the debate on this resolution, Lord Beaconsfield described it at a banquet as "a string of congratulatory regrets."

[1] Afterwards the Marquess Curzon of Kedleston.

in 9 cases out of 10 I feel what humbug it is and how undeserved, and that I endeavour to make the other person acquainted with the same fact. You ask and you repeated the question in London, what I like to hear about and to be written to about. I said anything. So I do. But I particularly like being told about character; faults in my own, good points in other people's. There is nothing I like better than the former; it is the province of a friend to correct and criticise one, at least I think so; and I owe to good friends of mine many little improvements or rather endeavoured abandonment of faults which I should not have noticed myself. Another thing or rather person I like to hear about is the person who is writing to me; not so much the actual movements, as the thoughts and aspirations; it is one of the best ways of interchanging ideas and finding things in common. So do tell me anything about yourself and what you think. I have little time for writing as I am working hard, but spare moments shall go towards filling a sheet to you, if you care to receive it.

Yours affec.,

GEORGE N. CURZON.

[*Journals.*]   STUDLEY ROYAL,
AUGUST 23RD.

*On
Manning.*   The Cardinal (Manning) came from Saturday till Monday. He was very pleasant, but is too academical not to be tiresome to me, who have had so much of dons. Since then we have had a shooting party. . . . We are alone again now, save Sir William Harcourt and Loulou.

[*Journals.*]   STUDLEY ROYAL,
AUGUST 24TH.

*Party
Intrigues.*   Last night I had a long talk with Sir William Harcourt. He claims to have invented Lord Hartington. When Mr. Gladstone

resigned the leadership in 1874, he announced his intention of not serving under Forster. He and Sir H. James offered the leadership to Lord Hartington. This did not please Lord Granville and the other leaders of the party. It, however, originated the contest between Lord Hartington and Mr. Forster. Lord Granville for a long time sat on the fence, ready to jump down on either side. He was in the habit of saying very sardonic things about Harcourt. Freddy Leveson [Granville's brother] too, was bitterly opposed to Lord Hartington's leadership. Harcourt after a talk with Freddy one day said, "Well, I don't care what you say, Freddy, it is unimportant; but you may tell your brother not to go on abusing me, for I won't have it. And if he doesn't mind *I shall not put him in the next Cabinet.*" Nothing is better proof of Harcourt's humour and big heartedness.

[*Journals.*]   BOLTON ABBEY,
                                          SEPTEMBER 1ST.

Left Studley yesterday sorrowfully. Besides the family there are here F. Cavendish, Leo Ellis, and the Granvilles. On arriving I rode up to the moors and was in time for two drives.

Lord Granville told us a good story of M. Dupin, once President of the French Academy. He was remarkable for keeping order and used to do so mainly by his satirical asides and observations. On one occasion a dull prosy speaker, M. Abraham, was occupying the time of the Chamber and met with considerable interruption. He appealed to Dupin to get him a hearing.

"That is your affair," said Dupin. He was reading his speech, and kept on shuffling his papers amid much ill-concealed impatience. "You may shuffle your cards as much as you like," said Dupin, "you won't find any trumps." Finally the uproar became so great that M. Dupin rose and said slowly and solemnly, "Abraham, Abraham, le moment de sacrifice est arrivé!"

In Paris, in September, Mr. Brett went to the Exhibition with George Curzon who then returned to England. By October, Curzon had entered on his life-long struggle against illness and pain. On the 9th he wrote from Cromford, near Derby, saying:

MY DEAR REGY,

Thanks for your kind words of enquiry. The facts are these. Since I came back from France, I have felt shooting pains in my side—in the region of the hip, and noticed the unusual prominence of that member. I went up to London about it and saw the best man. They said it was weakness of the spine resulting from natural weakness and over-work—and that I must give up Oxford for the present and lie down on my back. Paget, to whom it was settled I should go—as a final opinion—saw no harm in going to Oxford if I obey strict injunctions—wear an appliance—lie down a good deal and take no violent or indeed very active exercise. So I am respited and start tomorrow morning, to stay the night at Eton with Ainger, and go on next day to Balliol. I feel—myself—that I must be very careful and indeed Paget said if there is not improvement at Christmas I shall have to resort to the lying down. Will you some time, if possible or if you are ever near Oxford, pay me a visit? I should enjoy it above all things. (I write in pencil because I am lying down.) . . .

[*Journals.*]   CHATSWORTH,
                                           NOVEMBER 23RD.

Dizzy said to Dicky Doyle on one occasion, "Owing to circumstances I have sometimes had to talk a great deal, but nature made me a listener."

... Last night I dined with Lord and Lady Ripon; an informal entertainment in lieu of Lord Granville's usual party, which in accordance with a similar arrangement on the part of Ministers is deferred until after the recess. .... My Chief brought the *The* speech in his pocket to the dinner party in Carlton Gardens. *Queen's* There were the Granvilles, Northbrooks, Gladstones, Harcourts, *Speech.* and Mr. Forster. Lord Kimberley came in with the dessert. I sat between the late Governor-General and his daughter, Lady Emma. After dinner Lord Granville read the Queen's speech. The ladies had, of course, retired. It was some time before these magnates settled to their work. We did not leave the dining room till half-past eleven.

Lord Northbrook was admirably temperate and forcible; showing thorough and accurate knowledge of all the facts; together with a statesmanlike disregard of trivial points, and broad conception of every difficulty and risk. My Chief was finely accurate, and showed great clearness and coolness of head.

Much as I am attracted by Mr. Gladstone in his quiet subdued *On* moments, and great as he is, I am amazed that he should be the *Gladstone.* idol of our sober people. While he was speaking I felt he was an enemy in politics and morals. He has led men by their passions rather than by their intellects. On his part this has not been cunning, but unconscious action. ...

Just now a telegram arrived which was sent to us, announcing the capture of the Peiwar Kotal or Sherpur by Roberts,[1] after defeating the Afghans and taking 18 guns.

... For some while I stood on the steps of the Throne listening to Lord Granville, who was very piano.

[1] Afterwards F.M. Earl Roberts.

. . . Schouvaloff, the Russian Ambassador, stood next to me listening blandly to the courteous insults levelled against his Government. Later in the evening he was loitering at the stage door of the Alhambra; still bland.

[*Journals.*]   LONDON,
                                             DECEMBER 9TH.

Party Troubles.   I saw Harcourt this morning. The dissatisfaction of members below the gangway seems to have been graver than I thought. Some days ago there was a private meeting, at which it was resolved to take any opportunity which might offer to trip up and overturn my Chief. . . . Harcourt was severe. He thinks Lord H. deteriorated. Yesterday he was talking about him to Lady Ripon. She, who does not like Lord Hartington, tried to soften the severity of Harcourt's criticism by drawing his attention to my Chief's undoubted and irreproachable honesty. "Yes," said Harcourt, "but in this case honesty is not the best policy." Harcourt is really fond of Lord H., whom he looks upon as mainly his creation. . . . Of course we are in great difficulties. The extreme left will have no one but Gladstone. The left centre will have anyone but Gladstone. There must come a change in the personnel of parties.

[*Journals.*]   LONDON,
                                             DECEMBER 12TH.

Last night I dined with the Vernon Harcourts in Grafton Street. My Chief was there, the Bedfords, Schouvaloff, Cardwells, Dilke and Chamberlain. My Chief sat next to Chamberlain, and they talked a good deal; smoothing the way for the future I hope. Schouvaloff was very amusing. . . .

Berlin Congress.   At the Berlin Congress, Lord Beaconsfield spoke in English, but Lord Salisbury in French; "Foreign Office French" as Schouvaloff observed.

He says that Bismarck kept them in tremendous order. If any subject was discussed warmly, he used at once to say, "If this goes on, I shall go to Kissingen." "Go away, arrangez-vous comme vous voulez, come here when it is settled, but if this discussion goes on, I am off to Kissingen."

If someone tried to introduce the subject of the Montenegrins he at once broke out "Si cela continue, I shall go to Kissingen. Je ne veux pas entendre parler de ces gens là." What would Mr. Gladstone say if he heard the Montenegrins called "ces gens là"?

With the Bulgarians it was just the same; "I shall go to Kissingen." Never was a Congress so treated.

. . . The Berlin Treaty he declares, will not last. It will be destroyed, he says, by the exigencies of the case. "We shall fulfil it, but the moment that we quit Turkish soil, le traité ne sera plus."

[*Journals.*]   LONDON,
                                                DECEMBER 13TH.

I have heard the French mot better related. Someone speaking of modern French society said that the Legitimists were "le monde" and the Bonapartists "le demi-monde." "What then are the Orleanists?" "Ah! les Orléanistes sont la revue des deux mondes."

I had a talk with Lord Ripon last night on the strategical position in the North-West.

[*Journals.*]   LONDON,
                                                DECEMBER 20TH.

Yesterday my Chief left town. He went to Kimbolton, where he stays till Christmas. My brother Eugene dined with me last night. He had met, a few evenings before, Greenwood, editor

Bismarck.
of the *Pall Mall Gazette*, who told him one curious thing. Bismarck, hearing that he was in Berlin, sent for him, and praised the *Pall Mall*, saying that it was the only independent newspaper within his acquaintance. He offered him the run of the public offices, all the information he could give him, on the condition that once a month a German professor should be allowed to write an article in the *Pall Mall*, to state the "facts" of German policy; no argument, only facts. Greenwood refused. . . .

[*From Miss Ellen Terry.*[1]]   33, LONGRIDGE ROAD,
                                                 JANUARY 3RD, 1879.

It seems I've succeeded and *not* failed!! I send the scrawl written on that terrible night, so you may know I was not ungrateful for your kind thought of me. . . . I hurried home after the play on Monday convinced I had failed—failed—*failed*. Oh! the wonderful next morning! to find I was quite wrong. *I wasn't though.* I *had* quite failed to satisfy myself—and I played the mad scene so very much better on Tuesday. . . .

                                Very truly yours,
                                    ELLEN WARDELL TERRY.

[*Journals.*]   LONDON,
                                                 JANUARY 12TH.

*Russian
Policy.*
 . . . Harcourt in a conversation with Schouvaloff said to him "There are two things we shall never submit to: 1. that you should occupy Constantinople; 2. get command of the Straits; but with the rest of Turkey in Europe you may do as you please."
Schouvaloff said it would be possible to settle our differences with Russia on this basis. . . .

                    [1] On her first performance as Ophelia.

[*To Lord Hartington.*]   DEVONSHIRE HO.,
                            FEBRUARY 4TH.

If you wish to make fun, I think you might chaff Northcote about the *Sultan's Ball* in 1868 which he—then Sec. for India— charged on Indian Revenue. It was really a fantastical allegorical rehearsal of what he is doing now.[1]

If you get anywhere near the subject you might show that the *Foreign Policy.* Government do not understand—what Lord Palmerston knew so well—that the assent of the House of Commons strengthens the hands of the Foreign Secretary in dealing with a foreign nation. That the loud unanswered criticisms, which are the result of maintaining secrecy, weaken his hand. That if the Government adopt the foreign plan of secrecy they should, to be consistent and successful, adopt the further plan of restricting adverse criticisms in newspapers and at public meetings. Their half measures must always end in qualified success, if not in failure. . . . Bismarck in 1870 imprisoned Jacoby and others for openly criticising his action, as it tended *to encourage the French in their resistance.*

[*Journals.*]   LONDON,
                            FEBRUARY 8TH.

. . . Lord Dufferin goes to St. Petersburg instead of Augustus *Lord* Loftus. . . . It is good for England that Lord Dufferin should go *Dufferin to Russia* to charm the Russians. But from a party point of view I regret it. We shall probably turn him into a Tory, as we have done Sir Henry Elliott, and Layard and possibly old Odo Russell. It is clever of Dizzy to appoint him. One other Viceroy of the Dominion was Russian Ambassador. The Whigs ultimately destroyed and killed Lord Durham. *Absit omen.*

[1] The Government, in which Sir Stafford Northcote was Chancellor of the Exchequer, were of opinion that the cost of the Afghan War should be a charge upon Indian Revenue. The Opposition declared that the war was part of Imperial, and not of Indian, policy.

[Journals.]   LONDON,
                                         FEBRUARY 11TH.

Zulu
Battle.   There is sad news this morning from Africa. Owing apparently to great carelessness a convoy of our people was surprised
by Zulus[1] and after a desperate resistance was utterly annihilated.
The 24th Regiment with all its officers is cut to pieces, colours
captured, artillery, rifles, ammunition, and stores. I have no
heart to work to-day.

[Journals.]   LONDON,
                                         FEBRUARY 14TH.

. . . The newspapers have said civil things about Lord Augustus Loftus, which is quite proper; but someone has cynically said
that in order to get a Dufferin they had to get a duffer out. . . .

[Journals.]   LONDON,
                              ASH WEDNESDAY, FEBRUARY 26TH.

Last night I dined with the Freddy Cavendishes. We went
afterwards to the Lyceum. Ellen Terry as Ophelia proved herself to be the flower of actresses. Sarah Bernhardt would not
have played the part more exquisitely.

George Hamilton has made a great speech to his constituents,
the great feature of which was the following incident. He was
eloquently pursuing a worn theme: "And why did Mr. Gladstone do this? And why did Mr. Gladstone do the other? I will
tell you why. Mr. Gladstone has an eye on the Treasury Bench."
Upon which a man in the crowd cried out "Yes, and if you
don't look out he'll have his bottom on it very soon." This
emanates from the Carlton! . . .

I have been to one of the first of Lady Granville's *evenings.*

                    [1] Under Cetewayo at Isandhlwana.

She is *at home* in the foreign fashion four days a week. It was very pleasant. Lady Cowper picked me up at St. James' Hall after the Monday concert, and we drove to Lady G's together.

[*Journals.*]   LONDON,
                                                    MARCH 4TH.

On Saturday I dined at the German Embassy. The Granvilles were there, he rather less deaf than usual. Joachim dined. I talked with him after dinner, but he did not play.

Lord Chelmsford's despatch has arrived.[1] . . . The most *Zulu* ordinary precautions appear to have been neglected. They *Battle.* have recovered the colours of the 24th Regiment, which were supposed to have been lost. They were found wrapped round the body of Lieutenant Melville, on the Natal side of the river. He, together with a brother officer Coghill, had cut their way through the enemy, and crossed the river, but succumbed from the effects of their wounds. The *Pall Mall* publishes an article attacking Lord Chelmsford. There is not much to be gained by that.

[*Journals.*]   LONDON,
                                                    MARCH 14TH.

Last night I dined with the Ripons. Mr. Gladstone, who was *Gladstone.* there, talked a great deal about Seeley's *Life of Stein*, which though inartistic, contains many important things.

Mrs. Gladstone introduced the topic of the Royal wedding[2] which had taken place in the morning and to which Mr. Gladstone had not been invited, in spite of a private remonstrance made to the Queen through Dizzy. It is true that Mr. G. has been very injudicious. . . .

[1] From Africa.
[2] The marriage of the Duke of Connaught and Princess Louise Marguerite of Prussia.

[*Journals.*]   LONDON,
                                                 MARCH 18TH.

Last night the Derbys gave a party. Several Ministers were
there, contrary to general expectations. Afterwards I went to
the Bischoffsheims', where Lady Lonsdale[1] was incomparably
superior in beauty to everyone else. It was her first appearance
and she was shy.

[*Journals.*]   LONDON,
                                                  APRIL 8TH.

A few weeks ago I spent some days at Mentmore with
Rosebery. I have a sheet of notes scribbled in the evenings out
of which I have preserved the following:

Granville
Dicta.
Lord Granville gave us proof of Mr. Gladstone's mastery of
financial detail: that in 1853 when he brought forward his first
budget, he took four hours explaining it to the Cabinet, speaking
uninterrupted for that time, and that when next day he brought
it before the House of Commons, he did not make use of any
passage which he had used the previous day.

Lord Granville has always felt the "Cabinet" to be a great
bond between him and those with whom he has served. And
during all his public life, only one man remained a stranger to
him after they had been in a Cabinet together. This was Sir
James Graham. Talleyrand it appears, was dull in society, like
Dizzy, though he occasionally had brilliant sallies. Lord Melbourne said of him "a damned bore, that fellow Talleyrand,"
after a dinner at Holland House. . . .

Lord Aberdeen[2] was said to be very gruff and rude, and yet to
have been highly popular with men and women.

Dilke and Lord Granville agreed that Dowse was the wittiest
member who had addressed the House of Commons in their
time. . . .

[1] Afterwards Gladys, Marchioness of Ripon.
[2] Prime Minister in 1853.

[*Journals.*]   PARIS,
                                                       APRIL 10TH

Last night I saw *Ruy Blas* at the Théâtre Français with
Sarah Bernhardt as the Queen, Mounet Sully as Ruy Blas and
the admirable Coquelin as Don César. I have been reading
François Coppée's charming little plays, *Le Passant* being
quite first-rate in its way. . . .

[*Journals.*]   LONDON,
                                                        MAY 10TH.

I went to Newmarket; a pleasant week's racing; Lord Falmouth again succeeded in the great races. The season has begun;
but there is much grumbling at its slackness. People take advantage of their supposed poverty to dispense with entertainments. . . .

[*Journals.*]   PANSHANGER,
                                                         JUNE 7TH.

I went last Friday to Epsom, and enjoyed keenly watching
Lord Falmouth's beautiful mare, Wheel of Fortune, win the
Oaks. She has never yet lost a race.

Henry Calcraft[1] told us to-day that Dizzy has, for three
months, wished to send Wolseley to the Cape. But he was overruled in the Cabinet. . . .

The party here consists of the Northamptons, Elchos, Percy
Wyndham, Arthur Balfour, Henry Calcraft and Spencer
Lyttelton.

[*Journals.*]   LONDON,
                                                         JUNE 8TH.

I left Panshanger yesterday, travelling up to town with the *Dufferin.*
Dufferins. He certainly is charming, and I suppose the most
                    [1] P.U.S. Board of Trade.

popular man in Europe. But what a bore it must be having to keep up such a reputation.

On the 24th September he married Eleanor, youngest daughter of M. Sylvain van de Weyer, Belgian Minister at the Court of St. James. M. van de Weyer had formerly taken a leading part in placing the King of the Belgians on the throne, and had been the Belgian signatory to the famous "Scrap of Paper" which brought Great Britain into the Great War of 1914.

For two months Mr. Brett was in Paris on his honeymoon.

[*Journals.*]   HÔTEL BRIGHTON, PARIS,
                                 OCTOBER 18TH.

... We have been reading together the story of "Romola" and her sorrow. In elaboration, in sheer hard work alone, the book is a marvel.

To-day I met Mr. Gladstone in an antiquity shop on the Quai Voltaire and had some talk with him. He was searching for ivories. Last night he went to see *Hernani* and showed the keenest interest.

[*Journals.*]   PARIS,
                                     OCTOBER 29TH.

On Life.   Ernlé Johnson growls at being misunderstood by his teachers at Oxford. As if any life worth living ever was understood by contemporary critics. It is unwise to expect to be surrounded by sympathy of the more discriminating sort. The interesting thing, after all, is to understand your companions, not to be understood by them.

... There is not much glory in loving perfection; nor in reaching happiness if you are held safe from sorrow, like young people at the end of fairy tales. Ernlé is not to be pitied, though he cries with Keats: "O for a life of sensations rather than of thoughts." He really, like Keats, combines the two, which is the higher good. Strong feelings and a raging imagination are worth more than being understood and such shadows. . . .

[*Journals.*]   PARIS,
                                                        NOVEMBER 14TH.

Yesterday there came a letter from Gambetta's secretary to say   *On* that the President would see me to-day at half-past one. So, I   *Meeting* drove to the Palais Bourbon after breakfast. It is well guarded   *Gambetta.* by sentries, who present arms as one drives through the archway, and up to the palace steps. A servant in black asked for my card, and I was shown into an ante-room with an oak floor, and surrounded with red velvet benches, not unlike a smart waiting room at an Italian station. In a moment or two, however, an official appeared, who apologised for the delay, and showed me through a very stately room in white and gold Louis XV panels, into another room in the same style, where there were fine tapestry chairs ranged in rows, and a few men walking and talking in whispers.

An official in a sword and chain stood at the door, behind which could be heard Gambetta's voice. Shortly adieux were heard and there came out Sardou, the playwright, and I was immediately shown into a large room, furnished in much the same way, at a table in the centre of which sat Gambetta.

There were a few arm chairs placed about, to one of which he motioned me, after giving me his hand in a friendly way. After preliminaries, we talked about English politics. He thinks my Chief a man of more power than is usually admitted. Thought his speech at Newcastle very good, and the last one quite as good, which is not my opinion. He thinks him a better leader for the country's sake and for Europe's than Mr. Gladstone.

He does not think the Tories will be beaten, though in the last few weeks there has been a change of feeling. If Dizzy had dissolved after the peace of Gandamak, he thinks the Ministers would have had a large majority. All this might have been said by a well-informed newspaper correspondent. However, he added that he hoped our people would not come in, as it would perhaps be fatal to the country.

He cannot understand how we can effect any compromise with "ces gens là" (his way of describing the Irish) and without them we could not keep even a small majority.

As for Treaties of Commerce, he thinks this Government can manage them as well as another; and since the bad harvest, etc., the French people will look upon the treaties with no unfriendly eye.

Then we relapsed into personal matters. He is to send Arnaud, his private secretary, to me tomorrow to make acquaintance. I am glad of this. I think I did not bore him.

[*To Lord Hartington.*]   Paris,
                                 November 15th.

Gambetta.

I was invited yesterday to an interview with Gambetta; a regular solemn interview. (Through the instrumentality of Dilke.) It was rather amusing, and I have taken note how such things should be managed with a view to *our* arrangements. The great man was very affable and had a certain amount to say. . . .

His appearance is not quite what you gather from his pictures. He is not always dignified, being very short and decidedly podgy. His way of holding his head too, gives him the appearance, now and then, of a cunning Jew. On the other hand, an idea wakes him up in a flash, and you have a lion-like attitude— that pose of the head which is familiar to one in his photographs.

Tomorrow he is going to a "chasse" with Grévy, for the first time; and this is looked upon as an important political event. That is all my news.

Who is to be at Chatsworth when we are there? Anyone who will alarm Nell very much?

Gambetta resembles you in this (so his private sec. tells me) that he is the most indulgent and least "exigeant" of Chiefs.

[*Journals.*]   MIDNIGHT.

I have just finished reading aloud the last pages of *Romola*. *Romola.* It is incomparable, and increases one's pride in the human race. It is difficult to read aloud; almost too noble in parts to make it possible to stifle tears.

[*Journals.*]   CHATSWORTH,
                                          DECEMBER 4TH.

Harcourt spent this morning with me in my Chief's room. *Election* We made out a list of peers and M.P.s who may be asked to *Plans.* subscribe to a General Election fund. There are 114 of them. An average of £500 apiece would, Harcourt thinks, enable us to win 20 country seats. We further made out a list of men in both Houses, who aspire to places in a Liberal Government. . . .

Harcourt will only accept one of two offices; Chancellor of the Exchequer and First Lord of the Admiralty.[1]

He says he would make a better Chancellor than Goschen though he doubts whether the public would think so.

[*Journals.*]   DEVONSHIRE HO.,
                                         DECEMBER 17TH.

There is worse news from Afghanistan to-day. Telegraphic communication with Kabul has been cut. We shall not hear news from Roberts for some time. He has asked for reinforcements, which will no doubt be sent.

Tonight we dined with George Trevelyan.[2] I had a talk with

[1] He accepted the Home Office.

[2] Sir George Trevelyan, afterwards Irish Secretary.

Lecky on
Ireland.

Lecky the historian, an amiable man and pleasant companion. He thinks Ireland unsuited for Parliamentary Government. There is no natural leadership of the people by the squires as there is in England, and they are swayed about between the demagogues and the priests.

He says his countrymen are naturally a loyal people. A Government with a strong executive would suit them best, and a system of "préfets" like in France. This makes the outlook very black, as there is no chance of reform taking that direction. On the contrary, there is every probability that their liberty will be still further widened. And if so, troubles will come thicker. Material progress and the slow march of education are then the only panaceas in prospect. This means no political improvement for many years. It is a dark picture.

[*To Lord Hartington.*]   LONDON,
                                        DECEMBER 20TH.

Standing
for
Falmouth.

. . . Perhaps Adam told you that Lord Northbrook had sent to me a Falmouth solicitor, who has some political weight in that borough, to ask me whether I would stand at the next election in lieu of Cole Q.C., who retires.

The advantages are obvious, as the seat when won is a safe one. The disadvantages may be summed up in a few figures. It costs about £1,000 to fight an election, which is moderate; and £500 a year to keep the seat, which is a good deal. What shall I do? I am to see Lord Northbrook on Monday and give my answer. I should like to know whether you think it worth my while to accept.

[*To Lady Brett.*]   STUDLEY ROYAL, RIPON,
                                    JANUARY 14TH, 1880.

Falmouth.

. . . This morning I received a formal invitation from the Liberals of Penryn and Falmouth, to stand at the next election of their borough. I have discussed the matter with Lord North-brook and Lord Hartington, and they both very strongly advise me to say yes.

It is not sure that I shall be returned by any means, as Sir Julius Vogel is a good candidate.

However, I make out that the election will be a cheap one; costing me and my colleague about seven hundred apiece. . . .

It is an expensive seat to keep at the rate which the present senior member has been spending at; but, as Lord H. says, if I don't intend to stand again I can diminish expenses as much as I like.

He thinks it a good thing for me to stand, whether I am beaten or not. It improves my position in the country and the party, if anything were to happen to him. That is if he were to cease to lead the party, which might well happen. . . .

Mr. Brett was elected and sat in the House of Commons as M.P. for Penryn and Falmouth from 1880 to 1885. He re-mained, however, with Lord Hartington, going with him as his Private Secretary to the India Office.

[*Journals.*]   LONDON,
                                                   JANUARY 17TH.

Yesterday I left Studley, and came to town. A few days ago I showed Lord Ripon the list which Harcourt and I had made at Chatsworth, of candidates aspiring to office in the next Liberal administration. Next day, Lady Ripon told me that he wished to know why his name had been omitted; I said to her that neither Harcourt nor I had mentioned him throughout our conversation. I never for a moment supposed he had office in view; having, when he became a Catholic, abandoned the idea of it.

. . . The evening before we left we had a long conversation on the subject. He said after dinner that he wished to speak to me, and we adjourned to his room. Then he told me that Lady

Lord Ripon: Catholics in Office.

Ripon had told him the result of our conversation. He does not wish me to say anything to my Chief, or to Harcourt, although he does not object to my doing so if I think proper. He wished me to know that his views of his own eligibility for office, as a Catholic, are not what they were five years ago. . . .

Lord Halifax is the only man with whom he has ever discussed the probability of his resuming office, and he was strongly of the opinion that Lord Ripon might very well be placed in the Cabinet, notwithstanding his religious opinions.

Whether it would be wise for a Prime Minister to give him office he was not prepared to say; that would depend on circumstances; but he wished me to know that he did not consider himself "out of the running."

[*Journals.*]   LONDON,
APRIL 7TH.

. . . Victories come pouring in. In a few weeks we shall be in office. It is not a pleasant prospect.

[*To Lord Hartington.*]   CASTLE ASHBY,
APRIL 14TH.

Gladstone Dispute.   I cannot say that I expected to hear of any other resolve on Mr. Gladstone's part, than that which he has announced to Lord Wolverton. He said very plainly some months ago that he would not take office *under* anyone, and I do not see that anything has occurred or could occur which would make him swerve from that determination. Besides the position would be even more difficult with Mr. Gladstone in a subordinate position in the Cabinet than it is likely to be with him outside the Ministry altogether.

In a month he would be quarrelling with Harcourt at every meeting and in six weeks one or the other would have thrown up his place. At that dinner twelve months ago at Lord Ripon's just before the session, it struck me, and must have struck everyone else, that Mr. Gladstone, if he is to form part of a Ministry, could only do so in one capacity.

[*Journals.*]　　CASTLE ASHBY,
APRIL.

Been up and down from here daily. My Chief saw the Queen alone and told her plainly that Mr. Gladstone and no other could form a Government. He said that if *he* were to succeed it would be a more Radical Government than one formed by Mr. Gladstone, as *he* would have to give the lion's share to the Radicals, whereas Mr. Gladstone's Government would be predominantly Whig. *The Queen and Mr. Gladstone.*

The Queen was very obdurate. She insisted on my Chief returning to town and consulting Mr. G. and Lord Granville. He returned to Windsor after these interviews with Lord Granville. The Queen first saw my Chief alone, and then Lord Granville, who was waiting in the next room, was sent for, and endorsed what my Chief had said as to the impossibility of any one save Mr. Gladstone forming an administration. They then left for town, and the Queen sent for Mr. Gladstone.

[*Journals.*]　　1, TILNEY STREET,
APRIL 1ST.

We have returned here after a long stay at Castle Ashby, owing to Nell's illness and we are settled in Tilney Street.[1]

The ministry is now all but formed. There have been endless intrigues and counter-intrigues. . . .

[1] He had bought No. 1 Tilney Street, Mayfair, directly he returned from his honeymoon in Paris, but did not take up residence there till now.

Ripon to India.

That Lord Ripon should go to India surprises many and gives pain to several friends of his and hers. My brother goes with him and he has the good fortune to secure the services of "Chinese" Gordon as his private secretary.

[*From Sir Henry Ponsonby.*[1]]   OSBORNE,
                                          AUGUST 10TH.

DEAR MR. BRETT,

I am sorry to have given you the trouble of correcting so small a mistake. Your confidential Memo., which I have given to the Queen, was most valuable at this moment as it helps to remove some erroneous impressions that were being formed as to the action of the I.O.

                              Yours truly,
                                    HENRY F. PONSONBY.

[*To Lord Hartington.*]   LONDON,
                                 AUGUST 12TH.

This is General Ponsonby's letter which I mentioned to you. The Memo. referred to was a collection of telegrams *which had been sent to the Queen*—arranged in order, with notes drawing attention to the chief points, to show what had been done by you since news of the disaster[2] arrived.

I sent it to Ponsonby thinking it might be useful to him to explain the meaning of the short telegrams to the Queen.

These telegrams, unless read consecutively, are very ambiguous. The Queen has no doubt so much to read that she forgets their sequence. They are so concise, that her attention is not sufficiently attracted to the importance of each word. Hence

---

[1] Private Secretary to the Queen.
[2] The disaster referred to is the defeat of General Burrows at Maiwand, on July 27th, which was the occasion for General Roberts's march from Kabul to Kandahar.

misconceptions. I suppose you have no objection to my sending occasionally explanations to Sir H. Ponsonby. I think it is useful.

[*Journals.*] STUDLEY ROYAL,
SEPTEMBER 4TH.

To-day we received news of Roberts' victory at Kandahar. It does not yet appear, however, that it was of a decisive character.

The session is now coming to an end. The House of Lords did *Irish* their best further to prolong it, by throwing out another Irish *Affairs.* Bill, and giving great offence thereby to the Irish and to the Radicals. Mr. Forster made a speech threatening the House of Lords with "alteration." It was a clap-trap sort of speech without justification.

The Queen, who last week remonstrated at Mr. Forster's language about Ireland, will again be furious. He is supposed to be a tolerant and kindly man. His language in Parliament when contradicted or foiled . . . is supposed to be characteristic of honesty. . . .

Lady Ripon, who is fond of him, says he is only an overgrown baby, who did not have his fling when young.

[*Journals.*] 1, TILNEY STREET.
SEPTEMBER 5TH.

To-day I finished a biography which has recently been printed of "Sister Dora," who died at Walsall in December 1878. She was an unruly member of an "Anglican" sisterhood, and practically a hospital nurse at Walsall near Lichfield. She seems to have been a remarkable woman.

Part of the book is probably fabulous. But eliminate probabilities and still you have the character of a woman proud, tender, determined, passionate, religious, independent and eager for power. Her physical beauty considerable, her strength prodigious. Her cures were wonderful, her devotedness great. She was adored by all who approached her during her ministering to the sick. In the Middle Ages she would have been canonised. In these prosaic times she was unknown beyond her small town, but with all her faults has won for herself a place among heroes. Her death was of a piece with her life, full of beauties and shadows.

[*To Lord Rosebery.*]   LONDON,
                                        SEPTEMBER 17TH.

Kandahar.   Harcourt left here yesterday for Scotland. He, I think, is not so convinced as he was of the advantage of immediately evacuating Kandahar.

Putting other reasons aside I cannot see that it will be more difficult to come away six months hence than it is now. Who is to be blinded by the halo of Roberts' achievement? The natives of India or the English constituencies? The game is hardly worth playing. On the other hand a settlement, even nominal, *Indian Policy.* of the Central Asian question, is worth the expenditure of a good deal of Lord Granville's time, and the money it will cost to occupy Kandahar for a few months. Two things are at present clear:

1. Persia is alienated from us.
2. The temper of Abdur Rahman is uncertain.

In the course of the next five years you may have the Russians at Merv, the Persians avowedly friendly to Russia and hostile to us, and Abdur Rahman playing into the hands of Skobeleff.

I do not believe that India would be threatened seriously by such a state of things, as I am convinced that she is strong enough to resist such a combination if she is attacked. But is the present Government, or would any Government be strong enough to resist the pressure that would be brought to bear upon it and avoid adopting tactics which have cost India so much? If you are prepared to remain quiet in the face of such a state of things as I have described then you are justified in coming away at once from Kandahar. If you are not, then I cannot help thinking you would be wise to arrange beforehand to meet such an exigency by acquiescing at once cheerfully, before Europe and India, in a Russian occupation of Merv, and by making such terms with her and with Persia as will enable you to defy the Jingoism of Anglo-Indians and English Tories. . . .

Note: The course of the affair of Kandahar was as follows:

The siege was raised by General Roberts on August 31st, and Ayub's army was defeated by him on the following day. The Queen then became the principal bar to the evacuation. She first held that an undertaking from Mr. Gladstone on assuming office that there should be no reversal of facts debarred his Government from ordering the evacuation. The Liberals were able to show, however, that the Beaconsfield Government had not announced any permanent occupation and therefore there was no fact. The Crown Princess of Germany and the Duke of Cambridge were writing to the Queen in favour of the retention of Kandahar, but her Ministers were united in opposition to it. The decision was embodied in a despatch to Lord Ripon on November 11th in which the moment was left to his discretion, but he was directed to do nothing which would prevent the evacuation of Kandahar at the earliest opportunity. The decision was not announced to the public until the speech from the Throne on January 6th of the following year—in a very vague and reticent sentence. Lord Lytton, Ripon's immediate predecessor, obtained the publication of papers and arraigned the Government on their Afghan policy on March 3rd. The Lords passed a heavy vote of censure which was equally definitely reversed in the Commons. The evacuation was carried out on April 13th.

The bloody wrangling over the town prophesied by the Tories lasted six months and involved only two battles. Abdur Rahman's governor was defeated by Ayub in July, and Ayub by Abdur Rahman in person in September.

LONDON,
                                              SEPTEMBER 19TH.

The Queen   . . . The Queen has several times this session remonstrated
in Politics.   with her Ministers, and I must confess that on every occasion
I think her interference has been justified. She always gives way
before the authority of the Cabinet but she will not always yield
at once to the opinion of a single Minister.

Mr. Gladstone is indignant with her and asserts that he would
never be surprised to see her turn the Government out after the
manner of her uncles. But this is the impulsive side of his
character, rebelling against any interference from authority. He
is ready to obey those whom he looks upon as his inferiors, but
resents adverse opinion from anyone who is his equal or superior.
He is, in short, an amiable tyrant.

[*To Lord Cowper.*[1]]   LONDON,
                                              SEPTEMBER 25TH.

Free   I hope you will have nothing to do with suppressing agitation
Speech in   in Ireland by force or by law, call it which you will.
Ireland.   I do not maintain that the principle of absolute freedom of
speech is a good thing everywhere, but I am convinced that
wherever you have to do with Englishmen, either as a dominant
class or not, you cannot afford to ignore it. Observe how in
India the experience of the last few years has taught us that it does
not do to yield to the very natural desire to prevent people saying
what is disagreeable and what may be dangerous. In India the
experiment of muzzling sedition has been tried. It has failed,
and the old plan of allowing men to say what they please has
been resorted to.

It has failed because you never can really suppress sedition by
muzzling the seditious and you invariably, when you have to do
with Englishmen, enlist sympathy on their side. The only argu-

---

[1] Lord Lieutenant, the Secretary being W. E. Forster.

ment worth anything that can be brought forward in favour of interfering with agitations is that you interfere in the interests of the poor ignorant persons who may be led by seditious language into breaches of the peace. I admit the force of this argument, but my answer is that you cannot, in determining upon any course of action, be determined by one argument, however forcible, until you have weighed it against all that can be brought forward on the other side. I think these, which are familiar to you, are overwhelming; and I believe that the greater the latitude allowed to agitators in Ireland, the more you diminish their chances of success.

Repression has been tried for a great number of years, and we have had Ribandism and Fenianism and their bloody accessories. Let us loyally try, without fussiness or timidity, the magic of freedom, and I am sure you will do more to secure the tranquillity of Ireland than you will do by any Land Bills, however ingeniously devised.

Parnell said in the House of Commons that wherever the Land League of Ireland flourished, agrarian crime diminished. If that is true, and it is worth verifying, it means that wherever you allow the people to meet together, to march openly to meetings and talk over their real and imaginary grievances, you turn their thoughts away from conspiracy and crime.

You are ruling Ireland now in accordance with the narrow prejudices of the British middle-class. At least rule her then in accordance with their virtuous scruples. You refuse to recognise the fact that her people are Irish Catholics. The least you can do is to recognise that they are British subjects. Very soon the novelty of speeches like Mr. Dillon's famous outbreak will wear off and their influence will diminish in direct ratio. That is the end at which to aim. All men, even Irishmen, very soon sicken of exaggerated phrases, and when Mr. Dillon has run through his short vocabulary, the people will throw him aside like a sucked orange.

There is no knowing what men bound together by a desire for official existence may be constrained to do. But Lord Cowper is by his position free from any imposing force of this kind, and I sincerely trust that rather than lend himself to any further repression in Ireland, however specious the argument may be on which it is based, he will return to the quiet of Panshanger.

What think you of the things in the East? Les rites établis divisent aujourd'hui le genre humain, et la morale le réunit.

[*Journals.*]   LONDON,
                                                                SEPTEMBER 30TH.

Religion and Ireland.   . . . The Irish question is and has always been a religious question. And so long as we continue to govern Ireland as a Protestant country we shall govern it ineffectually. The stupidity of the British middle-class is not likely, I fear, to be overcome on this point.

Is it not strange that the English, who flatter themselves they can govern alien races better than any other nation on the earth's surface, should fail when they come to deal with Catholic Celts?

If the Irish were Mahommedans or Hindus we should have no difficulty with them. Every consideration would be then shown to their religious prejudices. Because they are Catholics they have been treated like dogs and are borne down by the vulgar bigotry of English evangelicism. Here in England, we insist, and we are entitled to do so, upon Protestant supremacy. We shall do no good in Ireland until we admit there the supremacy of the Catholics.

[*Journals.*]   LONDON,
                                                                OCTOBER 9TH.

Afghan Affairs.   Lord Ripon has sent home a memorandum on the annexation of the Afghan district of Pishin, which he strongly advocates. As I have said to him and to Lord H. [Hartington], the Government have, while Kandahar is in their possession, an opportunity of settling with Russia the Central Asian difficulty between the two nations.

. . . Lord H. says the Queen is very gracious. However, she *The* avoids discussing the subject of Kandahar with him, and he has *Queen's* hitherto failed to make her talk. He fears she is getting into the *Attitude.* habit of avoiding the discussion of subjects with her ministers which are unpalatable to her.

It appears to me there is wisdom in her course. For either she or her Ministers must give way, and as she knows she stands no chance against a united Cabinet, she prefers to avoid going through the form of yielding by tacitly ignoring the difference, after it has been once stated.

[*Journals.*]   LONDON,
                                          NOVEMBER 6TH.

The Queen has been influenced by those about her to post- *Kandahar.* pone as long as possible the announcement about Kandahar. To-day I had a long letter from Ponsonby in which the Queen's reasons are put for not desiring an immediate announcement, although he intimates that the decision has been taken and rather queries if that is not the case. . . .

Lord H. [Hartington] is engaged in fighting a battle with the *Indian* Duke of Cambridge about the Chief Command in India. He *Command.* wants it for Sir Charles Ellice, and opposes the nomination of Stewart, who has been recommended by Lord H. I am in favour of Wolseley, on the ground that he would be the best military and political appointment which could be made. He is one of the few soldiers I know who is at the same time a clever man. . . .

I regretted not to get down to Hardwick this week, but there was a press of work at the office, and I like to be there when Lord H. is away.

[*Journals.*]   LONDON,
                                                 NOVEMBER 21ST.

Yesterday I had a long interview with Sir F. Roberts.[1] He is very simple and plain spoken.

[*Journals.*]   LONDON,
                                                 NOVEMBER 22ND.

. . . This evening about 7 o'clock I went to see Harcourt. He was in bed in his dressing room. He tells me that for years past whenever he has wished to be alone and to think uninterruptedly, he has been in the habit of going to bed.

[*Journals.*]   LONDON,
                                                 JANUARY 5TH, 1881.

The Queen's Speech.

The Queen held a Council to-day to approve her speech. Harcourt and Lord Spencer went to Osborne. At about 1 o'clock Mr. Gladstone received a telegram to say that the Queen strongly objected to the stipulation about Kandahar; she had only agreed to the original despatch on the subject on the understanding that it should not be announced.

Here was an unexpected difficulty. The speech must be given to the Opposition leaders to-night, and to some of the papers.

Lord H. [Hartington] and Mr. Gladstone replied that four months have passed since then, and it is absolutely necessary to announce the fact of our retirement now.

This crossed another message from the Queen, which arrived about half-past two, to the effect that she would agree to any modification of the words which did not contain an announcement of the withdrawal.

----

[1] Afterwards F.M. Earl Roberts.

The prospect looked dark, and Lord H. was wondering whether Parliament would have to be further prorogued. At last, however—at 10 minutes to six—came a telegram giving her Majesty's assent. The only result is, therefore, that Harcourt and Lord S. [Spencer] will miss their dinner.

[*Journals.*]　　　　　　　　　　LONDON,
　　　　　　　　　　　　　　　　　JANUARY 6TH.

Sir H. Ponsonby was sent up from Osborne to-day by the Queen. He says she was never seen so angry as yesterday. Lord H. [Hartington] wrote a long letter, very dignified, but at the same time apologetic. No doubt there has been some forgetfulness in not keeping the Queen sufficiently well posted in Afghan affairs. I think Lord H.'s letter will mollify her.[1]

[*Journals.*]　　　　　　　　　　LONDON,
　　　　　　　　　　　　　　　　　JANUARY 7TH.

Gladstone spoke very well last night, and his defence of the Government was very good; but his voice got very weak towards the end of his speech. This is the first time his physical powers have failed him. . . .

[*Journals.*]　　　　　　　　　　LONDON,
　　　　　　　　　　　　　　　　　JANUARY 26TH.

For a week we have had a most severe frost. It began with a *The* snowstorm of exceptional severity, and driving winds which *Great* heaped the snow up into impassable barriers in the streets. For *Blizzard.*

---

[1] See *Sidelights on Queen Victoria,* by Sir F. Ponsonby.

three days no carriages or cabs could make their way. On Saturday I drove Lord H. [Hartington] to the Cabinet in my sleigh, the first time a minister ever went to the Cabinet in such a vehicle.

Last night, owing to a misunderstanding, the House became involved in a struggle with the Home Rulers, and we sat for twenty-two hours consecutively, coming to a decision this afternoon.

[*Journals.*]   LONDON,
                                                      FEBRUARY 1ST.

The clock in the tower has just struck 5 a.m. and we are wasting the night in sitting out the Irish, who are still struggling against the first reading of the Coercion Bill. . . .

The Ministers had agreed upon a resolution proposing the "clôture," and Northcote had consented to act with them; but under pressure from Randolph Churchill and a few of his friends he has backed out. In the end he will be forced into an agreement with the Ministers by the moderate men in his own party. If Dizzy were leading the Tories, he would ere this have taken advantage of the rising feeling in the country and posed as the champion of the dignity of Parliament.

[*Journals.*]   LONDON,
                                                      MARCH 1ST.

Majuba.   Came yesterday news of the disaster [1] at the Cape, Colley's death, and the consignment to the grave of all hope of peace with the Boers.

Roberts is appointed to the Command in South Africa. . . .

[1] Majuba Hill.

[*To Sir William Harcourt.*]   LONDON,
                                        APRIL 15TH.

Nellie went out for her first drive to-day, and we called in Grafton Street, to ask you to be Godfather to the boy, who is to be called Oliver Sylvain.[1]

Lord H. [Hartington] is to be his other godfather, and Mrs. Sturgis his godmother. If you will consent to join them, I don't see how the boy could start under better auspices. He is to be christened on Monday.

You will be away, but we hope that Loulou will come here about half-past eleven and take your place.

[*Journals.*]   NEWMARKET,
                                        APRIL 19TH.

This morning before I was out of bed, my servant told me *Death of* that Lord Beaconsfield was dead. He died soon after 4 o'clock, *Disraeli.* not unexpectedly, and very quietly. Monty Corry, they say, was holding his hand, and there was no suffering.

How will he be judged by posterity? No more curious figure ever appeared in English political life. He inspired affection, as well as admiration, in his friends and adherents. By all but his bigoted opponents he was held in regard and respect. He was the most magnanimous statesman of our time. He captivated the imagination of the English people, and triumphed over their not unnatural prejudices.

He leaves the Tory party disorganised, and there appears no immediate prospect of finding any successor to him. His death brings home to us possible contingencies of a similar kind, which will alter the face of political life. . . .

---

[1] Afterwards 3rd Viscount Esher.

[*Journals.*]   1, TILNEY STREET,
                                              APRIL 22ND.

This morning John Morley[1] called here and spoke very sympathetically of the Minister he did so much to displace. . . .

Dizzy is to be buried at Hughenden near his wife and *not* in the Abbey. So long as there is a statue to him in the Abbey, his burial place matters little. One never thinks of Mr. Pitt's poor bones when looking at his erect form over the west door of the Abbey.

The following reminder of the state of Egyptian affairs at this time may help to make clearer the letters and journal entries which touch upon Egypt during the next few years.

After de Lesseps obtained the concessions necessary for digging the Suez Canal (1856), Egypt, though politically a tributary state of the Turkish Empire, suffered an increasing intrusion of European finance. When Ismail brought the country to the edge of bankruptcy the Europeans, for the protection of their monies, obliged him to receive advisers at his Court and to establish a constitutional form of government on a Western model. It was against the influence of these foreign advisers (there were at the time an Englishman and a Frenchman in joint control) that Arabi led his revolt. The French refused to take action in suppressing him, and he was defeated by the English acting alone. In consequence of this, the English troops were almost at once withdrawn and an effort made to reorganise the country on lines consistent with its political status.

The revolt of the Sudan in 1884 compelled the English to further military action, the conduct of which was made difficult, and therefore dilatory, by the complications of the political situation. Throughout the period covered by this volume no change was made in the status of Egypt as a tributary province of the Turkish Empire, ruled by a Khedive whose government was in turn controlled, in the interests of their own finances and for the security of the Suez Canal, by a concert of European powers among whom only the English were prepared to take military action.

[1] Afterwards Viscount Morley.

REGINALD BALIOL BRETT.

From a painting by Julian Story, 1882.

[*Journals.*]   LONDON,
                                    JANUARY 18TH, 1882.

This morning John Morley called here, and I showed him *Egyptian Policy.*
Colvin's Mem. about Egypt. He thinks the Joint Note a
mistake.[1] So do I if the Government have not made up their
minds what is to come next.

Gambetta refused to agree to any explanation whatever. I
think he is right. We are committed to combined *action* with
France by the Note, if not before, by our whole policy. Bismarck pushes on the Turks, in the hope of breaking up the agreement between France and England. He first suggested to us to
take Egypt into our own hands. Finding this would not do, he
made a similar suggestion to France. Now he is trying to get
the Turks to interfere. At all hazards a rupture with France
must be prevented. In any dispute Bismarck will back up
France.

[*Journals.*]   LONDON,
                                    JANUARY 21ST.

Last night I dined with Dilke to meet Bismarck's eldest son.
There were ten guests, including Lord H. [Hartington], Courtney, and G. Trevelyan. The position of affairs in Egypt is
curious. Mr. Gladstone, of all men, will find himself in the position of having to defend an attempt to hinder a duly elected
Chamber from exercising control over public expenditure!

I have no doubt he will do it admirably, and will succeed in
showing to our complete satisfaction that it is in accordance
with the first principles of Liberalism!

We should still try to detach Italy from the German alliance. *Italy.*
She is alienated from us by our treatment of her in the Red Sea,
and our behaviour when Tunis was annexed by France. We
should "call in" not Europe, but the Mediterranean Powers,
Italy and Spain. It is high time to treat Spain with consideration.

[1] Sent under pressure from Gambetta on January 8th.

[*Journals.*]   LONDON,
                                          JANUARY 23RD.

Sir Charles Brownlow came from the War Office to see Lord
H. [Hartington] today. Arrangements are being most secretly
made, in view of its becoming necessary to send an army to
Egypt.

[*From the Rt. Hon. J. Chamberlain.*]   HIGHBURY, BIRMINGHAM,
                                          OCTOBER 18TH.

MY DEAR BRETT,

Egypt: I have been home a week. I did go to Russia but not to
Trial of Siberia. Where did you see this latter "canard"?
Arabi.
            I have been reading carefully the Egyptian papers, including
yours. Colvin and Malet are both trying to establish the old
system under a new name and in their endeavours to conceal
their intentions, or in their ignorance of what their own intentions really are, they get frightfully mixed and incoherent. The
enclosed contains my own conclusions, which I have sent to the
Grand Old Man. They are rather drastic, but it is as well to say
what you mean—and if we don't take good care we shall get
into a devil of a mess with some of the best men of our Party. I
am speaking of the Country and not of the House of Commons.
You can show the paper to your Chief, if you think he would
care to see it; but it is not good for weak eyes.
                                          Yours ever,
                                          J. CHAMBERLAIN.

[*To Sir Charles Dilke.*]   THE HUT, BRAY,
                                          OCTOBER 18TH.

We have got into a mess with this trial of Arabi. It is a misfortune that we ever mixed ourselves up in it, or permitted it.
What is to be done?

I agree with Malet that we ought to adhere to our original decision that no one should be executed without our consent, and then leave the conduct of the trial to the Egyptian authorities.

(1) In the interests of Arabi this is the safest course. If he is condemned to death, we can always say that had he been properly defended he would have proved his innocence. If on the other hand he is defended by English counsel, and condemned, it will be difficult for us to insist upon letting him off.

(2) In our own interests it is better not to allow all the old questions, by which his counsel will attempt to justify Arabi's acts, to be reopened. It will provoke a great deal of sympathy here, and will give the enemies of the Government at home and of the country abroad, "sense" (as we used to say at Eton) for their attacks.

(3) It will drag to light all the various intrigues of the Sultan, the French, the Khedive, and the present Egyptian Ministers, which are far better—in view of what remains to be done in Egypt—kept in the background.

I thought Malet's recommendation very sensible, and I hope it may be approved by Lord Granville. *The Times* is connected through one of its staff with Blunt. Hence the publication of Napier's letters, and the sort of personal interest kept up in Arabi.

Lord Hartington now consented to move to the War Office and Mr. Brett went with him. On December 8th, his brother, Eugene, died of typhoid fever contracted in Egypt.

[*Journals.*]   LONDON,
                                                                DECEMBER 5TH.

Dilke has told me that he has put forward my name for one of the two Under-Secretaries to be filled. I wrote to thank him.

[*From Sir Charles Dilke.*]   FOREIGN OFFICE,
DECEMBER 7TH.

MY DEAR BRETT,

I've not only this time, but always, put forward your name—because I think it the best name. But Chamberlain and Harcourt are just as keen about you as I am, and it must come soon, if it doesn't come now.

Yrs. ever,
CH. W. D.

[*To Sir William Harcourt.*]   NEW LODGE, WINDSOR FOREST,
SEPTEMBER 2ND, 1883.

*Title
for his
Father.*

I want your advice on a matter of personal interest to me. My Father completes this month his 15 years of service as a Judge. He is now—as you know—the head of the Chancery Division of the High Court, the President of the Court of Appeal.

He has not concealed from me, that both on personal and on public grounds he would like to be placed in a position of equal authority to that of the Chief of the other Division of the High Court, and like Lord Coleridge to be given a seat in the House of Lords.

Into the personal view of the matter I need not enter, but my Father feels also that the public advantage of placing the Master of the Rolls in the House of Lords would be, in the first place, to raise the value of the Judicial Office in the eyes of the profession, which at the present time is not an unimportant consideration: secondly, to give to the Master of the Rolls a more assured position of influence among the Judges themselves: and thirdly, to add to the House of Lords another lawyer altogether free from political trammels.

Then as to my Father's claims. He is well aware that he has none, from the political point of view, upon this Government; but 15 years' service on the Bench, and the position he holds, place him perhaps above any consideration of that kind, more especially as he would never consider himself entitled—so long as he held a high Judicial Office—in taking any part in political proceedings of the House of Lords. . . .

[*To Lord Hartington.*]   1, TILNEY ST.,
                                    JANUARY 29TH, 1884.

I had a talk with Harcourt last night. I think you know that it is only with great regret that I face the breach in my relations with you, which have been of such great advantage to me. And when I resolved to do so, it was only after careful consideration of your interests as well as of my own.

You know, as well as I do, that the end must come some day, and it was only the choice of time which was difficult to decide upon.

Harcourt thinks that if I were to resign my position with you, and take a more or less independent attitude in the House, at the present moment, it might give occasion for comment and questions of a tiresome kind; and he suggests that I should postpone the evil day until after this session, when he thinks a natural termination will probably be put to our official relations—as well as to the Government.

If you share this view, I shall be only too glad to continue to hold the position which I now fill, until the end of the coming session.

[*From General Gordon.*]   BRUSSELS,
                                    JANUARY 17TH.[1]

I saw Hobart, nice fellow, and Brocklehurst who is here, and heard much of you and yours. I was glad you and Mrs. R. Brett and children are well, and hope your father and family are also well.

[1] The day before his departure for Egypt.

Govt. and authorities have been exceedingly kind and I have every reason to be grateful to them, for I have often worried them and they have decided to let me stay in H.M.S.

I may say *I fear*, for people have been too kind. Did you ever read the *Ring of Polycrates*?

> "Wouldst thou escape the coming ill
> Implore the dread Invisible
> Thy sweets to sour."

Goodbye, my dear Brett, kindest regards to all. I will never forget you.

Yours sincerely,

C. E. GORDON.

[*To Mr. W. T. Stead.*[1]]   LONDON,
                                        JANUARY 29TH.

Egypt.   I am doing what I can to urge the Government to make the Khedive supersede Hussein Pasha at Khartoum, and appoint Col. Coetlogon to the command.

If a disaster occurs at Khartoum *before* Gordon's arrival, how can the Government say that they took all possible steps to prevent it, when they could easily, by putting pressure upon the Khedive, get an obviously unfit man removed from the post at this moment of supreme danger and importance?

[*To Mr. W. T. Stead.*]   HOUSE OF COMMONS,
                                        FEBRUARY 16TH.

Gordon.   Everything—thanks to Gordon—is going well. Where would the Government have been if they had not sent him? One of two things. Either defeated; or sending an army to relieve Khartoum, as well as Tokar.

[1] Editor of the *Pall Mall Gazette.*

It is satisfactory to us who have loved Gordon for years, and believed in him, to find those who have always treated him like a lunatic, now telegraphing to him their "increased confidence" in his judgment, and reliance upon his policy.

The Government are, I must say, behaving well to him. He is given "carte blanche." His telegrams are models of cheerfulness and self-possession. He might be, to read them, ensconced in the most comfortable of irresponsible offices in Downing St. By *June 1st* he hopes to have freed the Soudan from Egyptians.

[*To Mr. W. T. Stead.*]   LONDON,
                                                  FEBRUARY 16TH.

What everyone has foreseen has happened. I agree with every *Khartoum.* word of your article in this day's paper.

A possibility which should be faced is

(1) Gordon's capture (if not worse).

(2) The fall of Khartoum *before* he arrives there.

What is to be done then? Is not this stoppage of a transport full of time-expired men in the Red Sea a farce? We ought to send out to *Egypt proper* at once, a reinforcement sufficient to enable a flying column to move immediately to any point on the Nile.

No Indian troops. It is well-known here what men and material are wanted. And they are ready to go. But they ought to be sent at once to Alexandria.

Baker says that his squad of 3800 was attacked by 1000 Arabs. The Egyptians at once threw down their arms and fled, carrying the blacks etc. with them.

The police recruited at Alexandria etc. were the worst behaved of the lot. They lay down, and were speared through the neck. I hope Her Majesty's Government, in a like panic, are not going to lie down and be speared through the neck.

Nobody wants them to attempt to avenge Baker or reconquer the Soudan; but they should stand, sword in hand, ready to strike if anything happens to Gordon.

[*From Sir Evelyn Baring.*[1]]   CAIRO,
                                          FEBRUARY 19TH.
MY DEAR BRETT,

Many thanks for your kindly letter. Some passages of my despatches have been left out, which so far as I am personally concerned might, I think, as well have been left in. But if their omission will help the Govt. in Parliament I do not mind.

I do not like being praised by the Opposition as it makes me think that I must have done something stupid. If I get through the whole of this business without English responsibility being extended beyond Egypt proper I shall think I have been successful. I fear the folly and ignorance of Parliament and the English newspapers more than anything else.

Gordon is doing very well. That man was specially invented by Providence for the bewilderment of "able editors" and newspaper correspondents.

                                     Ever yours,
                                       E. BARING.

[*To Mr. W. T. Stead.*]   1, TILNEY ST.,
                                          FEBRUARY 23RD.

Egypt.   Zebehr[2] has been knocked on the head for the present, and it is suggested that there is no hurry, and Gordon may as well continue for a while "Lord Protector of the Nile Highway." I agree with what you say tonight that the people would not · stand Zebehr's appointment. It is putting rather too much faith in their logical faculty to suppose that they would.

With regard to Tokar, I think it is well-nigh settled that a considerable force is nevertheless to remain at Souakin to prevent the rebels threatening the place, and firing into the town as they did last week. Some of the troops will return to Alexandria,

---

[1] Afterwards Lord Cromer.
[2] General Gordon had asked repeatedly for this man to help him. He was a slave-dealer, but of great influence.

and shortly a force will be despatched to Assouan, where there is considerable ruthlessness among the Mohammedan population, threatening to the large number of Copts. This force must start while the Nile remains navigable. Some of Wood's Army would doubtless accompany it.

This is not definitely settled, but there is very little doubt that it will shortly be sanctioned by H.M.G.

[*To Mr. W. T. Stead.*]   HOUSE OF COMMONS,
FEBRUARY 25TH.

There are two points of *immediate* importance.   *Egypt.*

(1) Strengthen the British garrison at Cairo and Alexandria. In order to do this send troops at once from England. They are now ordered to be in readiness, so why not send them? Also, if force is required at Assouan send *Wood's* army. Because, first, doctors say you would lose 75% of men in summer. Secondly you would get Wood's force out of Cairo.

(2) Settle at once to defend Souakin from the place itself as a base, *unless imperative military reasons to the contrary*. Forbid advance to Jeb, and order whole force back to Souakin. From there it can operate more efficiently and safely.

Mr. Gladstone repudiated tonight the London Press, and public sentiment. If so, why did he flinch from the logical unpopular step of leaving Tokar to its fate. What is he *doing* now, though he *says* the reverse, but yielding to clamour if he attacks Osman Digna at Jeb, taking advantage of a subterfuge.

The moment has now come—unless we court disaster—to speak fearlessly. Sweep out the Turks bag and baggage from Egypt proper; Wood's army and all. Say to Europe, we make our sacrifice, you make yours. We guarantee peace and order for ten years.

You accept a composition for the Indemnities, and release the sinking fund. If not, we abandon Egypt to its fate. As for the Soudan, let Gordon effect the evacuation. Leave Khartoum in the hands of the notables, to the ultimate Zebehr or anybody else. As for Souakin, hold it.

[*To Mr. W. T. Stead.*]   1, TILNEY ST.,
                                         FEBRUARY 27TH.

Gordon.

The garrison of Sennaar is, Gordon reports, all right. There are rebels, however, on the line of communication between that place and Khartoum. He is apparently organising and despatching the "ever victorious" army to disperse them.

He is thus making the Government consistent "malgré eux." His proclamations will astonish many people. Do you think he carries the doctrine that the "end justifies the means" too far for the English public?

[*To Mr. W. T. Stead.*]   HOUSE OF COMMONS.

Gordon and Khartoum.

The immediate point of interest now is, not Tamaniet, but Khartoum. A decision must be taken at once. What are the alternatives?

Zebehr has been knocked on the head. Gordon then must decide. Let him say

(1) that he will stay, i.e. "Sarawak the Soudan."

(2) evacuate the place, and move with the garrison to Berber.

With regard to (1), it is obvious that he must judge. Rajah Brooke could hardly have been ordered or instructed to do what he did. It must be left to Gordon.

With regard to (2), it appears to me to be the only rational plan if Gordon refuses to carry out (1).

I should therefore propose to tell Gordon to remain at Khartoum if he thinks fit. If not, to evacuate *at once.*

In order to enable him to do this, if he elects (2), the route to Berber from Souakin must be opened.

The policy would then be

(*a*) hold the Red Sea littoral for Egypt. *No Turks.*

(*b*) evacuate the Soudan, including Khartoum, and *turn the key in the lock.*

[*To Lord Hartington.*]   APRIL 1ST.

I heard from General Gordon this morning.[1] Letter dated *Gordon.* March 3rd, Khartoum. He asks to be remembered to you. The following are extracts from his letter.

1. "As for Zebehr, I wish with all my heart that he was here. He alone can ride the Soudan horse, and if they do not send him, I am sentenced to penal servitude for my life up here."

2. "Bear this in mind, that it is impossible to hope for any compromise between H.M.G. and the Pacha tribe. I know it by experience, and I smite them with unrelenting severity because I know it is hopeless to try and deal with them. I rejoice in doing so. It is no use trying to work with them, and I wish our Government would see this."

3. "A French consul will be here in two days. He will not bother me, but you may expect he will push the French Government to bother our Government."

4. "We *must* evacuate the Soudan. It is absolutely necessary. In a year the slaves up here will rise and will emancipate themselves. What a wonderful dénouement! And how my prayers will have been then heard."

I wish again to say that nothing will, I am convinced, induce Gordon to leave Khartoum until all those persons who have been faithful to him can leave with him; and any policy based on the assumption that such an order would be obeyed is predestined to fail.

[1] General Gordon's letter began: "I am sorry you worry about me, for D.V. I am all right. I am comforted that if I try and do my best, one cannot fail. . . ."

I am also sure that Gordon neither wants nor expects an army to be sent to Khartoum to relieve him. At the same time it never would strike him that the Government could be capable of allowing it to be believed for twenty-four hours that "England had abandoned" him.

He would, of course, assume that the English Government would let it be known far and wide that they are prepared to support him with all the force at their disposal, if he should require and ask it; and the knowledge of this, permeating through Egypt and the Soudan, would in all probability be sufficient for his purpose.

If it were not, H.M.G. would only then have to do, what, if they were by some mischance to try and leave Gordon to his fate, they would have to do notwithstanding.

[*To Lord Hartington.*]   LONDON,
MIDNIGHT, MAY 28TH.

Egypt:
Anglo-
French
Talks.

I have been dining with Chamberlain, and Waddington was there. After a long conversation with Waddington, Chamberlain told me that he had got the Ambassador to admit that the only point in the negotiations about which the French care is the *time* of occupation. If you give way upon that, France would give way upon these points:

1. Multiple Control not to come into force until we evacuate.
2. An Englishman *then* to be president of the Caisse.

If this is true, to hold out for the whole time of five years is snatching at the shadow. But then what a condemnation of the F.O., that this attitude of the French Government should not have been appreciated sooner.

It would be better for you, I am sure, to say at once that, if the present arrangement is deliberately adhered to, you will retire. If the Government choose to reopen the *whole* negotiation, then you might give way upon the "term of years" provided that the other stipulations are modified to your satisfaction.

I am more than convinced that the Government will be turned out if the present arrangement is made. That it is possible that any such concession could be made to France appears incredible to most of our people. Your majority of 28 will be reduced to a minority.

[*Journal.*]　　　　　　　　　　　　LONDON,
　　　　　　　　　　　　　　　　JULY 11TH.

Camille Barrère[1] dined here this evening, and I had a long conversation with him about Egypt. . . .

*Barrère :
on Egypt.*

Have you considered, I said, the change in the foreign relations of this country, which would accompany a change of Government?

You mean, he replied, that Lord Salisbury would make an alliance with Germany; but is it so certain that Prince Bismarck, who has nothing to fear from England and not much to gain from her, would agree to such an alliance? For, he continued, the foreign relations of France might also undergo a change, and she might think it desirable to alter the whole course of her foreign policy in view of the Alliance you suggest.

I have no fear, he added, that a Conservative policy would be more hostile to France than a Liberal policy, because in my opinion Germany is at least as likely to favour an alliance with France as with England. If the Conservative party had a man like Beaconsfield to guide them, it might be different, he concluded.

You have not a high opinion of Lord Salisbury's courage and persistence? I asked. He said he had not, and then I told him he was completely in error, both as to Lord Salisbury's character and policy, and that Lord Salisbury's Egyptian Policy was "to govern it," and that were a Tory Government once established here in office, no impediment would be placed in his way, as far

*On
Salisbury.*

[1] Ex-communist, foreign editor of the *République Française* and afterwards French Minister in Rome.

as this country was concerned, in carrying his policy into execution.

Barrère, however, thinks that we should find it impossible to govern Egypt. We have been trying for two years, he said, to carry out a virtual protectorate, and we have failed. The Egyptians are like sand. They slip through the fingers. . . .

On Baring.

Of Baring he spoke without reserve. He admitted his qualities, his ability and honesty—qualities as he said, "of the stolid uncompromising Briton." But, he added, he is hated by the Khedive, and Nubar does not like him. Both natives and Europeans are unused to the manners which he has introduced into the diplomatic circle.

Barrère himself has had to treat him with great forbearance. Barrère—I may add—has formed the highest opinion of the services to this country by Sir Edward Malet, who, he thinks, has not been appreciated here at his value. Not even for Lord Dufferin, he said, do the Egyptians feel greater respect; and their respect for Malet is apparently equalled by their regard for him.

[*To Mr. W. T. Stead.*]   TRING PARK,
                                                        AUGUST 3RD.

Egypt.

. . . There will arise another problem, which is the Soudan. What is to be done? Is Gordon to be met at Berber, or not? Whatever happens now lies at the door of France. She has only herself to blame if we annex Egypt. The failure of the Government to come to any arrangement with the Powers is owing, as we have agreed all along, to their ignoring Prince Bismarck. They could not have managed better had they wished the Conference to be abortive from the first. . . .

Mr. Brett now finished building a country house on the property of his brother-in-law on the outskirts of Windsor Forest, which he called Orchard Lea, and he spent as much of his time there as he could spare, still staying at No. 1 Tilney Street when forced to remain in London.

[*From Sir Garnet Wolseley.*]   WADY HALFA,
OCTOBER 16TH.

MY DEAR BRETT,

. . . I have not yet had any answer from Gordon to the message I sent him from Cairo. I mean to get forward the mounted Infantry and Camel Corps as soon as possible; and when I get to Debbeh or its neighbourhood myself, I hope to get touch of Gordon and get him to formulate some practical plan for the future that will suit the views of the Cabinet. You may depend upon my sending home the troops as soon as I think their services can be dispensed with. I wish I saw my way to the withdrawal of all our men from Egypt. Thanking you extremely for all the aid and assistance you have afforded me. . . .

[*To Sir Garnet Wolseley.*]   ORCHARD LEA,
NOVEMBER.

. . . Thirdly, the *Standard* telegrams this morning have rather *Egypt.* frightened us. It appears from these that the difficulties of the Second Cataract were under-estimated in the first instance by the Canadians, and that the job will be more arduous and difficult than we were hoping it would be, judging from the earlier telegrams to the London papers.

All who know the facts, and how difficult it was to get the Government to move, will almost grudge them success. There is no doubt in the world, that if anyone but Wolseley were now in command, the anxiety in this country would amount to panic. And the Government cannot be sufficiently thankful that they secured your services for an undertaking, the difficulties of which have, I suppose, never been surpassed.

[*Journals.*]   ORCHARD LEA,
NOVEMBER 14TH. *Egypt :
Anglo-*
I have had a long letter from Herbert Bismarck, who says in *German* reference to Egypt, that we ought to let his father know our *Relations.*

plan (as if we had one!) *privately*, before communicating it officially. He gives me this hint as "a friend and a friend of your country." Then with reference to other matters he mentions the grievances of Germany against our Government:

1. Members of the English Government have, at different times during the last few years, confidentially asked advice of his father, which has always been given in a friendly manner, but has in no case been acted upon.

2. The violation "of one of the treaties" referring to Egypt for mere financial reasons.

3. An apparent desire, in colonial matters, "not to cultivate intimate and friendly relations with Germany."

He continues:

"If I had been in the place of the English Government I should years ago have tried, not to consult, but to ' bribe ' Germany. That means to say I should have given her manifest proofs of the value I attach to a solid German friendship. The means for this might easily have been found in the province of colonial questions. The German Government and people, which now are trying to find support elsewhere in order to try and carry out their colonial aims, would have felt very differently towards England if her attitude in these questions had been from the beginning a friendly and liberal one."

I sent Hartington the above for his consideration, as should the Cabinet agree upon a policy for Egypt, the approval of Europe will of course again have to be sought, and if the old tactics are adopted, I feel sure they will again fail.

[*To Sir Garnet Wolseley.*]   ORCHARD LEA,
                                     NOVEMBER 14TH.

Egypt :
Anxiety for
Gordon.

. . . Telegrams to the newspapers and to the French Government about Gordon's supposed destruction, coupled with the absence of news from Khartoum, cause much uneasiness. If the place has fallen, and Gordon is killed, the Government will try to stop the Expedition. No greater disaster conceivable could occur to my mind than that. It seems to me that every consideration forces us onward, even though the primary cause of the Expedition has ceased to exist.

But I am still sanguine that this further horror has not come upon us, and that Khartoum is safe.

With regard to our scheme for setting up a Government in the Soudan, my hope is that you will do nothing hurriedly, or give your sanction to a scheme of which you do not cordially approve, except by command of the Ministers. In my opinion they should not have committed you personally to the approval of your "instructions," which they have done by publishing Baring's despatch, in which he states that they were drawn up in consultation with you.

This course is not usual, and looks like an unconstitutional attempt to make you, who are the servant of the Ministers, share their responsibility. So I am afraid that when you get to Khartoum they may again try to make *you* responsible for a course which you may select, not as the best in your opinion, but the best subject to conditions imposed upon you by the Government at home.

... Resuming today, there is not much more to say. ... The recent news about Gordon has allayed public anxiety but the details of his letter are not known out of doors. We—who know them—cannot but be a little nervous at the prospect of a longer delay in reaching him than he perhaps contemplates; but personally I have great confidence in your star.

[*To Sir Charles Dilke.*]　　　　　Orchard Lea,
　　　　　　　　　　　　　　　December 14th.

Can anything be done to get the county "Divisions" under the new Bill called by the old name "Shires"? It would be perfectly and historically accurate.

Also could not some of the old names (Hallamshire for example) be revived, where no divisional name from a destroyed constituency is available?

And will you refer to the nomenclature of the new County Divisions to Freeman or Stubbs, as "advisers" to the Commissioners?

[*To Sir Garnet Wolseley.*]   ORCHARD LEA,
                                DECEMBER 29TH.

We are getting drearily through Christmas. I have no doubt that you are spending this insufferable season much more pleasantly at Korti than you would be likely to do in London.

Yesterday for the first time since your departure the telegrams in the newspapers were of a cheerful complexion. . . .

Lord Hartington has left town for a holiday, after a prolonged discussion with H.R.H. about the estimates for next year. He is not altogether free from anxiety about the expedition: but this is of course not surprising when his responsibility is considered, together with the novelty of the proceeding and uncertainty as to the obstacles still before you. . . .

Randolph Churchill's expedition to India deprives controversy of all raciness and zest. Next session will be exceedingly dull until he returns.

Reform of the Lords. Rosebery has issued a circular to the peers, asking each one individually whether he favours reform of the House of Lords—without pledging himself to any particular plan. I fancy his answers—if he gets any—will not impress him with any confidence in the desire of their Lordships to commit suicide. However, Rosebery apparently still retains the hopefulness of youth, as well as its charm.

[*To Lord Hartington*   ORCHARD LEA,
    (*at Sandringham*).]   JANUARY 1ST, 1885.

Egypt. The account of the start of the expedition from Korti is very exciting; but it is impossible not to feel a little anxious in spite of

the unbounded confidence of Wolseley in his letter. Earle wrote
to General Whitmore that Herbert Stewart is an incomparably
good soldier and leader of men.

[*To Sir Garnet Wolseley.*]   ORCHARD LEA,
                                        JANUARY 8TH.

There was a Cabinet all yesterday. All the Ministers were *Egypt.*
summoned suddenly in consequence of a series of telegrams
from Baring. The question was whether or no a force should be
sent to Suakin to thrash Osman Digna. The position of affairs
there is intolerable, and its effect is as bad in Europe as it is in
Egypt. Gordon's message to you has confirmed a belief long
entertained here, that Khartoum, though it will be speedily relieved, cannot be speedily evacuated. If this is so, everything
points to the desirability of getting rid of the wasps around
Suakin, and of opening the old trade communications with
Berber.

[*To Sir Garnet Wolseley.*]   ORCHARD LEA,
                                        JANUARY 9TH.

1. Your reply has arrived, and it certainly is very inspiring. *Egypt.*
I have never had a moment's doubt that you would achieve a
brilliant success, but I still adhere to my view about Suakin, and
the impolicy of leaving a small garrison besieged there.

The telegram of the Cabinet was the result—as you must be
aware—not of anything we heard from you direct, but of
Baring's reports of his correspondence with you, backed by
strong representations of his own.

2. The political atmosphere is still over-clouded. No reply
has come from the French, and none is expected before the 15th.
Mr. Gladstone is very angry, especially with Bismarck, whom
he looks upon as a personal enemy, and only second to the

enemy of all mankind. When the French reply arrives, it will probably contain proposals altogether unacceptable. We shall then be forced to take an independent line. I think by the time you are at Khartoum we shall very likely have established a virtual protectorate at Cairo.

The Cabinet— Gladstone.

3. Mr. G. is still bent on retirement immediately after the Seats Bill is through Parliament. It is doubtful whether Andrew Clarke will permit it. He is said to hold that excitement is indispensable to the old man's health.

If Mr. G. retires, Lord H. [Hartington] would naturally succeed him. The Radicals are opposed to Lord Granville, but they will support and serve Lord H. I was at Mentmore last Sunday.

Rosebery.

The Chief Commissioner of Works is still kept open for Rosebery by Mr. G., on the chance of his seeing his way to accept office. But there is no chance of the Egypt question reaching a stage which would enable Rosebery to join the Government, and colonial matters make it still more difficult for him. Besides there is nothing to be gained by joining a moribund government. After the next election, should he get a majority, the Ministry will require his brilliant personality.

There is absolutely no gossip. I am sending you a special umbrella. See that you get it.

[*To Sir Garnet Wolseley.*]   1, TILNEY ST.,
                                                      JANUARY 30TH.

Egypt: Abu Klea.

Many hearty congratulations upon your brilliant success.[1] Every one feels, even your enemies, how much the nation owes you. . . .

Poor Stewart. Will he recover? *I* have never for a moment doubted the success of your plans, and I never felt any anxiety except personal fear for my friends—for Stewart's little force. The best account of the march is in the *Daily Chronicle*. Lady Wolseley has been wonderfully cool and confident.

[1] Battle of Abu Klea.

Lord H. [Hartington] was very much affected by the news of Abu Klea; more moved than by anything I can remember except poor Freddy's[1] murder.

[*To Sir Charles Dilke.*]   THURSDAY MORNING, 3 A.M.
                                        [FEB. 5TH.]

Here is some bad news.[2] No Ministers in town except you *Egypt:* and Chamberlain! Have tried Lord G. [Granville] and Lord *Fall of* Northbrook. No results! So things must take their chance. *Khartoum.* There ought to have been a Cabinet tomorrow, but suppose it is not possible.

. . . Please return enclosed. Will send you a copy later. Have you any suggestions to make? You will see that W.[3] proposes to keep this *secret*. Not possible for *long* in this Office.

[*To the Rt. Hon. J. Chamberlain.*]   FEB. 5TH.

Please read the enclosed. My note to Dilke was written at *Khartoum:* 3 a.m., and by mistake I put *to-morrow* instead of *today*. I have *Absence of* telegraphed to Lord H. and Mr. G. is staying with him. I have *Ministers.* also telegraphed to Lord Northbrook to come at once.

I went to Lord G.'s in the middle of the night, and waiting in the hall for half an hour it was discovered that he was at Walmer, unknown to all his servants, except the valet who was got out of bed!

. . . It is absurd not to make them come up *today* in face of Wolseley's "It is most essential that I should have the earliest possible decision."

[*To Lord Hartington.*]   LONDON,
                                        FEBRUARY 5TH.

This miserable news arrived this morning about 1.30. We *Khartoum:* did everything possible to get it communicated to you and other *Military*
Plans.

[1] Lord Frederick Cavendish.   [2] The fall of Khartoum.   [3] Wolseley.

Ministers as early as possible, time being of such importance to Wolseley's movements. But there was no possibility of arranging a Cabinet before tomorrow. Lord Northbrook, whom I saw this morning, wished that a telegram should be sent to Wolseley conveying questions which he thought of importance. Sir Ralph Thompson[1] will show it to you. Upon your suggested telegram to Wolseley, I should like to make this observation. That you are not likely to hear of Gordon's fate for a considerable time, and that it is necessary for the safety of Wolseley's force that you should decide upon a course of action at the earliest possible date, and therefore you will have to act upon the assumption that Gordon is a captive. The main object will be to establish Wolseley in the strongest position from which he can put pressure upon the Mahdi. It may be that there are military reasons why we should fall back upon Debbeh, but the political effect of such a proceeding cannot fail to be very bad; and the military difficulty would, I should imagine, be considerable, owing to the demoralising effect upon our men, and the encouragement which would immediately be given to the enemy. I should have said, and Dilke agreed with this view, when I spoke to him about it this morning, that the best point of concentration would be Berber.

Earle's advance might continue, and Buller after taking Metemmeh would join hands with him. It might be necessary in the meantime to inflict a blow upon Osman Digna which would be a salutary way of wiping out the Mahdi's victory at Khartoum, which has in turn wiped out our victories at Abu Klea and Gubat. Buller's instinct appears to me to be the right one, that is, to reassert our superiority. I am sorry for Wolseley, to whom the abortive result of all his hard work must be a great blow.

I am very sorry for you, a feeling which will not be universally extended to your colleagues.

[1] Permanent Under Secretary, War Office.

[*To Sir Ralph Thompson.*]   LONDON,
                                     FEBRUARY 5TH.

This is the sort of telegram I think the Government should *Khartoum:*
send to Wolseley: *Military*
                                                           Plans.
"Until we hear certain news of Gordon's death, we are bound
to assume he is alive. We consider that you should place yourself in the most advantageous position for obtaining his release;
either by negotiation or by force. You should also have regard
to the defence of Egypt from invasion by Mahdi. Under these
circumstances do you think that the concentration of our troops
at Debbeh or an advance to Berber by the river from Abu Hamed
and Gubat would best contribute to the ends in view—or is there
any other course you would prefer? Reply fully upon the military situation based upon these conditions."

[*To Sir Garnet Wolseley.*]   LONDON,
                                     FEBRUARY 6TH.

The news of the fall of Khartoum was brought to Thompson *Khartoum:*
at one in the morning. He came here, and we went to the Office *Military*
together, where we gradually decyphered your melancholy   *Plans.*
budget of news. I endeavoured to find Lord Granville and Lord
Northbrook in the hope of getting a Cabinet assembled yesterday (for it seems to me the *earliest* decision should be taken), but
owing to the improper practice now in fashion of Ministers
rushing away when Parliament is not sitting, it was found impossible to get them together until this morning. So Thompson
agreed to send you the two telegrams you first received: 1, in-
forming you of the probable delay in sending you instructions;
and 2, asking for further information about your line of communication between Gubat and Korti, which seemed to us a
point of danger. The Cabinet are to meet at 11 o'clock today.
My opinion is that they have nothing to do with the military
situation; that their duty is to face the political situation; and to
make up their minds in the first place to put you in a position to

rescue Gordon (whom they are bound to assume to be alive till they know he is dead) either by negotiation or force, and secondly to provide for the defence of Egypt in accordance with our pledges. The mode of doing this should be left absolutely to your discretion without reference to them. I trust they may come to some such decision. Everyone should feel now how completely your strategy is justified by this event. Suppose you had been on the Suakin-Berber route, the Dongola province and Egypt would have been at the Mahdi's feet. We shall have, I suppose, a long and difficult series of campaigns in Africa, as we had formerly in the Punjab. It is perhaps not a bad tonic for the English nation.

Gordon may be safe with the Mahdi. My strongest sympathy is with you in your disappointment at this discomfiture.

[*To Lord Rosebery.*] LONDON,
FEBRUARY 7TH.

Rosebery takes Office.

You seem to have grasped at the possibilities; and upon considering them, I think your good impulse should not be checked.[1] Everyone will see that you have come forward at a moment of disaster, and will honour you for it. From the patriotic point of view, I should rejoice at your being in the Cabinet through the difficult year which is before us.

P.S. The present attitude of the Government *re* the Mahdi and Khartoum is all that could be hoped.

[*From Sir E. W. Hamilton.*[2]] 10, DOWNING ST.,
[*Private.*] FEBRUARY 10TH.

MY DEAR REGGY, I have thrown hastily together headings for a Govt. brief. I take it for granted that no sane man would have

---

[1] Joining the Government.
[2] Private Secretary to Mr. Gladstone.

advocated the despatch of a relief force (*a*) until the necessity for it was clearly proved, (*b*) until it could be undertaken without *reasonable* risk.

What I think ought to be established is

(*a*) When may that necessity be said to have been proved? X.

(*b*) What was the earliest date on which the expedition could have left Cairo? Y.

(*c*) What (1) was done, and what (2) might have been done (in reason) between the dates of X. and Y.?

(*d*) When, under C (2) could Wolseley have reached Korti? and when he *did* reach?

Dates, "chapter and verse," and references to authorities would have to be given with great care and accuracy.

Can you undertake to assist in having this done?

Yours sincerely,
E. W. HAMILTON.

[*To Lord Ripon.*]　　　　　　　LONDON,
　　　　　　　　　　　　　　　　FEBRUARY 11TH.

We have heard nothing definite from the Soudan, but after *On Gordon.* the detailed account in the *Daily Chronicle* I have no hope that Gordon is alive. I was looking this morning at his last letter to me before he left England. He describes the kindness with which everyone has treated him. He said it almost made him *afraid*, and then he quoted the *Ring of Polycrates*:

> Would'st thou avert the coming ill,
> Implore the dread Invisible
> Thy sweets to sour.

He drank the cup of bitterness to the dregs before the end came. Among Eugene's things which came from Egypt was a little volume of texts, which Gordon had given him, with an inscription written by him as he was leaving India: "To my honest young friend."

They both fell in the same cause, and what is that?

I hope Gordon's death will be good for the nation. George Eliot says: "The greatest gift a hero leaves his race is to have been a hero."

[*Journals.*]   LONDON,
                                                              FEBRUARY.

*On
Gordon.*   As is well known, General Gordon sailed for India with Lord Ripon, with whom he had accepted the office of private secretary to the Viceroy, on May 14th, 1880.

On June 3rd he resigned that appointment, and on July 2nd he arrived in Hongkong.

After visiting Pekin, and assisting his old friend Li Hung Chang, who was an advocate of peace and was in imminent danger from the War Party in China, Gordon returned to England in November.

I had made his acquaintance before he left for India and had introduced him to my brother, who as A.D.C. to Lord Ripon accompanied him on his outward journey.

Eugene and Gordon became great friends. The day he resigned his appointment he gave to my brother a little volume called *Clarke's Scripture Promises*—a book of which he was very fond—containing the inscription: To my dear and honest young friend, Eugene L. Brett. 3rd June, 1880.

In December 1880 Gordon came to see me at the India Office. From that time onwards he was always in and out of my home in Tilney St.

He would generally come in the morning, with a loose comforter round his neck, and a hat—by no means a new one—set well back on his head. The eternal cigarette in his mouth. His hair was brown and curly and his moustache tinged with grey. He was small—very small—and would have been unnoticed anywhere except for his eyes, which were of that peculiar steel-like blue, which seem to be characteristic of the enthusiast, and more especially when the enthusiast is a soldier. He would lounge into the library, and would stand—for he hardly ever cared to sit—for hours leaning against the fireplace, or he would walk up and down the room.

His talk was always refreshing. Full of humour, as simple as the Book of Genesis. Complexity of thought, confusion of ideas, prolixity of speech were impossible from him. He saw with wonderful clearness, although sometimes not very far.

He detested cant, and although he could be strangely indignant and was deeply roused by treachery, his charitableness knew no bounds. Repentance made up, in his eyes, for every crime. Although it amused him to be deceived, he was rarely taken in.

His religion was never obtruded, but it was as much part of his daily life as smoking cigarettes. He literally talked with God, and if it were not disrespectful, one might almost say that he walked arm in arm with Him.

[*To Sir Garnet Wolseley.*]   LONDON,
FEBRUARY 26TH.

This morning came the news of Stewart's death. It is a great sorrow. One more severe loss to the nation. We are paying a heavy penalty! *Khartoum : Political Effects.*

Early this week we began to realise that there was no hope of Gordon's having survived. The effect of his heroic life and death has been very good for the nation. It has brought men of all classes to view their responsibilities in a different and nobler light. Mr. Gladstone alone appears unmoved, as you will see by his speech last night.[1] It was very ill received by the House of Commons. I am asking Stead to send you a copy of his "Extra" about Gordon.

It is a terrible indictment against the Government. I cannot say that there is now a unanimous feeling that the Mahdi should

[1] The speech based upon the letter of February 10th.

be overthrown at Khartoum. The Dissenters all over England view the prospect with misgiving; so you must be prepared for reactionary symptoms in the Government. . . .

These are anxious times, and H.M.G. is unfit to cope with them. I am afraid, however, that the Opposition would do no better.

[*To Sir Garnet Wolseley.*]   MARCH 20TH.

Egypt :
Future
Policy.

Several mails have gone by without my having found time to write to you. Swaine has no doubt told you that the general sentiment here is critically hostile to the further advance of our force. No one seems to believe that we shall attempt to get to Khartoum, or that the railway to Berber will ever get beyond the hills. The feeling is strong, even in the clubs. It is stronger in the House of Commons, where man after man rose to denounce the campaign, in the debate on the railway vote. And it is strongest of all in the country, especially among the Nonconformists in the North. To keep you and your force in the Soudan throughout the summer, and to abandon operations when the autumn comes, would be a crime; yet a decent excuse for reversing the order of February 7th is at present wanting.

A few days ago it looked as if the Afghan difficulty would furnish this excuse; but the question now looks as if it would be solved without recourse to a military demonstration. No doubt Graham's operations may give a new turn to events, but I think you should be prepared for a policy based upon:

1. Defending Egypt proper at Wady Halfa and waiting there the Mahdi's advance.

2. Holding Suakin for ever with a railway and hill-station at Tambuk or Sinkat.

I am only now giving you an idea of the drift of public opinion, and by no means am I attempting to forecast any immediate change of policy on the part of the Cabinet. . . .

Mr. Brett now ceased to be Private Secretary to Lord Hartington.[1] He was defeated at the General Election in November and never stood for Parliament again. During the next ten years he spent most of his time at Orchard Lea, where he bred his beloved racehorses, or at Newmarket; but he kept in close touch with the political world.

[*To Lord Hartington.*]　　　　　ORCHARD LEA,
　　　　　　　　　　　　　　　　　　　APRIL 7TH.

I have never myself believed that we should adhere to our *Egypt.* resolve and go to Khartoum. The determination to do so, I never doubted, was right. And there is no question but that the decision greatly helped Wolseley by restoring the shaken morale of officers and men. But the state of facts are not what they were; and as months roll on, the resolve to push forward a force to Khartoum is fast fading. . . .

[*To Lord Hartington.*]　　　　　ORCHARD LEA,
　　　　　　　　　　　　　　　　　　　APRIL 15TH.

I am sincerely glad that you have passed through this fresh *Soudan* crisis,[2] although it must have been a trying ordeal for you, with- *Policy.* out having found it necessary to break up the Cabinet.

On other occasions I have doubted whether you were wise— in your own interests and those of the nation—to remain in office. But I have not the slightest doubt in this case; and I feel

---

[1] Mr. Hobart, Secretary to the War Office, wrote :
　　　　　　　　　　　　　　　　　　WAR OFFICE.

MY DEAR BRETT,—Your letter just received has made me very sad, tho I still hope there may be some mitigation to my sorrow at the step you announce.

Long as you have predicted it the blow is not one whit the less now it has come, and I feel it very severely. How will Lord Hartington take it? . . .

[2] The abandonment of the Soudan.

sure that it would be the opinion of every candid judgment to which the whole of the circumstances were submitted.

I never could see how "upon the state of facts then before you" your decision to go to Khartoum could have been other than it was. The fate of Gordon was unknown, and the condition of the force in the Soudan was perilous in the extreme. It was necessary to show the boldest possible front, both to discourage the enemy, and to preserve the morale of our men. An order to retire would have been indefensible at that time. Since then a wholly different "state of facts" has come to light; and the country has had time to make up its mind upon them.

There is very little doubt what the decision is; and if you had retired from the Government, you would have found yourself in the position of Athanasius—*contra mundum*.

I cannot see that you are specially more responsible for the *policy* of the campaign than any of your colleagues, though undoubtedly you are more responsible than they are for the conduct of it.

Then comes the question of the railway. If we are not to occupy Berber, a railway further than the hills is useless. It never could be preserved; it being so obviously the interest of the Hadenhowas—the carriers of the desert—to destroy it.

But a cardinal and indispensable part of your Egyptian policy is to hold the trade routes from the Upper Nile. For this reason we must hold on to Suakin, as we hold on to Cairo. The power that holds the one, should hold the other. The mercantile interests in this country would never forgive the government that allowed the trade of the Upper Nile to pass from French to German hands.

It would be indeed a farce, after all the fuss about the Cameroons and Angra Pequeñas,[1] to allow Suakin, which is the port of Khartoum and the Nile, to pass into the hands of foreigners.

If we are to hold Suakin, we must have a hill-station and a railway to connect the two. The approval of this policy will be very general throughout the country; and I am sure it will be

[1] Occupied by Germany in 1883.

thought to be the most prudent and advantageous settlement of the Soudan question which could have been hoped for, after the events of the last ten months.

The few persons outside the Cabinet who know what has passed within it during the last few days seem to have no doubt that you have acted wisely and patriotically in not giving way to the strong and natural feeling which you could scarcely avoid showing in this matter. It is, of course, heart-breaking to have to abandon an object for which so many sacrifices have been made. But I cannot admit that those sacrifices have been wholly made in vain.

They might have been avoided no doubt; but the fault—which necessitated them—was not committed yesterday. When the history of the past year comes to be written, I doubt whether the part played by this country will be considered a very noble one; but if the secret history of your relations to the government ever sees the light, I think you will not need to be alarmed for your reputation. Especially for this last act of self-abnegation.

[*To Sir Garnet Wolseley*.]　　　ORCHARD LEA,
　　　　　　　　　　　　　　　APRIL 17TH.

The question is decided. You are *not* to go to Khartoum. I am not surprised, and I do not imagine you are much astonished. *Soudan Policy.*

The feeling in this country—as I have told you before—is so strongly opposed to this Soudan war, that the Government would not have been able to carry it through. Of course there are great difficulties among the Ministers, but they have contrived to settle them for the present. Public attention is wholly engrossed in the prospects of war with Russia.[1] For my part I do not believe that Russia's objective is India. Consequently I *Russia.*

---

[1] The inclination to war arose out of the delays of the Anglo-Russian Boundary Commission in Northern Afghanistan. The Russians delayed the work of the Commission, but continued their military advance, and pro-

see no reason why, if war is staved off now, peace should not be maintained until war breaks out in Eastern Europe, when we should, in any case, have allies who are not now procurable.

The Turk no doubt is to be bought; but how can Mr. Gladstone consent to induce the Turk to recapture his lost provinces? Even Midlothian would rebel against such apostasy.

Strenuous efforts ought to have been made long ago to force Russia to come to terms. Now, if peace is maintained, it cannot help being to some extent humiliating to us.

Personally, I should prefer this to a war at the present moment, so convinced am I that we are not in a position to fight, with the full advantages which are our due. I am hoping that you will write to me from Cairo, as I am interested to hear in what condition you find the central Government.

This is only a short letter, but I feel sure that Lady Wolseley has forestalled me with every possible news.

[*Journals.*]   1, TILNEY STREET,
JUNE 23RD.

Bismarck.   Colonel Swaine, military attaché at Berlin, called this morning. Bismarck lives now the life of a hermit, never goes into society and sees no foreign Ministers or Ambassadors, except De Courcel, the Frenchman, to whom audience is always given. The others have to put up with Hatzfeld, the Foreign Secretary.

Lord Ampthill used sometimes to see Bismarck, but only when he had anything definite to say. When Lord Dufferin passed through Berlin, he asked to see Bismarck. Lord Ampthill, knowing that he had nothing of importance to communicate, tried to dissuade him, but Lord Dufferin insisted, and went to Varzin. He was received, and had some conversation with

posals for arbitration (advanced in the first place by Mr. Brett) were abortive. The state of popular feeling appears to have quietened without any specific change in the situation but merely because events nearer home, such as the changes of government and the general election, diverted the public attention.

Bismarck who, discovering that he came only for a "causerie," sent word next morning that he was too ill to see him again and begged to be excused.

The Prince of Wales when he goes to Berlin calls first on Bismarck and Moltke—as do all the other princes. The etiquette in other cases is for *subjects* to call upon Princes of the Blood Royal!

De Courcel, mentioned above, the French Ambassador, is a man of old family and elegant manners. A good talker, witty and refined. He is very acceptable, personally, to Bismarck.

Moltke is a "charming old man," but getting now past work, *Other* which is done by Count Waldersee, Quarter-master General of *German* the Army, about fifty-two years of age; a brilliant soldier and *Personali-* first-rate administrator. He was military attaché in Paris before *ties.* and after the war, and he will be Moltke's successor.

The Emperor is in very feeble health. Passes blood when anything goes wrong with him. However, he is the centre of everything German, especially of the Army.

When the Emperor fails to attend a Review or the Manœuvres there is no life in them. The General Staff, mostly composed of voluntary loafers, immediately diminishes by two-thirds.

Prince Frederick Charles, who recently died, was popular with the Army because of his dash and merit as a General; but he was a terrible martinet, and not favourably regarded by the Emperor.

The Crown Prince is fairly popular; a great admirer of England; not clever but sagacious.

The Crown Princess is disliked by the nobility for her liberal views. She has broken through all rules of etiquette by having architects, musicians, professors and such people to dinner. The Crown Prince tolerates this eccentricity, and is amused by it. He is, however, master in his own house. She wearies and disgusts Germans by her laudation of England and everything English. But he is fond of England and reads everything he can about her customs and institutions. He is a strong conservative.

His mother writes to his English relations that Prince William "hates England." He denies this strenuously in conversation. His abilities are great, and he is intimate with Bismarck, who treats him with all the affection and familiarity of a father.

The following are the particulars of the changes of government referred to in the next few letters. The second Gladstone Cabinet resigned on June 9th on account of the acceptance of an amendment to the Budget Bill. Since this was not a vote of censure or of no confidence they retained a majority in the House for most purposes. For this reason it was not until June 24th, and until he had obtained some assurances of co-operation from Mr. Gladstone, that Lord Salisbury could form a government prepared to take office.

The general election (in which Mr. Brett was defeated) took place in November, with a return of 4 Independents, 331 Liberals, 249 Conservatives, and 85 Parnellites. Parnell having transferred his allegiance for the moment to the Conservatives, this constituted a deadlock. Lord Salisbury decided to meet the House.

[*To Lady Esher.*]   STUDLEY ROYAL,
                                  SEPTEMBER 20TH.

. . . I have been very busy writing an article for the *Fortnightly Review* for October,[1] which the Editor bored me to send him, but it is over now. In a weak moment I consented. I saw Lord Hartington at Doncaster. I was asked to stand for Barrow-in-Furness, but I did not care to ally myself again closely to the

---

[1] The article was one of three grouped under the heading "From Three Platforms"; they expressed views which were all consistent with membership of the Liberal Party in the House. Mr. Brett advocated a clear and definite programme for social legislation for remedying abuses. Mr. Dicey protested that the social legislation favoured by some Liberals encouraged State interference at the expense of individual liberty and free competition. Mr. Labouchere prophesied that with the extension of the Franchise the Crown would be excluded from politics, the Lords reformed out of recognition if not abolished, and power remain—and rightly—with the toiling masses.

family, so I shall not fix up a constituency till November, and I shall then take my chance.

I wonder what you will think of Mr. Gladstone's manifesto. It is not a very exhilarating document, and certainly very mild in tone. The most serious thing on the political horizon is the insurrection in Roumelia. It may reopen the whole Eastern question. . . .

. . . We go from here this day week to Arthur Balfour's in Scotland. After that we shall return to Orchard Lea, and then I go to Newmarket.

[*From the Rt. Hon.*   LOCAL GOVERNMENT BOARD,
  A. J. Balfour.]   DECEMBER 4TH.

MY DEAR REGGY,

   I will show the P. Minister your letter—but I do not think you need trouble yourself about the controversial amenities of the Judge Advocate General. I am *very* sorry you are not in the House. Though destined no doubt to have a short life, the Parliament is likely to have a merry one—and in the general imbroglio which I foresee your peculiar gifts would I think have found a great sphere. You must look out for some new political bride—mistress would perhaps be the more appropriate term considering the brevity—and the cost—of the connection indicated. Remember me to Mrs. Brett, and believe me, etc., etc.

                                              A. J. B.

[*To the Rt. Hon. J. Chamberlain.*]   1, TILNEY STREET,
                                              DECEMBER 9TH.

   I am exceedingly grateful to you for your kind letter. Our fight at Plymouth was a good one, and although defeated, I shall never regret going there, or cease to congratulate myself on the experience I got in fighting a large city.

*Future
of the
Liberals.*

The impressions I formed of the future of the Liberal Party I should like to have the opportunity of talking over with you. The future looks rather grim at present. . . .

With regard to Ireland, there are but two alternatives; Coercion and Home Rule. The first is, I assume, impossible. It only remains to agree upon the form under which Ireland is to govern itself, and there appears no chance of arriving at any solution likely to be satisfactory and permanent without co-operation of the *three* parties. Indeed it is a *sine quâ non*.

You very kindly asked me what are my plans. For the present I see no chance of being of any service. But if the opportunity occurs I might endeavour to get into Parliament, although I do not desire it.

I hope that we shall never see again a Liberal Government composed like the last one, or held together by similar means. One might have imagined that there would be no great difficulty for men, plentifully endowed with the world's good things, to keep in view solely the advantage of the country, irrespective of petty considerations. But one would apparently have been mistaken.

I hope that Dilke will get out of his difficulty, and that you and Morley will be content to bide your time. *Tout vient à qui sait attendre.* Hackneyed, but none the less true.

[*To Lord Hartington.*]   1, TILNEY STREET,
DECEMBER 15TH.

*Chamberlain
Policy.*

I saw Dilke this morning. He says Chamberlain is determined not to take office, and to have nothing to do with Mr. Gladstone's Home Rule Scheme.

Chamberlain is full of fury against Parnell for having sold him. And he is very angry with Mr. Gladstone for having "negotiated"—which he says he has done—with the Irish and the Tories, without consulting him. He has heard a good deal of what has gone on at Hawarden, but not from the source from which he thinks he should have heard it. He has made up his mind to support the Tories so long as they behave themselves, and to help them to pass Liberal measures. . . .

[*To Lord Rosebery.*]   I, TILNEY STREET,
                                        DECEMBER 20TH.

I believe the Tories have definitely determined not to touch *Ireland.* H.R. [Home Rule] in any shape or form at present. Their proposal is to apply "county government" to Ireland, and to give Ireland equal and similar laws to those of Great Britain.

Churchill[1] thinks that this plan will come to nothing; that Mr. Gladstone's proposals will be unacceptable to the country; and that then the Tories will have to produce a third plan to which both great parties will agree.

It is not true that the Queen *made* them stay in, though she *The Tory* approved of their doing so. It appears that Lord Salisbury made *Cabinet.* an admirable speech to his Cabinet, in which he told them that he disapproved of the resignation of a Cabinet after a General Election, as tending to hamper the action of the party in opposition; that on this ground he thought Disraeli's resignation in 1868 a mistake; that if they were to resign now, their hands would be tied for two years, as they could not in fairness effectually criticise a new Government, having themselves *admitted* that they were unprepared to govern the country; but that if they were turned out by the House of Commons it was a very different thing. Consequently it was settled that they remain in office.

[*To Lord Rosebery.*]   I, TILNEY STREET,
                                        DECEMBER 21ST.

Hartington is very tranquil, but evidently determined to *Party* oppose Mr. Gladstone's scheme. It is just possible that he and *Politics.*

---
[1] Lord Randolph.

Chamberlain may come together in this matter, for their point of view is the same, although Chamberlain's objections are more complex than Hartington's. I presume, however, that Mr. Gladstone will not swerve from his opinion, so that we are in view of a break up of the party. . . .

But I find that many thoughtful people in London, and some of the ablest provincial journalists, are saying "Better total separation than Home Rule."

Chamberlain uses similar language. At present no public man says he agrees with Mr. Gladstone, but I fancy J. Morley will supply the deficiency to-night. . . .

[*Journals.*]   1, TILNEY STREET,
                                 JANUARY 16TH, 1886.

*Party
Politics.*

I saw Chamberlain on Friday last. At first he was hard and aggressive, although he thawed a little towards the end of our interview. It is clear that his feelings towards Mr. Gladstone are full of bitterness. His soreness in speaking of Morley was unconcealed.

"We have made Morley's position," he said, "and now he goes his own way. Well, let it be understood that, though our private friendship remains untouched, in future we act no longer together. I shall make this plain on the first possible occasion."

He thinks that Mr. Gladstone is determined to turn out the Government, "their holding office in a minority being unconstitutional and impossible."[1] . . .

[1] On January 27th the Government were defeated by a majority of 79 on a motion, opposed by the Government, for the compulsory creation of small tenancies. It was generally understood, however, that this was a piece of Parliamentary tactics designed to prevent the change of Government arising out of Irish questions.

[*Journals.*]   1, TILNEY STREET,
JANUARY 26TH.

Anniversary of Gordon's death and the fall of Khartoum. I *Party* wrote to Hartington, who is said to be going to vote with the *Politics.* Government and against his party to-night. I trust he will adhere to the determination not to serve under Mr. Gladstone again. It would only mean another term of unsatisfactory compromises and bitterness for him.

[*Journals.*]   1, TILNEY STREET,
JANUARY 27TH.

The Government was defeated last night amid wild excitement of the Irishmen.

[*Journals.*]   1, TILNEY STREET,
JANUARY 28TH.

I saw Rosebery this afternoon. We talked of Lord Granville. *The New* I urged him to refuse to join if Lord Granville returns to the *Cabinet.* Foreign Office. He alone is in the position to do this, as he opposed the foreign policy of Mr. Gladstone's late Government, and refused to join it on that ground. If he will take this course, he will earn thereby the gratitude of his fellow countrymen.

[*Journals.*]   1, TILNEY STREET,
JANUARY 29TH.

John Morley called this morning. He expects to be offered *The New* some subordinate place. I said "Of course you will refuse it?" *Cabinet.* He said "Certainly." He spoke in strong praise of Hartington's speech.

Natty Rothschild called this morning. He said Alfred [Rothschild] had been commissioned—as an old friend of Hartington's—to tell him that Lord Salisbury would serve under him as Foreign Secretary, and do everything to help him, if he would consent to lead the Tory party. There is no chance of acceptance, but he says H. was pleased.

The Queen's View.

The Queen is miserable at the prospect of losing her Ministers. She thinks Mr. Gladstone's Government will be the worst ever constructed, even by him. She, finding it was useless to send for Hartington, wished Goschen to go down to Osborne to advise her, and to see if any course was possible except to send for Mr. Gladstone. . . .

[*Journals.*]   1, TILNEY STREET,
                                                         FEBRUARY 1ST.

I dined with Chamberlain last night. He was in good spirits, but indifferent temper. J. Morley was there. He had seen Mr. Gladstone in the afternoon; not a very satisfactory interview. Mr. G. unfolded his views and offered Morley the Irish Secretaryship, an offer which he has taken time to consider. . . .

[*Journals.*]   1, TILNEY STREET,
                                                         FEBRUARY.

Harcourt.

Loulou Harcourt called and said that his father wished to see me. So I went to Grafton Street this evening. Mr. Gladstone told him that he could not part with him from the Commons, where he is to act the part of his first lieutenant, and offered him the choice of the Secretaryships of State.

Harcourt wished to know some details of the India Office, and asked me what I thought of the respective places. I pointed out that for a man in the House of Commons, with any responsibility there, the India Office work was exceedingly oppressive. He thought the Government of India was carried on mainly by the Viceroy. I pointed out to him that the Secretary of State has to stand between the Viceroy and a generally hostile Council at home. The Home Office work was familiar and easy to him. Rosebery is to go to the F.O. I have written to congratulate him sincerely upon it. He is fortunate and so is the country.

[*Journals.*]   1, TILNEY STREET,
                                                 FEBRUARY 4TH.

. . . Last night the Prince of Wales gave a curious pot-pourri dinner party of Radicals and Tories.

Had a long talk with Rosebery to-day. Discussed Under Secretaries, very difficult to find, and Private Secretaries.

[*Journals.*]   1, TILNEY STREET,
                                                 FEBRUARY 5TH.

Labouchère called here this evening, and asked if I would *Political* undertake to supervise the Editing of the *Daily News*. I declined. *Prophecies.* Labouchère thinks the Government will not survive many months.

Dined with Lord Ripon, Sir H. James, John Morley, Robert Browning, Sir D. Stewart, George Russell. Pleasant enough.

Mr. Gladstone told the Prince of Wales that he would be out of office "with ignominy" in three months.

Somebody said to J. M. "What is Joe playing at?" "Fast and loose" was the answer, which shows the feeling of tension between the two bosom friends of last year. Morley is modest and keenly full of responsibility. Ministers kissed hands to-day, the Queen looking very cross. Morley resented the ceremonial. Queer of him!

[*To Lord Rosebery.*]   1, TILNEY STREET,
                                                FEBRUARY 19TH.

I hope the F.O. will keep *The Times* well in hand. The *Daily News*, uninfluential and foolish, can be left to Arnold Morley and the small fry.

I hear nothing but praises of your appointment. It is a charming relief to hear that the F.O. is worked off its legs. May the Fates avert the necessity for sinking the Greek fleet in the Bay of Salamis!

I had a long talk with Chamberlain yesterday. What a curious state the Cabinet is in; and what a Fox is the G.O.M.

[*Journals.*]   1, TILNEY STREET,
                                                FEBRUARY 24TH.

Rosebery called here after breakfast, and we walked to Millais' studio where we found him with a stalking cap on his head and a short pipe in his mouth, painting from a model dressed as a kind of nun.

Chamberlain.   Chamberlain, when the Government was formed, received no offer of any post but that which he accepted.[1] He should have been given a Secretaryship of State. But it was fortunate for him he did not obtain it.

In 1882, when Forster resigned, Chamberlain was hurt at not getting the Irish Secretaryship; and then ensued the massacre in Phœnix Park. In 1886 he wanted the Home Secretaryship and immediately there occurred the riots of the Social Democrats. Two fortunate escapes! . . .

Gladstone.   Rosebery said five years ago, Mr. Gladstone had told him that it was time for him to retire, he was losing his constructive power. *Now* he is revelling in a constructive problem bristling with difficulties; plunging about in it, like a child in its tub.

---

[1] President of the Local Government Board.

[*To Mr. W. T. Stead.*]　　　　　ORCHARD LEA,
　　　　　　　　　　　　　　　APRIL 22ND.

I cannot compete with you in sketches of character. The *On Lord* inferior hand would be too distinctly traced. So you must *Hartington.* depict Hartington.

Perhaps, however, you will lay stress on the mythical Hartington; that is to say, the man who loves pleasure to the exclusion of work, who sacrifices statecraft to racing, who is *altogether* without personal ambition, whose mind turns away from long and serious contemplation of dull subjects. All this is fiction.

Apart from politics he has no *real* interest in life; and cut off from them he would be in reality as bored as he appears to be by them. No one I have known ponders longer over State problems; the bent of his mind is slowly critical, and very slowly constructive. This tendency of his, to see every objection to a proposal before attempting to gauge its advantages, has induced people—even his colleagues—to think him vacillating, which he is not, and more conservative than he is.

Chamberlain said of him, that the characteristic thing about him was his inability to be surprised or shocked. No proposition, however radical, ever seems to disturb his equanimity; but he considers it, weighs it, and argues against it, as if it were the most moderate and ordinary suggestion. He has Mr. Gladstone's habit of never accepting a statement of fact without examination and enquiry. A mere dictum, however apparently authoritative, never passes unquestioned by him; and chapter and verse are always asked for and insisted upon, before any value is placed upon a statement. His rough chivalry towards men is a strange feature in his character. Any "médisance" of a political or personal foe rarely passes unchallenged and without some exculpatory or qualifying phrase. His power of work is of a type which insists upon accuracy in detail, at first hand, and from original sources.

Of abstracts and superficial essays he has a horror. In this respect, officials who have known the two men say that he resembles Lord Salisbury, whose stupendous love of accuracy taxed the capabilities of the two greatest departments of State. Lord Hartington's strength lies in his nurture among a family with certain hereditary governmental instincts, such as a rough sense of the high duty which every man owes to the State, and a simple disregard for most of the ordinary social prejudices whenever they clash with this ideal. No personality, even the loftiest, and no sentiment, however pathetic, would prevail with him, against the plain, dry duty of man to man, or of a citizen to the State. On the other hand, his weaknesses spring mainly from the circumstances that he was robbed of the advantage of a public school, and consequently has been forced to go through life with certain chambers of the heart and mind hermetically sealed. The one supreme fact about him, however, is this: that upon every occasion, be the trial what it may, or however severe the test, Lord Hartington has risen to it, and has surpassed the expectations even of his warmest friends.

[*Journals.*]   ORCHARD LEA,
                                                    MAY 20TH.

*Home
Rule.*
Since the introduction of Mr. Gladstone's Home Rule Bill the storm has raged. Many private friends have gone down into the deep. With a rump of his old following the "Grand Old Man" has held his own. His support in the Cabinet and on the benches of the House of Commons has been weak. Morley alone has given him help. Up to a few nights ago not a single speaker had attempted to argue his case. Then Bryce's speech made a welcome break. It has raised his reputation and has strengthened the Government. But all the argument, all the authority, all the social influence are against Mr. Gladstone. This only drives him to fight the harder; and among the despondent hosts, he, with his 76 years of conflict behind him, alone is full of confidence and indomitable pluck.

Chamberlain has genuine feeling that the Bill is bad and can only produce mischief. For a considerable time the Government touts declared that his influence was not worth considering, and that his support was not worth the purchase.

As it happens, he holds the balance between the parties, and his sword in the scales will turn the division against the Bill. ...

[*To Lord Granville.*]   ORCHARD LEA,
MAY 22ND.

Will you allow me to make a suggestion to which I invite your favourable consideration.

Colonial Visitors : Hospitality.

The Colonial Exhibition will, it is to be hoped, bring many of our kinsmen to England, and already wise and thoughtful arrangements have been made, by means of a reception committee, to render agreeable their visit to the mother country.

This committee however will not probably survive the occasion which gave it birth, while every year the number of distinguished Colonists visiting England happily increases.

Readers of Froude's charming book which you recently quoted must have a conception of the hospitality shown by the Colonists to visitors from England.

Normally, I am afraid, reciprocal attentions are but rarely paid to distinguished Colonists in this busy city. Circumstances, proving unfortunately regrettable carelessness in this respect, must have come to your knowledge during the past few years. At the India Office, as you are aware, the Secretary of State considers himself responsible for the proper reception of distinguished natives of that great dependency. There is an Aide-de-camp, whose duty it is to act on behalf of the Sec. of St., and to see that the luxuries of friendly welcome and adequate information upon all points of interest, especially of social custom, are placed at the disposal of the Indian guests.

At the Colonial Office, where no doubt the circumstances are different, but where the need is nevertheless as great, there is at present no official of this kind. Yet the post of A.D.C. to the

Sec. of St. to the Colonies might be most usefully created and employed. No more favourable moment is likely to recur for obtaining the approval of public opinion to its creation, than when the warm feeling of Englishmen towards their colonial relations is accentuated by the Exhibition recently opened by the Queen, and by the reckless accusations so falsely brought against a patriotic Government, of a desire to dismember the British Empire.

To appoint an officer—whose duty it would be to help the Agent-General—by means of his close connection with the Secretary of St.—in discharging all functions of English hospitality to Colonists at all times, may appear to some a small thing. But no one can appreciate more truly than yourself the possibility of the silken fibres of affection and courteous dealing proving as strong to bind England to the Colonies as any legislative rope however skilfully woven.

There are evident signs that the new democracy will insist upon its ceremonial and its social duties no less than the Régimes of old times; and in asking your kind consideration of this modest proposal, I am confident I am not asking for more than Parliament and public opinion would cheerfully sanction.

[*Journals.*]   ORCHARD LEA,
                                                 MAY 24TH.

Home
Rule Bill.   . . . Gladstone and his whip, Arnold Morley, are said to be full of confidence. They still believe that they will carry the second reading. Unless some total change occurs in the situation, this is absurd delusion. Harcourt, Rosebery and Morley all recognise defeat as certain. However, Labouchère says "Mr. Gladstone has always two kings up his sleeve. The worst of the old man is, that he is not content with this, but is always trying to persuade you that God Almighty put them there."[1]

[1] "The division placed the Government in a minority of 30, the numbers being: for the second reading, 313; against, 343. No less than 93 Liberals

[*From the Rt. Hon. J. Chamberlain.*]   HIGHBURY, BIRMINGHAM,
DECEMBER 23RD.

MY DEAR BRETT,

What do you think of the "little rift" now? Salisbury is a bold man and is no doubt prepared for all the consequences. The old combination is irretrievably smashed. I hardly know what new ones may be possible in the future.

Yours sincerely,

J. CHAMBERLAIN.

[*To Lord Hartington.*]   1, TILNEY STREET,
DECEMBER 24TH.

I had written to you fully the details of the local government *Cabinet* squabble and the proposed basis of settlement between Lord S. *Split.* [Salisbury] and Randolph [Churchill], when the latter's determination to resign flung everything into confusion. The real reason was the refusal of the Cabinet to accept his Budget. This, on top of other differences, precipitated the inevitable catastrophe. I gave your address to H. Manners and advised him to tell Lord S. that if he desires to communicate with you he should do so direct and not through anyone else.

Churchill thinks Lord S. has got his back to the wall, and means to fight it out, regardless of what he may bring down with him in his fall.

voted with the majority and eight were known to have voluntarily stayed away. Next day the Cabinet met, and Gladstone persuaded his colleagues that Dissolution was preferable to resignation. He thought there was little chance, if any, of a Conservative majority in the new Parliament. The decision was announced in both Houses on June 10th, and after disposing of non-contentious business they rose on the 25th." Low and Sanders, *Pol. Hist. Eng.* xii. 384.

The result of the election was 316 Conservatives, 78 Unionists, 191 Gladstonian Liberals, and 85 Parnellites. The Government formed by Lord Salisbury was therefore a minority Government except on Irish affairs. Nevertheless, and in spite of the internal dissensions about to be mentioned in the *Journals*, the Government lasted until 1892.

Chamberlain told Churchill in the plainest way that if the government persisted with their local government scheme he himself would move its rejection. Lord S., I imagine, saw that one day he would have to make a stand, and preferred to do so at once.

Confusion of Parties.

The immediate future is very obscure. Churchill remains in town, unwell. Chamberlain distinctly holds out the olive branch to Mr. G. in his speech last night. J. Morley is much inclined for a rejunction of forces; but holds back from a large concession. Mr. G. is burning with ardour difficult to restrain —for denunciation of the "plan of campaign" and for a "conference" with the Unionists.

This is pretty well the situation, and a fine muddle it is. I think Churchill's case for his budget, on the face of it, very strong.

The Government will, I fancy, fall to pieces irretrievably.

[*Journals.*]   1, TILNEY STREET, CHRISTMAS DAY.

Churchill.

Yesterday Randolph Churchill asked me to call on him. He was lying on the sofa in his large grey library, smoking cigarettes, and completely prostrated by the excitement of the last two days. He said he was shunned like the pest and no one had been near him, not even those who owed everything to him.

He showed me his correspondence with Salisbury. . . .

R. C. pointed out that as usual when a Cabinet breaks up, the final breach is a developed outcome of a series of differences of opinion upon many questions. He was not in good spirits, and evidently doubtful of the result of his action.

[*Journals.*]   1, TILNEY STREET, DECEMBER 25TH.

Cabinet Split.

At Devonshire House, nothing is known of Hartington's return, but one of Lord Salisbury's private secretaries had said that he will be home on Monday and is prepared to join the Government.

I called on Randolph this morning at his request. He was still lying on the sofa smoking cigarettes, but in good spirits.

The tone of the newspapers and of the Clubs seems changing. Doubts are now expressed as to whether the man who led the Tory Party to victory may not perhaps be right. Then the hints as to the Budget—popular in spirit and brilliant in design—have their effect. . . . *The Rejected Budget.*

He said Chamberlain had dined with him, and he had mentioned the principal points of the Budget. "Chamberlain was very jealous; it was just the Budget he hoped to produce one day himself."

Extract:—

"We have reason to believe that the Budget drawn up by Lord Randolph Churchill contemplated a very considerable remission of taxation. It was proposed to lower the income tax to five-pence in the pound, to reduce materially the tea and tobacco duties, and to relieve the burden of local taxation to the extent of some two millions. . . . The Budget as framed necessarily involved a diminution instead of an increase in the Navy and Military Estimates, and was therefore inconsistent with the Estimates submitted by the Admiralty and the War Office."

This, which appeared in the *Observer* yesterday, is accurate; but he has no idea how it was disclosed. But in addition he proposed a *graduation* of the death duties and House Tax, which would have been very popular.

[*To Lord Hartington.*]   1, TILNEY STREET,
                        DECEMBER 31ST.

I meant to call this morning, but I am not feeling very well. If the newspapers are right, I am very glad of your decision. In view of the future there can be no two opinions. John Morley, whom I saw some days ago, hoped you would refuse on the ground that were you to join Lord Salisbury, it would leave the *Attitude of Liberals.*

Liberal Party, and consequently the destinies of the country, in the hands of those in whom he has no confidence. He said there was no one in public life with whom he so often agreed, and under whom he would sooner serve, than yourself.

"I look upon him as the strongest bulwark we have against all the strong socialist doctrine I hate," he said.

He told me that Mr. G. "expected you to join" Lord Salisbury and hoped that you would do so; which, from his point of view, is not unnatural.

He told me also that Parnell had sent for O'Brien, and had put an end to the "plan of campaign," in deference to Mr. G.'s strong opinion, which his late colleagues have with great difficulty prevented him from ventilating.

Harcourt rushed up to town, in the belief that the hour of triumph was not far off, but he has gone back, I think, sadder and wiser.

[*To Lord Rosebery.*]   1, TILNEY STREET,
                                                   DECEMBER 31ST.

*The
Cabinet
Split.*

This is to wish you a Happy New Year. . . . "The crisis" was quite unexpected. . . .

Randolph on Monday wrote from Windsor (the Queen was furious because he wrote on "Castle paper" and never said a word to her of his difficulties) to say that if the Estimates were adhered to he must resign. On Wednesday he received a letter from Salisbury to say that in the present state of Europe he could not agree that works of fortification, etc., should be delayed, and that—though he did it with regret—he must support Smith and Hamilton. Randolph replied that he considered himself as well informed on foreign affairs as anyone else, that he denied the risks to England of an European war, as we had no concern with the Balkan provinces; that in the present state of our finances, and the present condition of our commerce, etc., he would be no party to a war policy, and that this sentiment was shared by the Democracy; while he was confident that no reforms in the spending departments were possible until a Chancellor of the Exchequer had been sacrificed on the altar of economy.

This letter reached Hatfield at 1 a.m. on Thursday, and was handed to Lord S. in the middle of the ballroom as he was standing next to the Duchess of Marlborough. In the morning the announcement was in *The Times*, and Lord S. did not come down to breakfast to witness the consternation of the Duchess. Randolph was shunned like the pest at first by all his friends, especially his own pet creatures. A reaction has now taken place. Hartington, who arrived two nights ago, will probably refuse to take office in the teeth of manifold objections. Lord S. might force him by a threat of dissolution, but I don't think it probable.

Of course Mr. G. is very hopeful. J. Morley thinks the great obstacle to compromise in the Irish Question is Parnell's "hurry" lest Mr. G. should die, and his determination to make the most of him while he can. I expect this is the correct view.

Churchill may return to office like Palmerston in 1853. Of course, if H. had gone over to the Tories, Randolph might have gone over to the Radicals, and would have succeeded Mr. G. as the great embodiment of economy and anti-jingoism in politics.

I am sorry you are not here. It really is very amusing.

However I daresay there are newspapers to be found in the Khyber Pass.

It is said that you are returning to lead your extensive array of supporters in the House of Lords. I hope it is true. Meanwhile if Randolph goes back into the Government it is a *sine quâ non* that Iddesleigh should retire from the F.O.

[*To* ——.]   1, TILNEY STREET,
                               JANUARY 8TH, 1887.

I cannot consent to consider a proposal to stand for Penryn and Falmouth, until I am assured of the support of the united Liberal Party in the Borough, upon a platform including large

Mr. Brett's Political Platform.

measures of domestic reform—and a Foreign Policy Imperial and at the same time peaceful.

Domestic questions would include a wide extension of popular control over the government of counties, without class privilege of any kind.

Enquiry to be followed by energetic action into the administration of the great departments of State, especially the War Office and Admiralty.

Absolute freedom to support any measure, which might commend itself to my judgment, the effect of which would be to reform or abolish existing Ecclesiastical abuses.

Reform of the whole system of government in Ireland with a view to relieving the House of Commons of business it is unable any longer to cope with, consistently with maintaining intact the Unity of the State.

If after such an expression of my views, I were requested by my old supporters and friends to come forward as their candidate, to expound them to the constituency, and to advocate them in Parliament, I would give their request my earnest consideration with a sincere hope that I might be able to return an affirmative answer.

[*To Mr. W. T. Stead.*]   1, TILNEY STREET,
                                JANUARY 17TH.

On Lord Iddesleigh (Northcote).   . . . Don't you think you might do penance to-morrow—the day of the funeral—by giving us the "plain truth" about Lord Iddesleigh.

Of course you cannot speak ill of him, as there is nothing to be said against him as an individual, and his career was very meritorious until he was placed in positions for which he was in no way qualified.

(1) As a leader of the H. of C. he was a failure. No one denied this all through the last Parliament. And the journals, now more

sickening than usual in his praise, were then loudest in their criticism.

(2) As F. Minister he was, by the general verdict of foreigners as well as of Englishmen who had some knowledge, hopelessly inefficient.

Witness the general line of Foreign Policy towards Bulgaria, for which, of course, he was responsible, or too weak to resist; and especially Lord Salisbury's Mansion House speech, all the facts of which must have been and were supplied by the F.O.

The reference to "foreign gold" was not the invention of Lord Salisbury, and the Foreign Sec. was the person responsible for the statement.

That Lord Salisbury became alive to this is evident. As you explained the other day, Lord Salisbury is not capable of acting Foreign Sec. unless he has all the threads in his hands. When he found that he was provided with wretched material he came to the conclusion that, in the interests of the country, the Foreign Office must pass into other keeping.

To accuse him or Churchill of killing a man—who for 30 years had suffered from heart disease—and who had several dangerous fainting fits quite recently—is monstrous.

And the hysterics of the *St. James' Gazette* are disgusting when you consider the frightful responsibilities and burdens which rested on shoulders obviously—by the sequel—unfit to bear them. But then plain truth is so very unsensational as a rule.

[*To Mr. W. T. Stead.*]   1, TILNEY STREET,
                                                  JANUARY 21ST.

Thanks very much for the letter. XIII[1] has attracted considerable attention at the F.O., and I have had to discuss the article with a large audience, but without flinching.

I keep the secret because I have some things to say about the F.O. which will tell more anonymously than they would with my name attached.

[1] Mr. Brett himself was XIII.

[*To Lady Esher.*]   LAMBTON CASTLE,
                                          DECEMBER 8TH.

. . . Here there are no events which make it easy to write a
letter. We are a large party. I suppose about sixteen, but I have
not counted. Shooting every day, and bed about twelve
o'clock. Not an unhealthy existence but not wildly exciting.
Albert Grey is here. He still suffers from his head. I doubt
whether he will ever recover from the foolish neglect after his
accident. It seems to me that the French have issued from their
difficulties with a great degree of credit. Carnot from all account
will make a good President. I had hopes all along that neither
de Freycenet nor Ferry would be chosen. Both of them un-
trustworthy fellows.

The former especially being a horrid intriguer. . . .

Electric   The electric light here is quite charming. Especially in the
Light.   bedrooms. You touch a button, and your dressing-table is
illuminated. You touch another near the *table de nuit* and your
bed is as light as day. It costs £2000 to start, and they burn
about 5 cwt. of coals a day in order to produce it.

I hear that Coutts Lindsay has bought five acres of ground at
Greenwich, and intends supplying all London with electricity.
It will be ever so much *cleaner*, even if it is not cheaper than gas.

We remain here till Monday, and then we go to Tyninghame[1]
just over the border. . . .

[*To Lady Esher.*]   ORCHARD LEA,
                                          APRIL 1888.

. . . I went for a day to Newmarket last week, and sold my
mare "Lady Mine" for 300 guineas. So I did pretty well. . . .

Since the particulars of the Parnell forgery case are not so
well remembered as those of the divorce case, the following

[1] Home of Lord Binning.

THE HON. REGINALD BRETT AND "DANDY"
AT HEATH FARM, 1888.

summary may be useful for understanding the references in the coming extracts.

On April 18th, 1888, the day fixed for the division of the second reading of the Crimes Bill, *The Times* published the facsimile of a letter bearing the date May 15th, 1882, with the alleged signature of Parnell, in which the writer appeared to apologise for having as a matter of expediency openly condemned the murder of Lord Frederick Cavendish and Mr. Burke, though in fact he thought that Burke deserved his fate. The same night in his place in Parliament, Parnell declared the letter to be a forgery. Parnell took no further action through the conviction that he would not get justice from a Middlesex jury; and later, when *The Times* produced several more letters, on July 2nd, 1888, Morley urged the same argument upon him against instituting proceedings for libel. On this second occasion the Government offered to create a Commission of Judges "to inquire into the allegations and charges made against members of Parliament in the recent action"—O'Donnell *v. The Times*. Owing to the introduction after "Members of Parliament" of the words "and other persons" the inquiry was turned into a roving examination of Irish politics since the establishment of the land league. Its sittings dragged on from September 17th, 1888 to November 22nd, 1889. Its proceedings excited no interest except where they concerned Parnell. It did, however, in the course of its unnecessary work, establish beyond question that the letters were a forgery by Pigott. This decision was reached on February 22nd.

The leading dates in the second trial, the divorce case, were as follows: Parnell stayed with Gladstone at Hawarden to discuss the outlines of the second Home Rule Bill on December 18th and 19th, 1889. On December 24th O'Shea filed the divorce petition. The case appeared in the defended list; but when it was heard, on November 15th, 1890, it was undefended. The decree nisi was given on the 17th. Parnell was re-elected leader of his party on November 25th; but after much talk and intrigue, during which the Liberals compelled Gladstone to disown him in a public letter to the press, he was deposed from leadership on December 6th.

[*To Mr. W. T. Stead.*]   ORCHARD LEA,
OCTOBER 17TH.

Parnell :
First Trial.

. . . Are you sure about your ethical position? What higher obligation has man to man, than to help him save his life or his reputation?

If Parnell was a woman, would you keep silence? Perhaps you alone have the clue which will help him to prove his innocence. This you deny him. Can you justify it?

[*To Lord Hartington.*]   ORCHARD LEA,
FEBRUARY 22ND, 1889.

Parnell.

As you may, in the papers to-day, have seen my name in juxtaposition to yours, I think it right to explain a matter which occurred in June 1886, and which I never troubled to mention to you.

Albert Grey called upon me here at that time, and told me that an individual had some information for sale, which would connect the Parnellite members with the "physical force" party in America, and suggested that I should mention it to you. I said I was certain it was of no use, and that you would not entertain any proposal of the kind, and that I could not even suggest it to you.

Further that no prominent public man would care to embark upon transactions of that kind, and that it was otherwise with newspaper Editors.

Upon this he saw Mr. Stead, the Editor of the *Pall Mall Gazette*, and arranged an interview between him and the supposed Vendor at Dorchester House. This interview is reported in the newspapers to-day. I think, as the matter has been referred to in the trial, it is right you should know exactly the share which I had in it in reference to yourself.

[*To Mr. W. T. Stead.*]   ORCHARD LEA,
FEBRUARY 22ND.

Bravo Titus Oates Pigott.[1] How excellent it all is. Could not   *Parnell.*
be better. How superior are Archbishops to philosophers.

I hope that J. Morley and the others, under whom I have
groaned for months, will eat their prophecies of evil. Parnell
has a genuine triumph over them all. Heaven knows they
abused him enough for insisting upon clearing his reputation.

From the low point of view of mere into-office-climbing
tactics he is superior to them all.

[*To Lord Hartington.*]   MARCH 12TH.

I met Parnell at George Lewis's on Thursday, and spent   *Parnell.*
half an hour with him. His frigidity is wearing off under
the general influence of a sort of popularity. There is marked
change in his manner. His coldness and reserve were the outcome of insensate pride. They seem to be thawing rapidly. He
is fully bent on unearthing the conspiracy behind Houston and
Pigott. It will not transpire that there is much more behind
them than abject folly and the gullibility of arch-geese.

After dinner last night I sat near de Staal—the Russian   *Russia.*
Ambassador—who is always charming to me. He said that
Mme. Novikoff—whom he likes—has often asked why I have
not made her acquaintance. I said that in view of what was said
about her influence, the moment any Englishman professes any
regard for Russia, I thought it as well that one friend at least of
his country should not know Mme. Novikoff! He says she
never was a pretty woman. Always *épaisse*.

He spoke warmly of Stead. He had read *The Truth about
Russia* with interest, and personally approves the part about the
"Shadow of the Throne." He said it will have no effect.

He has a clever way of not asking questions which might be

---

[1] The forger of the Parnell letters.

embarrassing. He makes a statement as a half assertion, which enables one to reply frankly or not, just as it is convenient.

Mrs. Gladstone.

At dinner I sat near Mrs. Gladstone. She was full of ardour about him and all his affairs. She told me that she had, the other day, been, with a good deal of difficulty and a trifling risk, into the blue grotto at Capri. I asked whether Mr. Gladstone had accompanied her. "Oh dear no! I should not have liked him to come. I should not have thought it right."

[*Journals.*]   " SUNBEAM " R.Y.S., DARTMOUTH,
                                                    JUNE 9TH.

Mr. Gladstone, Mrs. Gladstone, Mrs. Yorke, Henry Gladstone, Cyril Flower; on board the *Garland* Mrs. Yorke's yacht, 250 tons auxiliary steam, schooner rigged.

Wolverton, Mr. and Mrs. Jack Pease, Arnold Morley, Lord Brassey; on board the *Sunbeam*, 565 tons. Arrived here 9.30 Saturday night. Left Portland 3.30. Hazy, Calm.

Gladstone's Memories.

Mr. Gladstone said that his first introduction to a peer of the realm was at Malvern in 1814. Lord Harcourt, an old man with a long green coat and top boots. He had with him two young ladies, his daughters, who gave Mr. Gladstone a pitch-fork with which he made hay. He described very minutely Lord Harcourt's appearance.

Mr. Gladstone said that at Eton in his day they taught very little general information. But what they taught was so carefully and accurately learned by the boys that it was not forgotten.

[*Journals.*]   1, TILNEY STREET,
                                                JANUARY 7TH, 1890.

Parnell : Second Trial.

I saw a letter from Davitt to-day in which he said, if Parnell is proved guilty of adultery, he not only must forfeit the lead of the Irish Party but would not be returned for any constituency.

In that case, the control of Irish politics would pass to the priests, which Davitt deprecates. Two men only are possible successors to Parnell in the House of Commons, as leader of the Parliamentary Party; John Dillon—with character but without capacity; Sexton—with capacity but without character, about which not much can be said. This is his view.

... Arthur Lyttelton (Master of Selwyn) came here last night. He had met Parnell at Hawarden. He was very self-possessed and cold and unenthusiastic. Almost indifferent. He appeared to know nothing of this charge (it had not been publicly made). Mr. Gladstone was nervous and not at his ease. The two men had some private talk.

Asquith—very clever—made an appeal yesterday to the leaders of the party to expound the details of their policy. Why should they?

[*Journals.*]　　　　　　　　　　　1, TILNEY STREET,
　　　　　　　　　　　　　　　　　JANUARY 15TH.

Rosebery called this morning and we talked. ... We talked about S. Africa. He told me that when Morier had fixed up the Lourenço Marques treaty, ceding Delagoa Bay to us, the King of Portugal telegraphed to the Queen that if we insisted on its fulfilment, he would lose his throne. The Queen showed the letter to Lord Granville who ultimately dropped Morier and lost Delagoa Bay. Probably pressure has been put upon Salisbury in a similar sense now, but he seems to have ignored it. *S. Africa and Portugal.*

Cecil Rhodes hoped that the Portuguese would give Lobengula a good thrashing in Mashonaland, and that then he would be enabled to step in as that potentate's protector. Now, however, if the Portuguese clear out, Lobengula will give trouble, and Rhodes' Co. may become involved in war. Although Rhodes has armed 1800 of his de Beers men with rifles and has got 250 mounted infantry, he would be considerably hampered by war. So would Lord Salisbury. Lobengula has an army of

Zulu mercenaries, armed with spears. Young, fine men, but not so fine as Cetewayo's impis.

[*Journals.*]　　　　　　　　　　　　　1, TILNEY STREET,
　　　　　　　　　　　　　　　　　　　JANUARY 17TH.

Yesterday was the anniversary of Abu Klea. Who remembers it? and all the terrible anxieties of that time!

[*Journals.*]　　　　　　　　　　　　　1, TILNEY STREET,
　　　　　　　　　　　　　　　　　　　JANUARY 23RD.

Parnell.　　Stead came to-day—very low—from an interview with George Lewis. Mrs. O'Shea *wishes* to be divorced and to marry Mr. Parnell. Mr. Parnell, whether he wishes it or not, agrees.

He is living with her now. Since 1880 he has always lived at Eltham. He takes the situation very coolly, and does not agree with Davitt that his adultery will lose him his hold over the Irish Party. But if it does, he prefers Mrs. O'Shea to the leadership. It is a bold stroke.

[*Journals.*]　　　　　　　　　　　　　1, TILNEY STREET,
　　　　　　　　　　　　　　　　　　　JANUARY 31ST.

Parnell.　　I was at Malwood staying with Harcourt from Saturday to Wednesday. *He* thinks Parnell is done for, Morley thinks he will be all right in Ireland but damaged in England. Stead thinks he will be all right in England but damaged in Ireland. Davitt thinks he will be ruined in Ireland. Parnell thinks he will be all right all round.

[*Journals.*]　　　　　　　　　　　　　1, TILNEY STREET,
　　　　　　　　　　　　　　　　　　　FEBRUARY 2ND.

Lord Dufferin defined the difference between a man and a woman's statement of the same fact: "One is history the other is her story."

Harcourt said the best bit of modern Vernis Martin is Sir Theodore Martin's *Life of the Prince Consort.*

[*Journals.*]   1, TILNEY STREET,
                                            FEBRUARY 18TH.

We spent three days—until yesterday—at Tring Park. Met there the Revelstokes and Arthur Balfour. Talking of fortunes, Guinness was said to have twenty millions. The Duke of Westminster's grandson will have an income of eighteen hundred thousand a year; nearly two million.

Arthur Balfour said he wished he could have two hundred thousand a year to spend in Ireland! A modest wish enough. I wonder how he would use it. Arthur looked weak after the influenza, but he is full of quiet courage. And more sanguine than formerly.

[*To Lord Rosebery.*]   NOVEMBER 7TH.

You can imagine the anxiety we have felt,[1] and the infinite relief which the last week has brought. I have constantly thought of you, with the futile wish to be of service which makes one realise how impossible it is to convey strong feelings in a practical form to one's friends. We have been for a few days in the New Forest with the Harcourts.

Charming as Harcourt is in private, friendly and affectionate, his talk always brings home the difficulties of our political prospects in the immediate future. Sometimes I am forced into hoping that our calculations may be upset, and that the General Election may exclude the Liberal Party from office for another Parliament.

Future of the Liberals.

[1] During the illness of Lady Rosebery.

The despairing forecast of a Liberal administration lies in the fundamental divergence of views upon so many important questions between Harcourt and Morley and yourself. It seems hard upon the rank and file of the Party, whose vision does not range beyond Ireland just at present, and whose cheerful work for electoral triumphs may be dashed by these disagreements, that a future Liberal Government will very probably either be wrecked or rendered powerless by the differences between their leaders.

In 1880, before Government had been in office three months, it had nearly fallen to pieces, and there is little doubt that the nation would have been spared much disaster if it had done so.

Harcourt used to say in 1879 that it would never be possible to serve under Mr. Gladstone, who would be a "dictator" to his Cabinet. As it happened, most of our misfortunes would have been prevented if Mr. Gladstone had played the dictator, instead of the eternal peace-maker and inventor of "accommodations" between the irreconcilable ideas of his colleagues. Should he be again P.M. can we hope that he will show greater firmness? Should he disappear, who is there that can be reckoned upon to be firm? And, if necessary, obstinate in defence of a principle? Perhaps Morley. But then he is not likely to be Prime Minister; and if he were, his opinions upon so many questions of foreign policy are opposed to the sense and habits of his fellow-countrymen.

It is specially with regard to these questions, which cannot be solved, that our difficulties will crop up. Salisbury has the immense advantage of being his own Foreign Secretary. To anyone who recollects 1884 the theory that "two heads are better than one" in foreign affairs must seem a perversion of bitter experience.

Salisbury's position is so enviable that it is almost too hopeful a view to imagine its acceptance as a precedent. We can only hope that the unexpected will help us out of our difficulties.

[*Journals.*]   1, TILNEY STREET,
                                           NOVEMBER 19TH.

What a season of disasters! Had Barings been allowed to   *Baring*
collapse, Natty [Rothschild]—who was here last night—says *Collapse.*
most of the great London houses would have fallen with them.
About 6 millions' worth of Bills are drawn daily upon London,
and an enormous proportion of this business passed through
their hands.

Last week, a Bill of theirs was as good as Bank of England
paper. To-day such a Bill could not be discounted. Everyone
will be sorry for Lord Revelstoke. He is the most generous of
men, as well as one of the most reckless. Yet he has a high
reputation for sagacity. It was mainly founded on good luck,
which finally deserted him.

Goschen, as usual, showed himself to be wanting in the highest
form of courage. In speech he is Bayard, in action Sancho
Panza.

[*Journals.*]   1, TILNEY STREET,
                                           NOVEMBER 21ST.

Lady Rosebery died at Dalmeny early on Wednesday
morning November 19th. Poor R., and the children!

When C. T. Baring heard of his late firm's disaster he offered *Baring's.*
them all his fortune to the last farthing. This was generous, as
he left the firm two years ago upon differences with Lord
Revelstoke in connection with their Argentine speculations.

He took the old-fashioned view.

[*Journals.*]   1, TILNEY STREET,
                                           NOVEMBER 25TH.

At 10 I went to Berkeley Square. A great number of friends
assembled. Singularly few peers or Members of Parliament.

Granville, Spencer, Reay, Herbert Bismarck, Mr. Gladstone, and friends and relatives of the Roseberys.

Natty [Rothschild] said Rosebery wished to see me. I spoke a few words to him, and kissed the boys, poor little fellows. He goes to Mentmore to-night.

We drove to Willesden cemetery. The Jewish service is very simple. It must have been framed in times of Israel's troubles, with a view to shortness and unostentation.

Baring's.

The indebtedness of the Barings amounts to 20 or 23 millions. They subscribed loans which they could not afford to hold, and could not place on the market.

Parnell.

Great excitement over Parnell.

I went to see Harcourt at midnight. The excitement in the Lobbies has been unprecedented. Harcourt says the Irish are raging against Parnell. But in spite of them all, if he is a strong man, he will stick to his guns.

Mr. Gladstone has, under pressure, written a letter which is to be published, the net effect of which is to say, "You must choose between me and Parnell."

[*Journals.*]   1, TILNEY STREET,
                                               NOVEMBER 27TH.

Parnell.

Mr. Gladstone was overwhelmed with telegrams and letters and glorifications from all over England. Still these men ignore that they violate the essence of Home Rule. They wish to dictate to Irishmen whom they shall not employ as their leader. What greater interference with liberty?

At the meeting of Irish members yesterday, Parnell was cold and silent. One of them said afterwards: "He treated us as if *we* had all committed adultery with *his* wife. . . ."

Contact with English has ever been fatal to Irish patriotism. Formerly we bribed with money, now we seduce with promises. Harcourt says that Home Rule will probably now be fixed upon the lines of District Councils—Chamberlain's plan.

If Parnell goes, the Irish Party is broken up. All the work is to be done again. Can the Liberal Party be trusted to do it? Very doubtful.

[*To Mr. W. T. Stead.*] LAMBTON CASTLE,
DECEMBER 2ND.

Parnell may have broken all the commandments, and every *Parnell:* rule of the code of honour, but one merit remains to him, *Effect* which is the courage and skill to fight against great odds with *upon* his back to the wall. *Ireland.*

Among *your* nonconformists up here the mischief is done and it matters nothing at all whether Parnell goes or stays.

Meanwhile, where is Ireland? Where is the Irish Party? And Home Rule?

Perhaps if mischievous intriguers like Labouchère and J. Stuart keep quiet, and Mr. Gladstone writes no more letters, in time there may be a rally. But it will only be on condition that Mr. G. puts into the form of Resolutions his scheme for Home Rule, and moves them in the H. of C.

Years ago he ought to have done this. The advisability has always been great. Now it has become a necessity.

Perhaps no effort may avail Ireland now, but absolute frankness is the only form of tactics which can have a chance of doing so. I go to Studley Royal to-morrow, and on Thursday to Tilney Street.

[*Journals.*] LAMBTON CASTLE,
DECEMBER 2ND.

It is impossible not to respect the courage and skill which *Parnell.* Parnell exhibits in his tremendous struggle. A man who can fight thus in a tight place deserves to lead his countrymen in spite of his breach of the 7th commandment. The Parnellite debate is very dignified, and remarkable for the high level of the speaking. . . .

Parnell. Parnell continues to score in Ireland. His energy, nerve and Napoleonic swiftness have won him a stronger position than any one expected.

Mr. G. said when the row began: "For the past five years I have rolled this stone patiently uphill, and it has now rolled to the bottom again, and I am eighty-one years old." It is a pathetic picture. The Tories are jubilant.

[*From the Rt. Hon. W. E. Gladstone.*] HAWARDEN,
JANUARY 2ND, 1891.

DEAR MR. BRETT,

I received yesterday your letter and enclosures; and as I reply under great pressure you will I am sure excuse my passing by matters which are of interest, to go to those which are of the more immediate concern. You assume not unnaturally that I "am aware" there are signs of wavering on H.R. But I cannot say that I know it. Our authorities did not *see* it in Bassetlaw. We shall probably soon know more. I have a kind of presentiment of it, and it is well to be on one's guard. I am in much correspondence with friends and am anxiously considering whether anything is to be said or done, also what or when. But I quite agree in the main propositions of your letter. There can be no relegations, even were it for the sole reason that we must still take our line as to coercion and on that there can surely be no doubt. The party has behaved admirably and I have good hope that it will not change. The "weak-kneed" have been pretty well riddled out. But it must be allowed that such a juncture tries some to whom that phrase is not applicable.

Heartily returning your good wishes for the New Year I remain,

Very faithfully yours,
W. E. GLADSTONE.

[*Journals.*]

There is much wirepulling going on, and many evil counsels *Liberal* are given. No one yet can foresee the sequel. Mr. Gladstone is *Attitude.* now in low spirits, and low spirits are dangerous in a man of his age. Morley is full of vigour. If he can be got to bind the party tight to its pledges, so much the better for them.

[*Journals.*] ASCOTT, LEIGHTON,
JANUARY 25TH.

Only the Leo Rothschilds, Duchess of Manchester, and Henry Calcraft. A good story:—

At Battle, the Duchess of Cleveland's, there is an odious custom under which every visitor, after writing his name in the book, adds a *sentiment*. Numbers have writhed under this infliction.

A young man was asked there from Saturday till Monday. He was thought by the Duchess and all the party, dull, a bore and *stupid*.

On leaving, he wrote his name, and was requested to insert a "sentiment." After his departure, the party left behind rushed to the book to see what common-place he had inserted. The Duchess read out the following:

"From Battle, murder, and sudden death, Good Lord deliver us!"

[*Journals.*] I, TILNEY STREET,
FEBRUARY 3RD.

Cecil Rhodes arrived last night from South Africa. I was at *Rhodes.* Stead's to-day when he called. I left them together. To-night

I saw Stead again. Rhodes had talked for three hours of all his great schemes.

. . . Rhodes is a splendid enthusiast. But he looks upon men as "machines." This is not very penetrating.

[*Journals.*]   TRING PARK,
                                                     FEBRUARY 15TH.

Rhodes.   Came here last night. Cecil Rhodes, Arthur Balfour, Harcourts, Albert Grey, Alfred Lyttelton.

A long talk with Rhodes to-day. He has vast ideas. Imperial notions. He seems disinterested. But he is very *rusé* and, I suspect, quite unscrupulous as to the means he employs.

[*Journals.*]   1, TILNEY STREET,
                                                     APRIL 2ND.

Lord Granville is dead.

The practical question, apart from all mysticism, is simply who is to take the lead of the Liberal Party in one of the Houses of Parliament which—with all its glaring demerits—still remains intact as part of the Constitution. I should like to see Rosebery the leader. However, it is a mistake, no doubt, to allow sentiment to enter into political life, although formerly "party spirit" involving personal loyalty, comradeship, etc., seemed to enjoin it.

[*To Mr. W. T. Stead.*]   1, TILNEY STREET,
                                                     APRIL 3RD.

On   There is a weird pathos about this craze for chastity. It is the
Chastity.   old monkish idea, useful enough in its way, even if it has only preserved us from the Indian curse of "caste."

But in the XIXth century, and in women, the idea assumes the shape of a fetish.

It is the last flicker of an old-world faith in the sanctity—the sacrament—of marriage.

All this is passing away very rapidly, thanks to beings like our excellent friend Garrett. Your new dogma is founded on reason, on convenience, etc. etc., and it is at the other pole, far away from Mrs. Butler's uneasy attempt to combine the passion for chastity with a most laudable desire to follow the merciful lead of Christ.

The election to which discussion now turns in the Journals and Letters did not take place until July 1892. The results were interpreted as a majority of forty in favour of Home Rule; and when the House met on August 8th, forty was the majority by which Asquith's vote of no confidence was carried. The session closed on August the 18th.

[*Journals.*]　　　　　　　　　　1, TILNEY STREET,
　　　　　　　　　　　　　　　　　　　APRIL 3RD.

J. Morley dined here last night. He remained till past mid- *Liberal*
night. We talked all round the compass. He surprised me by *Leaders.*
expressing a doubt whether he could ever serve with Harcourt, as his view and H.'s on Ireland diverged widely.

This morning I went to Colton's studio to see a statuette. Excellent. Colton is a very clever young fellow, and should go far.

After that I drove to the Cardinal's Palace in Westminster.[1] He came out on to the landing to receive me, and was more than cordial. We talked for two hours. He gave me a book with an inscription, and then came out again to the staircase to say farewell.

On getting home I found that Rosebery had been here, so I went to see him in Berkeley Square. He was more cheerful. A very satisfactory talk. He has no wish to be Prime Minister or to lead the House of Lords. "As P.M. in that house, a Liberal

[1] Cardinal Manning.

Minister is a mere cock-shy for his colleagues in the House of Commons." He prefers to be an unfettered Foreign Secretary.

"Place Harcourt in a position where it becomes his great endeavour to keep the Ministry together." This means H. should be Prime Minister. Then as F. Secretary, Rosebery would be unfettered, as H. would leave him alone for fear of breaking up the Ministry.

It is a well planned scheme; but will he, or can he, stick to it?

[*Journals.*]   1, TILNEY STREET,
                                                                APRIL 5TH.

Rosebery sent a note early to say he had not gone to Paris. I called there at 11.

He described Lord Granville's funeral as rather a melancholy pageant. No one of his late colleagues or M.P.s except J. Morley and himself, and George Leveson (a relative). He was glad he had gone.

It appears, however, that great difficulty was experienced in keeping Mr. G. away. I lunched with Rosebery, upstairs, with the four children and the governess and tutor.

We then talked till 3.30, i.e. four hours and a half. Traversed a good deal of ground.

[*To Mr. Grove.*]   1, TILNEY STREET,
                                                                AUGUST 2ND.

*New
Review
Proposal.*

I have carefully thought over your proposal and have considered it together with my idea of a Review, and I should see my way much clearer if we could devise a scheme under which the responsibility and control would be fixed more clearly upon me. If the *New Review* were to continue to be conducted upon the same general lines as at present, then your suggested arrangement would be a very fair one, but I am not sure that I should have the time or capacity to carry it on.

If the arrangement—with carte blanche—were to pass into my hands, the character or nature of the *Review* would be changed altogether, and might be a failure or an immense success.

[*To Lord Rosebery.*] HÔTEL DES DEUX MONDES, PARIS,
AUGUST 20TH.

I want you to see Alfred Milner, who just now is here, when he returns to London. Such a charming fellow, with a "culte" for you. Will you consent? He is home from Cairo for a holiday.

How clever of you to buy the Imperial dressing table, and the Napoleonic Sèvres which I came across in the Rue St. Honoré. The former is a very fine piece indeed. Fit for any Museum. Stolen, of course, from the Garde Meuble. I bought the statue of Voltaire seated in his chair, as at the Théâtre Français. Did you see it? Also one or two pieces of "Empire."

There is a most interesting exhibition at the Trocadero of "Art au début du Siècle" full of Imperial relics of all kinds. Beautiful furniture, and a cabinet of things which Napoleon had with him at St. Helena.

The weather here is not what it should be, but bears favourable comparison with that recorded in the papers from London.

We shall stay here until Saturday or Sunday and return home. . . .

[*To the Rt. Hon. J. Morley.*] 1, TILNEY STREET,
SEPTEMBER 1ST.

I won't press the point of "Compulsion," but you will not *Morley.* deny that you incur grave responsibilities when you endeavour to overturn a Tory Government, which has, on the whole, conducted our national ark safely through stormy seas unless you are prepared to take your turn at the helm.

There are some questions in politics upon which my opinion would not go with you. But on the Liberal side you are the only "Leader" whose motives lie outside the sphere of suspicion *and* conjecture.

If this feeling is widely held, which it is, you can imagine the shock if any Government were formed, based on a Liberal majority, and you were to stand aloof from it. From the first such an administration would be viewed with suspicion by the Stalwarts.

[*To Mr. W. T. Stead.*]   ORCHARD LEA,
                                OCTOBER 25TH.

Gladstone.

. . . Mr. G.—if he survives a General Election—will have reconstituted a majority for his party. On that he can retire.

If *Mrs.* G. were to die, most in the know think Mr. G. would retire at once. It is *she* who keeps him going in politics. He *hates* political life now.

You should see Arthur Balfour. He is nearer to you in most things than any of our people.

Morley.

I always except J. Morley, who represents, to me, the moral element in our party. No one else has the conception of it; and he will bear onward that torch when it falls from Mr. G.'s hand. All these things are not to be written about but pondered over.

[*To Lady Esher.*]   1, TILNEY STREET,
                            DECEMBER 30TH.

We had a very pleasant time at Tring. About 20 to luncheon on Saturday, and on Sunday we lunched at Alfred Rothschild's and were 24.

The weather was fine and both houses looked pretty. Everybody was very smart, although Lady de Grey did not look her best. She is not very well. . . .

Hartington wrote me a charming little letter—about the last I shall see of that familiar signature. But I could not go to the funeral. It was too far after a mild attack of influenza, which is not really well yet.

I saw the Duchess of Manchester yesterday. She is worried about Mandeville, who is dying, and whom she likes in spite of his slight deserts. But otherwise I think she seemed happy. She will now be Duchess of Devonshire! It is certain.

I have an article in the *XIXth Century* for January and will send it you when it appears. It is about Rosebery and Mr. Pitt, and supplements his book in one or two particulars. It is rather interesting I think.

[*Journals.*]   1, TILNEY STREET,
                                   JANUARY 19TH, 1892.

I wrote to Rosebery urging him to refuse the invitation to *Rosebery* stand for the County Council. Mainly on these grounds: *and the*
L.C.C.
1. He was, as Chairman, an unqualified success. Why not leave well alone?

2. His first duty is to Imperial politics, being one of the two or three men at the head of the Liberal Party.

3. Scotland has great claims upon him.

4. He is too big for the place. What would be said to the proposal that Salisbury or A. Balfour, or Harcourt or Mr. G., should become County Councillors?

5. Would it be fair upon London to become leader of the Progressives, and then, in a few months, because his party takes office, abandon the C.C. altogether?

6. As Chairman of the *first* C.C. there was good reason why he should serve, and inaugurate the Government of London. These reasons do not apply to leading a Party as an ordinary member.

I walked round the Temple Gardens for an hour with John Morley. He said, "I read your article on Pitt, and disliked it very much." I laughed, and said I thought he would, but did not ask his reasons, merely observing that he was not so wily as Mr. G. who read the first half of Rosebery's book, and then wrote to congratulate, knowing that he would not be able to do so after the second half.

Morley says the old man is astonishingly well. Enjoying himself in the South like a boy, reading Italian and French, and even glancing at the newspapers. Morley saw Ribot in Paris. He calls him a dull man.

I called later on the P. of M. [Princess of Monaco]. She described Maupassant's madness very pathetically. He has known for years that he would die mad. In one of his books, *Le Horla*, he almost foreshadows his own end.

[*Journals.*]　　　　　　　　　　　　1, TILNEY STREET,
　　　　　　　　　　　　　　　　　　　FEBRUARY 1ST.

On Friday Stead lunched here. Afterwards we went to his office, and from 3 to 7.30 John Burns talked to us about the County Council. He spoke with great fire and amusing power of incisive epigram.

[*To Lord Rosebery.*]　　　　　　　ORCHARD LEA,
　　　　　　　　　　　　　　　　　　　MAY 11TH.

Rosebery's Position.　　I agree with you that there is no necessity to take the public into your confidence. I was not arguing in favour of an open declaration. Hitherto you have kept comparatively silent upon the great political issues, and you have not taken a very prominent part in the struggle for power.

So long as you maintain this attitude, the private warnings to colleagues that you propose not to accept office are all that is necessary. Perhaps more than necessary. If men vote for Liberal candidates, assuming that you will be a minister, it is their own miscalculation they will have to blame. But if you enter just now into the political fray, in my view you give hostages to the Party. You are not a "plain and simple citizen" but a great deal more.

[*To Lord Rosebery.*]　　　ORCHARD LEA,
　　　　　　　　　　　　　　JULY 19TH.

The effects of the last fortnight are now possibly wearing off, *The* blown away by sea breezes. How glad you must be that what *Election.* for your sake I hope will be Mr. G.'s last election is over, and as well over as under all circumstances could be expected.[1]

I saw Arthur Balfour yesterday, and we had a walk after *Balfour.* luncheon. He was in excellent spirits. All the school-boy's delight at the prospect of a holiday. Apropos of Midlothian and Newcastle, he told me that he was going to propose to the Cabinet a short Bill abolishing re-election of Ministers. He was altogether uncertain how his colleagues would take it, but is determined to obtain their sanction if he can.

What view would *your* people take of it? Of course it would only pass *nem. con.* Harcourt formerly opposed this most sensible reform.

The whole situation is most amusing and interesting. A *State* Government without a working majority is such a novelty. *of the* It is the composite character of the majority and the large force *House.* of opposition, rather than the figure 44, which will make the Government Whip's life a burden to him.

I suppose the upshot will be Abortive Government of Ireland Bill (number 2).

[*Journals.*]　　　　　　　　HEATH FARM,
　　　　　　　　　　　　　　AUGUST 13TH.

We came here yesterday from Tring. At Tring were Ran- *Churchill.* dolph Churchill and Henry Calcraft. The former went up for

---

[1] The Liberals won the election in July and Lord Salisbury resigned in August.

the debate on Thursday and the Division. He had intended to speak on Tuesday. He gave as his reason for not fulfilling his intention, that Arthur Balfour had said everything he intended to say. His real reason he admitted to us. His nerve has gone, and the new House, full of strange faces, appalled him. Chamberlain's speech was extraordinarily fine. His rapier-like thrusts get keener and keener.

[*Journals.*]   ORCHARD LEA,
                                                    AUGUST 17TH.

*Rosebery
Foreign
Secretary.*

In the morning papers the Government appears. Rosebery is to be Foreign Secretary. It is good for the country just now, as his reputation stands higher than anyone else. May it stand as high two years hence! is the prayer to-day of all his friends. . . .

The thing of real interest in this morning's paper is the following announcement:

Marriage of the Duke of Devonshire to Louise, Duchess of Manchester.

For two years there has been much speculation about this. I have won a bet from N., who said it would never come off. The secret has been well kept. It will make life easier for him. He saw her every day and never took a step without her sanction or advice.

*Nellie
Farren.*

Heard from L. [Letty Lind] who had seen Nellie Farren in Manchester. "She looked like a rather pretty pathetic little old woman with her hands dreadfully distorted. She told me the whole of her once beautiful body was like it. It was sad to look upon her."

It seems only yesterday that Fred Meyers wrote of her:

> Swift as the swallow
> Soft as the dove,
> Hopeless to follow
> Maddening to love.

Ah! when she dances
Ah! when she sings
Glamour of glances
And rush as of wings.

Trill as of coming birds
Heard unaware,
Poise as of humming birds
Hanging on air.

[*To Lady Stafford.*]   ORCHARD LEA,
                                         AUGUST 19TH.

There is one attitude of mind I cannot understand. It is that *On Moral* in which a woman loses self-respect from her own act. Or a *Courage.* man either for that matter.

The ancients thought that it made a man servile to learn evil of his father or mother. That sentiment I understand. But if a man deliberately chooses a course opposed to the ordinary conventionalities of the world, he should do it seriously and be content to bear the consequences with his head erect. Think how defiant was our friend Shirley. Whichever turning she took she walked straight and courageously. If a woman mistrusts herself, she may be in danger. But if she despises herself she is lost.

There is my sermon.

What do you think of the new Ministry? Houghton's *Houghton.* appointment is interesting.[1] John Morley was most anxious to have him. He is a charming fellow, a poet and with a sound head.

Do you know Asquith?[2] It is said that there is a chance of his *Asquith.* marrying Margot. To be a Cabinet Minister and the husband of Miss Margot in one year, would indeed be to widen his experience of the world!

[1] Lord Lieutenant of Ireland.   [2] Home Secretary.

[*Journals.*]   ORCHARD LEA,
                                                AUGUST 19TH.

Anecdotes
of the   Two anecdotes of the Queen.
Queen.   She called on Lady Ponsonby at Osborne—especially to ask
her to tell Sir Henry that when the Queen makes a remark he
must not say "it is absurd." She would not tell him herself, but
she wanted Lady Ponsonby to tell him kindly.

She was shown in 1887 that grinning "Jubilee" photograph
of herself. Her daughters were indignant at its sale in the streets,
and wished her to have it stopped. All they could get her to say
was: "Well, really I think it is *very like*. I have *no* illusions about
my personal appearance."

[*Journals.*]   ORCHARD LEA,
                                                AUGUST 22ND.

The New   I heard that J. Morley was most anxious about Rosebery's
Cabinet.   decision until it was favourably given. He considered Rosebery
as indispensable to the Government as himself.

The Queen is delighted that the Buckhounds are to be abolished. She has always disliked that form of sport.

The   Labouchere writes to a constituent that he is not a Minister
Queen and   because the Queen would not receive him. This is true. But
Labouchere.   Mr. Gladstone should not have given this reason as an excuse.

Either he should have got the Queen to yield or have taken
the responsibility upon himself. That is the constitutional
position and doctrine.[1]

[*Journals.*]   ORCHARD LEA,
                                                AUGUST 23RD.

Went up to London. Saw Rowton, who speaking of the
Queen said:

[1] The Queen's objection to Labouchere was based mainly on his conduct of
Truth, a paper which she thought disloyal in tone. See her *Letters, Third
Series*, vol. ii, pp. 119 et seq. The question of Labouchere crops up in all
the letters concerning the formation of Gladstone's last Government.

That she has selected all over Europe the most intelligent *The*
member of the royal family of every Court, and upon any *Queen in*
question, domestic or foreign, which arises, she obtains by *Foreign*
letter an opinion. *Affairs.*

The German Emperor, the Queen of Spain, the King of
Denmark, the Queen of Italy, the Austrian Emperor, etc. So
that the Queen really gets the best opinion from the most
experienced foreign authorities who are "in the know," to use
a slang term.

[*Journals.*]   ORCHARD LEA,
                                            SEPTEMBER 4TH.

When Mr. Gladstone went to Osborne, at his first interview *Gladstone*
with the Queen he forgot to kiss hands. Subsequently he re- *and the*
membered his omission, and repaired it just before dinner. The *Royal*
Queen only said, "It should have been done this afternoon." *Family.*

She was very cold and distant to him. The Prince of Wales
was kindly and gracious. The Princess was so charming and her
treatment of Mr. G. was in such marked contrast to that of the
Queen, that Ponsonby said to her, "I believe, Ma'am, you are a
Home Ruler"; and she replied, "Well, I believe I am."

[*Journals.*]   ORCHARD LEA,
                                            SEPTEMBER 7TH.

Mr. G. has been knocked down in Hawarden Park by a mad
cow. The papers record it. It seems he said nothing about it on
his return home; but at dinner someone observed that there was
a strange cow—escaped from somewhere—in the Park, and
Mr. G. said "Oh yes! I met it, and it knocked me down," and
then related the circumstances.

Yesterday I went up to town. As I was writing in Tilney *Rosebery's*
Street, Rosebery walked in, and we had a stroll. He asked me *Acceptance*
to dinner, so—as he was alone—I remained in town to dine with *of Office.*

him. We dined at 8. About 10 we went out for a walk in the Park. A beautiful night. I returned by the 11.10 train, getting home about 1 o'clock in the morning.

Rosebery's final acceptance of office came about in this way. He had been pestered by everyone from the Prince of Wales downwards. He went to Mentmore—Saturday it was—with Primrose his cousin, who was once Mr. G.'s secretary. They wrangled all the evening.

On Sunday Buckle[1] came over from Humphry Ward's and implored him to take office. Talked for two hours. Then after he had gone he walked with P. for another two hours. On his return he found 16 pages of résumé from Buckle of all his arguments.

On Monday while the dispute still continued, Arnold Morley drove up with a note from Mr. G., who had gone to Osborne, saying, "As I have heard nothing from you since our conversation on Thursday last, I shall submit your name to the Queen this afternoon." At the interview in question Rosebery had definitely refused. So it came about, and Rosebery yielded, merely telegraphing to Osborne, "So be it."

The dodge was Eddy Hamilton's[2] idea, and it succeeded when perhaps everything else would have failed. It is not true that the Queen wrote to Rosebery. She suggested doing so and was prevented. . . .

He is absolute at the F.O. He informs his colleagues of very little, and does as he pleases. If it offends them, he retires. We shall remain in Egypt, and the continuity of Lord S.'s[3] policy will not be disturbed. All this is excellent. Meanwhile his spirits have wonderfully recovered.

[*Journals.*]   ORCHARD LEA,
                                              OCTOBER 5TH.

Yesterday I lunched with Rosebery.

The Cabinet scenes of last week were very stormy. "The

---

[1] Editor of *The Times*.   [2] Private Secretary to Mr. Gladstone.
                    [3] Lord Salisbury.

most exciting week of my life," said Rosebery. The Cabinet contains the last remnant of the Manchester School. Harcourt and Morley from conviction strong, and Mr. G. in a lesser degree. The old man is far the most susceptible to new influences.

[*Journals.*]   ORCHARD LEA,
                                               OCTOBER 7TH.

Yesterday Tennyson died. There is a deeply interesting *Death of* account—given in a few words—of his death, by Sir Andrew *Tennyson.* Clark, who was attending him.

The room quite dark, save for the light of the full moon streaming in through the oriel window on to the bed where the poet lay. He looked like "breathing marble" and his left hand clasped the Shakespeare for which he had asked, and in which he had found the play of Cymbeline. That wonderful death song was running in his mind. It is a fitting death. Like Gordon's.

[*Journals.*]   ORCHARD LEA,
                                               OCTOBER 17TH.

All last week we were at Newmarket. Nell with the Leo Rothschilds. I was at Exning with Durham as usual. Friday we went to the Durdans. Rosebery was alone there. He delivered a lecture to me on Esher Place; pointing out that having taken the title, and having the chance to acquire the Manor, Lord E. should do so for the benefit of his descendants. Saturday we drove to see the place. Rosebery was enchanted. The Wolsey Tower, of course, fascinated him. I do not care for it.

[*To the Rev. C. D. Williamson.*]   ORCHARD LEA,
                                               OCTOBER 21ST.
We went to-day to Esher.
Nell has told you of the reopening of the Esher Place question.

I cannot say what will come of it. Probably nothing. It will make no difference, at any rate for many years, to my keeping this house, which is dear to me for many reasons.

Tilney St. inspires me with no special sentiment. Rather the contrary.

On Thursday I spent half the day at Eton. Dined with my tutor.[1] Walked to Huntercombe with him, Arthur Benson, and Luxmore to discuss printing privately a *selection* of Tute's[2] letters—chosen by Canon Furse.

I am not favourable to the plan. What do you think? I don't like selections.

[*Journals.*]   NEWMARKET,
                                                OCTOBER 25TH.

Rosebery: Rosebery was offered the Garter on October 4th. He replied
the   to Mr. G. that he begged to be excused; but he could not conduct
Garter.   another controversy with him on a personal question; so that if
he *insisted*, he only asked that he should hear no more of the matter. And he never did hear any more of the matter until he saw the *Gazette*.

[*To the Rev. C. D. Williamson.*]   NEWMARKET,
                                      OCTOBER 27TH.

I am going home tomorrow. It has been pleasant here. Yesterday was a gorgeous October day; quite still, sunny and warm. A splendid race won by La Flèche of whom you have heard. I have been taking in draughts of Italian air through *Many Moods* which I brought with me. It is an audacious book. Louise, I am told, is going to present me with a copy of Symond's *Renaissance*, a welcome as well as a handsome present.

William   My difficulty about Tute's[2] letters is that Canon Furse *insists*
Cory's
Letters.   [1] A. C. Ainger.   [2] William Cory.

on editing any volume which may be printed. In a letter which I have seen, he deplores the "sentiment" in Tute, and I have no doubt would use the scissors freely. A bowdlerized edition of Tute's letters I could not stand, nor would a false picture of the writer, which such editing would present, give me the smallest pleasure. So I am not at all favourable at present to the scheme.

. . . You need not think much about Esher Place. It is more than doubtful whether it will ever become ours. I am indifferent. There is much to be said on both sides. . . .

[*Journals.*]   ORCHARD LEA,
                                             NOVEMBER 3RD.

To-day I lunched with Rosebery. He had just received a telegram from Constantinople, asking for leave for a certain lady who is there, to receive from the Sultan the female Order of the Shefakat. He was horribly embarrassed. When in office before, a similar application was made to him on behalf of a lady and her two daughters, he replied, "I can stand the Sheffy cat, but not the Sheffy kittens."

[*Journals.*]   ORCHARD LEA,
                                             NOVEMBER 21ST.

I went to London on Friday and called on Rhodes. He had *Rhodes.* asked me to do so. He was sitting with Captain Keene who has recently returned from a command on the Zambesi, and Sir James Siveright, the Commissioner of Public Works at the Cape.

They were discussing the new telegraph line up to Blantyre. It was curious to see with what rapidity and clearness decisions were arrived at.

Rhodes asked for the Government carriage of his telegraph poles, and 200 Sikhs at Blantyre. Then he will make the telegraph line. He would like a gunboat on Tanganyika.

I stayed there to lunch. Then saw Rosebery. He was in good spirits.

Dorothy and Sylvia[1] go to dancing lessons with Princess Beatrice's children at the Castle. The Queen sat all through their dance on Friday.

[Journals.]   ORCHARD LEA,
                                               DECEMBER 6TH.

On St. Andrew's Day we were at Tring. At Tring there was not a very lively party. I always enjoy the long talks with Natty [Rothschild].

On Thursday Rosebery asked me by telegraph to go to him. He was on the eve of starting for Ireland to visit John Morley. The mission of Gerry Portal to Uganda will be much canvassed, but it is good. Rosebery's colleagues commit themselves thereby to his views.[2]

At Windsor Castle.

On Saturday December 5th we returned to Windsor to stay with my tutor. Only Arthur Benson to meet us. Then we went to the Castle. The Waterloo Gallery had been divided into two by a stage and orchestra bowered in chrysanthemums. There

[1] Mr. Brett's daughters.

[2] "The Cabinet was hardly formed when differences arose within it regarding the retention or non-retention of Uganda. The decision was of importance in itself, and of interest in determining which school of Liberals was to prevail in the conduct of foreign affairs: the one group looking with distrust on the extension of imperial responsibilities and burdens which the other section surveyed with pride rather than apprehension. The crisis had arisen through the financial straits into which the British East Africa Company had fallen. Lord Rosebery's insistence on the necessity of retaining the territory overcame the reluctance of his colleagues, Sir Wm. Harcourt among them, who favoured abandonment. . . . After a mission of enquiry conducted by Sir Gerald Portal in 1893 the final decision to hold the country was taken, though the formal proclamation of a British protectorate of Uganda was not made until June 19th, 1894, after Gladstone's retirement." Low and Sanders, *Political History of England*, vol. xii, p. 418.

was a small procession. One arm chair for the Queen, and a few chairs for the guests, only 70 in all.

Presently, when all were assembled, the Chamberlain (Lord Carrington) entered with his wand, followed by the Queen, who walked fast, although with a stick, and her daughters and sons, and three small children, Connaughts.

The performance began at once. *Carmen.* Very well done. Word was passed that we were to applaud, and the command was dutifully obeyed.

After the homely performance was over, the Queen left for the drawing-room, in which she sat with her children behind her, while the guests passed her. She spoke to many; to Nell about the children; and when all had made their bow she left the room. There was supper with all the Princes and Princesses.

[*Journals.*]   QUEEN'S ACRE,
                                             DECEMBER 15TH.

I have finished the proofs of my little book[1] and it is finally in *Mr. Brett's* Press. It was first suggested by talks with T., and by finding *Book.* Eddy Dudley last summer in his library sadly puzzling over the *Student's Hume*, and complaining of ignorance, and his inability to get a notion of the modern history of our country. It has been a source of amusement and interest.

[*To the Rev. C. D. Williamson.*]   1, TILNEY STREET,
                                             DECEMBER 23RD.

Your grey weather is here black fog. You know the sort, quite opaque, electric light a necessity from early morn. Horrible. I shall be glad to be back at Orchard Lea, as you may well imagine. We got here on Monday. . . .

My booklet should have been sent off to you on Wednesday. It should have arrived before you receive this. I think *you* will

---

[1] *Footprints of Statesmen.*

like it. I care nothing about the public or the newspapers. It is well nigh impossible for me to read or write in this atmosphere. Unrest seems the natural accompaniment of dark days. I suppose it is the dark rooms so different from Orchard Lea. My books are dirty to the touch, and one is tempted to wash every half hour. London is not tolerable without *office work*. It is undeniable. So I am rejoiced that the house is let and that departure is necessary. . . .

Gladstone's Probable Successors.

I have no news for you, except that Mr. G. is showing signs of feebleness. His correspondence is in the hands of Mary Drew and she suppresses his colleagues' letters. There has been a storm about his journey to Biarritz, and whatever the fate of the H.R. Bill I doubt whether the old man will remain in office after Easter, even if the government survive that critical date. The choice of his successor will open the door to much unpleasantness.

Rosebery won't struggle; but the Queen and others will fight hard for him. Harcourt has in his favour (1) age; (2) being in the House of Commons; (3) Loulou. The latter is not a quantity that can be neglected. He has so many friends.

It will be an unpleasant rivalry, and I shall be glad when it is settled one way or the other.

Do you see that the Lord Mayor of London is going to visit Dublin, and is to be given the freedom of the city. That is a new departure. What will the London Aldermen say?

Of course you saw that Harry Chaplin welcomed Archbishop Walsh as an ally after his currency letter. Murray Finch-Hatton's remark that Bimetallism makes strange bedfellows was rather happy.

So much for politics—a dull subject.

[*Journals.*]   ORCHARD LEA,
                                                 DECEMBER 23RD.

Gladstone Half Retired.

. . . Mr. Gladstone's retirement is only a question of a short time, whatever the fate of the H.R. Bill. His trip abroad was

strongly opposed by the Ministers. Several letters from colleagues written to him, were stopped by his family. All his
letters are opened. They are suppressed or edited. It was strongly
desired he should take a private secretary to Biarritz. This his
entourage endeavoured to prevent. Thanks to Algy West they
failed. He tackled Mr. G. who said, "That subject is closed."

"I have reopened it," and he stated the case. Mr. G. yielded.
This state of things cannot continue. There will be a desperate
struggle for the leadership. Rosebery will have the support of
the Queen and some of his colleagues.

[*To Sir William Harcourt.*]　　　ORCHARD LEA,
　　　　　　　　　　　　　　　　　DECEMBER 29TH.

How can you ever have doubted that I should be otherwise
than gratified beyond measure at your kindly criticism. No one
could include *you* in Dizzy's celebrated classification of critics!
Besides if I were to object to anything, it would be your too
kind partiality.

If the little book pleases you and a few others, it will have met
with a greater measure of success than I ever hoped for. Everything that you say in your letter interests me, and I am more than
grateful. Curiously enough, you alone have hit upon the
passage which I like (of course one has preferences in paternity)
best in the book—I mean that which touches upon the relations
between Mr. Fox and the P. of Wales. No one else has noticed
it. Years ago the beautiful passage in Virgil about Pallas struck
me in some such connection, and I was glad to be able to use it.
Perhaps I do not share, though I say it with deference, your
strong opinion about the deterioration of Mr. Pitt; but then
statesmen—even the greatest—always seem to me so little able
to control their own destinies, and to be, more than other men,
the sport of time and circumstances. A workman is bound by
his material, and a statesman's materials are the passions as well
as the reason of his countrymen. To run away from the helm,

even though the alternative be to run the ship on the rocks, for the sake of apparent consistency, never appealed to me personally. But I don't defend my view, and merely hazard it.

The making of the little book was an amusement and its reception by a few friends, headed by you, has been a great pleasure.

[*To the Rev. C. D. Williamson.*]   ORCHARD LEA,
JANUARY 2ND, 1893.

. . . Yesterday I had tea with Letty [Lind] who gave a child's tea-party. Two Lonnen children—Jeanne Langtry[1]—Fred Story's little girl—Nellie Farren's niece, etc.

It was a most beautiful sight. Such exquisite dresses and such cleverness in the children. Some of the girls danced and sang quite perfectly. You would have been amazed at the difference between these Bohemian children and those belonging (as Letty says) to "ladies of high degree."

Mrs. Langtry looked as beautiful as she did 15 years ago. Her illness has given her once more all the beauty of her youth—refining away the coarseness of these later years.

[*Journals.*]   ORCHARD LEA,
JANUARY 9TH.

Visit to Tring.

We went to Mentmore. Took Oliver and Maurice to make acquaintance with Rosebery's boys.

Houghton was there for the night. Speaking of Lord Granville, to whom he acted as Private Secretary, he said that he worked diligently at the F.O. papers. All the F.O. officials maintain that he was lamentably idle.

Rosebery.   Rosebery reads everything. Did his boxes in the billiard room. He was humming a tune and suddenly discovered it to be

[1] Afterwards Lady Malcolm.

"Rule Britannia." He said it was desirable the Foreign Secretary should hum "Rule Britannia" while doing his boxes in order that he should not lose heart.

One evening he read aloud Harcourt's remarks on my little book *Footprints*. His comments were amusing. The following evening he went through the book with me, line by line, suggesting verbal amendments. He was at Osborne on Monday for three days. That the Queen likes him well is beyond question.

In 1886 Ponsonby asked himself to Mentmore, drove with R. and said to him: "Who do you think will be the Foreign Secretary when Salisbury resigns?" R. replied that it would probably be Lord Granville. P. said "The Queen wishes that it should be you." This was before there had been any public suggestion of R.

[*Journals.*]   ORCHARD LEA,
                                                JANUARY 13TH.

. . . When the Queen made her little speech at dinner the other night, proposing Princess Marie's health, she stood up. The diners were so *ébahis* that they remained seated. But they rose to drink the health. It was all very homely.

[*Journals.*]   1, TILNEY STREET,
                                                JANUARY 30TH.

Up to town. A long afternoon with Stead. Dined with Loulou [Harcourt] and Lady H. at 11 Downing Street. Harcourt dining officially with Mr. G. in number 10. He came in presently and ushered us in to Mrs. G.'s party with his sword drawn! He was in great spirits. Mr. G. looking younger than ever. I sat next Alfred Milner at dinner. We went on to Devonshire House. For the first time for 80 years a Duchess of Devonshire is entertaining there. A most interesting and delightful party.

[*To the Rev. C. D. Williamson.*]   ORCHARD LEA,
                                        FEBRUARY 12TH.

Irving's   . . . Last Wednesday—the night we went up to the Ball—we
"Becket."   went to see *Becket*. It is perfectly gorgeous, and Irving is
simply magnificent.

You know that I always admire him, but in this play he simply outdoes his very best, and even Nellie yielded to the fascination of his appearance and attitudes. I wonder if St. Thomas of Canterbury had his refinement. We know he had force and power and determination enough for ten martyrdoms.

[*Journals.*]   ORCHARD LEA,
                     FEBRUARY 21ST.

Gladstone   I went up to London. Returned in the train with Mr. and
at 84.   Mrs. G. bound for the Castle. *He* was wonderfully alert.
Nevertheless he complains that he cannot do a good day's work. "Only five hours to-day," he says; "I am unfit for my place; drawing my pay on false pretences." He did not sleep a wink the night before his speech, but he came down looking so fresh that none suspected it. His table was clear of letters. They had all been suppressed by his staff. He was furious. "There must be letters. I must have them at once." So a selection was found for him, and work had to be supplied all day. He had by that time his speech in his head, and had no occasion to think about it. That night (after his speech) he slept nine hours like a child. When told that a great crowd was collected in Downing St. he said, "All to see a wretched old man of 84 who is past his work."

He *walked* up to the Castle to-day. Mrs. G. drove alone in the royal carriage sent to meet him.

[*Journals.*]   ORCHARD LEA,
                                      FEBRUARY 27TH.

. . . Lunched with Rosebery. No one there but his two girls and Francis Villiers, his private secretary.

We talked of the "succession" to Mr. G. It is mere speculative talk, but interesting as all personal questions are interesting. R.'s opinion of Loulou is immensely high. He thinks it counts for two-thirds of Harcourt's popularity.

[*Journals.*]   ORCHARD LEA,
                                      MARCH 18TH.

This morning I went up to the Castle to see Rosebery; his rooms were in Edward III's Tower. A sitting room and bedroom. Furnished in the style of 1830. Very sunny with a splendid view. Outside the window the Queen's little pony chair was walking about waiting for her. She told R. last night that she remembered Mrs. Siddons and Sir Walter Scott. When a child she determined that if ever she came to the throne she would never have "mutton" for dinner; such was the surfeit of that article at the Duchess of Kent's table. *Anecdotes of the Queen.*

She asked who had most influence over Mr. G. R. said John Morley. She wished R. to go with her to Florence! but he thought it better to decline.

R. and the Empress Frederick agreed that the impressions from 10 to 18 were the strongest perhaps in life. She appealed to the Queen for agreement. "Certainly *not*" was the reply with very marked emphasis.

R. and I walked to Slough. We *ran* a quarter of a mile to catch the train but missed it. So waited on the platform for about 40 minutes.

To-night *Becket* was a brilliant success.[1] Hallam Tennyson *Irving at Windsor Castle.*

[1] Given at Windsor Castle.

was called by the Queen in the entr'acte, and she asked why Louis of France had "put away" Eleanor. "Because he was a very good king and she was a very bad woman" was the reply. She momentarily forgot who succeeded Henry II, but remembered all about it before Hallam could explain.

The party afterwards was very pretty. Ellen Terry was presented and talked for ten minutes to the Queen.

[*To the Duchess of Sutherland.*]   TRING PARK,
AUGUST 27TH.

Gladstone.   Yesterday Natty Rothschild and I drove with Mr. and Mrs. G. through Ashridge for an hour or so. The old man talked the whole time, incessantly, about Eton and Oxford, and literature, without any apparent effort or slackening. Get him off politics and he is very amiable and most reasonable. It is curious to watch him at his age, and to think he is governing this vast Empire with as much pluck and vigour (whether well or ill) as anyone half his age could do.

Mrs. Humphry Ward came to dinner, and he talked to her, but carefully avoided her novels. He thinks *them* quite hopeless —although he admires her intellectually and quite apart from her powers of invention. Harry Chaplin is here. Your friend Donald Wallace and the Marjoribanks, Eddie Hamilton, etc.

De Staal.   Dear old Staal, a charming old man, whom I have always liked. I heard him talking this morning about you. He said " Elle a une séduction de regard, qu'elle pourrait faire n'importe quelle folie à un homme." I suppose he is right. He is very entertaining. As you probably know he was for years at Wurtemburg and had a very intimate knowledge of the life of the mad King Louis of Bavaria. His description of his queer amours, and of the internal arrangements of his palace, all subordinated to his odd tastes, is most interesting and amusing. He is very immoral, and audaciously simple in his admissions about himself and others. I suppose this is one of the few pleasures left to a man of his temperament and tastes, at his age.

[*Journals.*]   TRING,
                                              AUGUST 27TH.

We have been here three days with the Gladstones. *She* is very frail. *He* shows no signs of age as ordinarily understood. I drove with him for two hours through Ashridge. He talked the whole time incessantly. About Eton, of which he speaks with ardent affection; and about Oxford. He seems very angry with the behaviour of the French in Siam. But the lines of his face are much softer than they used to be. This is very marked.

Gladstone at 84.

He was amused at Randolph [Churchill] saying "Mr. G. will be in his prime somewhere about the middle of next century." He talked a good deal about *dress*. He dislikes large sleeves in the modern female costume. Thinks the shoulders should *slope*. He complained in animated tones of the laxity of costume in the H. of C. Laments the old blue coat, and denounced Speaker Abercromby for having permitted members to dine with him in plain evening dress. Denison reversed this. Peel was the first man to wear *loose* sleeves. Before him all sleeves were tight.

It is said that the Queen has been writing brusquely to the old man of late. She never liked him. She wrote strongly after the row in the H. of C. "The Queen hopes Mr. G. will now see that it is *all his fault*," etc. etc., "and trusts that he will now withdraw the Bill."

He told Harry Chaplin that when a boy he lived in a house in Grafton Street next door to H. Chaplin's grandmother, and when she gave parties, he and his brother used to squirt water over the footmen and coachmen in order to hear their vehement discussions as to whether or not it rained.

There are two older men in the H. of C. Charles Villiers and Isaac Holden. The latter is 87. He is said to bathe in *oil* every day and wears six pairs of drawers one on top of the other.

[*To the Duchess of Sutherland.*]   TAN-YR-ALLT, TREMADOC,
SEPT. 4TH.

*Gladstone
at 84.*

. . . The end of the Tring visit was up to the level of the beginning. The old man talked for hours about costume. Did I tell
you? Denounced ladies' big sleeves! lamented the smart mas-
culine dress of his youth, and complained tragically of the round
coats and low hats now in the H. of C. He has always liked H.
Chaplin—and you can see his eye roving fondly over him, as if
he recalled to him the political sporting squires of his youth, the
George Bentincks and others, with whom he acted when he was
"the hope of the Tory party" himself.

His reminiscences of Peel are always charming. He goes back
to that period of his life with continued pleasure. He mentioned
the present Sir Robert as the possessor of by far the finest voice
he had ever heard within the House of Commons, and as being
second to none from the point of view of good companionship.
The former I have heard said. The latter I should doubt. But
then "taste" comes in where companionship is contrasted, and
some people there are who prefer men of the Donald Wallace
type to the Arthur Balfour type. This is not said to depreciate
the former, since *tous les goûts sont respectables*—but merely as an
illustration.

[*To the Rev. C. D. Williamson.*]   ORCHARD LEA,
OCTOBER 17TH.

. . . Loulou writes that the pathetic thing at Newcastle was to
see the old couple[1] standing with bended heads while the people
sang Auld Lang Syne. It seemed a farewell.

I hear sad accounts of Mr. G.'s health.

[*To the Duchess of Sutherland.*]   ORCHARD LEA,
DECEMBER 12TH.

*Mr. Brett's
Second
Book.*

It is curious that no one but you should have suggested the
"courtier-like" nature of that article; although I myself was

[1] Mr. and Mrs. Gladstone.

appalled by it! Indeed, after it was written and given to Knowles, I wished that I had put it on the fire. The idea was that it should be the first chapter of a little volume giving the personal history of the Queen in relation to her Prime Ministers.[1] For this relation *is* rather remarkable, and altogether different from that of other Sovereigns. Certainly such a book would interest foreigners, and might some day be thought readable by people who are fond of the "personal equation" in history. I don't know whether I shall go on although I am urged to do so.

. . . Did I tell you that I had let number 1 Tilney St. and propose to use number 2 as a *pied à terre*. It is *very* small but will be very pretty, I hope. You have sold *your* house if the papers don't lie. Here I have got a room I like. Quite warm, light and *upstairs*. It is a real Zoar, and perhaps it is the depraved taste for that kind of quiet which gives occasion for your blame! Although *why* should you wish me to plunge into the horrid vortex of "public life" once more, out of which I escaped with such joy? You can never again feel that you are *à l'abri du regard* of the world. But then you have so many compensations. I, on the other hand, should have none. All the rough and none of the smooth. And for what? Nothing that I could do, cannot be as efficiently done by others—if indeed anything is worth doing! And as for "popularity" and "fame" they are *tastes* like any other, racing or gambling, and they are not my tastes. There are things which I do think worth while having, and I try to get them, and this past year I have, oddly enough, wonderfully succeeded. So much so that I am frightened. . . .

Public or Private Life.

[*Journals.*]

ORCHARD LEA,
JANUARY 14TH, 1894.

Loulou [Harcourt] came down tonight just for the night. I felt sure he wanted to talk, and he did. It seems that on Tuesday last, at the Cabinet, Mr. G. showed terrible signs of failing.

Harcourt and Rosebery.

[1] *Yoke of Empire.*

From that and other symptoms, learned in close intercourse, Loulou thinks the old man will not meet the H. of C. again. So the struggle has commenced between Loulou and Rosebery for the Premiership.

Loulou does not talk to his father about it, but works independently. He has arranged a meeting at Derby; also on February 4th the "Federation" meet at Portsmouth. Harcourt and Rosebery were to be asked. The latter, however, is not to go. Loulou says he has worked for ten years at wire-pulling, and now he must reap the fruit. It is a painful personal question. Harcourt is 66 and for 30 years he has been in the thick of the political mêlée.

Powerful forces arrayed against him. (1) the Queen; (2) his colleagues; (3) the sort of interest roused by Rosebery. I am sorry for Loulou.

[*Journals.*]   ORCHARD LEA,
                                          FEBRUARY 26TH.

Gladstone Retires.   Mr. G. retires immediately after the session. Leaves Parliament. Rosebery will probably succeed him. Mr. G. has been most reticent with his colleagues. They were all furious with him. The Cabinet dinner was the first for 43 years. They were all expecting him to announce his demise.

Rosebery after dinner said "Have all precautions been taken to ensure secrecy?" Mr. G. said "The *usual* precautions." Then wine and dessert, and he told them *nothing*. The small fry of the Cabinet went away *furious*. Mr. G. is raging against his oculist who says his eyes are all right; and refuses to see him again. The fact is, he is determined to go, and told the Queen as much to-day.

[*Journals.*]   ORCHARD LEA,
                                           MARCH 3RD.

The anniversary of Eugene's birthday.

Mr. Gladstone was at Windsor—the Council—his last—met,

and all the town is agog over his successor. *That* is really the interesting point to most. He is half forgotten already!

[*Journals.*]   PARK STREET,
                                                    MARCH 4TH.

Rosebery is Prime Minister. I am sorry for Loulou. It is a blow for him, a devoted son.

[*Journals.*]   PARK STREET,
                                                    MARCH 9TH.

Nellie and I took Rosebery to the play and to dinner pre- *Rosebery.* viously at Willis' Rooms. He was in tearing spirits. I had been to see him at the F.O. His last day there. *So* sorry to leave. He would not say goodbye to anyone, but crept down the back staircase.

He is certainly grieved to go. He would have been content to remain there for a while under anybody.

[*To the Rev. C. D. Williamson.*]   ORCHARD LEA,
                                                    MARCH 18TH.

... The events of the past month have been very interesting, *Rosebery* and there is much that you would have been glad to hear. That *and* is your punishment! I suppose you were not sorry that Rose- *Harcourt.* bery's succession was assured. It is not a bed of roses, the Premiership—just now.

I was *really* sorry for Loulou, who has worked so hard for six or seven years with the one object in view of getting his father established at 10 instead of 11 Downing Street. But from the national point of view, it is creditable to England that R. was chosen.

I have always thought that the position of R. in the Lords and Harcourt as Leader in the Commons was impossible as a durable arrangement—and I still think so. The reverse would have been possible—for R. would have had a free hand at the F.O.—so that you may expect a breakdown and a dissolution in the summer.

[*Journals.*]   THE DURDANS,
                                                              JUNE 5TH.

I came here this evening; the eve of the Derby. Rosebery is in a state of suppressed nervous excitement. In very good spirits. Gerard, Durham, F. Johnstone, Lockwood, Colonel Forester and Arthur Sassoon.

[*Journals.*]   THE DURDANS,
                                                              JUNE 6TH.

Rosebery won the Derby.

Rosebery out at 6 to see Ladas canter. Then an enormous crowd on the downs. Twenty-five years ago he bought a horse called Ladas. He was at Oxford. The Dean of Ch. Ch. bade him choose between Ch. Ch. and the horse. He chose the horse and was sent down. Ladas was *absolutely last* in the race. To-day Ladas II started at 9 to 2 on and won the Derby in a canter. I stood next R. in his box. After the race (he drank a glass of champagne after the horse went to the start) he was genuinely moved. All he could say was "At last!" Such a reception never was seen at Epsom.

This morning he saw a hedgehog *run* across the path in the wood; a very rare sight; and he remembered that H. Chaplin had once a house with a garden in Park Lane. It was the first occasion on which R. met the Lad (Colonel Forester) who is here to-day. In the garden on a certain morning R. found a *dead* hedgehog. It was the Derby morning 25 years ago. He drew the Lad's attention to it who said it was a bad omen and

Ladas would be beat. To-day he told the story at breakfast, and the Lad said at once that Ladas would win.

Rosebery went up after the race to dine at Marlborough House, and left us alone.

[*To Mr. W. T. Stead.*]　　　　　　　　　JUNE 7TH.

. . . I admit the demoralization of racing and politics, but the former possesses more counterpoise!

[*Journals.*]　　　　　　　　　　　　　THURSDAY.

Thousands of congratulatory letters and telegrams. Some growling letters from Nonconformists. No telegram from the Queen. Herbert Bismarck turned up here yesterday. Chauncey Depew (the American wit) telegraphed "Many congratulations. Nothing left but Heaven."

After the race R. returned. We went to see Ladas in his box, then R. took me for a drive.

R. thinks that Harcourt will retire immediately the Budget is through, but will remain in the H. of C. "He will be potential to mischief then, but not much more dangerous than he is now."

Loulou, R. thinks, would be a model diplomatist. "Not scrupulous—charming manner—perfect tact." R. says there is no one he would rather employ on a foreign mission. . . .

If Harcourt goes, the question arises, who is to lead the H. of C.? Morley would expect it; but is he sufficiently in agreement with the Prime Minister? Very much the reverse, on Foreign Politics and some social questions. He is quick tempered and very sensitive. *Leadership of the Commons.*

Campbell-Bannerman is physically and mentally the best qualified. Asquith has not enough experience as yet, and is viewed askance by the Irish. These are R.'s criticisms. I think he is inclined to Bannerman. A good man; but very undistinguished compared with the others.

[*Journals.*]   ORCHARD LEA,
                                                      DECEMBER 15TH.

We returned to Orchard Lea, and this evening the Harcourts
came. Sir William in very good form. He told me two good
stories. One about the present Sir Robert Peel. Lady Peel's will
was read out after her funeral, and it was found that she had left
everything away from Sir Robert. He said aloud, "If I'd known
this, I wouldn't have buried her, and I've a great mind to go and
dig her up again." The Speaker and his brother didn't speak
to him for years after this.

The other story was apropos of the late Lord Grey. When he
was at the Colonial Office, a Kaffir war in South Africa was
raging much as usual. The whites had been used to say the
devil was black; the blacks that the devil was white. But both
now agreed that the devil was Grey.

[*To the Duchess of Sutherland.*]   ORCHARD LEA,
                                               FEBRUARY 11TH, 1895.

*On
Balfour's
Book.*

... I am reading Arthur Balfour's book, which will give an
infinity of trouble to many of his lady friends and admirers, if
they really try to understand it.[1] Probably a perfunctory read
over will suffice for most of them. It is really hard, when you
are the apostle of a charming sect, to trouble their minds with
abstract speculations. Concrete ones, as many as you like, but
not metaphysics! However, Mrs. Grenfell and the others will
no doubt feel that no one is likely to tackle them about details
—so they can pretend to know all about it.

Really—and trifling apart—it is a powerful and very interesting book. At Cambridge when all the "intellectual" set was
agnostic—Arthur used to be looked upon as a curious relic of an

[1] *The Foundations of Belief: being Notes Introductory to the Study of Theology.*
Longmans, 1895.

older generation, with affectionate pity. I could see his brothers', Frank and Gerald, brotherly patronage extended to him mentally, when he used now and then to come down to Trinity on a visit.

Arthur's opinions have not varied. He was then a "Christian" of a queer undefined sort, and in that faith he has abided. He has done more—for he has justified philosophically his faith—an operation not common as you know.

I should like to know what Mr. G. will say to the book. What is queer is that there is a strong resemblance between a portion of Arthur's argument and that by which Dr. Newman was ultimately landed in the Roman Catholic Church!

[*To the Rev. C. D. Williamson.*]　　ORCHARD LEA,
　　　　　　　　　　　　　　　　　FEBRUARY 18TH.

. . . I really think I shall be able without a pang to leave England for a month. However, probably something else will intervene.

One of the most important impediments shortly to doing any- *Cheap* thing will be inability to spare necessary cash—if money becomes *Money.* any cheaper. I suppose that people with "Interests" have just about half the income they possessed 10 years ago. This is getting serious—and the finding of so much gold in Africa and Australia ought—if theories of currency are correct—to make matters worse.

I am reading Arthur Balfour's book. *There* is a charming and attractive character! No wonder his party follow him with enthusiasm.

Loulou [Harcourt] and others tease about a "Mr. G." article, and insist that the series ought to stop, and that I must either be dull or indiscreet if I attempt to go any further.[1]

---

[1] The *Yoke of Empire.*

[To the Rev. C. D. Williamson.]   ORCHARD LEA,
                                            MARCH 5TH.

. . . Nothing has happened except that on Saturday I went up to see May Yohé in her new play. Dear thing, she was perfectly sweet—dressed as a middy and as a jockey! I must send you a photograph if they are successful.

I have plunged into the Mr. G. article. It is not easy because he has been so dissected, and every anecdote related *ad nauseam*. It is hard to avoid the common-place.

*L. Harcourt
Angry.*

Indiscretions—the Charybdis feared by Loulou [Harcourt]— are not nearly so dangerous. Loulou was here on Sunday. He is enjoying the defeat of the Progressives, and anticipating with intense satisfaction a complete rout at the general election. *He* is most vindictive, whereas Sir William has recovered his equanimity. Loulou has cut off *all* friendly relations with his father's colleagues. I rather admire the intense pugnacity in one so naturally gentle.

Rosebery Ill.

Rosebery has become sleepless again under the influence of influenza; possibly to some extent morbid inspection of his personal position for which—as he may not work—he has plenty of leisure. What a pity he did not yield the first place to the older man! However, it is not everyone who can refuse—like Mr. Pitt—supreme power with a view to a more certain and complete authority later. It requires the highest degree of self-confidence.

[Journals.]   ORCHARD LEA,
                        MARCH 11TH.

Rosebery is improved in health. He went to Windsor to-day. It would not surprise me if there were a dissolution in the offing. How can the House of Commons select a new Speaker in a moribund Parliament? With no majority! Will Rosebery ever be Prime Minister again? Or is he to be another phantom "transient and embarrassed"?

[*Journals.*]　　　　　　　　THE DURDANS,
　　　　　　　　　　　　　　　　MARCH 13TH.

Rosebery telegraphed "Would you care to come here for the *Rosebery on* night," and I answered "Yes." He has just come to this charm- *Mr. Brett's* ing home, still sleepless. No one here but Broadbent, the physi- *Position.* cian. R. walks with a stick and took my arm down to dinner. He is not cheerful.

He asked me whether I still wished for the Woods and Forests, and argued on two points:

(1) Is it a desirable place?
(2) Am I competent?

He thinks the Office of Works secretaryship more suit-able. I said that I had often felt that I had missed my vocation in not going into the Civil Service. He said, "No, you have missed your vocation in not going into the Diplomatic Service—*that* is the tragedy." I wonder! Anyway, I don't regret it, and I said so. It would have cost me many happy years. But as time passes one wants a *tie*.

R. was allowed by the Queen to *sit*. He remonstrated but he could not have stood. He knelt to kiss her hand when leaving and nearly fell over. "Take care," said the Queen.

I spoke of Lord Hertford's "George" which belonged to Charles Edward, and is now Aunt Adèle's; and he said that the "George" of Charles I was given by Juxon to Charles II, then passed to Cardinal York, who gave it to George IV, who gave it to the first Duke of Sutherland.

[*To the Rev. C. D. Williamson.*]　　THE DURDANS,
　　　　　　　　　　　　　　　　MARCH 14TH.

Rosebery telegraphed and asked rather piteously for a visit; so *Rosebery.* I came. Broadbent, the doctor, is here. He says in all his experi-ence he has never known so bad a case of insomnia; nor could he have believed any man would struggle so gamely. If it goes on, of course, there must be a fatal termination. During the last few days there has been some improvement—but very little. Last night he did not sleep. To-day is a gorgeous summer's day, as you sometimes get in the month of March. R. and I drove in a phaeton—with *postilion*—and another boy behind us (Quite a galaxy!) for miles this morning.

He was not cheerful, and we talked over every imaginable thing. He complains of loneliness. Marriage frightens him—he cannot believe in a fresh disinterested affection. As if that mattered to anyone who understands love! I tell him that he dried up the fount by becoming a man too soon. Pascal said that the happiest life—the life he would choose—begins with love, and ends with ambition.

R. has reversed the order. He has—while in the prime of life —everything that men toil for; wealth, power, position, everything! Yet he is a lonely, sleepless man! Up to now the fates have been too kind. He was spoilt by fortune and he forgot, or never knew, the story of the Ring of Polycrates.

Broadbent is not bad company. We were talking of women's morals and he told me of a saying of Ricordi's: "If a man marries at 50 *sometimes* he has children; if at 60 *always*." Fortunately he did not tell his anecdote in the presence of R.; for it might have confirmed him in his pessimistic views. You know I disapprove of second marriages; but I suppose the Prime Minister cannot in these days have a mistress. Certainly he requires an *intimate* friend. Or, he will die.

[*Journals.*]   THE DURDANS,
                                                      MARCH 14TH.

Rosebery.   We have just come in from a long drive. A phaeton, not driven, but in the old Daumont fashion, with a postilion and a boy behind. We drove past Givons Grove, and round by the house lived in by Madame D'Arblay, where Talleyrand took refuge.

People say of R. that he never hears the truth, or is spoken to with frankness. In point of fact, he knows and hears everything.

He admitted to-night that he made an error in not allowing Harcourt to try to form a Cabinet. He says that he did propose it, but it was vehemently opposed by M. [Morley] and others. He thereupon determined to spare them the pain of a scene! All previous experience shows that they would all have taken office like lambs. Rosebery has paid for the prejudices of men who will presently leave him in the lurch. He admits his extreme sensitiveness to newspaper criticism. It is sad but so human.

He complains of loneliness. His intimacies are intermittent. He denies that he was always "grown up" and reserved from early youth. But it is true nevertheless. He ought to marry again. He requires companionship. He said of the Queen that her chief influence lies in her womanhood. You cannot treat her as if she were Leonard Courtney! "She is an old lady with all the foibles and strength of one. . . ."

R. said to me "You think I am a spoilt child," and I could not deny it. My wish for him is a time of great stress, popular hatred, unsupported except by the loyalty of a few, and a triumphant resurrection.

I think that R. has ceased to value the personal equation in politics so highly as he did. He used to hold that the affectionate loyalty of a few friends was worth more as a source of power and as a political force than the applause of the people, and he would quote Dizzy. His rapid and early growth into manhood, with the aloofness entailed by it, and that necessary element of what is called "pose" in everyone who is a man at that age when others are boys, fitted him for oligarchic rule, but not to be Chief of a Democracy. He is curiously inexperienced in the subtler forms of happiness which come from giving more than one gets. He has been satiated with the sweets of life; and the long process has left him longing for affection, universal approval, omnipotent authority.

*Mr. Brett's
Position.*

. . . Rosebery telegraphed for me. I went down. He was worse than last week, after three sleepless nights.

He began "This is my wedding day!" That was depressing enough. He then said "I am worried about the Woods and Forests," and proceeded to argue the whole case again. Whether he expected me to discuss my qualifications, or to say "Don't think about it any more," I don't know. However I refrained. *He must* decide, and I care now very little what the decision may be.

He got very irritable and angry with the servants, and said to me, "I am unfit for human society." In reality he is broken down with illness and worry. He lies awake thinking all night. Whether it is temporary or permanent God knows, but it is terribly painful to witness.

Mr. Brett was appointed Secretary to H.M. Office of Works. This gave him the "tie" he was seeking and also, owing to the Royal Palaces, etc. being under his jurisdiction, brought him gradually into closer touch with the Royal Family.

At this point it may be useful to remind readers that the present King and Queen were known, after 1893, by the title of Duke and Duchess of York. On the accession of King Edward, they became at once Duke and Duchess of Cornwall, but were only known by these titles in official references. In these papers the York titles continue to be used in letters and informal passages. The investiture of the Duke of Cornwall as Prince of Wales did not take place until November 6th, 1901. Throughout this volume the two grandsons of King Edward are referred to consistently as Prince Edward and Prince Albert.

There are references also to the young Duke of Albany, who after 1900 was also Duke of Saxe-Coburg and Gotha. The line of succession to the German dukedom passed from the reigning Duke Ernest II to the sons of Queen Victoria. King Edward resigned his claim in 1863: the Duke of Edinburgh took the Dukedom in 1893 and died without heirs in 1900. The Duke of Connaught refused the title, thereby excluding his children also. The Duke of Albany had died in 1884, but left a posthumous son, the 2nd Duke referred to by Lord Esher later on. He therefore succeeded to the Dukedom of Saxe-Coburg and Gotha. He was deprived of the Dukedom of Albany during the war, abdicated from his German Dukedom in 1918, and is still living.

[*Journals.*] ORCHARD LEA,

MARCH 31ST.

Mr. G. has returned wonderfully well. Harcourt told him *Gladstone* that Leonard Courtney was strongly objected to as Speaker. *Anecdotes.* He could not understand why. One reason, Harcourt said, was his age. "What is that?" asked Mr. G. "About 63." "Ah! *that* is a very *grave* objection."

Mr. G. expressed himself delighted at the suggestion that he *might* be Speaker. "Only my deafness unfortunately prevents me," with a smile. He cares nothing for political talk, and thinks of nothing save Arthur Balfour's philosophic treatises! So Arthur was sent by Harcourt to see him!

[*Journals.*] ORCHARD LEA,

APRIL 1ST.

We came up to London this morning. Lunched at Willis' with Arthur [Balfour] and Teddie.

Arthur charming as usual. Told me about his interview with Mr. G. who talked incessantly for three hours. He was too deaf to hear Arthur's replies. He was much exercised because Arthur had forgotten Sir G. C. Lewis on "Authority in Matters of Opinion." Arthur was much impressed by the dignity of the old man, no longing for office, no regrets.

[*Journals.*]   ORCHARD LEA,
                                  APRIL 4TH.

The Queen, it seems, has been alarmed at the "tension" between England and France, and has expressed fears lest she should be detained as a hostage! She is at Nice.[1] We are in the middle of the Oscar Wilde catastrophe. A man of genius behaving like a fool.

[*To Lord Rosebery.*]   ORCHARD LEA,
                                  MAY 27TH.

Mr. Brett:
Office of
Works.

On leaving you I saw Herbert,[2] according to your wish, and had a long talk on the Terrace.

He explained to me all the duties of the Office, and described the work which it entails. The "Labour problems" I feel competent to deal with, and my relations with the Labour leaders have always, as you know, been pleasant. That part of the work would be very interesting to me.

The financial details I should not shrink from, and I hope I should manage as well as any ordinary mortal to cope with the rival arbiters of "taste."

Herbert was very cordial, and perfectly frank, so that I think he would receive me in a very friendly spirit.

Altogether, I have carefully considered the question all round, and although it is true that when you first suggested this appointment to me, actuated as I then was by a strong wish to have the Woods and Forests, I failed to be charmed at the prospect, I have changed my opinion, and now with open eyes,

---

[1] The tension referred to was caused by the speech of Sir Edward Grey (Under-secretary for Foreign Affairs) in the House of Commons on March 28th concerning French aggression in the regions of the Upper Nile and Upper Niger. The speech was answered by M. Hanoteaux in the Senate on April 5th.

[2] Mr. Herbert Gladstone.

should be glad to accept the place if you are kind enough to make me the offer.

I would do what I could in every way to justify your choice. Motives are very complex things, and mine are no exception, but perhaps some day I may be able to throw light on those which govern this decision.

Now, it is impossible for me to thoroughly explain them.

[*To Lord Rosebery.*]　　　　　ORCHARD LEA,
　　　　　　　　　　　　　　　　　　JUNE 2ND.

I have acknowledged formally to Murray your letter. You *Mr. Brett* may be sure that whatever views may now be taken of your *and Lord* choice, I shall justify your selection. *Rosebery.*

That will be a point of honour, as well as of other sentiments, which originated now many years ago, and have grown as years went by.

I will some day explain to you all the events of the past few weeks, and you will then see how mistaken you were, if you ever thought that the "intriguer" could be successful, which you suspected.

Want of confidence in a friend, I might have felt it hard to forget, had I been convinced that you felt it; but I have never for a moment thought that you were other than quite straight with me, or that you withheld your thoughts and wishes, or attempted to convey them to me otherwise than directly.

One of my earliest recollections is the stress laid upon your name by one who had the greatest influence over my youth.[1] From that time onward, you have always been more to me than anyone else in public life—representing something which every other man lacked.

For this reason, if for no other, I desired to be beholden to you, and to feel this tie in addition to those of private friendship.

---

[1] William Cory.

All this may be very sentimental, *mais voilà comme je suis.* You may always command me as before, and believe me affectionately yours.

[*To the Rev. C. D. Williamson.*]   ORCHARD LEA.

On his Office.   In to-day's paper, June 4th, you will probably see a gazette, announcing that Rosebery has appointed me Sec. to the Office of Works.

It is the headship of that office which has control of all public buildings, palaces, Royal Parks, etc., in England and Scotland; and the initiative in erecting public buildings, making improvements in London, etc.

It is not a post I have contemplated holding, but it has charm of a certain sort. It is a *permanent* office, worth from £1200 to £1500 a year. So it is not to be despised.

It has always been my wish to have, at a certain point in my life, definite service under the Crown apart from politics. I think the point is now reached!

[*Journals.*]   ORCHARD LEA,
                                                JUNE 4TH.

My appointment was gazetted to-day.

[*To the Rev. C. D. Williamson.*]   H.M. OFFICE OF WORKS,
                                                JANUARY 1ST, 1896.

Nellie has written to you about poor Griz,[1] who died in my arms yesterday. Nellie is miserable! She looks wretched and cried all night. I can understand this, as it is parting with a faithful unquestioning friend and companion of 13 years' standing.

[1] Her terrier.

She was a really great factor in Nellie's life. I wish all friendships were as simple and as absolutely untarnished. . . .

The following dates may be useful to remind readers of the course of events at this period. Dr. Jameson's raid on the Transvaal began on December 29th, 1895. The fight at Krugersdorp opened on January 1st, and Jameson surrendered at Doornkop on the 2nd. On the 8th Kruger surrendered Jameson and his men to the Imperial authorities. The leaders of rebellion in Johannesburg were arrested and charged with High Treason on January 10th; and of these four (not five) were sentenced in Pretoria to fifteen years' imprisonment. The sentences were not carried out.

During the course of their negotiations with the High Commissioner, the Transvaal Government published a number of Jameson's letters and telegrams which showed that Rhodes was the mainspring of the affair. These are presumably the documents to which Mr. Brett refers on the 16th.

[*To Sir William Harcourt.*]   OFFICE OF WORKS,
                                           JANUARY 16TH.

Have you seen Robinson in the *Daily News* to-day?

I am told by the Editor that Hawksley[1] has got the fellow who *Jameson* stole the Jameson letters to confess. It seems they were offered *Letters.* to Stead and Labby, and refused.

Then bought by Clarke M.P. and resold at a profit to Dr. Leyds. Hawksley wished to prosecute the thief, but the Chartered Co. people won't hear of it. . . .

[*From the Rt. Hon. J. Chamberlain.*]   HIGHBURY, BIRMINGHAM,
                                     Private.   FEBRUARY 1ST.
MY DEAR BRETT,

Many thanks for your note. If you are right in your anticipa- *Rhodes'* tion of Rhodes' defence, I do not think it will be considered very *Position.*

---

[1] Solicitor to the Chartered Company.

strong. After all, it is not Mr. Rhodes, but the British Government, that is responsible for general policy; and it will never be tolerated that pro-consuls in all the ends of the earth shall be allowed to have a war-making power of their own and to conduct both that and their diplomacy without consideration for headquarters.

If Rhodes were able to say (and to stand examination upon it) that he was, like everyone else, aware of the possibility of revolution in Johannesburg, and that he thought it his duty to be prepared, and even to have a force in observation, but he had no intention that this force should be used except upon an emergency and with the consent of the High Commissioner, I think it would be difficult to find serious fault with him. It might have happened that the Britishers at Johannesburg were in serious danger of their lives and that the vast property there was in jeopardy. In this case the High Commissioner might have thought it necessary to intervene for the purpose of protection and to keep the peace pending a settlement.

As I understand it, what Rhodes' enemies allege is that, with a view to improve the pecuniary position of the Chartered Company, whose property in Matabeleland and Mashonaland has turned out to be a failure, he desired "to rush" the Transvaal. With this object he fostered the revolutionary movement and assisted it with arms and money. Meanwhile he prepared a force intended to join the insurrection from outside; and Jameson's only disobedience consists in the fact that he went in a day or two too soon. Of course I do not adopt this charge, but it appears to me that it is substantially what Rhodes will have to answer. I may add that, although the existence of a German-Dutch conspiracy would hardly justify the action imputed to Rhodes, yet conclusive proof of it would undoubtedly tend to divert the issue and to share the blame. If therefore he can produce documentary or verbal testimony of such a conspiracy it would be of great use to him, and would be accepted, no doubt, by many people as a good excuse. But the question is, has he any evidence good enough for a Committee of the House of

Commons? I have marked this letter "private" but you may *show* it if you like to anybody interested in the question.

Believe me, yours very truly,

J. CHAMBERLAIN.

[*Memorandum.*]

Three days ago I had a letter from Chamberlain. It was difficult to get at Rhodes in time, but I asked Natty Rothschild to let him know immediately he arrived at Plymouth that it was most important that he should make no statement until he had seen him. Then I told Natty the substance of Chamberlain's letter. *Transvaal: Rhodes and Chamberlain.*

Yesterday morning Natty came to see me. He had seen Rhodes the evening before. He told him exactly what Chamberlain had said. Rhodes denied all knowledge of the Jameson Raid. He urges very strongly that Chamberlain should obtain the release of the five prisoners at present in Pretoria, and redress for the grievances of the Uitlanders. Rhodes promised that he would make no public statement at present. He talked of a large meeting at the Albert Hall, at which he proposed to address the shareholders of the Company.

2. In the afternoon Stead came to see me. He had just had a long talk with Rhodes, and his story was a very different one. Rhodes said that he was going to admit to his full complicity in the plot. That he could not deny it; it was true that he had no responsibility for the Jameson Raid. That he had no idea it would take place, that it was never intended. The idea was that the rising should take place in Johannesburg and that the Chartered Force should come in to restore order. *—and Stead.*

This preparation had been made in the interests of the Empire, as a successful rebellion of the Uitlanders would have meant an English in lieu of a Dutch Republic, which would have meant the nucleus of a United States, independent of the British Crown. This he determined to prevent. On the other hand, he had fostered and encouraged rebellion in Johannesburg. There might be documentary evidence of this. He had taken no trouble to cover up his trail. He had subscribed money and sent telegrams, if he had not sent letters. There might be heaps of evidence. It was of no use to deny all this, and besides he never told lies. He was quite willing to give up his office as a Privy Councillor and to cease to be a Managing Director of the Company. His personal position was of no importance. But it was essential that the English Government should show that they were not indifferent to the just claims for redress of men who had lain down their arms at the request of the High Commissioner. They must not think themselves abandoned, as that would leave a sore, which would take years to heal. That there, in the position of the prisoners who were shut up, in cells infested with vermin, were the considerations which weighed with him at the present moment. All this is very serious.

—and Brett.   3. I saw Rhodes this afternoon, Feb. 5th. He seemed altogether in better heart than I expected. I told him that I had said to N. [Nellie] that I rather despaired and that she had replied "you should never despair of a man like Rhodes till you see him swinging on the gallows!" He was amused at this. I asked him what he was going to say to Chamberlain. He said he should tell him the whole truth. That it was the worst possible policy to lie. That his brother Frank was in command in Johannesburg. That being the case, if he were to tell me sitting there that he had known nothing of the events leading up to the rebellion I should think him not only a liar but a fool.

He then repeated to me substantially what he had said to Stead. He had received my message from Natty and was aware consequently of what Chamberlain wished him to say, but he thought it better on the whole to be perfectly frank. I pointed out to him that there was one consideration which appeared to have escaped him, that was the position of Mr. Chamberlain, the Secretary of State. Chamberlain was obviously anxious to help and it would not do to embarrass him or to tie his hands. It appeared to me to be prudent to endeavour to ascertain how

THE HON. REGINALD BRETT AND MR. CECIL RHODES, 1891.

Chamberlain would receive a confidence of this kind. I said I would try and find out. On leaving me he said, "wish we could get our secret society."[1]

4. I found Chamberlain very tired, after a long day at Osborne. He had telegraphed to the Colonial Office, in response to Rhodes' request, that he would see him on the morrow at 3 o'clock. I told him that I had come to him to ask a question which he would not perhaps care to answer, and it was whether in the interview with Rhodes he desired him to be cautious or to be perfectly frank. Chamberlain hesitated to answer and looked very serious, so I thought it better to tell him what had passed between me and Rhodes. My telling him this committed him to nothing. After I had finished he pointed out the exceeding difficulty of the position in which he would be placed if Rhodes made these admissions to him. He might any day be asked whether he knew that Rhodes had been a party to the conspiracy, and if so, why he had not had him arrested as an accessory to the plot. He would have seriously to consider whether the Law Officers of the Crown should not be instructed to proceed against Rhodes as against Jameson. He could see no advantage in receiving Rhodes' confidence. *—and Chamberlain*

"Rhodes must remember," he said, "that by the position I hold I am virtually a judge in this matter." He then said that in his conversation with Rhodes he saw no necessity for discussing recent events. They had to look rather to the future. He was prepared to discuss with him the present condition of affairs in the Transvaal and the future of the Chartered Company, and it seemed to him the more their conversation turned upon these subjects, and the less upon recent events, the better. In any case, before they met, he strongly urged that Rhodes should take counsel with his legal advisers and very seriously consider the position in which he stood.

5. I wrote a line to Rhodes asking whether he would see George Lewis. With this he agreed, so I took George Lewis to see him about midnight. We had a long conversation. Rhodes *Transvaal: Immediate Policy.*

[1] See *Rhodes*, by Sarah Millin, pp. 32, 128, 172, 216.

was impressed by the point I put to him that whereas two months ago he and everybody else believed that the Boers were no longer the power they used to be, and that the Transvaal would be easily coerced, it was now clear that it would take an army of at least twenty thousand men to subdue them. He quite realises that this makes it more difficult to make terms with Kruger. He maintains, however, that although the difficulty may be great it has to be overcome, and that the Uitlanders who laid down their arms at the instance of the English Government, have got to be convinced that the English Government is prepared to befriend them. We then discussed Jameson's trial and Rhodes' position. George Lewis expressed his views very clearly and Rhodes said that he would be cautious in his conversation with Chamberlain, that he would not address any public meeting, and that he would, if he could get anything to show for his visit, return to South Africa, go to Bulawayo, and employ himself in the development of the great tract of country called by his name. Upon this we left him.

All this happened on Wednesday, 5th February, 1896.

[*To the Rev. C. D. Williamson.*]   MARCH 9TH.

Mr. Brett's Book.   I have been correcting the proofs of the Queen's Prime Ministers, which is to be published soon.[1] I want a few portraits for the volume. Shall I call it by the above title, which is descriptive enough? Or shall I call it *The Queen's Legacy*? Which is the real meaning of the book. People are so slow and stupid.

. . . The Cardinal [Manning] mentions an article of mine very kindly. Stan discovered the passage, which pleased me. I like to think of the old man reading what I wrote.

Yesterday I went to the Castle to see about some jobs for the Queen. I did not see her, but I saw her tea—such a queer little meal—being carried in. Just one cup and a plate of sandwiches!

[1] The *Yoke of Empire*.

An old "personal attendant" like Lord Palmerston in a white tie, and 3 gorgeous scarlet footmen to carry in this Belshazzar's feast!

[*Journals.*]　　　　　　　　　　2, TILNEY STREET,
　　　　　　　　　　　　　　　　NOVEMBER 4TH.

A bomb exploded on our doorstep in Tilney St. The door close behind which Nellie was standing, was blown in, and all windows broken. Nellie had a blessed escape. She was marvellously plucky and her coolness beyond praise.[1]

[*To the Rev. C. D. Williamson.*]　　2, TILNEY STREET,
　　　　　　　　　　　　　　　　NOVEMBER 8TH.

I will send you a newspaper account of the affair! It was a shave. Nellie showed wonderful pluck. She must have stepped over the bomb. Luckily she had stepped out of the line of fire, and was eating grapes near the table when the door came inwards.

It was a *French* bomb, full of melinite and French newspaper scraps and French screws.

An unpleasant experience. But it has brought *heaps* of affection and sympathy which compensates.

Teddie and I *walked*—imagine our horror when we found the street full of people—and the first fear of a horrible accident.

[*From the Rt. Hon. W. E. Gladstone.*] HAWARDEN,
　　　　　　　　　　　　　　　　JANUARY 2ND, 1897.
DEAR MR. BRETT,

I have now read your work with real interest and pleasure.　*Mr. Brett's*
To dispose at once of the part in which I am personally con-　*Book.*
cerned let me say that, were I to raise it absolutely in my own

---

[1] The motive of the outrage was never exactly discovered. The police theory was that the bomb had been intended for Mr. Justice Hawkins, a very severe judge who lived next door.

cause, I should issue from the ordeal with less to the Cr. and more to the Dr. side than you have liberally awarded me.

I cannot but regard as the central object of interest in the work the relations between the Queen and Lord Melbourne in the early years of the reign. But elsewhere, I think, as well as there, you have exhibited much care, tact and good taste.

Lord Melbourne has long been to me a figure of singular historic interest. The volume published under Lord Cowper's auspices is something, but is inadequate and, except as to M.'s short essay, not well done. It will be, I think, a reproach and a misfortune to us if we continue to be without a real Biography of this noteworthy character. With sincerest thanks I remain very faithfully yours,

W. E. GLADSTONE.

P.S.   You have inadvertently reprinted the now exploded error in declaring the Queen to be the Head of the Church. Queen Mary abolished the title which has never been renewed.

[*To the Duchess of Sutherland.*]   OFFICE OF WORKS,
                                          JANUARY 5TH.

Positively not a word of news here—except extraordinary rumours about the Queen—perfectly absurd—and much criticism of Rosebery's "flight"—for that is the interpretation put by even his party on his absenting himself at the opening of Parliament. I must say I think also that he is wrong. Even a suspicion of the white feather is as damaging as the real thing—which I am sure he cannot feel.[1]

[1] Throughout the fifteen months since the defeat of Lord Rosebery's government, the leadership of the Liberal party had been in dispute and the party in considerable difficulties. Rosebery himself was in very poor health; and it will be seen from the letters printed by the Marquess of Crewe that he was announcing in many quarters his intention to retire altogether from political life on this account.

These announcements had not, however, obtained sufficient currency to prevent the circulation of unnecessary reasons for this absence.

I had a most charming letter from Mr. Gladstone about that little book. The most characteristic thing you can imagine. Humble about himself in a stately old-fashioned way, and enthusiastic about Lord Melbourne, with a queer postscript on the ecclesiastical position of the Sovereign! I will show it to you when you come to London, as a literary curiosity.

Mr. Brett's Book.

Everybody has been kind about the book, which was sold right out at once! I admit that Xmas may have had more to do with this, than intrinsic merit. . . .

[*To M. V. B.*]   OFFICE OF WORKS,
FEBRUARY.

. . . I have only just got back from Sandringham. It is such a deuce of a way from London. I was *not* bored on the whole. Several things amused me. I saw all the thoroughbred horses yesterday; and walked there with the Princess, who was very nice.

Also the Prince has asked me to join his small committee to settle all the Jubilee festivities. I have a meeting at Marlborough House to-morrow, and it is rather interesting and not unamusing.

[*To Mr. W. T. Stead.*]   OFFICE OF WORKS,
FEBRUARY 19TH.

. . . I came up with Milner[1] from Windsor this morning. He has a heavy job; and has to start *de novo*. The Committee will leave few of the old gang on their legs. Alas! Rhodes was a pitiful object. Harcourt *very* sorry for him; too sorry to press his question home. *Why* did Rhodes try to shuffle after all we had told him?

S. African Committee.

[1] Appointed High Commissioner for South Africa.

His advisers are fools and knaves; some of both. The Russian Emperor will let himself go presently and there will be an end of the "concert." A good thing too.

[*From Sir Alfred Milner.*]   47, DUKE STREET,
                                                    FEBRUARY 9TH.

MY DEAR BRETT,

Milner to   Many thanks for your note. I am so glad that you are glad.
South Africa. For though personal friendship may have a good deal to do in the matter, you are much too keen about national policy to wish me to go if you thought I was the wrong man. "There is many a slip," so I shall believe in the thing when I land at Cape Town. But I hope there will be no slip, for, though I know perfectly well that I may break my neck over it, I am wild to go.

                                                    Yours ever,
                                                    A. M.

[*To M. V. B.*]   OFFICE OF WORKS,
                                                    JUNE.

I have had such a rush all day. Hardly a moment to spare. I just had time to tear in and look at a black fancy dress—time 1628—for the Ball[1]—all black velvet and trimmed with beads, and a ruff! And long silk legs in which I suppose I shall look as big a tomfool as everybody else—or more so! The d——d Jubilee is getting very much on my nerves to-day, as there have been no alleviations in the way of funny incidents.

[*To M. V. B.*]   OFFICE OF WORKS,
                                                    JUNE 16TH.

Jubilee   . . . The only alleviation was a luncheon with Letty [Lind],
Arrange-   who is in great dismay as they propose to have a performance at
ments.

                    [1] Devonshire House Ball.

2.30 on Jubilee day. She has promised me faithfully to chuck it —and I got this telegram just now, so I think she means to keep her promise.

I shall however try to get the whole programme put a stop to, as it is too hard on all the girls who want to see the show, and cannot possibly get to the theatre in time.

George Edwardes is a tyrant! All the rest of the day I was worried with all sorts of people—and did not get three minutes to myself. I backed Victor Wild for a place, which he got, as you will observe. There is to be a service in St. George's Chapel on Sunday morning, and the Queen is going to sit close to the altar steps on a sort of low throne. Very few people are to be admitted. I arranged to-day for the Tattoo on Saturday. Would you like to come ? If so I will ask Tutor whether he will allow it.

[*To M. V. B.*] OFFICE OF WORKS,
                 JUNE 18TH.

. . . I am getting through now rather better. All our tickets are sent off and the muddle is not so great as it was.

. . . I have tried on my fancy dress. It is black with puffed short breeches, which come very high up and stick out, and long black silk tights, and a black velvet jacket and coat. I want a dagger—but I don't know where to get a good one.

The medals which I bought for the school-children, I have got the Queen to present. Rather nice of her, and it will be very much appreciated. I only hope they will all be ready in time. It is a very near shave though.

This weather looks rather alarming. It will be awful if it goes on. The streets are a most curious sight. It is hardly possible to move. You will see it all on Monday. I doubt it being possible to get to the play that night.

Jubilee Arrangements.

[*From Sir William Harcourt.*]   7, RICHMOND TERRACE,
JUNE 23RD.

DEAR REGGY,

Letters of Congratulation.   Now that the great day is over and the big work done I must write you a line of congratulation on the admirable way in which your part has been played and the efficient and quiet way in which you have despatched a difficult business. To me there is nothing so grateful as the deserved success of my young friends.

Yours ever,
W. V. H.

[*From Sir Charles Howard.*]   METROPOLITAN POLICE OFFICE,
JUNE 23RD.

MY DEAR BRETT,

Just a line to congratulate you on the success of yesterday; and I wish to express my gratitude to you for the ready assistance you have given from the *very first,* which lightened my labours considerably. I have never had such warm and ready help from any Govt. Department before. Believe me, sincerely and gratefully yours,

CHARLES HOWARD.

[*From Sir Arthur Bigge.*]   WINDSOR CASTLE,
JUNE 23RD.

MY DEAR BRETT,

I hate to be behindhand in congratulating a friend, especially when the feeling is of so hearty a nature as I intended to express to you, had I not been almost overwhelmed with work during these last two days—indeed I can only keep abreast of the really pressing matters.

But no one could have been more pleased on your more than well-earned C.B. I consider that the success of Tuesday was to a great extent due to you, not only what you did, but the way you did it in dealing with your fellow creatures. Don't

"A GENTLEMAN OF FRANCE IN 1628."
THE DEVONSHIRE HOUSE JUBILEE BALL, 1897.

write. Edwards has shown me your kind letter. It was entirely
through your thoughtful hint that the Queen gave the medals
and refreshment to the children on Tuesday.

Yours very truly,
ARTHUR BIGGE.

[*To M. V. B.*] JUNE 24TH.

. . . I want to tell you all about the children's fête in the Park, *Jubilee.*
and the Queen's arrival. But I can do this to-morrow. It was all
a great success. I have had scores of congratulatory letters about
the Jubilee. Very flattering some of them. And when I got to
the station this morning *Ormond* was the first to tell me of the
Queen's recognition in the papers.[1] I knew nothing of it.

[*To M. V. B.*] OFFICE OF WORKS,
JULY 2ND.

. . . To-night is this infernal Ball. I will tell you all about it
to-morrow. I expect it will be a fiasco. At Chamberlain's great
party—to which an instinct warned me not to go—there was a
fearful bearfight. Impossible to get into the house through the
crowds in Piccadilly. Princess Maud nearly got torn to pieces.
The footmen were the great offenders—ragging all the guests
and using most filthy language—especially to respectable elderly
ladies. The Princess of Wales drove up and had to drive away.
You can imagine Chamberlain's wrath.[2]

[*To M. V. B.*] OFFICE OF WORKS,
JULY 19TH.

It was a very sweet half hour under the trees by Fellow's
pond, and I should like to renew it one day. . . .

[1] He was given a C.B.
[2] The occasion was a reception given for the Colonial Premiers who were
all in London at the time. It is not to be understood that there was any public
congestion in the street or any public riot. The guests exceeded the accom-
modation; that is all.

Royalty and
Finger-bowls.

I found the Princess [Louise], and Lorne when I returned, and made my excuses. They dined with us, and went off after dinner. Both very nice and gracious. No contretemps except that there were finger-bowls at the dessert!

Do you know that it is not etiquette when you entertain a member of the House of Hanover? The custom dates from Jacobite times when the health of the "King over the water" (the Pretender) used to be drunk. I ragged the Princess about it! People who were friendly to him were afraid of drinking that toast boldly, so used to say "The King" and pass their glass over the finger-bowl full of water!

It is a queer custom to maintain—that of not having finger-bowls—but I like queer customs!

[*Journals.*]   JULY 31ST.

. . . Thursday night Oliver and Maurice came home, and yesterday I made them come up to London to see their Grandfather at the Law Courts for the last time, as he retires in October. He wrote announcing it to Lord Salisbury, who wrote a perfect letter in reply, alluding to his "splendid service" and well-earned repose. . . .

The summer half has passed very happily for the boys. We had the electric launch again, and many jolly evenings we took them down to see the eight, or up-stream to see races. I had two rows with Maurice in a gig, with Neil Primrose to steer. Neil is Rosebery's second son, an attractive little fellow. (N.B. I omit all references to the hard work of the Queen's Jubilee. It has lost all interest, and the really beautiful pageants in London and at Eton, with which I had necessarily much to do, have passed from memory.)

Mr. Brett had been up to Callander in Perthshire every August for several years and had now bought The Roman Camp, the old hunting lodge of the Dukes of Perth, which ultimately became his real home.

[*Journals.*] THE ROMAN CAMP,
AUGUST 9TH.

Slept here for the first time to-day. Nellie, Maurice and I
went with Chat [Williamson] to Lochearnhead, and then drove
along the loch to Comrie and got back to dinner.

[*Journals.*] OFFICE OF WORKS,
NOVEMBER 2ND.

I went to Windsor to make arrangements for the Duchess of *The Vaults*
Teck's funeral. Inspected the vault where repose the descen- *at Windsor.*
dants of George III. It is in a deplorable state. The partition
between this vault and that in which Henry VIII, Charles I and
Jane Seymour were buried is bricked up. But I saw an old man
who was present, as a boy, when George IV opened the vault,
and the coffin of Charles I. This man told me that when the lid
was removed, King Charles' face seemed that of a living man,
absolutely perfect. In a few minutes, exposed to the air, it fell
to pieces. There was a piece of black ribbon to hide the sever-
ance of the head from the body.

[*To M. V. B.*] NOVEMBER 16TH.

. . . I saw your grandfather to-day. He had a tremendous *First Lord*
reception yesterday—and made a very good speech. It was *Esher Retires.*
nice and manly, and not silly and mawkish as those things
usually are. Viola[1] attended with Lady E.

[*Journals.*] 2, TILNEY STREET,
NOVEMBER 21ST.

My father has been created a Viscount, and has bade farewell
to the Bar.

[1] Viola Dudley-Ward, afterwards Lady Erskine.

[*Journals.*]   2, TILNEY STREET,
                                        NOVEMBER 24TH.

Dinner with   Dined with the Queen at Windsor. Invitation came when
the Queen.   we were in London. Dorothy[1] replied by the orderly of the
Blues: "The Lord Steward. I hear from my mother Hon.
Mrs. Brett that she will obey the Queen's command. Yours
sincerely, Dorothy Brett." An original document!

Arrived at 8.45. Drove to the entrance in the N.E. corner of
the quadrangle. Shown into the corridor where we waited. A
few chairs before the fire at the north end. Sir Fleetwood and
Lady Edwardes, Pelham Clinton, Lady Downe, Lord Denbigh,
the latter a new Lord-in-waiting. Other members of the household passed through the Corridor on their way to their separate
dinner. After a while at a sign from a page we moved to the
southern end of the Corridor near the staircase across the top of
which are the Queen's rooms. The Queen walked in supported
by her youngest Indian—a handsome youth. She bowed to the
company and Nellie kissed her hand. We went straight in to
dinner. Previously we had been shown our places upon a card
by the Master of the Household, which card was placed by the
Queen for reference.

Gold plate, and beautiful Sèvres. Indian servants behind the
Queen. A Highlander to pour out the wine. The Queen ate
everything. No "courses." Dinner is served straight on, and
when you finish one dish you get the next, without a pause for
breath. Everyone talked as at any other dinner, only in subdued
tones. The Queen was in excellent humour. After dinner the
Queen rose, and we stood back against the wall. She went out
and we followed. Immediately to the left of the doorway in the
Corridor was placed a chair, and in front of it a little table.
There the Queen seated herself. We stood in a circle at a considerable distance away from her. Coffee was brought and
liqueurs. The Queen sipped her coffee while a page held the
saucer on a small waiter. Then the Princess spoke to the Queen

[1] His daughter, then aged 14.

for a few minutes, and afterwards moved to Nellie. The Queen talked a while to Lady Downe, who was sent to fetch Nellie. Meanwhile the circle whispered discreetly! Then the Queen sent for me, and she talked to me for half an hour of her affairs and her family! Finally she bowed, and I retired. By that time it was nearly eleven. In a few moments she rose. Nellie kissed her hand and she went away. We remained a few moments, had some lemonade, and departed.[1]

[*Journals.*]   2, TILNEY STREET,
                                                  NOVEMBER 30TH.

I lunched in New Court; heard lots of talk about the wretched *Dreyfus.*
Dreyfus, whose case is racking the French nation; he is possibly guilty although that is doubtful, but in their desire to convict him the military caste is falsifying evidence and making of this uninteresting Jew a Christian martyr.

[*Journals.*]   2, TILNEY STREET,
                                                  JANUARY 18TH, 1898.

John Morley expressed a desire to call in Tilney Street. It was a surprise, as I have not seen him for ages. He came from Macmillan to ask if I would undertake to write Dizzy's life! Very flattering. But I pointed out that my whole time was absorbed. He spoke of 3 or 4 years to do it in. Much depends on the state of the papers. Natty Rothschild always told me that there were 15 boxes at New Court in wild confusion. J. M. thinks they are arranged. I doubt it. Also I am not sure whether Monty Corry or Natty really wish this book to be written. They have been so dilatory in taking the obvious steps. *I* have taken time to consider.

[1] This was the prototype of many similar dinners to which all reference is omitted.

[*To Sir Arthur Bigge.*]   OFFICE OF WORKS,
                                            JANUARY 27TH.

... I was at Kensington Palace this morning with Sir Spencer [Ponsonby Fane] and he will propose to the Queen to get rid of a lot of rubbish, leave for which will I hope be given. Such a mess! A hopeless quantity of broken things. Quite valueless.

On the other hand there are some of the Queen's old toys, a doll's house, etc. etc. lying about, which I hope H.M. will hereafter allow us to put into glass cases, and place in the room to which the public will be admitted.

Finally. When I saw the Prince of Wales a short while ago, he asked me to suggest to you, from him, that if an opportunity arose for sounding the Duke of Edinburgh as to the possibility of his exchanging Clarence House (which must be a great expense to him as a *pied à terre*) for York House it would gratify H.R.H. who cannot, of course, suggest the thing to him.

[*Journals.*]   ORCHARD LEA,
                                           JANUARY 29TH.

Chamberlain on Rosebery.   I lunched with Princess Louise yesterday, and went all over her house at Kensington Palace. A pleasant home. Then in the evening I dined alone with Chamberlain. Talking of Morley, he praised the latter's speeches, but, he said, "He never concludes." Of Rosebery he said, "I shall never forgive him for having known, when he became P.M., how to revive the old Liberal Party, having tried to do it, in the right way, by his 'predominant partner' speech, then having funked, and destroyed his own handiwork and the Party for ever." A characteristic "boutade."

—on Foreign Affairs.   He talked of China and West Africa, and of France and Russia, with an amplitude of view and phrase that would have astonished Birmingham ten years ago. He has lately had a strong difference of opinion with Lord S. [Salisbury]. He believes we

are at the parting of the ways, and that we must stand fast for Imperial expansion now or never, whatever the result.

I told him of Morley's visit to me, and his proposal. He thinks in any eventuality I must remain in the Civil Service.[1]

[*Journals.*]   ORCHARD LEA,
                                                    FEBRUARY 8TH.

Parliament opened to-day. Lord E. took his seat as a Viscount, looking very dignified in his peer's robes, but frail. . . .

I had an hour's talk with Rosebery this morning. He talked   *Rosebery.*
of the disillusions of political life, and the lesson he was so grieved to learn, that private friendship was incompatible with political loyalty. Alas! It is *he* that has lost the power of binding people to him. He is too lacking in frankness for perfect intimacy. . . .

[*Journals.*]   FEBRUARY 21ST.

Went to the Levée with my Father, who was presented! Age 82. Rosebery's first ball for Sybil and Peggy, a brilliant success.

[*To the Rt. Hon. A. J. Balfour.*]   OFFICE OF WORKS,
                                                    APRIL 1ST.

I was at New Court yesterday and heard certain rumours   *Warning to*
which may or may not be true.   *Balfour.*

I only write a line to remind you that all the disasters of 1880–1885 came from the Government of the day allowing themselves to be swayed by the newspapers. Never once did they hold straight on to the end with the policy which (right or wrong in its inception) they had adopted.

[1] This he decided to do, and refused Mr. Morley's proposal.

The public generally have no notions about the Far East. They never use maps. You can do exactly what you believe to be right with impunity.

The opportunists of to-day are *morally* the descendants of the Doctrinaires of 1798!

Forgive me for writing. Burn this and don't answer.[1]

[*Journals.*] OFFICE OF WORKS,
APRIL 4TH.

Up to town early. Saw the Duke of Cambridge for an hour at Gloucester House. He was pathetically enthusiastic and juvenile about his estimates. Although 80 he is as ardent as a boy of 18.

[*To M. V. B.*] OFFICE OF WORKS,
MAY 9TH.

. . . The party at Ascot ended in my playing Bridge last night till 12, after two rounds of golf in the afternoon with Mungo Herbert (Reggie's uncle), whom I defeated quite easily! You will perhaps as usual think he must have been a very inferior player. Among the guests were the Scotts, who now own the Isle of Harris. She was a Cadogan. They want us to go to Harris this autumn from Pinkie. It is the finest sporting place in Great Britain.

If you can come with me, and care for me still by that time, I will go. Glorious fishing.

I have been harried to death to-day to get Kensington Palace ready for the visit from the Queen. And at the last moment she

[1] Mr. Balfour was at this time First Lord of the Treasury; it seems probable, however, that this letter refers to agreements about "spheres of influence" in China which were being much discussed in the House and the country on account of the Russian occupation of Port Arthur.

cannot go! I lunched with Ivan Caryll at the Grill room, which was so full I couldn't get a seat—so he asked me to lunch "gratis."

The new piece at the Gaiety comes out on Saturday. He thinks it is the best he has done yet. He says Seymour Hicks is rather a difficult person to manage, but that *she* is charming. Apparently there is a charming duet for Payne and K. Seymour —as Piccaninnies—with blackened faces. And he has also dug up some good new singers. The scene is first in Corsica and then in Venice. It sounds pretty—he described the dresses and the choruses both of which sound very attractive. He told me that he sold 250,000 copies of *My Honey* and made £9000 out of *Christopher Columbus*; that wasn't bad. He is a very clever fellow.

[*To the Duchess of Sutherland.*]   ORCHARD LEA,
                                            MAY 11TH.

. . . All the gossip you will have heard from others. Note, *On Gladstone* however, in to-day's papers, the accounts of Mr. Gladstone's *Dying.* final leave taking of the world. It is a really noble ending to a noble life from your Christian point of view. The intense pain, the intense resignation, the intense faith in the God he not only professed, but apparently has really adored. What is also touching, is the responding chord touched in the hearts of the great nonconformist masses who have always been his followers in politics, but who differ so keenly on matters spiritual. In the face of suffering and death these differences sink into nothingness. Perhaps before you get this, the end may have come. I wonder meanwhile what you are doing. . . .

[*Journals.*]   ORCHARD LEA,
                      MAY 11TH.

My mother went to the Drawing Room and *fell* when passing the Queen. She will be 84 years old next month.

The Prince of Wales sent for me this morning, and I was with him for about half an hour in his room on the first floor of Marlborough House, up the staircase decorated with frescoes of Marlborough's victories. We discussed family business as usual. The Duke of York was there for a while, frank and charming. Finally two messages came from the Princess to say she was waiting, the second so peremptory that the Prince left hastily.

This afternoon I had three-quarters of an hour with my old Chief, the Duke of Devonshire, who was brighter than he has been of late. To-night I came down with Wolseley, the Commander-in-Chief, to Windsor. Lord Salisbury was in the next carriage. Wolseley talked all the time. Praised Kitchener highly; also Gatacre; said how superior these younger men were to the older Generals. K. will move to Khartoum in August. . . .

The Queen Ageing. . . . As the Queen ages she does not see her secretaries sufficiently often. Her ladies read papers to her, and bring down messages. It makes complications. There was a pathetic moment at Netley yesterday, when the Queen was wheeled up to Findlater and the other wounded V.C., both sitting in chairs. They were ordered to rise, but the Queen said, "Most certainly not," and raised herself without help (a very unusual thing) and stood over them while she decorated them with the Cross. The Queen won't see her Ministers because they argue with her, and she says, "You know I cannot any longer argue." A month or two ago she failed to come to dinner, the first time within living memory.

Death of Gladstone. After a long lingering illness, Mr. Gladstone died at 5 o'clock this morning. Very peacefully. He has been saved all pain of late, under the influence of morphia. Will his relations accept the proffered public funeral? It is thought that they will. Precedents are hard to find, and it will lead to much confusion. The F.O. party on Saturday postponed. Will the Queen postpone the Ball on Monday? Here again there is no precedent. A ball was postponed when the *Victoria* sank, and again when Lord Clarendon died, but he was Foreign Secretary at the time. Mr. Gladstone is not a "Minister." We shall hear to-morrow. In the *Yoke of Empire* I have written down all I feel or can ever feel about Mr. G. It is a mighty figure gone.

[*To M. V. B.*]   TURF CLUB,
                                                   MAY 21ST.

It is impossible for me to get away until late to-night. I hope to get back by the 12 train, but don't feel confident even of this.

I hoped to get an "off" day but this morning I was telegraphed *His Funeral.* for, and have been all day worrying about the funeral. The Duke of Norfolk as Earl Marshal has control, and all the arrangements have to be made by Saturday. I have suggested the Eton boys as a guard of honour. Mr. G.'s old school. I don't know if the idea will be adopted, but I hope so. Perhaps the Head will object! He seems to be in a very particular mood, from what I heard yesterday.

. . . This is not a letter in the real sense of the word, only a scrap scrawled in the interval between tiresome conclaves in Westminster Abbey, and a still more tiresome dinner.

[*Journals.*]   ORCHARD LEA,
                                                   MAY 21ST.

To-day all day busy with the funeral, the whole strain of which is necessarily borne by my office. Dined with the Chancellor of the Exchequer, and came home late. Queen's birthday was kept to-day.

[*Journals.*]   ORCHARD LEA,
                                            MAY 22ND.

The Prince   Not a word from the Queen on the subject of Mr. G. The P.
and Glad-   of W. very nice about it all. Asked me to propose him as Pall
stone.   Bearer, which I did. There is no precedent for a P. of W. acting
in that capacity to a "subject," and I had great difficulty, but it
was finally overcome. I suggested that the Eton Volunteers
should form a guard of honour at Westminster Abbey.

[*Journals.*]   ORCHARD LEA,
                                            MAY 28TH.

Funeral.   Mr. G.'s funeral. The Eton boys came up. Yesterday there
were two striking scenes in Westminster Hall. (1) March past
of the Liberal Delegates. Very solemn. Men and women who
really felt the parting. Not sight-seers, a last farewell to their old
Chief. (2) Then the midnight watching. The silence of the
great Hall. The kneeling figures. The simple dais and coffin.
I fetched Rosebery down at 12 o'clock, knowing he would
appreciate. He said, "May I kneel for a minute?" He is such
an enigma.

[*From Sir Francis Knollys.*]   MARLBOROUGH HOUSE,
                                            MAY 28TH.

MY DEAR BRETT,
   I am desired by the Prince of Wales to write to you and say
that he never knew anything go off better than the ceremony
yesterday. He thinks all the arrangements were excellent, and
that all those who had to do with them deserve the greatest
credit.
                                    Yours sincerely,
                                    FRANCIS KNOLLYS.

[*From the Rt. Hon. Herbert Gladstone.*]   HAWARDEN,
                                        MAY 30TH.

MY DEAR R.,

We are all grateful to you for your invaluable help last week, not only for your official work done as was to be expected, but for personal kindness and the thoughtful suggestiveness which believe me we have very deeply appreciated.

                                    Yours always,
                                        HERBERT GLADSTONE.

[*Journals.*]   ORCHARD LEA,
                                        JUNE 2ND.

D.[1] returned from Balmoral. The Queen was very angry at *The Queen* the attempts made to induce her to write in praise of Mr. G. It *and Glad-* would have been in the nature of a recantation. She absolutely *stone.* refused to be dictated to by the newspapers. Salisbury backed her. The message to Mrs. G. she had already written in her own hand. She was willing to put something in the Court Circular, but only if not to do so "would hurt the Ministry!" She was displeased with the Prince of W. acting Pall Bearer, and kissing Mrs. G.'s hand! She said, "I am sorry for Mrs. Gladstone; as for him, I never liked him, and I will say nothing about him!" Her regard for what she thinks the truth, and her courage, are as characteristic to-day as they were in 1838.

[*Journals.*]   ORCHARD LEA,
                                        JUNE 30TH.

Dined with the Queen at Windsor Castle, and I was gently rebuked for misdirected enthusiasm over the Ceremonial last month.

[1] The Rt. Hon. Akers Douglas, afterwards Lord Chilston.

[*To the Duchess of Sutherland.*]   ROMAN CAMP,
                                        SEPTEMBER 16TH.

I ran up to London on Tuesday and returned on Wednesday
night—not a very long visit. But long enough to be depressed
by the atmosphere in the south. All your pity for humanity
would be required of you, if you could see the wretched
wearied-out autumnal faces of the people who pass you in the
street. Otherwise life has been quite uneventful. I had one
charming sail in a small boat, over to Mull with a fine breeze
and bright sunshine.

The Bones of   Yesterday, in Edinburgh I opened the royal vault where the
Scots Kings.   Scottish Kings—a few of them—lie. The vault was desecrated
by the mob in 1688, and the bones of James V, his wife, his
children, of Darnley, etc. all lie in confused heaps on the floor,
and on one poor wood shelf, over the coffin of Mary of Gueldres,
wife of James III of Scotland—whose place of burial was elsewhere—and was only moved to Holyrood after the revolution.

I have suggested to the Queen the propriety of having all
these poor relics of departed greatness collected, and placed in
a decent manner in some closed place. . . .

[*To M. V. B.*]   ROMAN CAMP,
                        SEPTEMBER 20TH.

. . . I started directly after I wrote to you, and walked right
up to the burn, about two miles from the empty shepherd's
house, where you went off shooting by yourself.

I lunched in the corrie, with Fred and Donald sitting a little
way off. Then began to fish. I got 21 trout, all—except one or
two—bigger than those caught by Loulou [Harcourt] that day.

I only fished for two hours. Walking back I had milk at the
farm, and then counted 60 blackgame in those two corn
patches. 35 on one, and 25 on the other! The corn is all cut,
the place quiet, and the birds swarm there.

[*To the Duchess of Sutherland.*]　　ROMAN CAMP,
　　　　　　　　　　　　　　　　　OCTOBER 2ND.

. . . In Paris no one can mention the name of Dreyfus, nor *Religious* say of Brisson otherwise than that he is a scoundrel. All the best *Bigotry ;* *Dreyfus.* Frenchmen, the most religious, the most humane and generous, are on the side of the apparently gross scoundrels who have hounded down this unfortunate Jew. Is it not a queer state of things?

Do you not detest religious prejudice? It even gives one an *—the Mahdi.* uncomfortable feeling to read of the desecration of the tomb and body of the Mahdi; who, after all, was (whatever he may have really been, or judged by our standards) believed by his people to be a holy man, sacred and saintlike. I doubt whether we are justified in playing the Herod and Pontius Pilate, and trampling on the faith of thousands of human beings, merely because that faith is an inconvenience to us politically. What will Arab and Sudan tradition hold? Quite possibly we have (unwittingly) started some new theory or some new religious enthusiasm, which will give us more trouble in the future. That anyhow is the lesson of all former religious persecutions. . . .

[*To M. V. B.*]　　　　　　　　　ROMAN CAMP,
　　　　　　　　　　　　　　　　　OCTOBER 5TH.

I had a glorious day yesterday. You cannot imagine anything *Deer* more splendid than the weather—cloudless and as hot as sum- *Stalking.* mer. I drove to the "Bees" and then walked. The ponies and men were waiting at Arrie Bridge. Not a deer in sight. We went straight up over the hill. I rode a pony some of the way. It was grilling hot. When we got over the other side we saw a great many deer. Not lying well. All very inaccessible. How-ever, we went right up to Ben Voirlich and down the Ruchill— walking; close to the river, to get round some deer. Suddenly we saw some on the left, and I had a very difficult stalk.

We couldn't get near them, but I was persuaded to have a shot *up hill*—always very difficult at about 200 yards—and missed! I was very sick. We went on expecting all the deer would be put up. As we got up a burn away from the Ruchill, walking for a long way in the water, we crawled up a mound, and just caught sight of a hind and a young stag about 10 yards away. We had to lie absolutely dead still for a quarter of an hour. Then they moved off, and we saw the other stags about 60 yards away. I crawled to a hummock, and killed one, "shot him dead."

After this the ponies came down and we had lunch and a cigarette; a still, glorious, unclouded day. After a rest we walked back over the hill, and I got a beautiful shot (after a long crawl) at a good stag, with 10 points. "Shot him dead" and he rolled yards and yards down hill.

The stalker insisted I should fire my second barrel at another big fellow, after he had moved 250 yards away. I hit him and he separated from the rest. We should have got him easily, only two damned tourists that had been on Ben Voirlich—one a woman in knickers—came past and scared him. Walked right away up the Stronetrichan Burn for miles; however, ultimately we got him. A most successful day. Donald met me with some milk at Arrie Bridge and I walked home. I longed for you all the time. *Do* come with me once next year and have a shot.

[*To M. V. B.*]   OFFICE OF WORKS,
                                             OCTOBER 10TH.

Fashoda.   . . . To-day I came up early, and have never been out of this office. I lunched here off cold chicken—and have rather a head-ache in consequence. Perhaps it is the result of the war scare this morning; although I cannot think the French will push the thing to extremities. They are in such difficulties about Dreyfus and other domestic matters that they might welcome war as a distraction. It would be too silly to quarrel over a place which is nothing but a swamp in central Africa: and which not one man in ten thousand had ever heard of a month ago.[1]

[*To M. V. B.*]   OFFICE OF WORKS,
OCTOBER 12TH.

. . . To-day there were two telegrams from Egypt to Lord *Fashoda.* Salisbury—one from Kitchener—opening the door of retreat to the French—and making a suggestion that we should give a little island down the Nile to Marchand to which he could retire. Lord Salisbury has sat upon the plan, and insists that he should retire unconditionally.

The other was a very funny telegram from Lord Cromer saying that the effect of our having killed etc. 30,000 dervishes, is that the Sirdar has 30,000 women on his hands and would be very much obliged if he could be instructed how to dispose ot them, as he has no use for them himself!

[*To M. V. B.*]   OFFICE OF WORKS,
OCTOBER 28TH.

One cannot tell what this day will bring forth—but at the *Fashoda.* Cabinet it was settled that Goschen was to concentrate his fleet and that the French were to be told we could not negotiate until Marchand is out of Fashoda. So that they will have to recall him or fight. It is an anxious moment.

Lord Salisbury was the most worried of the Ministers. The others seemed to take the view that the row would have to come,

---

[1] The decision to reconquer the Sudan was taken in the spring of 1896, and operations were begun in September. They culminated in the battle of Omdurman, in September 1898. It was not until early in 1897 that Major Marchand, with a force of native troops quite inadequate to deal with the Mahdi, left the Congo and forced his way through Central Africa to the Upper Nile. On the other hand he hoisted the tricolor at Fashoda before the victory of Omdurman, in July 1898.

and that it might as well come now as later. This is a state of mind I never quite sympathise with, for it always seems to me that it is so much better for a row to come *later* than sooner.

It is most difficult to see how the French are to get out of this mess, with honour. Of course we shall *do* nothing and Marchand, poor devil, will starve, for they cannot succour him. However, I think that Salisbury's interview, which is to take place with the French ambassador this afternoon, ought to bring the thing to a head.

[*Journals.*]   2, TILNEY STREET,
                                                         OCTOBER 28TH.

Rosebery.   The Eton dinner to George Curzon, Minto and Welldon was a great success. Welldon and Hornby spoke excellently. Of course Rosebery was *hors concours*, as he always is! He and I walked the streets after the dinner from 11.30 until just now (1.30 a.m.). He in his blue ribbon. We talked much about politics, about foreign affairs, the past and the future. He spoke kindly of Harcourt. He still repudiates all desire for office. He feels more physically capable than he did; of that I am confident. He is inclined to think that a war with France now would simplify difficulties in the future. But Bismarck's aims are different. He was making a Nation, not competing for a mudflat. Perhaps this was bravado or paradox on his part.

[*To M. V. B.*]   2, TILNEY STREET,
                                                         NOVEMBER 5TH.

Kitchener.   . . . What a success was the Sirdar's [1] dinner last night. He seems to have made a wonderfully good speech for a soldier.

You saw that at the Gaiety two nights ago he was recognised and all the house rose and cheered him. "Miss Vaughan" was

------
[1] Lord Kitchener.

there, in the front row of the pit, and was perfectly enchanted. The war has blown over for the present, although the risk still remains.

It seems that the French cannot fight at sea in *winter*. They were so advised by their Admiralty experts. The engines of all their ships are too light and cannot stand the wear and tear of bad weather!

[*To M. V. B.*]　　　　　　　　2, TILNEY STREET,
　　　　　　　　　　　　　　　　NOVEMBER 25TH.

. . . After the Quaker[1] party had left, we dressed in the usual quiet finery for the Castle and went to the entertainment. The Waterloo Gallery was beautifully arranged, with a huge orchestra, and a very tiny audience. The Queen wore an unusually low gown, and looked very well. It is curious to see her giving precedence to her daughter, the Empress of Germany, which the latter accepts in a deprecating sort of way. The music was really splendid. I had no idea an orchestra could be so good. In the intervals odd drinks were handed round, among them hot mulled port! Very old-fashioned! We had supper after the usual march past the Queen, and got home about one o'clock.

[*To M. V. B.*]　　　　　　　　OSBORNE,
　　　　　　　　　　　　　　　　JANUARY 26TH, 1899.

. . . We came from Southampton in lovely weather; and *Visit to* were met at Cowes by a royal carriage. When you get to the *Osborne.* door you are met by the Housekeeper, who shows you to your rooms. The Master of the Household—Lord Edward Clinton (Francis Hope's uncle)—also met us. We have a sitting-room as well as a bedroom, and they brought us tea. Then the

---

[1] Queen's Acre, the Windsor home of Howard Sturgis.

Duchess of Roxburgh (Innes-Kerr's mother) carried off Nellie and I went to the equerry's room.

At 9 we dined. It was more "homey" than Windsor—but still very royal. I sat next to Princess Henry and next but one to the Queen. She talked and laughed a good deal. After dinner we all went to the drawing-room—and the women all sat down. I had a long talk with the Queen. It was not nearly so stiff as at Windsor.

To-day there was hockey in the garden. The Princess and the children and the elderly people in waiting all rushing about like maniacs.

We breakfasted with the household and lunched with them. The equerry is Charlie Harbord (Jacob's uncle). After lunch Nellie and Miss Cochrane and I drove with Princess Beatrice to Carisbrooke Castle, where Charles was shut up. A lovely old place (in my charge) of which the Princess is "governor."

We have just got back and had tea. This is our day. I thought you might like a short account of it. I have taken some photographs.

[*To M. V. B.*]   OFFICE OF WORKS,
                                   JANUARY 27TH.

. . . After I wrote to you yesterday I had an interview with the Queen and found her in a queer little room, sitting up at her round table—and then we dined again with her and I had another talk. She was very forthcoming altogether.

. . . It was lovely crossing the Solent this morning—a brilliant sun and not a bit cold. I got back about two, and have not left this office since. Now I am off to O. Lea.

[*To M. V. B.*]   MIDNIGHT,
                                   JANUARY 31ST.

The Theatre: . . . I was interrupted, and forced to go off and see the Duke
A Court   of Devonshire. Since, I have dined at the Berkeley and been to
Scandal.   the Court Theatre, where we found all the rank, beauty and

fashion of London assembled. It is a pretty play,[1] and when you come for leave you must see it. Of that there is no doubt. There is much about it that will captivate you—like my tutor's lecture—and there are at least two beautiful faces to look at.

I will tell you about it when we meet. Seymour Hicks plays it quite intelligently, and looks very well. . . .

In the play I saw to-night, one of the most effective people is Miriam Clements, that girl admired by George Edwardes. She is wonderfully handsome. Fanny Ward was in a box, most smartly decked out as usual. There were rows of beauties in the stalls!!

Tomorrow I lunch at Stafford House and had hoped to come down and see you for tea—if convenient to you—but perhaps I shall get hitched up by my friends—or perhaps you may not want me.

On the death of President Faure it was feared that the various forces in alliance against Dreyfus—the Clericals, the Royalists, the Militarists, the Anti-Semites—would attempt to overthrow the Republic. Had the President died less suddenly they might have done so. In the event, nothing occurred but some shouting in the streets.

The Duc d'Orléans addressed a deputation of French artisans at Brussels on January 30th, and a deputation of 200 Royalists from Hérault at San Remo on February 17th. Both speeches were anti-Semitic. They were also confused and pointless. For a very caustic account, see *The Times* of February 18th.

[*To the Rev. C. D. Williamson.*] ORCHARD LEA,
FEBRUARY 19TH.

. . . Faure[2] was lucky to die. He would have hated private life—after his inevitable dethronement. He was on the verge of a series of attacks in his domestic life—just the sort of thing that

---

[1] *A Court Scandal.*   [2] President of the French Republic.

would have made him wretched. Did you ever read anything more imbecile than the Duc d'Orléans' speech? However, I am glad to see that the Bourbon continues to "forget nothing, and remember nothing." They are natural foes of England.

[To M. V. B.]   OFFICE OF WORKS,
                                        FEBRUARY 21ST.

. . . Also a letter from R. Lister, and one from Oliver. You will glean all the Paris news. Evidently Nolly saw all that was to be seen from the outside, and I daresay had the best of the fun. I hear that there were several charges of cavalry in the Paris streets, in which the men used their sabres. But no shots were fired. There is a queer account of the new President's mother, an old peasant woman with sabots, and a white cap and mahogany face. I don't think he will last long, unless he develops some wonderful latent strength of character.

I went to lunch in New Court with the Rothschild family; and have been frightfully pestered all day.[1] I shall only just have time to catch the train when I finish this letter.

[1] A typical but unusually humorous letter runs:

                                        FOREIGN OFFICE,
                                        FEBRUARY 8TH.
MY DEAR BRETT,

We have incurred Lord Salisbury's displeasure!!! His clock stopped at 2.30 p.m. and deceived him! As he has lost two trains lately through the vagaries of this uncertain instrument, he lowered his voice to a threatening bass when I entered his apartment and demanded the execution of the clock-winder and the substitution of another time-piece.

I duly sharpened the official axe but discovered to my discomfiture that some time ago in a fit of economy our official clockman was discontinued and that the clocks are now wound by the Head Office Keeper and regulate themselves.

Could you give us back our clockman? The clocks are very nice presentable ones and only want an expert, I imagine. Everyone admires our room and we daily bless the name of Benefactor Brett.

                              Ever sincerely yours,
                                        HENRY FOLEY.

[*Journals.*]   ORCHARD LEA,
                                              MARCH 3RD.

Went to a Ball at Stafford House last night. M.[1] at the top of
the staircase all in black with the gorgeous Marie Antoinette
necklace round her throat was a sight not easily forgotten.

[*To M. V. B.*]   OFFICE OF WORKS,
                                              MARCH 8TH.

. . . I have been lunching at Willis' with Arthur Balfour,
Gladys and de Grey. Soveral—the Portuguese minister—whom
they call the "Blue Monkey"—came in after and joined us. He
is a sort of Cyrano—a very ugly but hyper-smart person—who
is so attractive that all women love him. I think I have pointed
him out to you often. I went up to see Vi. Rosslyn for a moment—but she was having her arm tattooed! an extraordinary
mania. The portrait of her terrier was being reproduced on her
arm. *So* silly. She will probably regret it frightfully hereafter,
as I don't see how she can wear a low gown! Gloves, I suppose
will hide it.

[*To M. V. B.*]   OFFICE OF WORKS,
                                              MARCH 17TH.

. . . On Sunday there are to be notices in the newspapers of *On Plays.*
George Edwardes' new play for the autumn; and puffs of Letty
[Lind]!
I think she is only *half* pleased at the honour of starting on a
new line of business. Really rather frightened, as she is not sure
whether she can make a success or not. However, I am tranquil,
as she is one of those people who always rise to the occasion.
. . . One of the things we will go and see in the holidays is
Martin Harvey in *The Only Way*. He is the coming Irving.
However, there are many things we have to see this holiday.

[1] Millicent, Duchess of Sutherland.

[*To M. V. B.*]   THE DURDANS,
                                                  APRIL 30TH.

There is no one here but Sybil and Rosebery. I think Asquith
comes tonight about dinner time. When I got here I found
Rosebery just prepared to walk or drive. A carriage with a
postilion very smartly dressed was waiting. We chose a walk
and went round the Derby course, which is just outside the
grounds, and talked hard all the time, so that the mile and three-
quarters seemed nothing, and I never noticed Tattenham Corner.
The house is fuller of pictures and relics and books than ever.
The latest arrival is a set of shutters from the house at St. Helena
in which Napoleon lived, with holes bored in them through
which he could point his gun. You remember that he had to
shoot at a mark in the garden.

After dinner we sat and gossiped until half-past 12—a great
deal about Eton past and present.

. . . Rosebery asks endless questions about you, but how
can I explain that you and I walk side by side through life,
and that you are not dragged behind with a rope, after the
fashion of such relationships generally. Our friends are the
same, our interests the same, and there is complete confidence
and mutual help. And all that is an education in itself is it not?
But how difficult to explain to outsiders! Rosebery is full of
ambition for himself and the boys.

[*To M. V. B.*]   OFFICE OF WORKS,
                                                  MAY 1ST.

After I wrote to you from the Durdans, we drove, and returned to tea, when Asquith arrived. His son has got the
Brackenbury at Oxford, a Balliol scholarship, and all sorts of
things.

. . . To-day we came up early, and I went at 12 to Kensington
Palace. The P. of W. turned up, and Princess Louise came out

of her apartments. We went all over the Palace, stopped opposite the lovely Marlboro' picture, and then lunched with Princess Louise—only four of us including the Prince. I did not get here till 3 o'clock.

I see that Georgie Grossmith's play is only a half success, but I daresay they will work it up into something good. I never care very much for those screaming burlesques.

[*To M. V. B.*] OFFICE OF WORKS,
MAY 5TH.

. . . To-day I lunched with Mr. Stead whom I had not seen *On Stead.* for four months. He is off to Russia to see the Tzar again—on Monday. He is wild and odd as ever, and thinks he has inherited the spirit of Charles II, who—through him—is making amends for his previous life on earth!

Pretty good loony! All his female friends he endows with the attributes of Charles' mistresses! If he wasn't so sane in other matters he would have to be shut up. I shall try and see you as I cross the bridge tonight. Lord E.[1] comes up tomorrow to London. It is really a most wonderful recovery. If you had seen him that first day, you would not have thought it possible. I am going to Ascot tomorrow and shall leave by the 7.42 on Sunday morning. It is the only way in which I can get down to Windsor in time to see you. But for that I would start at any hour.

[*To M. V. B.*] ORCHARD LEA,
MAY 8TH.

. . . You really *must* get Tutor to suggest something for the Queen's birthday. Anyhow, if nothing else is done, you should have all the volunteers in the quadrangle for the trooping of the Colour—and then march past the Queen.

[1] His father.

I think I shall suggest that to the Head! I have just been to Ennismore Gardens. The invalid[1] is much better but of course very weak. He was down in the drawing-room, and went out for a drive. We dine with Rosebery, and I don't feel much interested in the dinner. I have a sort of notion that it will be exceedingly dull! It is clear that until after the 17th when the Foundation Stone business[2] takes place I shall be overworked. Such a nuisance—as it cannot be a great and interesting thing like the Jubilee and yet it gives as much bother. I lunched with Bigge at Willis'. The de Greys were there and a few more society people, but no one interesting.

Victoria and Albert Museum.

[*To M. V. B.*]   OFFICE OF WORKS,
MAY 9TH.

I am in *such* a bustle over this function on the 17th that I have hardly a moment in which to write to you. The dinner with Rosebery went off well. I sat between Lady Helen Vincent, whom you met at Esher Place, and Lady Essex. Two very pretty women, so *I* was all right.

To-day I lunched at Willis' with Gladys [de Grey] and

[1] His father.
[2] Victoria and Albert Museum. Six months previously Sir Arthur Bigge had written:

BALMORAL CASTLE,
OCT. 15TH.

MY DEAR BRETT,

The Prince of Wales is very glad to hear that there is every reason to think the foundation stone of S. Kensington can be laid in the Spring. I think H.R.H. regrets the change of name as he says Sth. K. Museum is as familiar as Buckingham Palace or St. Paul's Cathedral. However he is consoled that it is to be "Victoria and Albert" and not "Albert" alone.

I will let H.M. know about Kensington Palace. Meanwhile Spencer Fane has sent up proposals among others that you, he, and Robinson should form a Ctee. to arrange what shall be sent to Kensington. I hope the Queen will approve of this. . . .

ARTHUR BIGGE.

Juliette. She is taller than her mother! Isn't that awful? Then Maysie [May Yohé] called in her victoria to ask me to luncheon on Thursday. Too sweet for words. *So* smart and pretty.

The Queen comes to Kensington Palace on the 15th—another scurry. Still I hope to get down to you tomorrow at tea at 6.

[*To M. V. B.*]   2, TILNEY STREET,
MAY 15TH.

. . . I went down to Windsor mainly to avoid newspaper *The Queen's* reporters who are making life a burden. Down by the 7 train, *Memories.* and back by the 10.10. For all day I have been on and off at Kensington Palace. This morning with the Queen in the home of her youth—and after 60 years. She came with the Hesses, and Princess Beatrice. She would have no one to meet her except me. She was carried upstairs in her chair, and I received her at the door and never left her chair until she re-entered the carriage. She talked all the time of her childhood, her accession, and her dolls! It was a queer and interesting experience. I had to go afterwards to Marlborough House to see the Prince, and meet the Duke of York who—with Princess May—insisted *Princess May.* on coming to Kensington Palace this afternoon, so returned with them. He is a good fellow, very boyish. *She* is educating herself carefully, and will be a woman of much importance later on. The Queen's memory and knowledge are quite wonderful. I like to tell you my day, and hope that it is not wearisome.

[*Telegram.*]   MAY 18TH.

The Queen wishes me to say how much she appreciated your excellent arrangements to-day.[1] H.M. was very pleased with everything. Edwards.

[1] At the Victoria and Albert Museum,

[*From Sir Francis Knollys.*]   MARLBOROUGH HOUSE,
MAY 18TH.

MY DEAR BRETT,

The Prince of Wales desires me to repeat in writing what he said by word to you yesterday, that he thought nothing could have gone off better than the ceremony, without a single hitch or drawback, and that all the arrangements were admirably carried out. I have sent up the tickets to see Kensington Palace tomorrow to the Prince of Wales. Many thanks for them.

Yours sincerely,

FRANCIS KNOLLYS.

[*To M. V. B.*]   OFFICE OF WORKS,
MAY 18TH.

. . . I had a very appreciative telegram from the Queen about yesterday. I send you a letter to read. You are the only person in the world who sees all my letters. Is not the writer an attractive friend? I also send you another note, which shows that my plans for to-day were upset. I am just off to Ennismore Gardens, where I fear things are not going over well.[1] They want to have another doctor. I think it is *so* useless to worry over the inevitable. What good can a doctor do? And it only fusses him needlessly.

[*To M. V. B.*]   OFFICE OF WORKS,
MAY 23RD.

Dinner with the Queen.   The dinner was a great success. It was really quite an amusing and pleasant dinner for me. I was two off the Queen, between the Duchess of Connaught and the young Duchess of Hesse, who is called "Duckie." . . . She was very shy at first, but we got on capitally later, and by the end of dinner there was quite a rag.

[1] His father.

The Queen was extraordinarily vivacious, full of smiles and chaff—a most wonderful thing.

She is devoted to Hesse, who is very attractive to look at, and nice to her. After dinner I had a long talk with the Queen who finally asked all about you and Noll. I had to describe you (fairly) accurately!

[*To M. V. B.*]   TURF CLUB,
MAY 23RD.

I went to Ennismore Gardens at about 6 and found the poor invalid very ill indeed. The doctor injected something and he rallied a little. They did not think he could live through the night, but there is now a hope that he may get over it. If he is better in the morning, I shall run down to see Nellie at O. Lea and you. If not I shall telegraph to you the news in the course of the day. Violet [1] has come up to London.

Lord Esher's Death.

I *hope* he will survive a little longer for Mama's sake, though hardly for his own.

[*Journals.*]   2, TILNEY STREET,
MAY 23RD.

This night my beloved father died.

[*To M. V. B.*]   2, TILNEY STREET,
MAY 24TH.

Only a line, I am so overdone. I have just been down to Esher to see Uncle Wilford [2] and make necessary arrangements. It was a peaceful death. As I told you he was sleeping when I left Ennismore Gardens at 11 last night, and at 4 o'clock this

Lord Esher's Death—

[1] His sister, the Hon. Mrs. Dudley Ward.
[2] Sir Wilford Brett, K.C.M.G.

morning he merely ceased to breathe. There was not a movement of any kind. He said good-bye to me yesterday, and
sent his blessing to Noll and you.

It has been a wonderfully successful life, and happy—and he
dies, as he wished to die, peacefully, and without seeing Mama
go first. So all is well, and there need be no regrets. I shall go
down home to-night—and come up to-morrow.

On Monday, I think at 11, at Esher, he will be buried. I shall
hope to have you and Noll there, and the Ward boys, and
Uncle Wilford. We don't want anybody else.

I shall do all I can to keep the others away. You go on with
your rowing and your usual life. It is what he would have
wished, and what I would wish, were I in his place. Death has
no terrors.

[*To M. V. B.*]   OFFICE OF WORKS,
                                             MAY 25TH.

—and
Funeral.   . . . *He* looks very beautiful lying among a lot of flowers—
and I wish you could see him. Oliver is coming over for Monday. I think it is right he should. I mean everything to be very
simple and quiet and no strangers. I shall not be allowed to quit
the office—I can see that—although it is an unusual proceeding to
remain on, as a peer. It *bores* me so, being in a new dress under
a new name!

[*From Sir Arthur Bigge.*]   WINDSOR CASTLE,
                                             MAY 25TH.

MY DEAR BRETT,

To-day I wrote to P. McDonnell to say that the Queen and
Prince of Wales are most anxious that you should remain at the
Office of Works. The Queen spoke to me of you and your work
there in the highest terms this afternoon. I cannot see what

objection can be raised so long as you take no active part in the H. of Lords.

Yours very truly,
ARTHUR BIGGE.

[*From Mr. Balfour to Sir Francis Mowatt.*[1]]

10, DOWNING STREET,
MAY 25TH.

MY DEAR SIR FRANCIS,

I should be very sorry indeed to think that there was any probability that Lord Esher's accession to the title should deprive the public of his services in his present place. So far as I am able to judge he does his work admirably, and it is not, I think, a prejudice born of five and twenty years of unbroken friendship which makes me think that future First Lords of the Treasury will have very special reason for congratulating themselves if, when they have to do business with the permanent head of the Office of Works, they find that Lord Esher has consented to retain that position.

Yours very sincerely,
ARTHUR JAMES BALFOUR.

[*To M. V. B.*]

OFFICE OF WORKS,
MAY 30TH.

I must address this letter in the new way to you—I don't enjoy my new name. The old signature seems to rest on so much that was dear to me. These landmarks on the path of life that thrust themselves into prominence, are not happy or cheerful ones. We were so happy as we were! . . .

On taking the Title.

---

[1] Head of the Treasury.

[*To M. V. B.*]   2, TILNEY STREET,
                                                        JULY 1ST.

I have a few minutes before catching my train, so I may as well tell you what I have been doing, *in case* I miss you to-day.

This morning I signed Loulou [Harcourt]'s settlement at the splendid Burns home in Brook Street. He wasn't there when I arrived and Walter was in bed, so I was received by the girl. She is young and fresh with nice hair.

. . . I saw all the presents, which are gorgeous. Such jewels and things. Almost too gorgeous.

. . . I then had to go and see Lansdowne for a bit of business, and then lunched at Willis'. All the seats crammed. Kitchener was there with a large party. That beautiful Miss Kitty Clarke (now Mrs. Martineau), Vi Rosslyn, Molly Sneyd, Mrs. Hwfa ; in fact all the fashion. I lunched with Gladys and de Grey.

The Duke of York wants to go to Studley to shoot, and they were fussing about that. He will get a good shoot in August.

I wonder if you remember *our* day on the moors. It was a long time ago. Do you remember the huts, and our walk over the heather home—and lying out on the heather before we started the homeward drive. I remember every detail.

[*To M. V. B.*]   OFFICE OF WORKS,
                                                        JULY 3RD.

. . . I had a very nice letter from the president of the Leander Club—saying that in memory of old oarsmanship, etc. they wanted me to be a member of the club. I have, of course, accepted. Very nice little compliment. I can therefore use the lawn, or whatever they call it, at Henley, if the spirit moves us.

[*To M. V. B.*]   OFFICE OF WORKS,
                                                        JULY 10TH.

The Tower.

. . . This morning I have been to the Tower to investigate a new secret passage just discovered between the White Tower and the river—a sort of oubliette like those of Catherine de Medici at the Louvre. It was a horrible descent down a steep ladder, with water at the bottom, just as Dumas described it in La Reine Margot. Very unpleasant.

[*To M. V. B.*] OFFICE OF WORKS,
JULY 11TH.

. . . There is very different news to-day from S. Africa. And it looks as if the Government will cave in to Chamberlain. In that case there will be war. Such a horror—and a crime too— so that the atmosphere is rather depressing. *The Boer War Looming.*

[*To M. V. B.*] 2, TILNEY STREET,
JULY 18TH.

. . . Just returned from *Lord Quex*. It bears seeing a second time wonderfully well. Sophy Fulgarney[1] was as fascinating as ever—and Lord Quex[2] himself has improved. No acting could be more finished. I still think the ending unnecessarily cynical, and rather inclined to be stagey; but the third act is incomparably good. *" The Gay Lord Quex."*
. . . I lunched with Mrs. Leo Rothschild and met the little French woman who knew all about the latest Dreyfus scandals. Several good stories and interesting details about Faure's death. The lady was a very pretty woman (I mean Faure's lady) called Mme. ——, with gorgeous hair. His fit was so sudden that his grasp of her hair was inextricable, and a great lock of it had to be cut off and remained in his fingers.

[*To M. V. B.*] ORCHARD LEA,
JULY 26TH.

Lord Kitchener came to see me to-day. He wants help to build and furnish the Gordon Palace at Khartoum, where he is *On Kitchener.*

[1] Played by Miss Irene Vanbrugh. [2] Played by Sir John Hare.

to live. It is strange, after all these years, to be connected with the raising of that house, where Gordon fell, and from which he wrote to me just before his death.

Kitchener is not attractive. None of the men who served with him were attracted to him. I should doubt anyone loving him. It is the coarseness of his fibre, which appears in his face in a marked degree. The eyes are good—but the mouth and jaw and skin are all those of a rough private. Some of Napoleon's marshals, sprung from the ranks, were such men as he. He is to come and see me again on Saturday. Nothing else happened to-day.

[*To M. V. B.*]   OFFICE OF WORKS,
                                        JULY 27TH.

. . . Luckily this day has been crammed up with ordinary business. Lord Cromer came this morning and remained about two hours, going through all his business. He shares the personal coolness towards Kitchener which appears to be felt by everyone who comes in contact with him.

Then I had to go to the Treasury, and was bored to death for two hours. It is all very wholesome and reduces one to a proper level of insignificance before the stars. When Adam was turned out of Paradise, he found work the only solace—good hard delving of the soil.

[*To M. V. B.*]   THE ROMAN CAMP,
                                        SEPTEMBER 26TH.

You certainly carried off the sunshine, and you would find it difficult to imagine the soaking I got on the Burn yesterday. I went up alone, and thought of you all through the solitary walk, and of our happy life together. Meanwhile the rain came down and the wind blew! I got half a dozen trout, rather good ones, and then was too frozen to go on. My gun was at the Farm, and

Nellie had walked up there and left me some short-bread, which was an unexpected treat.

As I got to the "Bees" I saw a queer elongated figure crawling up the hill towards the stooks on the field where you so often walked round the corner for blackcock.

It was Stanley stalking! He was drenched to the skin, but wildly excited. He crept on his tummy from stook to stook— and about 40 blackcock were in range of him the whole time— he could see them but could not judge the distance. They were suspicious and moved slowly away—he in pursuit.

The spectacle was irresistible and I watched him for about 40 minutes. At last he made up his mind, loosed off his two barrels, and the cock flew majestically away—unharmed.

. . . To-morrow, if the weather is possible, I go stalking.

[*From the Rt. Hon. J. Chamberlain.*]   HIGHBURY, BIRMINGHAM,
OCTOBER 3RD.

MY DEAR ESHER,

Whatever other faults the War Office may have, I do not think anyone will be able to accuse them of trying to do things on the cheap at the present time. The bill will be something tremendous. I am afraid we have a tough job, but the fight had to come sooner or later.

The Boer War.

Yours very truly,
J. CHAMBERLAIN.

[*To M. V. B.*]   THE ROMAN CAMP,
OCTOBER 4TH.

. . . I send you two very interesting letters. I wrote to Joe [Chamberlain] about the numbers of troops.[1] He seems satisfied. I hope he is right.

Need of Troops.

[1] For the Boer War.

Cook is the Editor of the *Daily News* and is in close touch with Milner and his friends. I think 50,000 men *may* do the job if it has to be done, but with less it would be very risky.

The "poor old War Office" is a precious long time about mobilising their Army Corps.

[*From the Rt. Hon. J. Chamberlain.*]   40, PRINCES GARDENS,
OCTOBER 11TH.

MY DEAR ESHER,

Many thanks. I heard from Eckardstein this morning to the same effect. I am not in the least anxious about foreign complications. It is a pleasant habit of our dear friends on the Continent to show their teeth when we are engaged with another dog. But in certain tempers of the British public these demonstrations are dangerous, and if I were "a Frenchman or a Roosian or a Proosian" I should be inclined not to twist the lion's tail at this precise juncture.

Yours very truly,
J. CHAMBERLAIN.

[*To M. V. B.*]   OFFICE OF WORKS,
OCTOBER 13TH.

There is a big fight (so it is thought on White's telegram) going on at the moment.[1] I only hope it will go well. If it doesn't, all the Foreign Powers will squeeze us, and we shall have a lot of blackmail to pay.

. . . It will be most unpleasant if we get a check. I feel all the sort of tingling which one feels before a house match. It is nervous work. The French are making themselves very disagreeable, and are moving a big fleet to the Mediterranean.

[1] There was actually no engagement yet in progress except an attack on an ammunition train, resulting in the capture by the Boers of an officer and fifteen men. This was the first engagement of the war.

Lord Salisbury ordered the Channel Fleet to the Mediterranean to-day. Which is a very unusual step.

Altogether, it is difficult just now to think of anything else but war. Of course, if we score heavily in an engagement with the Boers, the atmosphere will clear but if we have a check, the jealous powers of Europe will make it very hot for us.

[*To M. V. B.*] OFFICE OF WORKS,
NOVEMBER 2ND.

No news to-day except that the French fleet have gone *The* through the canal to Madagascar, and George Curzon telegraphs *French* from India that he thinks they mean an intrigue on the Persian *Fleet.* Gulf and wants them shadowed. Lord Salisbury won't do this. But he sent for the French Ambassador and told him that we were very hard up for coal in S. Africa, that we had bought every available ton, and that he hoped the French ships would not ask for coal from our captains, as they would be forced to refuse! This is rather an ingenious way of hampering their movements, for they have no coaling stations except Madagascar, which is insufficient.

No one knew if Buller has gone to Durban. He has not informed the W.O. of his movements. I think it quite likely that he may have gone there—but he would not wish it to be known.

[*To M. V. B.*] OFFICE OF WORKS,
NOVEMBER 3RD.

George Binning came to see me last night. He will be *"The* gazetted Colonel of the Blues in a day or two. Old Brocklehurst *Blues"* has gone off with most of his capable men, and the Regiment is *Going* rather decimated. George, as Colonel, cannot go to war. He *Out.* sends a contingent—including Reggie Ward and Marjoribanks. He refuses to send Castlereagh as he is just going to be married. Tullibardine has gone. His wife saw him off, and then came

straight up to George with a message to urge him to get Tullibardine sent up to the front—as he is at the *Base* on some
business or other.

George thought it very plucky and sweet of her. George was
shooting at Mellerstain. Got home wet through at 6.30, found
a telegram "Rg. for service" and caught the 7.30 at *Kelso*! Not
bad. Left Katie in tears, of course. He is not going himself so all
is well. Brock is a Major-General! I asked how Herbert [1] was
getting on. George says he is very quiet and shy, but doesn't
seem a bad fellow! That description would have surprised
Herbert a few months ago. I think George likes being in command. He will be much more severe, and much "smarter" than
old Brock. I only hope he won't be too hard on fellows.

. . . I went to the Turf Club last night after George had been
here. It was crammed with fellows all talking about the war.
Jack Durham was there, proud of Hedworth of course. The
arrival of the sailors at Ladysmith raised the spirits of the Army
20%. They were full of fun, jolly as if it was all a picnic.

[*To M. V. B.*]   OFFICE OF WORKS,
                                        NOVEMBER 6TH.

. . . The Government have settled to mobilise another 10,000
men, and it is not too soon to do so. All our troubles come from
not taking time by the forelock. I saw Reggie Lister to-day,
who says it is awful in Paris—à bas les Anglais is shouted everywhere. Very disagreeable for him. He was rather funny about
White. "I hate your dashing generals. Give me a good
poltroon who makes plans!"

[*To M. V. B.*]   2, TILNEY STREET,
                                        NOVEMBER 9TH.

. . . I have just come back from the Guild Hall. I sat between
Admiral Douglas—who responded for the Navy—and a

---

[1] Afterwards Lord Pembroke.

foreign ambassador. The sailor was a good chap. Hedworth *Hedworth*
Lambton *is* shut up in Ladysmith. It appears that he made up *Lambton.*
his mind coming back from China that he would go to the front
—bought khaki for his sailors, and went up *without orders*! Sent
his application for leave *after* he had started. There is a Nelson
ring about that. Also he found a regiment at the Mauritius
(where he bought his khaki!) under orders for war, waiting for
transport. He packed them all on board the *Powerful* and took
them with him! Also without orders. Wasn't it dashing?
Lord Salisbury made an excellent speech. No one else was good.
The thing began at 6 and I am just home at 20 to 11. Beastly
long. All day I have been fussed about the Queen's gift to her
soldiers. I think it will be chocolate, but it can't be done under *The*
£5,000. It is a lot of money. There are, or rather will be, *Queen's*
100,000 men in S. Africa. What an army! I am wrong— *Chocolate.*
Wolseley made an excellent speech.

[*To M. V. B.*]   OFFICE OF WORKS,
                                    NOVEMBER 14TH.

. . . I am going to the Castle in about a quarter of an hour and
I was prevented from writing my letter in London by having to
go and see Wolseley just before I started. He is in good spirits *Wolseley*
to-day, and believes that the Boers have shot their bolt, and will *on the*
soon collapse. He is, however, an optimist, just as Buller is a *War.*
pessimist. So I suppose the truth lies half way between, and
that we shall win very soon now, only it will be after one or
two hard fights. He was very nice.

[*To M. V. B.*]   ORCHARD LEA,
                                    NOVEMBER 19TH.

I send you a dear little poem by Newbolt; the sort of thing
which must appeal—like that chapter in Stalky about the "old
boy" match—to every school.

Anyone who can read that chapter without a lump in his throat must be made of iron. It seems that Baden Powell, just before being shut up in Mafeking, wrote a little book on scouting which I shall get to-morrow, and if it looks interesting, shall send it to you.

[*To M. V. B.*]   OFFICE OF WORKS,
                                         NOVEMBER 23RD.

There was an element of flatness at the Castle last night. The Queen did not dine—owing to the death of Princess Leiningen. She dined alone with two ladies. The Artillery band played splendidly and looked so nice. C. would have been proud of his gunners.

There were some Etonian representatives there. Hornby, the Head, Austen Leigh, and Arthur Benson. I have got to meet the

Kaiser   Emperor at the Wolsey Chapel on Saturday at a quarter to
Wilhelm II.   eleven. I wonder what he will be like? The girls [1] saw him shooting on Tuesday. Biked to the rendezvous; and remained there for hours, quite close. He was dressed in light blue with a tyrolese hat, and a blackcock's feather. He has four men also in blue, with four guns. The gun is handed to him full cock, and he shoots with one arm (the other is withered as you know). He shoots wonderfully well—but I daresay the gun-handing is a bit dangerous. He killed 178 pheasants and 330 rabbits. Not so bad.

[*To M. V. B.*]   OFFICE OF WORKS,
                                         NOVEMBER 24TH.

Chamber-   My journey down yesterday with Chamberlain was rather
lain on   interesting. He is such a devil of a fellow. So frank and straight
the War.   and unlike the ordinary politician or official.

[1] His daughters.

He is disappointed at the result of the war so far—and no wonder. But he won't express any final opinion until all the facts are known. Buller tells them nothing. His interview with the German Emperor will be interesting. Both strong, frank men. Very different from their kind. I daresay there was much mutual respect.

To-day I took Wolseley to lunch at Brooks'. He also had a talk with the Emperor; who told him that the Germans had made a plan of campaign for S. Africa, which they would have carried out, had they been in our place; that they knew all *our* plans and numbers of troops, etc.; that they also had spotted all our mistakes. They put the Boer forces much higher than we do. Wolseley told me that White had muddled the whole thing, that it is elementary strategy when you see that you may be cut off from your base, to retire towards it; and that when he found he could not hold Ladysmith, he should have retired to the Tugela—blown up his magazines, and destroyed his food. As it is he is caught in a trap, and it takes an army to get him out, dislocating all Buller's plans by the way! Even now it would be better for him to break out and lose a quarter of his men. He is a gallant fellow but no strategist. Wolseley says that French asked for old Brock [Brocklehurst] as the best cavalry leader in England. That is good!

The Kaiser on the War.

Wolseley on Lady-smith.

[*To M. V. B.*] ORCHARD LEA,
NOVEMBER 26TH.

. . . I rather enjoyed my morning with the Emperor. . . . He is like an ordinary man, with genius, and not hidebound by conventionalities. He asked me to send him some sketches of houses like O'Lea to Berlin, as a present. He noticed the house driving past, and he wants red houses of that kind built in Germany!

The Kaiser.

[*To M. V. B.*]   OFFICE OF WORKS,
NOVEMBER 27TH.

The 9th
Lancers.

. . . The news in the papers is rather disquieting, although we win "victories." The 9th Lancers are a worry. It may be that they have got into some trap. You see Methuen's first fight only drove back the Boers *six miles*! Hardly further than from O'Lea to Windsor. That is not a very big "victory." When you think of Napoleon riding from Waterloo to Paris ! ! !

[*To Mr. W. T. Stead.*]   ORCHARD LEA,
DECEMBER 3RD.

. . . I have been offered the Aquarium for the Government. We do not require it—but think of it as a sight for (1) Newspaper office. (2) Club. (3) Library. (4) Meeting hall with the finest organ in Great Britain.

I tell you, Harmsworth would be knocked out! So would the Primrose League.

[*To M. V. B.*]   ORCHARD LEA,
DECEMBER 6TH.

Schemes
for Eton.

. . . I wrote yesterday to Cust, who has published a book upon Eton, that he should get up a subscription limited to £5 per head, for building a new speech room at Eton, and turning Upper School into a school library—in memory of Myers and of Etonians fallen in this war. I think there would be at least 2000 Etonians and O.E.s who would give a fiver apiece, and that would produce enough to do the job. Upper School would make a splendid library—with book-cases at right angles to the wall leaving all the old benches and names as they are.

There would be nooks and corners with tables, and it ought to be very comfy.

The position of the new speech room would be more difficult, but I don't see why it should not be built in the region of Weston's Yard, sticking out into the playing fields beyond the College Buildings.

Do you think the Ed. of the *Ch.* [*Chronicle*] would take up the subject? I shall send you Cust's reply if I get one.

[*To M. V. B.*]   OFFICE OF WORKS,
                                         DECEMBER 8TH.

... The dinner went off well. The Queen was in good spirits *The* and talked to me a good deal at dinner and afterwards. I was *Queen.* next but one to her, between Princess Beatrice and Lady Dudley. The latter looked very well, stately and young to be the mother of all those Wards! A telegram came at dinner and the Queen turned quite pale. She said it made her ill to open telegrams about the war. She talked to me after dinner about you, and was interested to hear that you were going to serve her. She said she was glad you were not in the Army just now. She asked me if I had seen her new portrait by Angeli, and when I said no, had it sent for into the corridor. It is wonderfully like.

I think you will have to be presented to her before she dies. We must manage it in the summer.

[*To M. V. B.*]   OFFICE OF WORKS,
                                         DECEMBER 12TH.

So sorry I cannot get down to-day. I should have liked to so *Colonial* much—as I want to talk to you badly. *Office*

I was offered yesterday the Under-Secretaryship of State to *Declined.* the Colonies. It would mean leaving my office and going under Joe [Chamberlain]. Of course it would be interesting and it is a very high post. But I don't fancy Joe much as a Chief, and I think all the Colonial bosses I should have to cope with are second rate.

Just now, with this African affair going on, it would be interesting—but—I doubt whether, with a man like Chamberlain, one could do much to influence the result, when it comes to settling the country. If it had been the War Office, I think I should have said yes.

However, I will explain it all to you in detail when I see you. I enclose my answer to Mowatt. I consulted Rosebery and he agrees with me.

[*To Sir Francis Mowatt.*]   OFFICE OF WORKS,
                                           DECEMBER 12TH.

Colonial
Office.

I have thought over the question you put to me, and while full of gratitude to you for the suggestion, there are personal reasons which incline me to stay where I am. Of course, it would be absurd to deny that I should like to take a hand, however indifferently played, in S. Africa after the war, but other considerations which I will explain to you when we meet, outweigh this one.

For the Colonial Office I have never had much fancy, and the work would not be congenial to me, as would be the case at one or two of the other great offices. Nor am I vain enough to think in my case there is any call of public duty to make me abandon the Works.

I have given the matter as much consideration as I could in the time, and I think that when I have an opportunity of explaining to you my reasons, you will not altogether withhold your sympathy.

[*From Sir Francis Mowatt.*]   DECEMBER 12TH.

MY DEAR ESHER,

Many thanks for the friendly tone of your letter. When a man in my position is so near his setting, his constant anxiety must be to have each of the great depts. in the strongest hands he can find.

Whether you stay at the Works or are transferred elsewhere, I shall always know that I have a colleague with whom I can work, and in whom I can trust.

Yours very truly,
FRANCIS MOWATT.

[*To M. V. B.*]   OFFICE OF WORKS,
DECEMBER 13TH.

. . . Miserable news about Methuen. A repulse is a serious *Lady-* thing just now. I don't think Buller will be surprised, but he *smith.* will be vexed. He will be a long time before he can do anything himself as the road to Ladysmith *direct* is impassable. He will have to go round about 50 miles, and it will take a long time. What a job the whole thing is! Little was the difficulty foreseen. . . .

. . . It makes it difficult to think or write of anything else. *Chamber-* The more I think it over, the gladder I am that I refused the *lain's* Colonial Office. It would have been very disagreeable to go *bility.* through all this, to have to work for Chamberlain, at whose door so much of this trouble lies.

Sometimes one is justified in refusing another colour. I think this is the case! A telegram has just come saying that Andie Wauchope has fallen. Poor chap—a gallant fellow. He was the man who proposed to Ces Baillie-Hamilton, George Binning's sister, and she refused him. He married about two years ago.

This war will do two things—change our whole military *Strategic* system in England, and alter military tactics throughout the *Lessons.* world. The old war of "sieges" will begin again. It is clear that a direct attack, with modern weapons, against good and brave men entrenched, is impossible.

[*To Sir William Harcourt.*]   OFFICE OF WORKS,
                                        DECEMBER 15TH.

*The
Colonial
Office—*

   I like to let you know my varying fortunes, as you have counted for so much in my life. Mowatt sent for me two days ago, and asked me if I would like to go to the Colonial Office. Herbert is doing the work temporarily, but he cannot go on with it, and Wingfield is permanently hors de combat. I asked for 24 hours to think it over, and regretted that you were not near, as I should have been glad of your advice.

*—and
Chamber-
lain.*

   After talking it over with Nellie, I decided to remain here. Under other circumstances, and auspices other than Chamberlain's, I would have accepted, in view of the great interests which must be involved when this lamentable war is over. But I do not think that with Chamberlain, any opinion of mine would carry weight, and I should have been in the position of a "devil" to him, which seems a particularly low place in the Inferno for anyone voluntarily to occupy.

   So I remain perhaps more humbly, certainly more peaceably, among my bricks and mortar.

   Of course this is a very private matter, and I have not given any definite reason to Mowatt. I shall tell him quietly, some day, my real motive. Do you approve?

[*From Sir William Harcourt.*]   MALWOOD,
                                        DECEMBER 16TH.

DEAR REGGIE,

*Harcourt
on
Colonial
Office.*

   I was most pleased to receive your letter as a proof that you appreciate the true interest and affection I have always felt in all that concerns you and yours. I feel sure that you have made a wise decision. . . . I am very glad the offer has been made to you because it shows the high estimate which has been formed of your capacity and sense by Mowatt—than whom there is no better judge, and you have had placed at your disposal what may be regarded as at this moment the first place in the profession. What news to-day. The plagues of Egypt are indeed overtaking Pharaoh. Was there ever such crass ignorance and presumption. . . .

[*To Sir William Harcourt.*]   OFFICE OF WORKS,
                                                    DECEMBER 18TH.

I am very grateful to you for your letter, and pleased at your approval. I think I was right; although it seems at first sight incumbent upon everyone to help at this juncture; but I don't think I *could* help, and that is the point.

Buller telegraphed an absolute non possumus on Saturday, *Buller* in regard to the passage of the Tugela. His supersession is the *Superseded.* reply. It may restore the morale of the Army which has been rudely shaken. But *what* a national fiasco so far! The series of horrors culminating with the yielding of the Government to the pressure of those who insisted on the holding and the relief of Kimberley.

And what a justification of the unfortunate Butler! However, it is all too wretched to write about.

[*To M. V. B.*]   2, TILNEY STREET,
                       DECEMBER 18TH, VERY LATE AT NIGHT.

Only a line or two. . . .

. . . I send you Jack Durham's letter and speech which will interest you. The appointment of Roberts and Kitchener is the reply of the Government to that pessimistic telegram from Buller of which I told you. These names will restore the morale of the Army which has been rudely shattered.

Bobs is a tower of strength in that way. Poor little chap. But you see how gallant a death his son died, with a certain V.C. to his credit.

The splendour of our fighting is beyond compare, but the tactical errors have been awful.

[*From Lord Ripon.*]   STUDLEY ROYAL, RIPON,
                                    DECEMBER 19TH.

MY DEAR REGGIE,

Lady Ripon has shown me your letter and I hasten to tell you how right I think you have been in refusing to take the appointment at the Colonial Office. You could have done no good there; nobody could, with Chamberlain at one end of the South African cable and Milner at the other. You would have been in a false and hopeless position which you were in no way called upon to accept. . . .

                                    Yours ever,
                                    RIPON.

[*Journals.*]   OFFICE OF WORKS,
                              DECEMBER 20TH.

Ladysmith.   There are some telegrams from Buller to-day. White telegraphs that he can hold out for a month longer than he thought, i.e. a month from Xmas—so that the hurry was not so great after all. It is astonishing that every detail, and on every occasion, information, vital to the issues involved, should be fallacious.

White also suggests employing Indian native troops, to which the Government of course will not agree. They have troops enough. What they want is leadership.

Roberts.   Roberts was very sweet—very dignified and calm, when he was offered the command. Arthur Balfour sent for him, as the appointment was settled against the will of the War Office, by the Cabinet. Roberts, when the offer was made, thought for a few minutes, and then said he would go. He said he had always kept in training, thinking he might be wanted, and was as fit now at 67 as he was ten years ago.

Nothing was said to him about his loss—only business was talked. He evidently had determined to fix his mind exclusively on the work before him. He is a fine fellow. The offer to

Kitchener was made through Cromer, who telegraphed back that Kitchener accepted with delight. He is personally devoted to Roberts, so they will work well together.

[*To Sir Arthur Bigge.*]   OFFICE OF WORKS,
DECEMBER 21ST.

It occurs to me that the Queen might like to place temporarily *Bushey* at the disposal of the sick and wounded, Bushey House, which *House for* would make a capital convalescent Home, owing to the capa- *cent.* cious character of the house, containing, as it does, large rooms, the sheltered gardens, and the fine range of Bushey Park. During the summer no place could be more healthy or more accessible.

Perhaps some of the funds available for such purposes could be used to put the place in proper condition. Of course a certain outlay would be required—not, I think, very large. The house contains no furniture, which is an advantage, as only a certain sort of furniture is desirable, and this would have to be supplied by the committee who have these matters under their charge.

I have not said anything to anyone about this proposal as Her Majesty would of course make the first suggestion, should the idea commend itself.

[*To M. V. B.*]   HOUSE OF LORDS,
JANUARY 30TH, 1900.

... There is nothing but worrying war news to-day. *War* Roberts has telegraphed for the VIIIth Division, and I suppose *News.* it will go. That will leave literally no one in this country. About three battalions! Is it not ludicrous? Now, all depends on Kitchener! He is really our last line of defence. He is *lucky*, which is everything, and this may pull us through.

If he fails it is difficult to see what the result will be. I am sure that very serious difficulties will arise next autumn with France and Russia, unless we are well through this war by that time—

and even then! So that you can imagine the depression of it all. What a horrible fiasco the whole thing is.

. . . I am writing to you from the House of Lords, which is crammed. All anxious to hear Lord Salisbury. They have seldom met under such gloomy conditions. We have to go back to the end of the last century to find comparison.

[*To M. V. B.*]   OFFICE OF WORKS,
                                   JANUARY 31ST.

*On
Rosebery.*

. . . Last night, after I wrote to you, I heard Lord Salisbury, who did not shine as much as usual, and then Rosebery—who made an unpremeditated but extraordinarily good speech. I had not heard him for a long time, and the improvement was very marked. He spoke with much fire, and his gestures, which were so awkward, have got quite good. His voice strong and clear. It was a really first-rate performance. If his character has strengthened since 1896 as much as his speaking he is fit to be Prime Minister. We may want a change badly a few months hence, if things go steadily wrong. I hear that Bobs estimates that the war will last two years. That is rather a sad outlook.

[*To the Rev. C. D. Williamson.*]   OFFICE OF WORKS,
                                         FEBRUARY 8TH.

*On
Buller.*

There is no final news about Buller's last attempt. Everyone is most anxious to hear. Buller has shown no real grip. He eats too much. Roberts, although 67, is twice as hard. The thing will come right finally I suppose.

Did I tell you that the Colonial Office had been again pressed on me—under Sec. of State. But I persist in refusing. I will not "devil" for Joe [Chamberlain].

[*To M. V. B.*]　　OFFICE OF WORKS,
FEBRUARY 13TH.

. . . There is not much news to-day. Just a real good row on *The* between Buller and Bobs. Evidently Buller wants to put some *Generals* of the blame of his failure on to the little man—so he complains *Quarrel.* that reinforcements which were to have gone to Natal have gone to the Cape. Bobs sent a very clever Kitcheneresque tele-gram asking him to specify the date when he asked for the troops (he never asked for any!), also asking him why—when he had been requested to delay his attack until Bobs moved, he had nevertheless attacked—and finally whether Warren approved of abandoning Spion Kop. There is no answer yet. I fancy Buller will be rather stuck up! All this is secret of course. I think a fight has probably taken place with Cronje. I *hope* Bobs is moving to his right, towards Jacobsdaal, and attempting to relieve Kimberley direct. No one knows. He has been asked by the Government not to let even them know his plans. It is a very sensible request.

The old Duke of Cambridge has just been to see me here. He asked about you, and said he hoped you would go into his Regt., that it was altogether the best and happiest life! . . . Everyone, when feelings are strongly engaged, is apt to lose their sense of proportion, and sound judgment. No one of us is exempt from weakness. You see clearly the path along which your friend or acquaintance should walk—but your own way is obscured by roses and thorns, and you tread invariably to the right or to the left. You become so absorbed by the excitement of pursuit, that opinions of others, ordinary rules which you yourself admit in cooler moments to be valid, are all swept to the winds. Everyone else sees that you are walking down a thoroughfare with the white paper round your hat, while you neglect to notice it, or if it occurs to you as a possibility you are too engrossed to take it off for examination. Such is the blinding power of that mischievous little god.

This is not mockery, for heaven knows I have suffered and

still suffer these things. But occasionally a friendly voice will help us to realise what we have for a while forgotten, and save the unwary from falling over the cliff.

[*To M. V. B.*]   ORCHARD LEA,
                                                   FEBRUARY 18TH.

. . . Remember that to love is an art, as we have often agreed. And that one of the really artistic things is not "to tear a passion to tatters," but to establish reserve, even if it did not exist. I know this is hard; but beware of the danger of excess—even in affection. Let the beloved one occasionally hunger for you, as you for her; and be not too prodigal of favour. You see the difficulties; and the obstacles which the conventional world places in the way of your free intercourse have endless advantage.

"Stolen fruit," etc. and numerous other ancient adages are singularly true. You must watch and protect, and beware of yourself as of others. Two things destroy love, which is based on a foundation of passion. One is the absence of reciprocal feeling. The other is satiety. Both kill. "To teach love" as that letter you so often read observes, is so to train the beloved one that gifts are occasionally granted, but never lavished! And this applies to the presence of your friend as well as to the more ardent demonstrations of your affection. "Il faut se faire valoir," as the French masters of the art often impress upon its votaries.

[*To M. V. B.*]   OFFICE OF WORKS,
                                                   FEBRUARY 21ST.

Progress of the War.

. . . I send you a collection of documents to give you all my news. Roberts telegraphs that Cronje has been largely reinforced and that his position is very strong. It will be a more difficult job than he thought to move him again. We shall lose a lot of men, but it must be done. The successes of the last few days have led people to think the war is all over; but it is far from that.

Roberts' estimate of next November for his advent at Pretoria will not be far from the mark.

. . . As I write Roberts telegraphs that he was to attack Cronje at daybreak this morning, to storm the position, and that the losses would be heavy. I hear Macdonald was badly wounded yesterday. Bad luck. There are other serious losses; but none are known yet. It makes one horribly nervous to know that this is going on. I am afraid that the job is very difficult. I only hope that neither Bobs nor Kitchener will be killed. Poor Douglas is in great anxiety about his boy. The suspense is so horrible. It is cruel to let us know that a very serious battle is in progress. However, it is perhaps as well that those at home should be made to suffer. I am not in a mood in which I can write to you much that is interesting.

You can understand the difficulty of thinking about anything but this accursed war. I am glad that it is to-morrow and not to-day that I shall be with you. The thing will then be decided one way or the other.

[*To M. V. B.*]   OFFICE OF WORKS,
                                                      FEBRUARY 22ND.

Still the anxiety weighs upon us. If Bobs stormed the position yesterday morning, we should have had some message before now. Yet nothing has come in. As far as we can judge it is a case of a bad repulse, or a solid victory. No half and half business. Let us hope for the latter.

For the first time yesterday the Queen was a little depressed. *War:* All through the early disasters she kept up her spirits. Yesterday *Feeling* the long list of casualties, and Roberts' not over-sanguine tele- *at Home.* gram, came as a violent reaction after the good news of the previous day—and she showed much feeling and anxiety. She

has lost confidence in her Ministers and looks much to Rosebery! I am not surprised. I cannot imagine what has happened
to Lord Salisbury. His speeches show much weariness and
entire misunderstanding of the people's mood.

What an absurd thing to say that the militia ballot would
drive young men to America, in order to escape duty. This,
too, in the face of the great wave of patriotism. Any other
argument would have been more suitable at the present. I
think the losses will be terrible in Roberts' fight—but we cannot
help that, if only he has won!

[*To M. V. B.*]   OFFICE OF WORKS,
                                   FEBRUARY 27TH.

Surrender   Isn't Bobs' telegram a model of what such things should be.
of Cronje.   Just exhilaration and no swagger. It is a neat coincidence that
the surrender should come on the anniversary of Majuba. It was
tactful of Cronje to wait until this morning to make his bow
to Bobs.

[*From Sir Arthur Bigge.*]   WINDSOR CASTLE,
                                      FEBRUARY 25TH.
MY DEAR ESHER,

The Queen has seen your letter to me of yesterday for which
H.M. desires me to thank you. She is receiving congratulations
from all corners of the world. I hope we shall hear of dear old
Buller at L. Smith.

                              Yours ever,
                                ARTHUR BIGGE.

[*To M. V. B.*]   OFFICE OF WORKS,
                                   MARCH 1ST.

. . . I also saw the Duke of York who was talking about the
impropriety of the Queen going to Italy at this moment. I
thought that he talked a good deal of sense.

They none of them dare, however, to tackle H.M.! The German Emperor has written some very interesting letters to the Queen commenting on the returns published by the W.O. as to the numbers of men in Africa—and I think the War Department are shown up as usual—counting men twice over, etc.!

[*To the Rev. C. D. Williamson.*]   ORCHARD LEA,
                                                      MARCH 8TH.

What events have occurred! I have privately heard that Steyn *News* has asked for peace, but it is impossible unless the surrender is *of the* unconditional. Still, it shows that the Boers weaken. How well *War.* all has gone since Roberts and Kitchener arrived. You will be interested to hear of the wonderful energy and spirit shown by the Queen. Will her visit to Ireland be appreciated there? Anyhow, it is a recognition of the splendid fight made by the Irish soldiers. Division VIII go out next week.

. . . London was a wonderful sight to-day. A spontaneous demonstration of loyalty. Thousands of orderly people. No police, no soldiers. A domestic nation on a gigantic scale.

[*To M. V. B.*]   ORCHARD LEA,
                            MARCH 10TH.

. . . He has just told me of a "subaltern court martial" which was held on —— for various offences.

The wretched fellow had to eat an egg raw; get two cuts each from every member of the court on his behind; and have his room dismantled. It sounds like bullying—but on hearing the charges, I'm inclined to think it was deserved.

They were all quite nice to him afterwards—and the thing is never alluded to. If he does not improve, he will have to leave the Regiment. Two other fellows were had up. One for being dirty and untidy—and he was jawed. And the other, quite a kid —for having, through ignorance, got drunk the first time he dined on Queen's Guard. He is very young—only 18. He was spoken to *alone,* by the senior subaltern, and told he must not do it again. He turned ashy white, and burst into tears. Rather pathetic.

The trials are very solemn affairs, and all the proceedings written down and kept. The senior subaltern is held responsible by the Colonel for the behaviour of all the younger lot, as you are held responsible by Tutor. After the Colonel the senior subaltern has the greatest responsibilities of anyone in the Regiment. All this seems well managed, and *ought* to prevent bullying. If a fellow ever *is* tried by a subaltern court martial it must be very much his own fault, and he must be very tactless.

I will tell you ——'s offences when I see you. They were quite hopelessly unpardonable.

[*To M. V. B.*]   ORCHARD LEA,
                                      MARCH 21ST.

. . . I forgot to tell you that I paid Letty [Lind] a visit. She was learning two new songs from two composers, who were superintending the operation. I am going to remonstrate *hard* as she is far from well. Probably I shall get myself into terrible hot water, but I mean to try and stop her going on the Halls. It is *so* silly to wear herself out for nothing. So you must be prepared for my being really unpopular in that quarter.

For the sake of all that has been, I shall make a fight. Rose [Cardross] came to luncheon at the Berkeley and was very sweet. She is a little wonder, so perpetually youthful—and perpetually sweet.

This evening we are remaining in London, as we go to see *Richard II*, a play I have never seen, then supper at the Carlton. Such a Gala. I seized the opportunity to tea with Lady Harcourt.

[*To M. V. B.*]   OFFICE OF WORKS,
                                              MARCH 22ND.

The play at the Lyceum was excellent—*Richard II.* Very
interesting—even Nellie, to whom Shakespeare gives a back-
ache, was thrilled. Then we had supper at the Carlton—but
there was not a human being there I had ever seen before. . . .
There is no news. Buller has been complaining that he was sup-   *Buller's*
plied with a rotten staff. Funnily enough, at the W.O. they have *Complaints.*
unearthed a letter from him written from Aldershot when his
staff was suggested to him by Wolseley, saying that he approved
of the names, making one or two suggestions and adding
"If I can't beat the Boers with such a lot of officers as you
propose, I ought to be kicked!"

[*To M. V. B.*]   ORCHARD LEA,
                                              MARCH 29TH.

I saw Letty [Lind] for a few moments last night and had   *Letty*
rather a pathetic talk. I tried—very tactfully—to warn her   *Lind.*
against music halls—for her own sake—and for Jackie's—but it
was very difficult. She shrinks from solitude, from her lonely
thoughts, from the inevitable contemplation of what has been
rather than of what is to come. Youth is the only great joy that
is given to women. As it fades, all life seems to them finished;
and harsh fate has decreed that the youth of women is so short-
lived. I have seen it so often, this melancholy struggle against
cruel and inevitable decree; and it is always intensely pathetic.
Men have so much to fill their lives. To love always rather than
to be loved; a so much happier state.

Then the comradeship of other men. And finally the battle
of life and all the various ambitions which lie ahead, even to life's
ending. Whereas to one like Letty, all triumphs, all joys, all
ambitions disappear with the fresh bloom of the skin and the
flash of bright eyes.

So I am depressed to-night: for there was a tragic pathos about the sad little figure that I left crouching over the fire in that room downstairs, which you know so well, and will always remember.

I have no news for you, except that Baden-Powell has privately told Roberts that he can hold out until May 15th. This is good news. Roberts has written a despatch on Spion Kop rather severely criticising Buller and Warren; but not more than I fancy they deserve. I don't know when it will be published.

[*To H.R.H. the Prince of Wales.*] [1]   OFFICE OF WORKS,
MAY 24TH.

Imperial Service Order.

I would submit for his Royal Highness' consideration the case of Civil Servants of the Crown who have performed long and distinguished service, but not of a sufficiently conspicuous character to entitle them to enter the Order of the Bath. Officers who have served the Crown throughout their lives frequently retire without receiving any mark of Her Majesty's favour, or recognition of meritorious work. It also not infrequently happens that conspicuous duties are performed by a Civil Servant, who, for reasons hard to define, but clear to his superiors, is not properly qualified for the Order of the Bath.

His Royal Highness is probably aware of civilians, not actually members of the Civil Service, who have done work for the Crown which well entitles them to some distinguishing mark of favour, who also come into both the categories to which I have referred.

Her Majesty has recently been graciously pleased to institute a medal for services in India of an exceptional character, and I would venture to suggest that the claims of civilians in other portions of the Empire may receive consideration, under circumstances not wholly dissimilar. There are, of course, serious objections to the multiplying of "Orders," but His Royal

---

[1] This letter resulted in the Imperial Service Order.

Highness will recollect that the Bath, originally a Military Order, was divided into two branches, and I would humbly suggest that the Distinguished Service Order, now purely military, could be extended to Civilians with salutary results.

The Distinguished Service Order meets the difficulty in the Military Service of the standing rule under which no officer under the rank of a Field Officer may be recommended for the Bath; and it is to meet the case of Civilians, who either from their position, or from the precise nature of services rendered, do not come within the category of those upon whom Her Majesty could properly confer the higher order, that a civil branch of the D.S.O. would prove so useful. I am sure that His Royal Highness will appreciate the regretful circumstances under which the Head of a Public Department is obliged to bid farewell to an old and faithful servant on his retirement after 40 years spent in the Service of the Crown, without it being possible to approach the Sovereign for a recognition of long and distinguished service.

His Royal Highness is well aware that the Civil Servants of the Crown are underpaid in comparison with men of the same class in private employ, nor have they much leisure, nor are the avenues of advancement and promotion wide or facile. The favour of the Sovereign is the sole recognition which they can hope to obtain for special and deserving merit.

His Royal Highness will perhaps, should the opportunity occur, and should this suggestion, made with great deference, be favourably received, approach Her Majesty in the interests of a fine and loyal body of men, for there is no one except His Royal Highness who can forcibly and effectually plead their cause.

[*To M. V. B.*]　　　　　　OFFICE OF WORKS,
　　　　　　　　　　　　　　　MAY 24TH.

. . . I have just come back with Nellie from having seen Mrs. " *Magda.*" Pat Campbell in *Magda* and am still under the charm of a wonderful play and a wonderful bit of acting. I wish you had seen it. Of course it is not very pleasant, but it is extraordinarily powerful. There are two plays in London which you have not seen and ought to see. This one, and *Ib and Christina* is the other.

[*To M. V. B.*]   OFFICE OF WORKS,
                                                      MAY 25TH.

I have just been to see Nellie dressed for the Drawing-room. She looked very well. I then drove to Stafford House, and saw Millie [Duchess of Sutherland], also resplendent, with Marie Antoinette's necklace and other brilliant things about her. . . . Young A. Douglas told me some wonderful stories about the thirst madness which overcomes the men in battle. One of the worst wounds anyone got in his company was from a man who rushed at him and *bit* him, under the arm, to try and get a drink of his blood. Many of the men sucked their own blood, driven mad by thirst.

[*To M. V. B.*]   OFFICE OF WORKS,
                                                      JUNE 13TH.

*The
Casualties.*
The telegram from Roberts has just been put into my hands, and I have telegraphed to you about poor Charlie Cavendish. It brings the whole thing back to *us* more than almost anything which has yet happened. It seems so short a time since he was ragging about my tutor's, and one met at every turn his nice blue eyes. However, he has met with a gallant death—although he has "left the world too young." Airlie was a most gallant and splendid soldier. A real fine officer, and a very fine man.

It is an irreparable loss too. I cannot think of poor Charlie's unfortunate relatives. It would have been so much better if Chesham had fallen, as he has lived so much of his life. The fates are very cruel sometimes.

Roberts' telegram is in other respects very satisfactory and although there will be desultory fighting, the war—as a war— is over. Of course in this sort of hedge and ditch business there may be great loss of valuable lives. I don't suppose many fellows will be killed, but the few will probably be the pluckiest and most interesting. It is not sad for them, but sad for those left behind.

[*To M. V. B.*]　Office of Works,
JUNE 22ND.

... I am going first to Hertford House to see the opening by the P. of Wales, but I shall get away in good time.

[*To M. V. B.*]　Orchard Lea,
JUNE 23RD.

... Hertford House was lovely yesterday. A very smart party. I must take you to see it on the morning of the second day of Lords. It is on the way. You will think it perfectly superb.

I have been offered £800 for the table at which I am writing to you. I cannot make up my mind whether to accept it or not, and buy an electric motor!

[*To M. V. B.*]　Office of Works,
JUNE 27TH.

The opera was great success. Calvé more flirtatious in *Carmen* than words can describe—but the Queen was enchanted with her and held her hand a long time, when speaking to her afterwards.

[*Journals.*]   2, TILNEY STREET,
OCTOBER 24TH.

. . . When it was suggested to the Queen that I should go to the War Office as Under-Secretary of State, she said she could not possibly allow me to give up my present office. . . .

The Houses of the Royal Family.

I spent some time with the Duke and Duchess of York. The Queen has offered them Clarence House. The Duchess is very practical, and takes both pride and interest in her surroundings, wishing to create a sort of Hanoverian atmosphere. With her I went all over Clarence House. She discussed every detail. It is a grief to her to migrate from her charming rooms in York House. It seems—in view of the Queen's life chances—an unwise proceeding. The Prince of Wales, however, insists. The Princess of Wales is said to have declared that she will never give up Marlborough House!

[*To Sir William Harcourt.*]   OFFICE OF WORKS,
OCTOBER 25TH.

War Office Proposal.

I am afraid I cannot get away. I wish it were possible. I wish, however, very much to have a talk with you. Should I be definitely asked to go to the War Office as Under-Secretary (a renewal of a different office of the proposal made some months ago) I shall run down and talk it over with you. I have been "approached" and the Queen has been asked whether she would approve. At present she objects strongly—so the matter may end there—and it will be a relief to me if it does. She has said such nice kind things that it would be difficult for me to give up my present office. At the same time, the Government may press it, and then I shall have to decide, which I have not done yet!

There was no difficulty in refusing the Colonial Office, but in this case I am harassed by a feeling that it may be shirking a duty to try and avoid the unpleasantness of the W.O. and the certitude that nothing but kicks without halfpence can be got from going there.

It is upon the course I shall take—if the proposal comes in definite form—that I should like your advice. In normal times I would not exchange this office for the War Department, but if the Government mean seriously to tackle that office, it is a different matter. However, you will easily weigh the pros and cons.

Of course, I may be *driven* to accept or refuse, by some condition or circumstance of which I know nothing, so you must not mind if ultimately I do not act on your friendly advice; but I should like to have it.

The Government reshuffle has been very difficult. Lord S. [Salisbury] was determined to keep the Foreign Secretaryship but the Queen has intervened so strongly in the contrary sense that I think Lansdowne will go there. Probably Lord S. will be P. Minister and Privy Seal. . . . *Cabinet Reshuffle.*

[*Journals.*]   2, TILNEY STREET,
                                            OCTOBER 25TH.

I saw Rosebery this morning. We had a long walk, and talked about the Government changes. He strongly opposed my going to the W.O. He says I should make no sacrifices for "these people," meaning the Government. That point of view never occurred to me. I never thought of Ministers. My reasons for refusing these offers are quite personal and private— and I never give them. Never, never, will I harness myself to a "political" office. *War Office.*

[*Journals.*]   2, TILNEY STREET,
                                            NOVEMBER 9TH.

The new appointments have been well received on the whole. Lansdowne only has come in for a large share of abuse. Why, no one can explain, who knows him and his sound diplomatic instincts and his experience. I saw him yesterday. He was unmoved by criticism. He has been accustomed, as an Irish land- *Lansdowne.*

lord, to be pelted by the Press. I called on him to arrange what
can be done for Lord Salisbury's comfort. He has no "office,"
no place to lay his red boxes. As Privy Seal he is minus a salary
and as Prime Minister minus a bureau! We proposed to give
him three large reception rooms at the F.O. He accepted gratefully, subject to Lansdowne's consent. This was rapidly obtained, although L. is aware that ill-natured critics will say
that Lord S. remains there as Mayor of the Palace.

There is an advantage in the P.M. occupying rooms accessible
from the principal offices without the necessity of running the
gauntlet of prying reporters. We have made the F.O. to
communicate with the Colonial, Home and India Offices.

I saw Arthur Bigge, and he at once began about the W.O.
I told him that I had no wish to leave my present office.

[*Journals.*]   2, TILNEY STREET,
                                                NOVEMBER 10TH.

Goschen.   Lunched at Windsor Castle. Goschen desires to take a
personal leave of the Queen although he has no official reason
for seeing her! She has consented to receive him on Tuesday.
Ridley.   Ridley, on the other hand, asked to be excused from personally
surrendering the seals of the Home Office, as it was painful for
him to do so. The Queen, however, desires him to come. He is
grieved at giving up office, and has no wish to become a peer.

There seems to be a chance that Kitchener may go to the
War   W.O. after all. That might tempt me into the hornet's nest.
Office.   The difficulty is Evelyn-Wood, who has two more years to
serve as Adjutant-General.

[*To the Rev. C. D. Williamson.*]   ORCHARD LEA,
                                                NOVEMBER 11TH.

The W.O. negotiations are going on again. I shall not go
there unless (1) the Queen approves; (2) I can make terms on

the basis of (*a*) free hand to reform internal administration; (*b*) assurance that H.M.G. mean business.

It is a galère into which I shall not run myself, *if* muddle is to continue.

[*Journals.*]   2, TILNEY STREET,
                                             NOVEMBER 15TH.

. . . In the evening I had half an hour with Brodrick at the W.O. He is full of vitality, and keen to sweep out his Augean Stable. All his life his desire has been to occupy the Secretary of State's room at the W.O. It comes to very few men—in the early forties—to realise their political heart's desire. His main trouble will be with the older generation of soldiers and with the Crown. *Constitution of the War Office.*

The Navy is a constitutional force. Every commission is signed by the Board. The Army is a royal force and, while the Queen never interferes with the Navy, she interferes very much with the Army. As she listens to soldiers rather than to Ministers, the task of the Secretary of State for War is never easy. Hence the importance of a good understanding between the civil and military advisers of the S. of S. This has never been realised in my recollection—i.e. since 1882.

[*Journals.*]   2, TILNEY STREET,
                                             NOVEMBER 21ST.

I wrote a short note to Lord Salisbury last night at Hatfield, saying that if he saw no objection, I proposed to take my seat at the opening of this Parliament, but that I should not vote nor speak, and should sit on the cross benches. *Lord Esher takes his Seat.*

I had a reply this evening, an interesting letter, approving the proposal.

[*Journals.*]   ORCHARD LEA,
                                                 DECEMBER 1ST.

Army   Went to the Castle. Met Professor Osler,[1] who had been
Medical   sent out to the Cape with a letter from the Queen, and had an
Service.   opportunity of comparing the medical arrangements with those
of other armies, with which he is familiar. His account was not
pleasant. Antiquated appliances, and few of them. Not enough
doctors. Red tape. Deficient in medical practice. Organisation 30 years in arrears.

The   The Queen has been unwell. *Elle a beaucoup baissée* in general
Queen's   health. She felt deeply the death of her grandson, the little
Health.   Christian boy. However, the Canadian officers dined with her.
She talked to them all, and the Adjutant, when he left her, said
with emotion, "I could die for her!"

[*Journals.*]   2, TILNEY STREET,
                                                 DECEMBER 4TH.

. . . Lord Salisbury, at the last three Cabinets in the autumn,
when he was Foreign Secretary, sat a crumpled heap—like
Grandpa Smallweed—evidently wearied out. Since giving up
the F.O. he is brisk and attentive. A changed man.

Lord Roberts telegraphed that his "young Colonels" have
overdone their job, and exceeded his orders by burning too
many farms. Bobs proposes an "African Order" to spare the
Bath and St. Michael, for his list, he says, is 18,000 long! Even
divided into three, it is portentous. The Cabinet were all hostile
to the Order. Even though the old Orders are temporarily
swamped, they think it is better so.

[1] Sir William Osler, Regius Professor of Medicine at Oxford.

[*Journals.*]   2, TILNEY STREET,
                                                            DECEMBER 11TH.

My official Chief [1] told me that Chamberlain is anxious to get   *Offer of*
a Governor of the Cape, and asked him to put out feelers to   *Cape*
see if I would care to go! . . .   *Governor-*
                                                                    ship.
The Queen of Holland is now so much in love with her   *The*
husband, that she has rather cooled off politics. . . .   *Queen of*
                                                                    Holland.
The little Queen has had a medal struck to commemorate her
wedding. Two heads on the obverse side, and on the reverse,
a boat putting out to sea, with two figures in the stern, but *she*
is steering!

[*To H.M. the Queen.*]   OFFICE OF WORKS,
                                                            DECEMBER 28TH.

Lord Esher presents his humble duty to Your Majesty and   *On*
hardly knows how adequately to convey his deep sense of   *becoming*
gratitude for the high honour which Your Majesty has been   *K.C.V.O.*
graciously pleased to confer upon him.[2]

He can only say that as his prayers have always been for the
long continuance and happiness of Your Majesty's reign, and
for the support of Almighty God in Your Majesty's many
troubles and cares, so his own humble efforts will always be
directed loyally to ensure, so far as in him lies, Your Majesty's
comfort and ease, as well as those of the Royal Family.

Lord Esher begs most humbly and gratefully to thank Your
Majesty for this additional mark of Your Majesty's great kindness to him and his.

[1] The Rt. Hon. Akers-Douglas, afterwards Lord Chilston.
[2] The K.C.V.O.

[*From Sir Arthur Bigge.*]   OSBORNE,
                                          DECEMBER 28TH.

MY DEAR ESHER,

I am so truly delighted that the Queen has given you the
K.C.V.O. and I congratulate you with all my heart. It is such
a personal proof of H.M.'s appreciation of your valued services
to her and to the country.

The Editor of the *D.T.* telegraphed last night to know if it
were true that the Queen had instituted a new African order!
I replied "Not that I am aware of," but I do not see how the
Bath can be so extended as to meet all the demands upon it on
account of the S.A. War!

                                          Yours ever,
                                            ARTHUR BIGGE.

[*From Sir Frances Knollys.*]   SANDRINGHAM,
                                          JANUARY 1ST, 1901.

. . . The Prince of Wales desires me to congratulate you
very sincerely on having been appointed a K.C.V.O. by the
Queen, and to say he is very glad you have got it.

I also wish to congratulate you, and to say I am sure you
deserve it after all that you have done for the Queen and the
Royal Family. . . .

[*Journals.*]   ORCHARD LEA,
                                          JANUARY 1ST.

*The
K.C.V.O.*

On Friday, i.e. December 28th, I received a charming letter
from the Duke of Connaught, written in the Queen's name,
saying she was ill and tired, or she would have written herself,
and sending me the insignia of a K.C. of the Victorian Order.
It is a *gift* from the Queen—on her own initiative—and I am
very glad to have it.

through Ponsonby an instruction that at her death her successor should not be present at the Public Proclamation, a ceremonial that "had been peculiarly painful to her." I told Douglas of this paper, and it was found at the Home Office last night and handed to Arthur Balfour who will show it to the Prince. . . .

I saw the Duke of Norfolk, and arranged with him exactly what steps are to be taken, if, as Earl Marshal, he has to conduct the funeral.

The Lord Chancellor and the Speaker had put their heads together, and arranged that they would ignore the Council, and sit at once in their respective houses to take the oath of allegiance, forgetting that it is the Lord Chancellor who administers the oath *at the Council* to the Sovereign, and that the Sovereign must take the oath *before* anyone is justified in swearing allegiance. No one seems to have taken the trouble to look even at the Annual Register, to ascertain what took place when William IV died.

I showed D. [Douglas] all the precedents, and we also went at some length into the arrangements preparatory to the Civil List discussion, for which I shall have to prepare for him a memorandum.

What a series of political and social changes this event will produce! It is like beginning to live again in a new world.

[*To Sir William Harcourt.*]   OFFICE OF WORKS,
JANUARY 22ND.

I have telegraphed to you, with Douglas' strong approval, *General* lest you should, by mischance, not be here in time for the *Confusion.* Council.

The Prince of Wales has telegraphed to say that the end is near. If the Queen dies to-night, the Council will be held at St. James's Palace to-morrow. The question of *uniform* is undetermined at present.

Loulou [Harcourt] told me of Ponsonby's letter to you of

which *nothing* was known. It was found at the H.O.[1] last night, and Arthur [Balfour] took it to Osborne an hour ago.

Ritchie is *not* sent for—has been at Eastbourne all along, and apparently is not wanted! I cannot describe to you the ignorance, the historical ignorance, of everyone from top to bottom —who should know something of procedure.

You would think that the English Monarchy had been buried since the time of Alfred. There has been a great rush to get everything ready—but we are in smoother water to-day. The Queen has had a return to consciousness and has recognised her children, but still there seems to be no hope of any strong revival, so that the end will be a release. It is really merciful that her illness has been so short. You know well what endless confusion is already created by the accumulation of documents for signature. Some of the Judges even have been unable to proceed on the Assize for want of the Queen's authority.

What changes, political and social, this event will produce! The idea is that it will be impossible to escape from a great national demonstration of respect and sorrow *in London*.

No one knows yet what the Queen's own wishes may be upon that point. I hope you will come up.

[*Journals.*]　　　　OFFICE OF WORKS,
JANUARY 24TH.

The Council.　The Queen died on Tuesday evening, 22nd of January, at 6.30. Yesterday the King came to London. I was asked to attend the Council. It was not held in the Throne Room but in the Banqueting Room at St. James's. Everyone in uniform. There were about 150 people there. Some curious old fossils.

The Act of Homage.　The ceremony was unimposing, but the King was very dignified. He spoke exceedingly well; began in a broken voice, but gathered strength as he proceeded. Then a cushion was put at his right hand, and the Royal Dukes did homage. All knelt and kissed his hand, except the old Duke of Cambridge. Then at

[1] Home Office.

his left hand another cushion was placed, and the Duke of Devonshire and Lord Salisbury, followed by others, performed the same ceremony. He raised Lord Salisbury very tenderly and respectfully. Rosebery was rather in the cold. This made me sad.

At night, at 10, the King summoned me and Clarendon to discuss the funeral arrangements. All the Royal Dukes were there. A curious gathering to those who remember interviews with the Queen.

An odd thing happened. Almeric Fitzroy sent for the King's speech to have it printed in the *Gazette*. No copy existed. The King had spoken it impromptu, showing great nerve. It certainly was excellently done. The King suggested that Rosebery and Akers-Douglas should be asked to supply a copy from memory! *The King's Speech.*

To-day the King was proclaimed, according to the ancient ceremonial. Lord Roberts was at the head of the show, on a fine horse. *The Proclamation.*

The funeral arrangements having been entrusted to the Lord Chamberlain, the Earl Marshal claimed his rights. This the little Duke did with so much energy, that he overcame all opposition. The Lord C. was much chagrined. *Funeral Arrangements.*

The general plan of the ceremony is settled. I suggested a "sea procession." It would have been a fine thing to have brought the Queen the whole way to London by sea. However, she seems to have given certain directions which are to be followed. No black—no hearse—only a gun-carriage. A military funeral. It is fixed for Saturday, February 2nd, so we have only 10 days in which to make mighty preparations. I have been very hard at work all day.

[*Journals.*]　　　　　　　　OFFICE OF WORKS,
　　　　　　　　　　　　　　　　JANUARY 31ST.

. . . I saw the King on Tuesday night from 10.30 to 1.30 a.m. I was with him alone for half an hour, and he was very gracious. *Funeral Arrangements.*

Then Pembroke and Clarendon and Victor Churchill arrived. The King was dignified but perfectly simple. After a while he made us all sit down. He also asked us to smoke, but no one availed himself of this latter permission.

Since then I have been occupied in London and at Windsor all the time. I have control of all the Windsor arrangements.

Maurice went off to Sandhurst yesterday.

To-morrow we have a rehearsal at Windsor of the actual arrangements in St. George's.

[*To M. V. B.*]   ORCHARD LEA,
                                                        FEBRUARY 4TH.

*The
Final
Ceremony.*

... We rehearsed until after 12. I got to bed at 1. To-day has proved a brilliant success. This morning I walked down to Frogmore with Lorne and was introduced to all the young Princes and Princesses. Played about with them for some time. Princess Beatrice of Coburg is a beauty. Margaret of Connaught a sweet. The Crown Prince is *charming*. Speaks English beautifully. But I fell in love with Albany. He was quite unshy. ...

In the Mausoleum this afternoon, he was sweet, the only one, besides the Princess of Wales, who was in tears. The ceremonial was lovely to-day—and perfectly arranged from start to finish. I had to receive everybody at the Mausoleum. It was beautiful, interesting and pathetic. I brought away a laurel wreath that hung over the grave, which I shall have framed, and some lovely lilies of which I have kept some for you. The procession down the long walk was most striking. ...

... So ends the reign of the Queen—and now I feel for the first time that the new régime, so full of anxieties for England, has begun. Keep always in your heart the memory of the Queen whom your immediate forefathers served so closely and faithfully and well.

[*To M. V. B.*]   ORCHARD LEA,
                                                   FEBRUARY 5TH.

The German Emperor had a noble reception to-day from the   *The*
citizens of London, who have forgiven him his telegram to   *Kaiser in*
Kruger, in consideration of his behaviour during the past 10   *London.*
days. I was in St. James's St. The cortège was a pretty sight.
The Blues splendid. Very few police. Large crowds. Much
cheering. Very hearty. The Kaiser acknowledged the cheers,
the King sitting quietly beside him—which showed fine taste.

So the new reign starts under good auguries. I have been busy
all day with the Civil List. A tiresome but necessary duty. Also
arranging the House of Lords for the opening of Parliament.

I sent a list of queries to the King to-night—about a throne
for the Queen. She objects to being called Queen *Consort*.
She means to be the Queen—although she says pathetically
she would prefer a peaceful and quiet station.

I had a talk with Douglas about the Army and Navy Estimates. *Apart from the wars* they have risen since 1895 from 35 to
nearly 60 millions. This is bad, as it may produce a reaction
against Imperial ideas. We *must* face militia ballot—or some
sort of compulsory service for *home* defence—not conscription
—as we have often agreed—for that is impossible.

[*To M. V. B.*]   ORCHARD LEA,
                                                   FEBRUARY 6TH.

. . . At dawn this morning an orderly arrived with a note to   *Changes at*
say that the King would see me at 12. I was obliged to remon-   *Windsor.*
strate. It was not inconsiderateness, only ignorance. So I suggested 7, of which he approved. He lives in his old rooms in the
Castle, small and convenient. The Queen Alexandra came in,
quite in homely fashion. The Corridor and the Palace looked
much the same—but all the atmosphere was changed.

The Indians—who were there—were wandering about like
uneasy spirits. No longer immobile and statuesque, as of yore.

It may be my imagination, but the sanctity of the throne has disappeared. The King is kind and debonnair, and not undignified—but too *human*!

Knollys thinks he will not live much at Windsor. That he would be bored there. He goes back to London to-morrow to reside at present at Marlborough House. Later he will occupy Buckingham Palace.

. . . With me to-night he went through every detail of the opening of Parliament, scribbling notes, which he handed to me. Ceremonial has great charm for him.

[*To M. V. B.*]   OFFICE OF WORKS,
                                   FEBRUARY 8TH.

. . . The King telegraphed up that Pembroke, Clarendon and Portland were to meet him at Marlborough House at 4! They were all scattered through the country; and he was furious.

These gentlemen are not going to hold sinecure offices under the new régime. Hitherto they have been paid large salaries for doing nothing.[1]

[*To Sir Francis Knollys.*]   OFFICE OF WORKS,
                                   FEBRUARY 8TH.

Advice on the Coronation. As I don't suppose I shall be here when the Coronation takes place, I want—while the subject is still fresh in my mind—to suggest that if the Earl Marshal undertakes it (and it may be impossible to prevent this) he should be given the control, on the understanding that the four departments concerned—i.e.

The Master of the Horse   The Lord Steward
The Lord Chamberlain   The Office of Works

[1] These Lords held the offices of Lord Steward, Lord Chamberlain, and Master of the Horse.

place their staff *absolutely at his disposal*. That he should be the nominal figure-head, but that the Departments should do the work in their usual fashion.

This is exactly what happened in 1897, and resulted in a great success. There could be a committee room—and I would suggest St. James's Palace as a convenient place—in which the Heads of the Departments would meet.

The Duke of Norfolk could preside, just as the Prince of Wales presided in 1897.

If this plan is adopted all will go well.

If the Heralds have anything to do with it, failure (or less) is inevitable. The Duke is all right, not at all a bad man of business.

[*Journals.*]   ORCHARD LEA,
                                                                              FEBRUARY 9TH.

... To-day I walked down to the Mausoleum, still embowered in flowers, to see the recumbent figure which has been placed in position. It is a graceful effigy. The Queen as she was in 1861.

I met Princess Louise there. The dying scene was stately and dramatic. The Queen now and then recognised those about her, and spoke their names. Her difficulty in breathing was the only painful symptom. Reid—the doctor—passed his arm round her and supported her. *Details of the Queen's Death.*

The King knelt at the side of the bed. The German Emperor stood silently at the head, near the Queen. The other children and grandchildren were there, all calling their names to her at intervals. She died quite peacefully. After the King had left for London, the Emperor took charge of everything. His tenderness and firmness were extraordinary, so unlike what was expected of him.

He refused to allow Banting's men to measure the Queen for her shell. He turned them out of the room. He sent for Reid, and took all the measurements himself. He and the King and the Duke of Connaught lifted the Queen into her coffin.

The day before her death, while the Prince of Wales was in the house, but not allowed to go near the Queen for fear of alarming her, she said, "The Prince of Wales will be sorry to hear how ill I am. Do you think he ought to be told?" Another thing she said was, "I don't want to die yet. There are several things I want to arrange."

The Mausoleum Ceremony.

Of all the ceremonials, that of Monday was the simplest and most impressive. The procession from the Sovereign's entrance, the Princess of Wales leading Prince Edward of York, the other children walking, was very touching and beautiful. At the Mausoleum, the arrangements were left to me. Everyone got into the Chapel, and the iron gates were closed, showing the soldiers without. Teddie and his guardsmen brought in the coffin. The King and the Princes and Princesses standing on the right. The choir on the left. The Bishop and Dean, and the two great Officers of State, at the head of the coffin. I stood close to the foot, but below the platform, in order to lift the rollers at the end of the service. When all was over, all the Princes and Princesses and servants walked past the tomb. They could see the two coffins side by side. When they had gone, I remained to see the stone placed over the tomb, and sealed. I brought away the wreath that hung over the grave near where the King stood. Of all the mourners the Princess of Wales and the young Duke of Coburg displayed the most emotion.

The Recumbent Figure.

Last year the Queen mentioned to me that there was a recumbent figure of herself in existence at Windsor. Last week, I asked the Clerk of the Works where it was kept. He had never heard of it. No one had heard of it, and there was much scepticism. After a minute enquiry, an old workman remembered that about 1865 the figure had been walled up in the stores at Windsor. The brickwork was taken down, and the figure found. It is now over the tomb, a really impressive thing by Marochetti. It was pure chance that it was discovered.

I had a long talk with Bigge to-day. Talking over the Civil

List, the Household, and many other things. He becomes Private Secretary to the Duke of Cornwall. The "pension" question is full of difficulties.

A Memorial is on foot for the Queen. A Committee pro- *A Memorial* jected, on which it is suggested that I should serve. There is a *Proposed.* desire for the memorial, but no practical scheme is proposed. I suggested "Duke of York's Schools"—to be called Queen Victoria's Schools, to train boys for the Army at Edinburgh, Dublin, Melbourne, Quebec, Calcutta (the Indian one on a different footing). It is a thing the Queen herself had thought of, and would have liked.

[*To M. V. B.*]   ORCHARD LEA,
                                   FEBRUARY 10TH.

I drove to Windsor to-day with Nellie. She called on Howdie [Sturgis] and I went to see Arthur Bigge. I told you about the *The* proposed memorial to the Queen, and my idea about the *Memorial.* military schools all over the Empire.

Bigge pressed me to think of an alternative scheme, and driving home it occurred to me that Osborne might be purchased from the King, and preserved as a shrine in honour of the Queen, uncontaminated by domestic uses, and filled with memorials to her. The idea would appeal to the oriental and possibly to the colonial mind. . . . To-night I have been reading *Greville* Greville's memoirs, and I see that it was settled by the Duke *and* of Kent to call the Queen "Alexandra Georgiana," when *George IV.* George IV said that he would not permit Georgiana as a *second* name—so mercifully it was changed to Victoria.

Greville is worth reading if only to see what an unmitigated cad ruled the nation in George IV. How his Ministers stood him, I cannot think.

[*Journals.*]   ORCHARD LEA,
                                              FEBRUARY 10TH.

Possible
Biography
of the
Queen.

... Bigge talked to-day of an official *Life of the Queen*.
Roland Prothero has been thought of, and Arthur Benson.
Such a task is impossible during the life-time of certain persons,
and until the shadow of passing events grows longer. Justice
could not be done to the Queen's character, unless her later
years were thrown into strong relief, for it was during her later
years that her judgment mellowed, and her influence over her
people and over the Empire became so powerful.

The only possible thing to do is to (1) collect and arrange all
her papers, (2) print selections from her journals up to a certain
date, (3) print correspondence *very fully* up to a certain date. All
this "pour servir" the historians of the future. Far more
interesting than any expurgated biography. The truest service
to the Queen is to let her speak for herself.

[*To M. V. B.*]   ORCHARD LEA,
                                              FEBRUARY 11TH.

... To-day I was fussed all day by emissaries from Marl-
borough House. Great excitement over the height of the
Queen's footstool! ... We finished our report on the "Civil
List" for the King to-day, and sent it to the Ch. of the Exch.
Would you care to see it?

[*Journals.*]   2, TILNEY STREET,
                                              FEBRUARY 16TH.

Opening
of Parlia-
ment.

The opening of Parliament went off without a hitch.
Cholmondely—the new Lord Great Chamberlain—performed
his duties well. He has written me a grateful letter of thanks.
My people at the Office of Works certainly were wonderful.
The whole success of the arrangements was due to their intelli-

gence and devotion. The King most dignified. The Queen looked beautiful, with all her jewels and the Kohinoor—upon a black dress. The contrast between the red robes of the peers, and the black dresses of the women, was very effective. The Queen was a little nervous, and her entry—led by the King— created a well-justified sensation. . . .

Princess Christian, whom I saw yesterday, told me that the Queen had my letter of thanks for the K.C.V.O. read her twice, and called it a "beautiful letter." She wished to write to me herself, but was dissuaded by the Duke of Connaught, as the effort was thought too great for her. I cannot help feeling a personal regret. . . .

[*Journals.*]　　　　　　　　　　　2, TILNEY STREET,
　　　　　　　　　　　　　　　　　FEBRUARY 17TH.

The King sent for me at 12.30 to-day, and with him and the *Arrange-* Queen and the Duchess of Cornwall, we walked through the *ments at* State rooms and all the private rooms of the Castle. The Queen *Windsor.* desired to live in the State rooms, but the King insisted on occupying Queen Victoria's old rooms, and he means himself to occupy his Father's room. There was quite a smart difference of opinion. Every detail was discussed. The Queen showed excellent taste. The Duchess was very gentle and appreciative. We finished about a quarter past two.

At 3.30 the King ordered a carriage, and I drove with him and Prince Louis of Battenberg to the Mausoleum. Then we visited the Memorial Chapel and the Vault, and parted at 5.30. A long day.

He was very gracious, and said, "For God's sake don't give *On the* up your appointment." He talked over some very private *King.* affairs with me, and I shall not venture to write down the conversation. He is certainly a great-hearted King, and when he stood by his mother's grave, I could see that he inherits her romantic spirit—without display!

[*To M. V. B.*]   OFFICE OF WORKS,
                                              FEBRUARY 21ST.

The
Memorial
Committee.

... To-day I attended the Memorial Committee. I refused
to go until certain points of procedure had been cleared up; so
it ended by my having to walk in and take a seat next to Lord
Salisbury, when the séance was half through. *This* was done
without loss of dignity. There was much gas without any
practical result—except that a conference of artistic experts was
settled. This I have to manage on Monday next. Rosebery and
Chamberlain "bickered" a good deal. They do not love one
another. I have several schemes for the memorial, but am not
enamoured of any of them.

I have been reading *Footprints of Statesmen*. It is a very good
book although you despise it, and the characters of Marlborough
and Bolingbroke are quite excellent. I cannot imagine how the
author combined to know so much, and to put what he knew
so well.

[*Journals.*]   ORCHARD LEA,
                                              FEBRUARY 23RD.

Lord
Esher
and the
King.

This morning I had not intended going to London, but I had
a telegram from Knollys, saying the King was much disappointed at not seeing me last night, and that I should be
there at eleven. So I went.

The King was more than kind; warned me that I should
never leave his service. He then went into a quantity of details,
things he wished done, as he leaves for Germany to-night, to
bid an eternal farewell to his sister the Empress.

I am now fully empowered to act as Hon. Sec. of the Committee of the Queen's Memorial. In my letters to Maurice I
have written an account of our first meeting.

Queen
Victoria's
Gift.

The Queen left a list of persons to whom she wished
memorials to be given. I received a curious old ring, of twisted
serpents and coloured stones. I am glad to receive this gift.

[*To M. V. B.*]　　　　　　　OFFICE OF WORKS,
　　　　　　　　　　　　　　FEBRUARY 26TH.

As it is Sylvia's birthday we slept in town, and went to *Twelfth Night*. It is perfectly sweet, especially the girl who plays Olivia.[1] You would love it, and must go some Saturday afternoon or evening.

... I was busy all yesterday with the Memorial Cttee. It looks as if it would give me a good deal of trouble. I think the scheme which I suggested of statue and arch in the Mall will probably be adopted. I have got Cust the place which he wanted: "Surveyor of the King's pictures." He ought to do very well, and it adds to his income.

[*To M. V. B.*]　　　　　　　OFFICE OF WORKS,
　　　　　　　　　　　　　　FEBRUARY 27TH.

... The Committee to-day decided nothing about the memorial. Rosebery and Chamberlain contradicted each other perpetually—and that was all. Lord Salisbury likes Rosebery and is amused by him. It is rather a queer experience seeing this composite "cabinet" of the Government and the Opposition seated round the same table. *Queen's Memorial Committee.*

In no other country could political opponents thus meet in friendly fashion for a common cause.

It is creditable to us as a nation.

[*To M. V. B.*]　　　　　　　ORCHARD LEA,
　　　　　　　　　　　　　　MARCH 4TH.

... This morning I had an hour with the King, who read me some curious papers written by the Empress Frederick on what must prove her deathbed—asking him to look after *Empress Frederick Dying.*

---

[1] Miss Maud Jeffreys.

pictures and things she loved in her youth, and the exact pictures which are at Windsor and at Buckingham Palace, she describes—she has her mother's memory.

This afternoon I went with the King for a drive to Westminster where we met A. Balfour and Douglas, and walked through the slums, inspecting sites for the Queen's memorial.

He was recognised everywhere, and treated with the greatest respect. He is very *simple*, as well as dignified.

[*From Sir Francis Knollys.*]   MARLBOROUGH HOUSE,
                                                            MARCH 5TH.

MY DEAR ESHER,

The King and Queen would like to meet you *alone* at Buckingham Palace (Prince Consort's entrance) to-morrow. Please tell no one.

Yours ever,
FRANCIS KNOLLYS.

[*To M. V. B.*]   OFFICE OF WORKS,
                                  MARCH 7TH.

. . . I was tired to death yesterday after two hours *alone* with the King and Queen at Buckingham Palace. They were fussing over domestic plans. *She* had never been before into Queen Victoria's rooms. Queer was it not? She examined every detail; and made all her own little domestic arrangements.

[*To M. V. B.*]   OFFICE OF WORKS,
                                  MARCH 10TH.

*Hampton
Court*

. . . I did not record for you my visit to Hampton Court with the King. He was amazed at the splendour of his possession. He had not seen it for many years. At once he wrote off to the

Empress Frederick, who, although on her deathbed, is still keenly interested in all the places and things she once knew so well. . . .

[*To M. V. B.*]   OFFICE OF WORKS,
                                              MARCH 11TH.

I got through my committee to-day, and carried my scheme *unanimously* for the Queen's memorial in the Mall. I then went to the King, who was very gracious. He was delighted to get the thing settled on these lines. I suggested he should give a subscription to the memorial himself—and he thought it a good idea.

. . . I had a present from the Duchess of York, rather a nice bust of herself. I told her at Windsor that I collected and she sent me this little bronze to-day.

[*To M. V. B.*]   OFFICE OF WORKS,
                                              MARCH 12TH.

. . . I spent the morning with the Queen at Buckingham Palace. She was in tearing spirits and will enjoy her new home, when once she begins to arrange her rooms. *Buckingham Palace.*

Then, this afternoon, the King came, alone, and went all over the ground *she* had traversed in the morning. Then he drove off.

[*To M. V. B.*]   ORCHARD LEA,
                                              MARCH 18TH.

. . . Early, I spent an hour with the Duke of Connaught gossiping about the Army. He was just off to Sandhurst, and I wonder if you came across him. Prince Edward of York came in while I was there. Rather a sweet little person. Then after luncheon I saw Teddie decorated. A pretty sight.

The ceremony took place inside Marlborough House. All the Tommies were hopelessly shy. Especially after they had received their medal, and were walking away. Kinloch got an M.V.O. after all, and he thoroughly deserved it. Then I had an audience of the Queen, and went all over her rooms with her looking at her treasures. She has some beautiful things, and is in sore distress, because she has so many, and nowhere to put them, unless she spreads over more rooms in Buckingham Palace than she is really allowed to absorb.

Numberless possessions are no doubt a curse. I am still in doubt whether to appeal to Eton and Sandhurst for subscriptions to the Memorial, and if so whether to limit to a shilling. What do you think? *All* the public schools might be asked to follow suit.

The King read my memo. on the C. in Chief, etc. (which I showed you some time ago) and gave it to the Duke of Connaught to read, with much commendation. There is no doubt that my views were right.

[*To M. V. B.*]   ORCHARD LEA,
                       MARCH 19TH.

Memorial   What have I done to-day? We had our memorial meeting—
Committee.   and the very distinguished committee was as inept as usual.
Rosebery was sore that his idea had been snuffed out. He takes a beating badly. Chamberlain, on the other hand, accepted *his* defeat, and finding that they would not stand his plan, fell in loyally with the other. This is much more practical, and better behaviour.

[*To M. V. B.*]   ORCHARD LEA,
                       MARCH 26TH.

I lunched with the Lord Mayor, rather an appalling affair, and then we had our meeting for the Memorial. Arthur

[Balfour] spoke well, and old Harcourt was rather good, but Chamberlain simply surpassed himself.

I wish you could have heard him. It was extraordinarily well done. I shall get a certain amount of money, but not very much.

[*To M. V. B.*] ORCHARD LEA,
APRIL IST.

I got back late to-night, having been to the Castle. The King plays bridge after dinner, and keeps people up till nearly one, which is very tiring. He insists on having all his letters brought to him unopened, about 400 a day, and sorts them by the envelopes. He tried at first to open them all, but found that impossible.

[*Journals.*] ORCHARD LEA,
APRIL 8TH.

We dined at the Castle last night for the first time, under the new régime. There was a large assembly as the whole household in waiting dined with the King and Queen. The oak dining-room is no longer used, and the quiet impressive entrance of the Queen into the corridor is as obsolete as Queen Elizabeth.

Dinner at Windsor: New Style.

We assembled in the Green drawing-room, and the King came in unannounced with his daughters and his sister. He took the Duchess of Fife in to dinner. We dined in the White room, which looked very well. He retains the Indian servants. The dinner was like an ordinary party. None of the "hush" of the Queen's dinners. Afterwards we left "arm-in-arm" as we entered.

Then the party remained in the Green room, and he took me into the White drawing-room. It had been furnished with the famous Gouttière Cabinet that belonged to the Comte d'Artois, and with tapestry chairs, and other fine French things. The King began with the Queen's memorial, going back upon his approval of the scheme, persuaded by X——, who was angry because she had not been consulted, that there was danger "of mobs in front of the Palace"—"Trafalgar Square"—etc., a tissue of rubbish. I said what I thought, but I would not argue. I wrote strongly to Knollys to-day. Later he sat down to bridge; the Princesses slipped away, and I made my bow.

I regret the mystery and awe of the old Court. However, the change was inevitable.

[*To M. V. B.*]   ORCHARD LEA,
                                                            APRIL 18TH.

I am running through the new edition of Byron's letters. He, too, was a mixture of genius, of splendid intellectual brilliancy, and of sordid heartlessness.

But this is a more common form of contrast. His great score was that he loved and admired Sir Walter Scott. That makes up for a multitude of sins.

Queen Victoria's Papers.

I saw the King this morning. The other day, when we drove to White Lodge, I had no opportunity to refer to his request that I would arrange the Queen's papers. To-day I did so, and he was very complimentary and generous. . . .

[*To M. V. B.*]   ORCHARD LEA,
                                                            APRIL 22ND.

The King's Car.

I came down with Marcus Beresford in the train to-night—fresh from Sandringham. On Saturday he drove with the King to Newmarket, in the latter's new motor car, 50 miles in 2½ hours. Not bad. He says the *dust* was something portentous. They were white as millers.

[*To M. V. B.*]   ORCHARD LEA,
                                                APRIL 24TH.

. . . No love is strange. It is all, in whatever guise, so very *On Love* human. I remember finding somewhere the review in *The* *and "In* *Times* of "In Memoriam." Vials of ridicule were poured upon *Memoriam."* Tennyson, and his affection for what the reviewer called "this Amaryllis of the Chancery bar." And I remember also reading a letter, written by one of the most splendid English writers and preachers upon that same reviewer—a letter full of magnificent wrath. "Of course," he wrote, "the love of 'IN MEMORIAM' appears exaggerated to those who feel feebly. This is ignorance of human nature. The friendship of a school boy is as full of tenderness, and jealousy and passionateness, as even love itself. I remember how my heart beat for ——; how it beat at seeing him, how the consciousness of his listening while I was reading or translating, annihilated the presence of the master; how I fought for him; how to rescue him from prisoner's base, turned the effect of mere play into ferocious determination as if the captivity were real; how my blood crept cold with delight when he came to rescue me; and this miserable quill driver in the very spirit of flunkeyism calls this poem exaggerated, because all the poetry of the affections is made ludicrous by remembering that this Amaryllis was a barrister at the Chancery bar. If the Chancery bar or any other accident of a man's environment destroys the real poetry of life, then the human soul has no worth but that which comes from its trappings—an idea which I reckon about the most decisive proof of a vulgar soul which can be found!"

If ever you feel inclined to scoff at love which you think exaggerated, will you remember this passage.

[*To M. V. B.*]   ORCHARD LEA,
                                                APRIL 25TH.

. . . The Government are afraid that when Milner leaves S. *State of* Africa, Kitchener may grant Botha too easy terms! Not one's *the Boer* *War.*

preconceived idea of K. But his troops are worn out. The whole point is now one of *amnesty* for the rebels in Botha's force. If it is granted, he surrenders. Milner is opposed to it on the ground that it is unfair to the loyalists. That is always so in civil war. But there never was civil war yet, that did not end in the long run in amnesty.

After the American war the rebels were pardoned—or they would have been fighting still.

[*From the Duke of Argyll.*]   KENSINGTON,
                                            APRIL 23RD.

MY DEAR ESHER,

Deputy Governor, Windsor Castle

If I die gubernatorially I am glad my swan song shall be of your Deputy Governorship, and herewith enclose a formal epistle. Lord Edward has been told that there will be a change now that he has resigned the Mastership of the Household. If you make any holes in the outer walls I may be liable to a hanging over said aperture.

I have sent the King a Memo. on the appointment of the Governorship of which I will send you a copy later when I get back to London. It points out that the office at the Tower of London is a little like that at Windsor—that the G. ship is a military command (which in peace in a minor fortress can always be styled a sinecure)—and that the Police and military have to send in regular reports to the G. of anything occurring within precincts of Castle. Pole Carew reported to me for H.M. information for instance the other day. The Police report that all is well before the Sovereign arrives, etc. In short I have kept up the forms belonging to a commandantship which has lasted since the Conquest.

                                            Yours, etc.
                                            ARGYLL.

[*To M. V. B.*]   ORCHARD LEA,
                                   APRIL 26TH.

... My appointment as "Lieutenant and Deputy Governor of Windsor Castle" arrived from Lorne—who is the Constable —with the King's approval. So that is settled, and I have the right of "pit and gallows" and should like to use it on one or two of our Windsor and Eton worthies.

... I hope you read the Kaiser's speech which I marked for you.[1] No man living in any country could have made so eloquent a one. Do you not agree? It struck the right note for boyhood blossoming into manhood.

[*To M. V. B.*]   ORCHARD LEA,
                                   MAY 5TH.

... I drove to Frogmore this morning, to see the house vacated by the Munshi, and then to the Castle. Laking had found some splendid armour in a back room in the Round Tower.

[*To M. V. B.*]   ORCHARD LEA,
                                   MAY 6TH.

... I only got back at 9 to-night. The King came to the garden at B. Palace at 4, and stayed till 7. I could not escape. *Ascot Committee.* He has put me on to the committee about Ascot, where all sorts

---

[1] The Kaiser had visited Bonn and made an address to the Corps of Students which was not only charming in its reminiscent tone and lofty in its idealism, but was also welcome to the English and to some sections of the German Press by its stress on the national Germanic basis of the Empire. It was held to be a corrective to the hints of expansion and world dominion which had been read into his earlier speeches. *The Times* leader, however, gave a caution against drawing wide general conclusions from the speech, and reminded the public that the Emperor commonly spoke out of the mood of the moment.

of changes are proposed. I fancy it will be a very tiresome enquiry; as there are tremendous differences of opinion as to what should be done.

[*To M. V. B.*]   ORCHARD LEA,
                                                   MAY 15TH.

. . . The King was queer to-day. He walked about the garden knocking dead wood out of trees with his stick—saying, "I always do this *at home*. It is the only way to get it done." Rather pathetic his speaking of Sandringham as "home." He looks upon these other possessions as encumbrances, I think—although I am sure that he will get to like Windsor.

He says I am to wear rather a nice uniform as Deputy-Governor of Windsor. Blue and scarlet, a tunic and a hat with a straight plume, with a sash round the waist. It sounds rather smart. No wonder the guard turns out!

[*To M. V. B.*]   ORCHARD LEA,
                                                   MAY 16TH.

. . . I was examined before a committee of both Houses this morning upon the King's opening of Parliament. I had to sit in a chair for about ¾ of an hour and be badgered by silly questions.

[*To M. V. B.*]   ORCHARD LEA,
                                                   MAY 20TH.

. . . All this morning I was on the Committee about Ascot racecourse which the King has appointed.

We arrived at no conclusion and have to meet again. I saw the King afterwards. He was sitting and examining a bust of himself—and was rather exercised about the nose. He thought

H.M. KING EDWARD VII AT BATSFORD, 1905.
From a drawing by the Hon. J. Mitford.

it was too short! I assured him to the contrary, but I do not think he was convinced.

[*To M. V. B.*]   ORCHARD LEA,
                                   MAY 21ST.

... Saw the King again after luncheon—sitting in his room upstairs with his after-luncheon cigar. Looking wonderfully like Henry VIII, only better tempered.

Then I went to the House of Lords and listened to Lovat making a halting speech about his S. African experiences. Although he can't string three words together, everyone, including Lord Salisbury, appeared enthralled. Such is the force of a man having some *facts* to relate.

Demosthenes is not in it with him!

[*To M. V. B.*]   ORCHARD LEA,
                                   MAY 27TH.

I am going into Windsor with Reggie Lister. We shall be muddling about in the Library most of the morning.

Lady Gosford told Reggie that at bridge there was a wrangle as to what points they should play. The Queen said she would not play for money, as her income had not been voted by the Government yet. In the end they fixed on pennies. When the game was over the score stood:

The King plus 11*d.*
The Queen minus 7*d.*!

[*To M. V. B.*]   ORCHARD LEA,
                                   MAY 28TH.

Yesterday I drove early to Windsor with Reggie Lister. We found Lady Gosford and walked through all the rooms—to the

Library—where we were engrossed in miniatures for a long time. There are beauties, which you must see. Notably one of Monmouth—who was a real beauty; and a queer nude one of Nell Gwyn painted for Charles II.

After a while the Queen sent for us, and we met her in the corridor. She was in excellent spirits, full of rag and mischief. She is coming over to tea some day this week—so she says! We drove home to luncheon, and then I bicycled up to Ascot.

. . . Reggie's spirits had been depressed since morning, from having been to the Castle in *brown* boots, and having noticed Princess Victoria's eye fixed on them!

The Queen had on a most extraordinary hat, like a squashed mushroom, and yet she looked perfectly regal as usual. I am not going to London to-day, being summoned to Windsor.

[*To M. V. B.*]   WINDSOR CASTLE,
                                             MAY 31ST.

Yesterday I was all day here, and in the afternoon we drove to Ascot. Four grey horses in a brake, and two outriders. As I was waiting for the King, I saw a little hatless figure near the gate, talking to the footman, and recognised John.[1] Then Sandy appeared. As we drove off I waved to John, and the King asked who he was. We had a beautiful drive through the Park, and walked about at Ascot—for hours. His energy is untiring. He is at it hard again to-day.

[*To M. V. B.*]   ORCHARD LEA,
                                             JUNE 2ND.

. . . I am glad you were here to-day to meet the King and Queen. It is a reminiscence and an interesting one. You received three generations! The Queen—retaining her grace and beauty—does not strike one as a grandmother!

[1] Lord Roos, afterwards Duke of Rutland.

... Did I tell you that the Windsor court has stiffened up *Etiquette at Windsor.* very much since we dined there last? The King takes in the Queen—and everyone else takes in a lady.

You come out of dinner the same way. Then after an interval comes bridge. The King's table is in one room and the Queen's in another. She does not play for money. The non-players *sit* and talk. When the Queen retires the guests leave—but I went and bid good-night to the Monarch—after my game with the Queen.

All day yesterday he muddled with pictures—and all this morning he was at it again. His energy is untiring. I think he will prove a good master to good servants. However that we shall see later. The only blot on the past two days has been that I have not been enough with you.

[*To M. V. B.*] ORCHARD LEA, JUNE 5TH.

I send you some very fine lines by Kipling from to-day's *Kipling.* *Times.* How wonderfully he reads the soldier's character, and the pathos of a soldier's life. He ranks with Napier, and with Kinglake, at their best.

With the former rather than with the latter, in his sympathy with the genuine "Tommy."

[*To M. V. B.*] ORCHARD LEA, JUNE 11TH.

... I have been worried all day about this ceremony for to- *On Corona-* morrow.[1] The military authorities were too stupid for words *tion Cere-* and I had to go to the King who damned them all in heaps. *monial.* Heaven knows how we shall get through the coronation, which

[1] Presentation of South African War medals on the Horse Guards Parade by the King.

began to-day! I think it will take place on one of three dates. 24 May, 20 June or 28 June.

At present the King inclines to the former. I have just written to him a very "conservative" letter, urging him to adhere to all ancient practices and traditions unless they are "ridiculous."

It was the revolt of the young *noblesse* against the old fusty customs which materially helped to bring the fall of the French monarchy.

[*To M. V. B.*]   SANDRINGHAM,
                                                JUNE 20TH.

Etiquette at San-dringham.

. . . I arrived here very late—and found a brougham and a note from General Probyn—which I enclose—giving me full directions. After dinner I went to the dining-room, and sat next the King, who got very excited over one or two things, using rather more vehement language than usual. However, he was quite pleasant. It is altogether different here from Windsor. No ceremonial at all. Just a country home. After dinner the Queen played "patience" with Gladys de Grey and Nellie.

The King sat on the sofa and talked for about half an hour, then the women went to bed—and the King led the way to the billiard room. He sat down to bridge, and the rest of us sat and talked, while de Grey performed miracles on the billiard table *à la Cinquevalli.*

I talked to Soveral, who was charming and witty as usual. About 1 o'clock we went to bed. All the clocks here are half an hour fast. It is an old custom. When Queen Victoria came here she had them all put back. She thought it a ridiculous habit and a "lie"—so characteristic of her!

[*To M. V. B.*]   SANDRINGHAM,
                                                JUNE 21ST.

I have been driving with the King most of to-day. We went to Houghton—Cholmondeley's place—a splendid house built by Walpole but frightfully neglected owing to poverty. A sleepy hollow of a park. Possibly the Duke of York may rent it. I wonder if George[1] has ever been there. We drove 8 miles in 19 minutes in the King's motor—really very pleasant—only you have to wear spectacles.

Last night I sat between the Queen and Princess Victoria at dinner. I talked mainly to the former about books and the war. She is very attractive.

This morning I played about in the garden with the children and took lots of photographs. The second boy is the sharpest— but there is something rather taking about Prince Edward. He wants a walking stick with a horse's head on it for his birthday.

Soveral is very charming and Paget tells wonderful stories about the war. Life here is very simple. The King walks about like any country gentleman, and there is no pomp. Only *before* dinner there is an attempt at ceremonial. We never get to bed before one.

[*To M. V. B.*]   ORCHARD LEA,
JUNE 27TH.

. . . To-day has not been very interesting. I lunched with Mrs. Leo [Rothschild] *tête-à-tête* and heard all her gossip about the party, and I bought a lovely sword at auction—worth £60. I found it myself and Laking was enchanted. I got it for £3 15! and he was furiously jealous.

. . . To-morrow I am going to Hampton Court to meet the Queen about 5 o'clock. In the evening I return here.

[*To Lord Knollys.*]   OFFICE OF WORKS,
JULY 15TH.

Will you inform His Majesty that the Executive Committee met to consider the Architects for the Memorial, and that they

The Queen Victoria Memorial.

---

[1] Lord George Cholmondeley.

had before them Mr. Brock's sketch, and several other schemes.

The Committee at their second meeting which took place after His Majesty's visit to St. James's Palace adopted the following resolution.

"The Committee recommend that Mr. Brock's Memorial be accepted, subject to such modifications as may be necessitated by the scheme of the Memorial as a whole. That Mr. Aston Webb's plan for the general treatment of the space in front of Buckingham Palace be accepted, subject to certain necessary changes.

"The Committee further recommend that the consideration of the remainder of the Mall scheme be postponed until the amount of the subscription to the National Memorial has been determined."

I have consequently sent a copy of this Resolution to Lord Salisbury, who will no doubt summon a meeting of the General Committee, after which he will doubtless lay the decisions of that Committee before His Majesty.

[*To M. V. B.*]　　OFFICE OF WORKS,
JULY 15TH.

. . . To-day I have been hard pressed, as usual. Fools weary me. I lunched with Cairns and Colonel Kitson—the Military attaché at Washington—a very clever fellow, who will accompany the Committee to Sandhurst. He knows all about West Point—and much about Sandhurst.

You will receive this visit on Thursday for certain. I saw the old Duke of Cambridge to-day, who was full of recollections of two previous coronations. I am writing down all that he told me.

[*From Sir Arthur Bigge.*[1]]   H.M.S. "OPHIR,"
                                         AUGUST 2ND.

MY DEAR ESHER,

It is exactly 20 weeks since we came on board this good ship; please God in 13 weeks more we shall be at home again. I have often wished to have a good talk with you; for I felt that were I at home we could mutually appreciate the changes which from necessity must have been made so quickly, and yet continue to be made, and it would be interesting to compare our views on so interesting a subject. In fact I know nobody whose opinion I would sooner hear; for you thoroughly knew the past order of things and I expect you have much to do in the creating of the new—if I am right in my surmise *tant mieux* that you are there! . . .

                                         Ever yours,
                                         ARTHUR BIGGE.

[*To M. V. B.*]   THE ROMAN CAMP,
                                         SEPTEMBER 22ND.

. . . I have just been writing to Knollys about S. Africa. The *State* shrieks of *The Times* for more men are so silly. We have got *of the* so many men there now that they are a prey to the Boers. *War.*

We try to do too much. The problem is not understood. It is really similar to that which had to be faced in the Lennox 1700–20 when Rob Roy was the Botha of the District.

Every British force moving about Africa should be superior to any possible Boer force. If we guarded the frontiers of the C. Colony and Natal, and the big towns, it is sufficient. Of course loyal farmers would suffer here and there for a time— and the railway it is absurd to guard. A prominent Boer on every train, passenger or luggage, who would be shot through

---

[1] Now Private Secretary to the Duke of Cornwall.

the head at the first sign of an attack would soon protect the line. We want:

(1) An Administrator—like Lawrence of the Punjab.
(2) Fewer soldiers.
(3) Patience!

That is my prescription.

[*To M. V. B.*]   OFFICE OF WORKS,
                                                    OCTOBER 3RD.

Kitchener   . . . He thinks that these last two fights will shake the Boers a
and   good deal. It appears that Botha—who has many friends here—
Milner.   is heartily sick of war—but is kept going by Steyn and de Wet.
Ward[1] quite agrees that Kitchener is too big a man to be in the
same country with Milner, also a big man, and that the settlement being more administrative now than military, K. should
come away. He is to be the C.-in-C. in India.

[*To M. V. B.*]   ORCHARD LEA,
                                                    OCTOBER 10TH.

I was in Westminster Abbey all the morning, making pre-
liminary plans for the coronation. I think it will be a fine
ceremony, and my Swan Song as far as the Office is concerned.

I lunched with the ineffable Sidney Greville—who came and
routed me out. He was full of court gossip. They want a
Master of the Horse for the Duke of Cornwall. I suggested
Brocklehurst. If the Queen will give him up, they will not do
better. He is *her* equerry, and she is very tenacious!

[*To M. V. B.*]   ORCHARD LEA,
                                                    OCTOBER 14TH.

I am very tired to-night. And I cannot imagine the cause.
There is no reason that I can think of. The motor-car went

[1] Col. E. Ward, Permanent Under-Secretary to the War Office.

beautifully to-day, and I am thinking of taking Nellie to the station to-morrow.

. . . I lunched with Arthur Ellis who has returned from Balmoral. The King wears his kilt in the daytime as well as in the evening. He is very well, in spite of rumours to the contrary. Only suffering from lumbago.

There is a coronation medal which he will give people to wear. It is to have a crown on the top and a wreath round it (like the French medals). The King and Queen's heads. More like an order than a medal—which is perfectly correct.

The only other news is the probable abolition of "drawing-rooms." This will not be popular. The idea is to have five enormous evening parties instead—to which people will be invited. *"Drawing-room" and "Courts."*

This is not at all the same thing as a "drawing-room" at which the dentist's wife was presented by Mrs. M.P. for Slocum Pogis.

It has been suggested that when young ladies are "presented" at these parties—the *Queen* should kiss them, at which the King kicks strenuously!

[*To M. V. B.*]   ORCHARD LEA,
OCTOBER 15TH.

The news to-day is that Buller is on the verge of dismissal. Roberts telegraphed very indignantly to Brodrick for an explanation—such a speech was contrary to the rules of the service —and his reference to a secret telegram, and his proposal to produce it, a breach of discipline so serious that it would be necessary, if no explanation was forthcoming, to place the culprit on half pay, and relieve him of his command. *Trouble over Buller.*

Brodrick, from Balmoral, says that the King strongly supports Roberts—so I imagine Buller is doomed—although Lord Salisbury has not yet given his decision.

I confess I think the man deserves his fate. His example will be a most salutary one. There will be no more "surrenders" in future, either advised or accomplished.

The telegrams from S. Africa are more hopeful than they have been for many a long day.

[*To General Sir Arthur Ellis.*] ORCHARD LEA,
OCTOBER 20TH.

Suggestion for Court Ceremonial. I am much honoured that you should think my humble criticisms worth writing down. Since you have asked me, I should like to make one or two suggestions on the "pageantry" of the King's reception, and then the observations which occurred to me in reference to presentations.

1. I have always thought the *mise-en-scène* of a Drawing-room and a Levée spoilt, owing to the Sovereign not standing more conspicuously forward. After the Windsor entertainments the Queen used to receive her guests, sitting *alone* in the centre of the room, with the Royal Family grouped behind her. This was very effective.

If His Majesty will stand before a Canopy—even though on the floor—at Buckingham Palace, in the Ball Room—and the Queen stands about four feet away on his left—with all the Princes and Princesses grouped *behind* them, the effect will be very fine.

2. There should be a wide space left in front of the Sovereign, between the dais and the general circle; and some of the great Officers of State could stand facing the Monarch, which would enhance the spectacle.

3. If His Majesty would receive the Ambassadors in the Ball Room, before receiving the rest of those attending, it would then be possible for him to stand on the step of the dais. This gives at once a nobler air to the spectacle.

It is quite easy to kiss the King's hand under those circumstances, and any other form of salutation is as *démodée* as the embrace by the Peers after the Coronation, which the King has very properly abolished.

4. Perhaps the Queen may modify the form of "low-necked dress" worn hitherto—and allow women to wear sleeves—at any rate to the elbow. The *décolletage* hitherto in vogue being one of the most trying and unbecoming costumes ever invented for women.

5. Perhaps His Majesty would consider whether a "train" should not be a regular official garment, of some selected material—i.e. velvet or satin—whichever is selected—and *not* sometimes of one, sometimes of the other, and often of "chiffon" which looks like an elongated housemaid's duster.

6. If the King abolishes Drawing-rooms and institutes "Courts" by invitation, a difficulty will arise in maintaining the old plan of "presentations." It furnishes a good opportunity for revising a system full of abuses; notably the receiving of payments for presentation at Court, and the irresponsible introduction for political or social reasons to the Sovereign of persons who should not be admissible.

The obvious reform would be to allow introductions to the Sovereign to be made only by official personages.

The Mistress of the Robes.

The wife of the Foreign Secretary.

The wife of the Colonial Secretary. . . .

[*To M. V. B.*]   ORCHARD LEA,
                              OCTOBER 20TH.

. . . I have just finished a long letter of ten large sides to Arthur Ellis on the new "Courts." He asked me to give him on paper my ideas of presentations, etc. I have aired all my fads.

I don't know that the abolition of the "drawing-room" will be popular. I rather doubt it. Still, the present system is an abuse. Will you remember that all Tuesday and Wednesday

I shall be in London—sleeping in London on Tuesday night. This is only in case you want to telegraph.

The King returns to-morrow from Scotland, arriving Tuesday morning. There will be no peace until he goes off to Sandringham after Prince George returns on November 1st. The coronation business will then begin in earnest.

On the Tudors.

. . . While you were at Windsor I went to the Farm, and sat in the room upstairs reading the accounts sent by the foreign ambassadors to their courts of Henry VIII when, quite a young man, he became King.

He must have been an engaging creature—quite splendid to look at, and a noble athlete. With all his supremacy at games and sport, he combined a wonderful love of music and poetry, and high skill in both. Those Tudors were an extraordinary race. Henry's sister, Mary—who married as a girl the decrepit King of France, Louis XII, and after his death insisted on marrying the man she had always loved, Charles Brandon, Duke of Suffolk, was a regular heroine of romance. There was not one of the brood but was full of character—standing out in bold relief from among all the lay figures of history.

If I go on writing in this strain I shall weary you. It is a lapse into the style of old days.

[*To M. V. B.*]   ORCHARD LEA,
                                   OCTOBER 21ST.

The Buller Case.

. . . To-night there was a sort of "rump" Cabinet at the W.O. to settle the fate of Buller. Timid spirits advise that he should be let alone. Of course every day that lapses makes it more difficult to punish him.

[*To M. V. B.*]   OFFICE OF WORKS,
                                   OCTOBER 22ND.

The Buller Case.

The Cabinet Committee decided nothing about Buller, and they met again to-day. Roberts was very fair but strong and emphatic. Buller defies them, and tries to blackmail—threatening all sorts of disclosures and that he will "drag down many others with him." Roberts is prepared to relieve Brodrick of all responsibility, and to take the blame of dismissal on his own shoulders. He says, in truth, that after calling on Buller to explain and the latter's refusal either he or Buller must go. Otherwise his authority as C.-in-C. is forfeited.

He is not vindictive but very firm. Although not a good administrator, and fond of "jobs"—he is a courageous, honourable and straightforward gentleman.

I don't think Buller is any of these things. You will be sorry to hear that B—— *was* one of the cavalry leaders he was forced to dismiss—very reluctantly. He says that French[1] was the only *first-rate* cavalry-man he had with him.

We had a long "coronation" confab to-night. A quantity of queer points, but I think we made a start. I am to see Norfolk to-morrow and arrange the next move. *Coronation : Early Arrangements.*

The Queen has settled to have four Duchesses to stand near her in Westminster Abbey, and to arrange her crown. She is to select the four herself—tall and well matched. . . .

I believe that it is settled that the Princesses are not to wear anything on their heads, and are to put on their crowns when the Queen puts hers on.

[*From Mr. A. G. Harmsworth.*]　　THE "DAILY MAIL,"
OCTOBER 22ND.

DEAR LORD ESHER,

You may or may not know that rumours about the King's health, which I believe to be absolutely untrue, are worrying the West End tradespeople a great deal. Yesterday for example, one of Poole's men who attends to me, told me that he did not think there would be a Coronation; to-day one of Catchpole and William's partners said the same thing. My own impression

---

[1] Gen. Sir John French, afterwards F.M. Earl of Ypres.

is that the King was never better. Do you think it would be wise for me to contradict these rumours emphatically? They have already appeared in print in provincial papers.

Yours faithfully,

A. G. HARMSWORTH.

[*To M. V. B.*]   ORCHARD LEA,
OCTOBER 27TH.

The drive home last night was perfect. The moon was full and the roads solitary and smooth. But it was cold, and the result is to-day I am not fit for human society. To-morrow the King comes down by the 10.15 train, and I meet him at Windsor —always providing I can get out.

. . . I suppose the King will give us a long day to-morrow. On Thursday at Buckingham Palace he looked at everything— but my remembrance of him principally is sitting on a turned-up table in the middle of the Ball room, surrounded by masses of bedroom furniture, smoking a cigarette, and gossiping to me about old Wetherby, the Sec. of the Jockey Club, who has just retired. . . .

[*To M. V. B.*]   ORCHARD LEA,
OCTOBER 28TH.

Such a day. By dint of smelling and sucking camphor I patched up my cold, and was able to drive in the brougham to Windsor. The King came down in the ordinary train at 10.45 and I met him. We spent a long day, looking at everything. Lunched in the equerry's room, very cosily—an excellent lunch —and drove to Frogmore. I accompanied him to the station amid quite a thick crowd. He was very well received. There were not many Eton boys, and when I saw the train *arrive* at 5.40 this was explained—as the whole school had evidently been on leave.

... This evening came the enclosed telegram. You see it reached me very late. Poor old thing,[1] I hope he will die suddenly and peacefully—the happiest of deaths. I shall go up to-morrow morning to London, and probably down to Esher in the afternoon. I shall possibly sleep in London, but of this you shall hear by telegram.

I shall have to look after him, as there is no one else—and you can imagine how this fits in with the multitudinous duties that no one else can perform, many of them fixed for to-morrow! However, I must manage somehow. The King seems to take no interest in the coronation at present. It is, I suppose, too far off. Or, he may have some haunting superstition that it may not take place. Yet, he looks very well, and appears very well, although I have seen him in better spirits. I think the "yoke" begins to make itself felt a little. This is a good thing.

[*To M. V. B.*]   ORCHARD LEA,
                                   OCTOBER 29TH.

... I have had rather a hard day. A meeting with Norfolk this morning to prepare for the bigger meeting in the afternoon. Then I lunched with Harmsworth—a clever, vain man—not very intelligent about anything except organisation and money-making; but full of aspirations for power. The man rather interests me, as all self-made men do. ...

In the afternoon we had our big committee. Settled a few coronation ceremonials, but the body is effete! Little Bradford[2] poured out all his grievances to me. The people about the King send messages through the War Office—which infuriates him—as he takes orders from no one. He is not a bit touchy, but the stupidity of the thing annoys him.

... Then at 5.20 I went to Esher. Uncle Wilford knew me, and laughed in his jovial way, but he could not speak. He is not likely to live through the night.

[1] Sir Wilford Brett, K.C.M.G., his uncle.
[2] Sir Edward Bradford, Commissioner of Police.

"Sea
Power in
History."
You will not find the *Sea Power in History*[1] clash with your notions about the navy. Fisher,[2] who is perhaps the best of our seamen, thinks this book a classical work. So it has the approval of an expert. I gather from it that a modern sea fight might give one a sensation, in spite of the ugliness of a modern line of battleships.

The great point of the book, however, is what constitutes the real mastery of the sea. It is in this portion that you will find an echo to some of your ideas. "Fast cruisers" to protect commerce will never give us supremacy. It is weight of metal, seamanship, seagoing qualities, etc. that tell in the end. The account which the writer gives of Colbert's policy and its success and failures, is very instructive.

I thought Rosebery much better in spirits and health. He goes abroad immediately his "proofs" are supervised. . . .

Newmarket was delightful. . . .

I saw Arthur Balfour after his return from Germany, where he had been on a musical tour with the Elchos. Lady Elcho captivated Bismarck, who thinks her the most beautiful and charming of women. Had he been still Chancellor this might seriously have affected the Triple Alliance. Arthur, however, was a great success with Madame Wagner. So there were compensations. . . .

There was an enormous amount of betting on the Cambridge-shire. More than for many years. A fortune was won by three obscure individuals who planned and brought off a clever coup. Most people lost. I won a little, Loulou [Harcourt] will be pleased to hear. So I can afford to play piquet with him next time we meet. Always a most expensive amusement. . . .

---

[1] By Capt. Mahan.   [2] Afterwards Admiral of the Fleet, Lord Fisher.

[*To M. V. B.*]　　　　　　　　ORCHARD LEA,
　　　　　　　　　　　　　　　NOVEMBER 3RD.

. . . We have been looking through some old pedigrees to-
night and found that we have, a *very* short way back, a common
ancestor with Shelley. His grandfather, and my g.g.grand-
mother were brother and sister. Her name was Frances Shelley.
I will show it to you next Saturday.

[*To M. V. B.*]　　　　　　　　OFFICE OF WORKS,
　　　　　　　　　　　　　　　NOVEMBER 5TH.

. . . To-night I had to go and see Arthur Ellis, who showed *Orders of*
me rather a nice book containing pictures of all the "Orders" in *Chivalry.*
Europe. The Russian cross of St. George, first class, not a single
living Russian—not even the Emperor—can wear. At one
time there were three in the world, of which the Duke of
Wellington was one, and neither of the others were Russians.
The qualification is to have "commanded a victorious army in
the field."

The "Order of Maria Theresa" is Hungarian, and the
qualification is to have "broken into an infantry square."

The Austrian "Golden Fleece"—a very sacred order—can
only be worn by catholics, who take the oath always to wear
some badge of the order. So they have a collar made in which
they sleep at night. This oath, or promise, used to be made by
our Knights of the Garter, but I believe that they no longer
adhere to the pledge. Ellis gave me a most interesting medal,
by Fuchs, commemorative of Queen Victoria.

[*To M. V. B.*]　　　　　　　　ORCHARD LEA,
　　　　　　　　　　　　　　　NOVEMBER 7TH.

. . . My day was altogether without adventure. I saw de
Grey, and asked him if Shankland[1] did harm by shooting grouse

---

[1] His keeper at the Roman Camp.

*Thomas
Brock.*

too late, and he says no. Keepers lie in wait and shoot the grouse sitting on the walls. They rarely walk across moors. The season is over on the tenth of the month.

I went up to see Brock the sculptor to-day, and he has given me two little works of his. One a bust of Leighton, the artist, and the other a statuette of "Eve"—very nude and pretty.[1] If I get anything out of the wreckage of Uncle Wilford's estate, I shall make him do me a bust of my father. He has done a splendid one of Lord Russell of Killowen from a photograph.

[*To the Vice-Provost of Eton.*]   ORCHARD LEA,
                                          NOVEMBER 10TH.

*Schemes
for Eton.*

I understand that on Tuesday next there is to be a meeting of the Governing Body to discuss, among other matters, the question of a S. African Memorial to Old Etonians who have fallen.

If the scheme, as I hear is not improbable, takes the shape of a "Speech Room," let me urge upon you the conversion of Upper School into a School Library.

As you are aware, this is not a new idea. It has commended itself for many years to Etonians, and is desirable mainly on the ground that it will perpetuate the use of an historical room, full of association, to a practical purpose, connecting the Eton of the past with the Eton of the future.

---

[1] Mr., afterwards Sir Thomas, Brock wrote :

                    THE STUDIO, 30, OSNABURGH ST.,
                              REGENT'S PARK,
                              NOVEMBER 28TH.
DEAR LORD ESHER,

I am sending by bearer the little bronze bust of the late Lord Leighton, which you honoured me by accepting when you were here last. I do hope you will like it. "Eve" shall follow as soon as I can get a really satisfactory casting,

                    Believe me, yours very faithfully,
                              THOMAS BROCK.

The best judges of the requirements for a Library have held Upper School to be eminently adaptable; and I can safely quote J. W. Clark, who sees no difficulty in placing bookcases in the mediaeval fashion at right angles to the walls, and far enough from them to enable visitors to read the names cut on the panels. As you know, this method enables a room 95 feet long and 30 feet broad—which I believe to be the dimensions of Upper School—to be arranged so as to contain quite as many volumes as the School Library is likely to be required to hold. The recesses thus formed would be open, and as the bookcases would be low, and would not stand out more than 9 feet from the wall, the view down the room would be uninterrupted.

From the historic and economic points of view the scheme possesses advantages upon which I need not dwell; and I should like to add that I am confident many would subscribe to a Memorial which included this conversion in the general plan, who would hold aloof from what to some might appear a more ambitious scheme of endeavouring to erect a Speech Room and Library upon one site.

If you can urge these considerations upon the Governing Body I should be grateful.

It occurred to me to send these remarks to the Press, but I prefer on the whole to leave the matter in your hands in the hope that your colleagues may share the views which so many Old Etonians hold upon this point.

[*To the Rev. C. D. Williamson.*]   ORCHARD LEA,
NOVEMBER 12TH.

All is well. Rosebery threatens a speech as you see. Does he know what he would do, if he returned to power. If he does, and explains, he would serve the country well just now.[1] But I doubt.

[1] It is probable that Lord Esher had in mind no particular crisis, but the general situation—a situation thus described in *The Times Survey of the Year*,

I am up to the neck in a variety of work. Coronation, a War Office Committee on the Engineers, of which I am Chairman. The King's private affairs. All my office work, and my uncle's executor. So I have no time to write—but I think of you often.

[*To M. V. B.*]   ORCHARD LEA,
NOVEMBER 12TH.

Rosebery's
Position.

. . . To-day I lunched with Cairns and Spencer. They have both seen Rosebery, who cannot make up his mind what to say when he makes this impending political speech. If he really means business and to return to politics, I should have thought his course was easy. Some people are trying to tie Buller round his neck. If they succeed he will sink under the weight. The case *against* Buller is overwhelming. From his first telegram to the Colonies "unmounted men preferred," to his heliogram to White.

What the country wants is to know what Rosebery would do if he came into office. If he knows, he should say. If he doesn't know, he is not fit to succeed Lord Salisbury. That seems unanswerable!

[*To M. V. B.*]   OFFICE OF WORKS,
NOVEMBER 15TH.

All yesterday I was at Windsor. The King came up to the Castle from Frogmore with the P. of Wales—and they looked at everything. Then we went to Frogmore for lunch. There

December 31st, 1901: "The Parliamentary history of the year is not specially memorable, nor has it been such as to raise the reputation of the House of Commons or of Parliamentary institutions. A hostile critic might describe the composition of the House as a tired Ministry, a perfunctory majority, a divided and inconsequent Opposition, and a deliberately obstructive Irish party; not encouraging materials considering that the House was elected only fifteen months ago and that this is the first Parliament of a new reign."

was quite a large party. Two tables at luncheon. I sat next to the Prince of Wales—who has very much improved since he left England last spring. He has gained much in gravity from hard work and the experience of the colonies. Then we went into the garden, and got away for tea at Howdie's. Returned to Frogmore for dinner. We wore the Windsor uniform, and it was very well arranged. The guests assembled, as at Windsor, and the King is announced in proper style. He came in with the Prince of Wales and we went straight in to dinner. A long table this time. The King sat on one side of the table, with the Austrian and German ambassadors, and I sat again next to the Prince of Wales. He told me a good deal about his journey, *The Prince* especially about the Cape. He found the Dutch very civil and *on South* they showed a good deal of loyalty. Some of the prisoners *Africa.* made little presents for him and the Princess—so they visited the prison at Simonstown to thank them. He shook hands with a lot of them and made a little speech. He is firmly convinced that after the fighting is over, the Dutch will settle down as loyal subjects.

After dinner the King talked mainly to me and old Bridport. Then he had his game of bridge, and I asked leave to go at 11.30.

[*To M. V. B.*]　　　　　ORCHARD LEA,
　　　　　　　　　　　NOVEMBER 17TH.

... What a terrible thing is the drifting apart of friends. *On* Clough's poem of "*Qua cursam ventus.*" You remember it. It *Friendship.* is always in the night that the drift occurs, i.e. during absence. Separation—not knowing all the small varying moods and episodes of life—that is the fatal thing.

Of course it is possible to be faithful even though the widest seas separate you from one you love—but that fidelity is altogether different from the highest kind of intimacy. It is always half a pose of the heart, a constraint of the imagination. Of course, with very young souls like J—— you cannot expect a continuance of affection even—much less unbroken intercourse. They are always on the lookout for pastures new.

Then, fidelity is always an effort of the elder—and if the friendship is to remain unbroken, it can only be managed by the exercise of unusual tact and above all patience.

. . . It is a painful process, at least I have always found it so.

[*To M. V. B.*]   ORCHARD LEA,
                                                   NOVEMBER 18TH.

. . . I saw a charming letter from the Queen to-day, to Arthur Ellis, about her dress at the Coronation, saying " I know better than all the milliners, and antiquaries. I shall wear exactly what I like, and so shall all my ladies—Basta!"

She *will*, too, do exactly what she pleases! Anyway she will look charming.

[*To M. V. B.*]   ORCHARD LEA,
                                                   NOVEMBER 21ST.

German Annoyance.   . . . All the excitement in London centres round the burst of ill-feeling in Germany at Chamberlain's remarks about the war of 1870. He has never learnt the French proverb "*Toutes les vérités ne sont pas bonnes à dire.*" What he said about the Germans was perfectly accurate, but it was certain to provoke a storm.[1]

We are not so strong in friends on the Continent that it is worth while to excite the hostility of the least unfriendly to us of all nations. The Emperor will have a hard job to restrain the

[1] In the Speech referred to Mr. Chamberlain had spoken carelessly; that is all. The outcry in Germany was due to the effect of the most preposterous stories of "outrages" supposed to have been committed by the British troops —stories which had been constantly circulated and largely accepted throughout the previous two years. For particulars of this situation (interesting in view of what was to happen in 1914–18) see *The Times'* leader, November 20th.

fury of his people. Chamberlain's faults all come from his *Chamber-*
lain. upbringing. Clever as he is, he has never learnt the self-restraint which everyone learns at a great public school or at a university. I mean everyone with his immense capacity.

The Government has grown so weak from old age—is so *Rosebery.* worn out—that if only Rosebery possessed Lord Beaconsfield's indomitable courage and perseverance, they would be out of office in a few months. I fear, however, he is soft-hearted. His head is all right but his soul is not tempered. He wanted the fire of adversity. Until 1895—when he became Prime Minister —the hand of man had never been raised against him—and the hand of God but once—when he lost his wife.

[*To M. V. B.*]　　　　　　　ORCHARD LEA,
　　　　　　　　　　　　NOVEMBER 25TH.

. . . If the Government really made an effort, I think they *Progress*
of the
War. could arrange a peace. Lord Cromer was asked the other day his views and he said something might be done.

His interlocutors said it was a pity the Government did not send him out, and added "Of course you might not succeed in achieving anything." To which Cromer replied very drily, "At any rate I might *try*." By which he meant that the Government do not.

I heard to-day of a curious talk between Chamberlain and *Chamber-*
lain on his
Mistakes. Morley, who in spite of violent political antagonism still manage to remain private friends. Chamberlain admitted that he had got into a devil of a mess in S. Africa—a remarkable admission. Morley said, "You admit this to me in private, why don't you have the courage to say so in public?" "No," said Chamberlain, "that would never do." I think he is right. No good would come of such a confession, but his knowledge of his mistakes does him credit. Most men would not admit such a thing to themselves in the silence of the night. My committee begins to-morrow.[1] Such a labour.

---

[1] On the Royal Engineers.

"Last of the Dandies."

. . . Granny has been to see *The Last of the Dandies*. She says it is excellent. When she says a play is good, it nearly always is so. The converse is not however to be trusted. D'Orsay, she says, looks younger than she remembers him at the end of his life—but wonderfully like. Of course Lady Blessington is much too youthful. Granny remembers her with black ribbons tying up her double chins! She says Dizzy is very like what he was at that time of life. D'Orsay drew the head of the picture of Granny in the *Book of Beauty* published in 1840 by Lady Blessington.

[*To M. V. B.*]   ORCHARD LEA,
                                                  NOVEMBER 26TH.

Committee on the Royal Engineers.

I had four hours of my committee to-day, and examined the Deputy Inspector-General of Fortifications. He was a friend of General Gordon's, and I knew him in old days. We take his chief to-morrow. I rather fancied my cross-examination. My colleagues are very friendly so far. General Leach V.C. quite intelligent and amiable. I must find out how he won the V.C.

Foreign Feeling on the War.

There are rumours of a cabal against us among foreign powers to stop the war, instigated by Russia. I am very sceptical about their coming to an agreement. They could not agree about Armenia a few years ago, and only half agreed to coerce China —so I doubt their acting in accord against us.

Still, the situation is not pleasant, and must be dangerous until peace is achieved. There are, on the other hand, excellent telegrams from French—who thinks that in another few weeks we will have cleared all the Boers out of the Cape Colony Kitchener seems also more cheerful—but he is very much bored with Milner!

[*To M. V. B.*]   OFFICE OF WORKS,
                                                  NOVEMBER 28TH.

Sir William Nicholson.

I have been on my committee all day. We had Sir William Nicholson before us to-day. The cleverest soldier I have yet seen. No wonder that Bobs relies on him. Such a hard-headed man. Most clear and determined and explicit. We had also Sir Frederic Stopford, a charming ex-Grenadier. Very intelligent and attractive.

. . . The play *When we were Twenty-one* is one of the best I have seen for a long time. It is by Esmond, and acted by Americans—a Miss Maxine Elliott—a beautiful and talented woman. But the whole company is first rate. It is such a good play that I should like you to see it on Saturday afternoon. The last day of the performance, as the Company leaves for America. You would enjoy it immensely.

[*To M. V. B.*]   OFFICE OF WORKS,
                    DECEMBER 2ND.

I have been harried all day. I had no time to telegraph until this evening.

. . . My committee is very tiresome.

. . . I have just finished a huge bag of papers, and long letters to George Curzon in India, about one or two things. He is one of the greatest of Viceroys, if not altogether *the* greatest. Certainly, except Cromer, no other Englishman possesses his qualities as an administrator and possibly none as a statesman. He has enormous capacity for work, and a brilliant imagination, with supreme gift of expression.

On Curzon as Viceroy.

[*To M. V. B.*]   OFFICE OF WORKS,
                    DECEMBER 3RD.

Although I shall see you to-morrow, I want to tell you one or two things in case we get no chance of talking alone together.

Sir Ernest Cassel—who is one of the greatest of financial magnates—and whom I met at dinner at Frogmore, called on me to-day—and made me much the same sort of offer that Pierpont Morgan made Dawkins. If I would leave the office,

Offer from Sir Ernest Cassel.

and associate myself with him in great enterprises in Egypt and America—to give me a large share in his business. *I* have taken time to consider. If it comes off, it will not be till June next. If I accept it will be for your sake.

This evening I saw Bobs, and had a long talk about the Army and Sandhurst. He was charming. I went to his house in Portland Place. A picture of Nicholson—the hero of Delhi—hangs over his writing table. I asked about him. Roberts praised his extraordinary strength, determination and gentle smile—and tenderness to those he liked. He says that Nicholson took Delhi. Without him Wilson would never have succeeded. Evidently Nicholson was his hero. The other picture in the room is Julian Story's posthumous portrait of young Roberts. It is very pleasant and brilliant for Julian.

. . . To-morrow night I dine with the King, and so shall miss my dinner with you.

[*To M. V. B.*]   ORCHARD LEA,
                                                  DECEMBER 5TH.

. . . It *was* thick near Frogmore, and nearly made me late. I sat next the King at dinner—on his left hand, and he talked to me all the time. I broke gently to him the Cassel affair! He is going to talk to him about it. Of course he objects, but not vehemently—to my leaving my present post.

Then we talked a good deal about the coronation, and I told him all the ancient customs, of which he is profoundly ignorant. After that we passed to a much more delicate topic—the handing of Osborne to the nation. He could not get from anyone a clear idea of what was to be done with it. *I* am clear. An *officers'* convalescent home; keeping part of the house as *state* apartments.

The Future of Osborne.

Poor officers have not a hole or corner into which to run. Many have no relatives, or they are too poor to take them in. I am sure it would be a great boon. The King liked the idea.

He has commissioned me to speak to Princess Beatrice about it. Now I am off to Windsor for the day.

[*To M. V. B.*]   OFFICE OF WORKS,
DECEMBER 9TH.

. . . This evening I called on Cassel as arranged. This is his *The* offer. An arrangement for 3 years—in case we fail to get on. *Cassel* During that 3 years he guarantees me £5000 a year, and also *Proposal.* 10 per cent. upon any profits made in enterprises in which he is engaged. It is really a very handsome offer, as this means a large sum if things go right.

His one stipulation is that the King should be got to acquiesce. It is a nuisance having to arrange and manœuvre this, but I think Cassel is right. A quarrel would be foolish. I think I shall get more time free than hitherto—and always August and September.

Next winter I may have to go to Egypt for a month, which will involve a separation from you, which I *hate*. Still, take it all round, I think the arrangement is a fortunate one. Tell me what *you* think. I must know that. Anyhow if the King can be squeezed, the die is cast.

[*To M. V. B.*]   ORCHARD LEA,
DECEMBER 11TH.

Tired to-night. Cross-examination all day is very wearisome. It takes it out of one having to keep one's attention fixed. I must show you some of the evidence, then you will realise the sort of strain. I had some rattling good soldiers before me. Hardly a duffer among them.

I had a letter from the King this morning, on his new note-paper, with a queer cypher. As it is on business I must keep it till to-morrow. Then I will send it to you to look at. You will be unable to read it. His writing is so crabbed.

[*Journals.*]   ORCHARD LEA,
                                            FEBRUARY 14TH, 1902.

I went by appointment to Marlborough House at 3.45 to-day. . . . Presently the King came down. Just as we were starting the Prince of Wales came in; but the King would not wait. He was quite kindly but the Prince was shy. Then the King got into the French brougham, and I followed him. No *Inspection* servants on the box. We drove to the Abbey. At the entrance *of the* we got out unseen, and walked along the cloister. In five *Abbey.* minutes the King had settled that the "screen" could not be removed. Some idiot had proposed this should be done! We visited all the important points of the Abbey and especially the shrine of St. Edward. Then we drove away.

The Levée on Tuesday was a successful affair, arranged quite differently from previous Levées, far more effective. I wore my new uniform (Lt.-Gov. of Windsor Castle) for the first time. Oliver was present. Maurice unfortunately could not get his uniform in time.

Coronation   That evening I called at Marlborough House casually, and
Arrange-   sent up my name. The King was disengaged, and kept me well
ments.   nigh an hour. He made me sit down and talked with less "distraction" than usual, about the Coronation and family matters. All small points, but interesting enough. He discussed his own dress, the procession, the form of service. We settled a good many things, and I was glad to persuade him to *return* by the longer route, going by the shorter to Westminster Abbey, thus reversing the published order.

The previous day I had a long talk alone with the Princess of Wales, who has much of the force of character and tact and a good deal of the sound sense of Queen Caroline. In fact she reminds me of Queen Charlotte, only much handsomer.

[*To M. V. B.*]　　　　　　　ORCHARD LEA,
　　　　　　　　　　　　　　FEBRUARY 22ND.

. . . I had an "audience" of the King yesterday, and settled a　*Future of*
lot of small coronation details. Also, a really important thing　*Osborne.*
if he sticks to it, that he will give Osborne to the nation—on
the day of his coronation.

He wants me to go down there next week and report on the
place generally.

I shall do this. I shall stay with Princess Henry at her house.
Just for one night. He wants me particularly to look at the
things which can be brought away. There are *tons* of rubbish!
Of course the part of the house in which the Queen died will
be kept as a shrine. It is, in fact, the scheme which I originally
proposed to the King.

I want to go and see the young King of Spain crowned on
May 17th. Just to get hints. It ought to be magnificent for the
splendour of Spanish Palaces is unequalled. I don't know if it
will be possible to get away.

[*To M. V. B.*]　　　　　　　OSBORNE COTTAGE,
　　　　　　　　　　　　　　MARCH 8TH.

. . . I have been all over Osborne, and the property. There is　*Osborne.*
a sadness hovering over the whole place. It is like the grave of
somebody's happiness. I suppose it is because one realises that
it was everything to the Queen, and is nothing to those who
come after her.

Still, I don't think it *can* be given up, and I must tell the King
so. I am glad I have come here *alone*, and have seen all the
innermost recesses!

[*To M. V. B.*]   ORCHARD LEA,
MARCH 16TH.

Treves[1] never hesitated, and after seeing Doll, came down and explained that left alone she must die,[2] and that the operation alone could save her. Even that was 10 per cent. risk.

It was all well managed, as you shall hear, and I think he was fairly satisfied. It was a difficult operation in a way, as there was a complication. All this I will explain.

There is danger for 48 hours of course; great danger. One can only hope for the best.

[*From Sir Francis Knollys.*]   MARLBOROUGH HOUSE,
MARCH 20TH.

MY DEAR ESHER,

The King and Queen desire me to say how very glad they are to hear your most satisfactory report about your daughter and they trust that everything will now go on well. The King wishes to know whether, when your daughter is able to be moved, Lady Esher would like to take her to Barton's Cottage, Osborne, for a little change, as if so he will be very glad to lend it to you. He hopes you will go with him to Cowes on Thursday next for a day or two, living on board the Royal Yacht, as he proposes while he is there going over Osborne and settling various things in connection with it.

Yours ever,
FRANCIS KNOLLYS.

[*To M. V. B.*]   H.M. YACHT "VICTORIA AND ALBERT."
MARCH 28TH.

The Royal Yacht.

Yesterday was an interesting experience and I wished for you to share it. We travelled down in state. The King in naval

---

[1] Sir Frederick Treves.
[2] His daughter, Dorothy, was operated on for appendicitis.

uniform. Soveral and I travelled with him. The others in the next carriage. He talked for a while, and then went to sleep. Soveral gibbered very pleasantly all the way to Portsmouth. Lots of people along the route saluting. We ran on to the jetty alongside of which the yacht was lying. A fine guard of honour —and the Admiral and General in full uniform. Hedworth Lambton resplendent as captain of the yacht. The King inspected the guard of honour and we waited. Then we came on board.

She is a splendid vessel, done up quite regardless! Very large and very luxurious. As we left Portsmouth all the ships were manned, and a salute fired from the *Victory*. The sun was bright, and the "spectacle" was pretty. Excellent tea—and on to Cowes. I have got a charming cabin—with everything you can think of, including a white satin quilt, and a "hot bottle" warmed by electricity! We had dinner, and the King played bridge. I sat next him at dinner, and Hedworth next to me. He was in his most nautical form, and very good fun. Two of his officers came to dinner. I went to the ward room with Hedworth and was introduced to the lot.

To-day we had service on deck, read by Hedworth remarkably well. The singing of the crew was queer, but not unimpressive. They rig up canvas sheets all round the deck, and make quite a good chapel. The *Minerva* guard ship is quite close to us, and we have boats in command of middies coming off perpetually. All these sailors seem very good fellows.

After luncheon we shall go ashore. Cowes is not looking lively. There are a few yachts, very few—and charming little 5-raters rushing round us all the time—like seagulls.

We dress in blue serge and dine in a queer sort of smoking-jacket with brass buttons. Rather smart—E.R. and a crown on them. The King wears his navy mess kit—which oddly enough does not sit ill upon him.

[*To the Rev. C. D. Williamson.*]   ORCHARD LEA,
                                                        APRIL 23RD.

. . . I am overburdened with work. No time to write nor think. I quit the office on 30th June!

[*To M. V. B.*]   OFFICE OF WORKS,
                                                        APRIL 30TH.

. . . Doll was moved on to a sofa yesterday, to the surprise of Nellie when she returned. She was none the worse. The wound is healing fast. I have just lunched with old Harcourt. Very nice the old man was. I am in a shocking temper to-day, owing to the stupidity of everybody. Such a series of rows.

[*From Lord Rosebery.*]   GREAT NORTHERN RAILWAY,
                                                        MAY DAY.
MY DEAR R.,
    Many thanks for your confidence. I do not doubt your judgment for a moment. It is best to give up office in a blaze of credit when that is possible; which is rare. I always look back to your appointment with unalloyed complacency, more especially as it was made in the teeth of opposition led by yourself. Had I ever returned to Office I should have forced another appointment on you.
    I hope that all is well with Dorothy. You have become such a Grand Vizier that I can hardly hope to see you.
                                                        A. R.

[*To M. V. B.*]   WINDSOR CASTLE,
                                                        MAY 19TH.

I have been here since eleven—and it is now five. This morning we went all over the gardens, arranging about the garden party, which will be very pretty. Then we went to Frogmore Gardens—and back along the Park. The King was very amiable. This afternoon he is still amiable, but has a toothache!

I am now waiting to see Rosebery before going home. They have a large dinner party to-night. The band has been playing on the terrace—and crowds of people. The P. of Wales played golf, watched by hundreds, and made rotten shots rather in my style!

. . . I sat next to the Russian Ambassador at luncheon, a dear old thing, who has always been most charmingly frank about people, and he got on to the subject of Lady Granby! . . .

[*To M. V. B.*] ORCHARD LEA,
MAY 20TH.

. . . I was with Rosebery most of to-day. We went over the Castle with the King—who was in *very* good humour. Then R. and I walked down to Eton—and "did" the sights. Your photograph is in a most conspic. place in Kissack's. The queer-eyed girl played you false and me true. We visited Upper School, Lower School, and all sorts of queer places. R. showed me the room he *first* occupied at Eton. Such a hole. We went to the O.E. Club and left an insulting note for Tutor[1] about the paper and pens.

Bobs came over the Castle with us. He asked after you *with much interest*, and wished you all success. Arthur Balfour was there too, and so the party was most pleasant.

To-morrow I go up to town early, and then return to lunch at Frogmore with the P. of Wales. The King asked me to dine with the 2nd Life Guards to-morrow, but I got off, as I want to return and dine in London.

[1] A. C. Ainger.

[*To M. V. B.*]   OFFICE OF WORKS,
                                                  MAY 31ST.

. . . I am harassed to-day. The Head[1] came to see me about the Eton celebration, and followed me into the Abbey. He was very pleasant and friendly. I think the Saturday of Ascot will be quite a pretty day.

[*To M. V. B.*]   ORCHARD LEA,
                                                  JUNE 2ND.

Peace.   Your telegram gave me the blessed news of peace. What a triumph Kitchener has had. A soldier diplomatist. I saw Chamberlain to-day. He was quietly and happily triumphant. Thank heaven it is all over. There will be a thanksgiving in St. Paul's on Sunday, to which the King goes.

. . . There is a rehearsal on Saturday, but the Duke of Norfolk says you need not come, as you are to be there with the Children.[2] You can come to the next one. They are dreadfully behind with the rehearsals; I only trust they will not bungle.

[*To M. V. B.*]   OFFICE OF WORKS,
                                                  JUNE 4TH.

The   I did not go to the Derby, nor the 4th June. Far too busy to-
Prince's   day. But I was amused to-day by taking the Wales children,
Children.   two boys and a girl, to the Abbey. They climbed on to every tomb, and got very dirty, but were thoroughly happy. I wished for you as you would have enjoyed it.

I hope you will have charge of the boys on the day of the Coronation. Prince Edward remarked of the Duke of Buckingham that he was a "wicked man"—and when I asked why, he said he gave bad advice to Charles I. He knew that Buckingham

---

[1] The Rev. E. Warre.   [2] Of the Prince of Wales.

had been murdered at Portsmouth by Felton. I think he must have been reading Dumas!

To-night we went to see Réjane in a very unpleasant play. Most disagreeable. Liane de Pougy was behind us. She came on to the Carlton where there was an enormous crowd. Cleo de Merode, and Fanny Ward, and Mrs. Brown Potter, etc. etc.

[*To M. V. B.*]   OFFICE OF WORKS,
                                                        JUNE 5TH.

. . . To-day I have had the usual amount of rushing about. *The* This afternoon the Queen telegraphed for me, and showed me *Queen* her rooms, which are quite pretty. Then she and Miss Knollys *Inspects the* and I drove to the Abbey. Only Stanley [Quick][1] knew we were *Abbey.* coming, so there was no one about. We went all over the Abbey and looked at everything. The workpeople were more interested in her than in anyone-else who has gone with me. As we went out, all the Westminster boys, many in change flannels, had congregated, and clerics and servants, and they cheered for about five minutes. Such a row. The Queen was *delighted*. In that respect she is unlike the King, who dislikes a "reception."

. . . *We* go to Lady Howe's ball. That reminds me that you must order, on Monday, some knee breeches for Windsor. You will also want some for Stafford House. There is a ball there on Monday July 7th to meet the King and Queen. I send you an invitation which I opened in case there was any hurry, but there isn't.

This morning I gave the final orders to Stanley to send off all our invitations for the Procession.

[*To M. V. B.*]   OFFICE OF WORKS,
                                                        JUNE 6TH.

. . . I am here until evening to-morrow, as we have that rehearsal—rather a one-horse affair—in the afternoon. In the

[1] Lord Esher's Secretary.

morning at 11, the P. of Wales is coming to the Abbey. I have had a very full day. I saw the King this evening, who read me out a telegram from K. [Kitchener] giving the best possible account of the friendly feeling between us and the Boers. The King spoke very warmly of K.

He had been to Epsom, and looked as fresh as paint, and was going through his letters and papers as if he had done nothing all day.

He *never* refuses an audience, and never seems tired. To-night he will be three hours at Court. Another pouring wet night.

[*To M. V. B.*]   OFFICE OF WORKS,
JUNE 10TH.

. . . I had such a day. A most interesting two hours at Cassel's with Lord Inverclyde, and Furness and Sir Alfred Jones—three great shipping owners, over the British "combine." I hope it will come off, as it is a very big and interesting thing.

Then I went to St. Paul's after a hurried luncheon, to arrange the function for July 3rd.[1] After that the Thames Conservancy people called, and we settled the Eton Gala. Then the Abbey till 6. Then I had to go to the Palace and only got home just in time for dinner.

Pertab Singh.   . . . Pertab Singh was at dinner—very attractive. A typical Indian Beau Sabreur. A sort of Saladin. He rides a three-year-old every morning in the Row at 6 a.m. He talked a good deal in Kipling English about his campaign in China. He regrets peace, and would love to be always fighting. These Rajputs are splendid fellows. He is so splendidly high bred and loyal.

[*To M. V. B.*]   OFFICE OF WORKS,
JUNE 11TH.

. . . We went to the Albert Hall to-night. I wish you had been there. An enormous crowd, military bands, Melba, and

[1] Thanksgiving Service, afterwards postponed till October 25th.

good singing—quantities of waving flags, and great "go"
about the whole performance.

It revived me after a long day. I was asked by the King to-day   *Coronation*
to "stage manage" the ceremonial in the Abbey, and *refused*!   *Arrange-*
Of course, very politely, on the ground that the little Duke of   *ments.*
Norfolk would be horribly hurt! So I shall help, but nothing
more. We met your Colonel in the Grill-room at luncheon. I
told him you were to look after the little Princes, and he was
enchanted! Early to-day the D. of Connaught and all his staff
came to the Abbey.

[*To M. V. B.*]   OFFICE OF WORKS,
                                              JUNE 12TH.

. . . The King and Queen came to the Abbey to-day. It was   *Coronation*
an interesting rehearsal. They went through a good deal of the   *Rehearsal.*
ceremonial. I turned everyone out of the Abbey. Only the
Bishop of Winchester, the Duke of Norfolk, Canon Duckworth
and myself. He said I was to assist as much as possible at the ceremony. So I must have a smart robe! as I shall evidently be very
conspicuous. It would have amused you. We are to practise
with the Knights of the Garter and the four Duchesses to-
morrow.

[*To M. V. B.*]   OFFICE OF WORKS,
                                              JUNE 13TH.

Such a day. A *very* long rehearsal, with nearly everyone   *Rehearsal.*
there. George Cholmondeley very sweet, and Macclesfield, a
nice pretty Eton boy, Geordie, and Millie [Duchess of Suther-
land]. Quite amusing, and on the whole we made progress.
Then a rush off to dine at the Civil Service dinner. The P. of
Wales excellent, and the Admiral Sir Edward Seymour, and
Rundell both made admirable speeches. The Prince has a great
gift.

The Rajputs at the Court.

Then home to dress and to the Court! It was the most brilliant of all. The Rajputs quite splendid. Such a splendour of uniforms and jewels. Kuch Behar smothered in diamonds and Raj—in turban and silk dress—with necklaces and aigrettes, looking most oriental. It was queer, especially to hear him talk like an Eton boy.

I went on to Baroness Meyer—to the Dan Leno party. Maurice Farkoa, Louie Freer, Huntley Wright, etc. The latter much the most finished artist; that "Yo ho little girl" is very pretty. Never heard it before. Connie Edis was good. I had a talk with Louie Freer who was most amusing.

[*To M. V. B.*]   NORFOLK HOUSE,
                                                      JUNE 20TH.

The King's Illness.

The King's illness has been the one absorbing thing. He was not well before he went to Aldershot, and the damp and misery of the Royal Pavilion plus the Tattoo produced violent pains— very similar to those from which Doll suffered. The Queen and Princess Victoria, with the Prince of Wales, sat up all night. Laking arrived at 4 in the morning and found him very ill.

Princess Victoria told me that the Prince of Wales was, beyond all praise, good, helpful and quiet. He managed every-thing. They had a miserable time. The King and Queen drove to Windsor on Monday after the review in a travelling carriage with 4 horses in three minutes under the two hours. He was very weak but slept. I saw him arrive—and he looked feverish and feeble.

Next day Soveral stayed with him when the others went to Ascot, and they had a drive. He was much better; but on Wednesday his temperature rose again, and Treves saw him. Not more than three people knew this. Treves was very uneasy. Yesterday morning his temperature was 102. He sent for me and received me in bed. He was looking feverish and flushed, but was quite cheerful. He was lying in his charming bed-room, very bright and gay, overlooking the East Terrace.

Jack, his terrier, was lying on the bed, and when I kissed his hand, growled at me, just as Teddie's dog used to do. The doctors had warned me not to bother him with questions, so I did not transact much business. He postponed the Eton Gala, then gossiped.

. . . I stayed about a quarter of an hour, sitting on his bed, and then rose to go, and kissed his hand again. He was very friendly and gentle. In the evening I returned to London, and found that his temperature had fallen. Still, we had a consultation with Barlow, the surgeon, and Laking about the *possibility* of putting off the Coronation. The King told me that he would prefer to die in the Abbey. Still, they thought the necessity might arise. I said that if there was danger of life, they would be justified in insisting, but if a risk only, then—in his great position—he should be allowed to take it. We settled that—should the necessity arise—the Bishop of Winchester should be sent for, and we should have a consultation with him and Francis Knollys, before making any proposal to the King. I told all the circumstances to the Bishop to-day, and he was very strongly in favour of the view which I had expressed to the doctors.

Yesterday I saw the Queen and the Prince of Wales, who were both sensible and charming. They went to Ascot as usual. The doctors want to have the Ball put off, for fear the King might insist upon going, so the King of Saxony's death came opportunely.

This evening, when I got to the Castle, his temperature was normal.

The difficulty now will be to avoid all the tiring receptions *before* the coronation of Thursday. After that, we need not care. Little else matters. Treves is to see him again to-morrow, and I think Laking will put him up to insisting on complete quiet.

In these abdominal troubles there is always a fear of recurrence. The King's popularity—his personal popularity—is extraordinary. There is no doubt that in spite of the Queen's presence, Ascot was *manqué*.

18, WILTON STREET, S.W.,
JUNE 27TH.

K.C.B. MY DEAR REGGIE,

No one deserves a "Coronation Honour" so well as you, and I am only sorry that it comes at such a dismal moment. All your work was so splendidly done, and the organisation of the Great Festa seemed quite perfect.

What next! Miserere Domini. The festive look of London jars quite horribly.

Ever yours,
GEORGE RUSSELL.

[*To M. V. B.*] OFFICE OF WORKS,
JUNE 27TH.

I went down by an early train yesterday to Windsor with the Crown Prince of Portugal. Rather a sweet, aged 16. He was most intelligent and interested, and yet quite a boy, and full of a new watch he had bought that morning, which was also a pedometer and half a dozen other things.

. . . I lunched at Stafford House and there was a good deal of quiet pleasure even in the unemotional Strath [Duke of Sutherland] at his K.G.

I am being inundated with letters about my K.C.B. of which I will show you the most interesting. It is queer how the letters coincide. I am now off to Cassel's where there is a meeting about the shipping combine, and then I pick up —— who takes me in her motor to Windsor. I have half a fear that she drives herself, in which case I have not much hope of getting there alive.

[*To M. V. B.*] OFFICE OF WORKS,
JUNE 30TH.

. . . We have just got back from *Paolo.* It is a poor weak play in spite of the fine subject. Miss Millard very sweet as

Francesca. Paolo too feeble as an actor and graceless of figure and movement. I thought Alexander decidedly good. Anyhow he is a whale among minnows in that company. He would play Richard III well. How curiously his early training with Irving comes out. The play is tedious, and Phillips is far from being Shakespeare. The play leaves one unmoved. How different from Maeterlinck.

. . . This morning I saw Treves. He wants the King to be crowned during the first week in *August*, while H.M. is still an invalid, and while the doctors have control. He says dinners are far worse than a coronation service, and he is frightened of the galas which would be inevitable in October and impossible in August. The decision is to be taken in a fortnight from now. The King is a very difficult patient, and will hardly allow the wound to be dressed. He is going on astonishingly well. I am having a row over the Office. The Government will not make a fresh arrangement and want to postpone my leaving. I am fighting hard, and do not mean to lose.

Date for the Coronation.

[*To M. V. B.*] OFFICE OF WORKS,
JULY 1ST.

Of course it was a great disappointment that you should have been able to get over home to-day and that I was not there. The fact is that I am winding up my Office work, and that Thursday and Friday I am obliged to be at the Castle to receive all the Mahratta chiefs one day, and the Rajputs the other. So I am fixed here till then. The King has insisted upon my keeping all the Coronation work, although I relinquish the Office work on Saturday. So I move into a new room and house, with the Coronation business, until the ceremony is over. The show this morning was splendid. Such a show of Imperial force—a wonderful object-lesson.[1] It was perfectly done by the Queen

Lord Esher Resigns Office.

[1] There were at this moment in London some 2000 colonial troops, representing twenty-eight colonies. These were reviewed by the Prince of Wales on the Horse Guards' Parade, and twenty-three D.S.O.s and V.C.s were presented.

I—22

and the Prince of Wales. His manner to the men he decorated was quite perfect. He shook hands with all the officers. Altogether it was a fine performance, and must have impressed all the foreign princes.

Albany looked charming in blue. I wished for your presence all the time. Ward, to whom I lamented your absence, said that it was these sort of self-denials that made, in the end, the successful soldier. That he had talked over with Kitchener, in Pretoria, all the abnegations of their respective youths, and had agreed that the end was worth the sacrifice.

The King is very well to-day, and will sign a paper or two tomorrow. I regret that he has not seen and will not see these magnificent colonial troops. This evening I had an interesting interview with Chamberlain about the shipping combine. He was, also, very proud of the colonial show.

[*To M. V. B.*]   ORCHARD LEA,
                                                      JULY 6TH.

. . . I am glad to be free of the Office. After 6 or 7 years one has done all the work that is possible in an office of that kind— and it is a comfort to change the sphere of activities. I don't think I *could* lead a purely idle life; but I am sure to find many things that interest me in the Cassel connection. Indeed, I am already interested.

[*To M. V. B.*]   ORCHARD LEA,
                                                      JULY 7TH.

. . . I rather like my new room overlooking the Park.[1] I was not in it for long to-day, as I went on to the city, and did my first day there. It was interesting and novel. The two subjects were, the shipping combine, about which Cassel was to see Chamberlain this evening, and the proposal of George Curzon to

The Cassel Interests.

---

[1] 1, Chapel Place, Westminster, used for the Coronation work.

start great steel works in India. Cassel is sending out a very clever German expert in mineral to prospect.

[*To M. V. B.*] ORCHARD LEA,
JULY 9TH.

I went to the Palace this morning. Knollys has seen the King, *The King's Health.* who looks 10 years younger, and sleeps eight hours at night without moving, a thing he has been unable to do for years. He recognises that he has been living too hard, so his illness may—after all—prolong his life.

He is far less irritable too, which is a sign of health. A date is to be fixed to-morrow. They talk of the 9th. Everyone seems to be in favour of a procession on the second day, as before. I told them that it was only fair to the King to warn him, before a decision was taken, of the changed circumstances and the changed aspect of London in the East and South, since he went to bed.

I think a procession would be very unpopular now. However, we are to wrangle all this out to-morrow. This afternoon I went to a meeting of the King's Hospital where I had to represent His Majesty as one of the Trustees. Then I came back to Windsor and caught a glimpse of the colonials. The Maoris are a splendid body of men.

. . . I went to the city for half an hour to-day—a very short spell. I think Cassel rather likes me. He is very kind and considerate at present. I don't know how long it will last.

[*To M. V. B.*] ORCHARD LEA,
JULY 14TH.

. . . I saw the Queen to-day who was perfectly sweet, pale *The King's Health.* and affectionate, and tender about the King. They are off to-

morrow. The sailors are practising in the corridor how to carry
his chair. He goes off through the side entrance by Buckingham
Gate; quietly to the yacht. The Queen is anxious about the
9th and thinks the doctors were in too much of a hurry! *Nous
verrons.*

*Balfour's
Leadership.*
... What do you think of Arthur Balfour's succession? It has
all happened as we thought. He has taken the lead without
question from anybody. Although a great influence is withdrawn by the retirement of Lord Salisbury, still in great measure
this is mitigated by the supreme energy of Arthur. For some
time the Cabinet has had no active head. Now, fresh vigour will
be infused, and this should be good. Joe Chamberlain has
behaved with great loyalty and good feeling: the Duke of
Devonshire, although he must be disappointed, like the patriot
and gentleman which he has always shown himself to be.

[*To M. V. B.*]   ORCHARD LEA,
                                                   JULY 15TH.

The King's departure was very well managed. He was
carried down by sailors, put into a huge omnibus with drawn
blinds, and taken through Victoria Gate privately to Victoria.
No one saw him. I got this telegram this evening, so all has
gone well. Buckingham Palace looks deserted. Not a soul
hanging about. Such a change after the past weeks.

*Chamber-
lain and
Balfour.*
... Joe Chamberlain was more seriously hurt than was
known. Very nearly killed, in fact. The skull was bruised at a
very thin place, and he has not been able to read or think since.

He saw Arthur Balfour, however, and expressed his complete
loyalty to him. He was so touched by Arthur's loyalty to *him* all
through the most difficult moments of the S. African war, that
he determined—at any cost—that Arthur should succeed Lord
S. [Salisbury] and that he would serve under him. It is a pretty
story, and quite true.

[*To M. V. B.*]   1, CHAPEL PLACE, WESTMINSTER,
JULY 16TH.

. . . I lunched with the Princess of Wales to-day—only Lady Airlie and her. Very pleasant. She was charming as she always is when alone. She said something about taking Guy Laking to the Imp. Inst. on Sunday morning. She is coming over to O. Lea next week some day from Frogmore. Her children went down there to-day.

There was an excellent telegram from the King, who lies on deck on his couch, and is very comfortable. It appears that the meeting with Kitchener was very touching. K. knelt down by the bed, and kissed his hand, and the King put the Order of Merit round his neck. The Queen burst into tears, moved by the great contrast.

The poor little Duke of Norfolk came to see me to-day. He looked very ill. Broken down with sorrow. He said all *peace* and *joy* in life was gone for him. The only thing he ever looked forward to when work was done, was to go quietly down to his boy. He cannot yet realise what life will be without him. When you think what the boy was, it is marvellous. So strange is the heart of man. So Godlike in its sympathies, love and pity.

[*To M. V. B.*]   ORCHARD LEA,
JULY 17TH.

. . . This morning I settled a lot of Coronation details, and came down with McDonnell[1] and F. Ponsonby by the 2.20. Then we went to Frogmore, and found the little Princes playing about in the garden, too mischievous for words. We looked round the place with McDonnell, and got back about 6 o'clock.

[1] Sir Schomberg MacDonnell, his successor at the Office of Works.

[*To M. V. B.*]   ORCHARD LEA,
                                                    JULY 20TH.

. . . How dull the lives must be of people who are hide-bound by conventionalities. No wonder that women like —— rebel, and that some are tempted to rush to the other extreme. The really attractive thing is to enjoy the current and undercurrent of life; and not to float exclusively in one or the other.

Visit of Indian Troops.

I wrote to the King to-day, and told him of the successful visit of the Indian troops. Colonel Dawson and his officers laid great stress upon the value of the day's work. The visit to the tomb of the Queen, and the presence of her great-grandson would be talked of in nearly every Indian village, and would do great good in cementing the loyalty of the nation's troops to the Empire. It certainly was pathetic and stirring to see the emotion of the native officers, and the reverence of the privates as they saluted, one after the other, the last resting place of the Queen; as well as their pleasure in the greeting of the boy.

[*To M. V. B.*]   I, CHAPEL PLACE,
                                                    JULY 22ND.

I have just come back from Alfred Rothschild's dinner. Not unpleasant; a very good band—his own private band—playing all dinner and afterwards. Rather a terrible female who sang, but she was redeemed by Princess Pless who sang two or three songs quite charmingly—and by Evie James (please remember she is a cousin. *Forbes* married a *James!*), who did imitations, only *not* of favourite actors, but of the Queen and Princess Christian, etc. dangerously well.

I saw Arthur Ellis who says that the King is wonderfully well. Treves declares on his reputation that he will go through the ceremony, bar a cold.

Pembroke has been offered the Viceroyalty of Ireland and has refused. Wise man. It now rests with Dudley, Zetland and Marlborough. If you could send Dudley and the Duchess of

Marlborough—they would do very well! They are wrongly sorted. It is not important politically as George Wyndham is to be in the Cabinet, and the Lord Lieutenant is to be a mere figurehead.

[*To M. V. B.*]   ORCHARD LEA,
JULY 24TH.

. . . We did a lot of Coronation work this morning—with Bradford and the little Duke of Norfolk. The police arrangements are by no means easy. I hear the King has telegraphed for my star and badge of the Bath, and proposes to give it me privately on the yacht. I am rather glad, as it is better than being herded with a crowd!

. . . I still like Cassel, he is very nice to me.

[*To M. V. B.*]   H.M. YACHT "VICTORIA AND ALBERT,"
JULY 27TH.

We were still on deck after breakfast in bright sunshine, when *The* suddenly a storm of tremendous violence came on, and we were *King's* drenched before we could possibly get back into a cabin. The *Health* Roads are full of yachts, and the scene is gay enough, but the weather is *not* good. I was sent for by the King directly I arrived last night, and sat with him for two hours. He is very comfortable, dressed in his yacht clothes, with a white cap, and looking wonderfully well. He *sits* up now—in a huge chair specially constructed—and he reads and writes all day, quite happily, not a bit bored. He is on a very sparse diet—hardly anything—and he is proud of a reduction of 8 inches round the waist, and a loss of certainly over 2 stone in weight. His face is improved, and grown younger—much fined down. He is to be allowed to stand up on Tuesday, just five weeks from the operation. The wound is now about the depth of a two-shilling piece. No tube

—only packing. Treves thinks him a much healthier man than before the operation.

This yacht is perfect for an invalid, and the King sits practically in the open air all day. The Queen presides at dinner. I sat next her, between her and the P. of Wales, who ragged all through dinner, and was in excellent spirits. We did not dine till 9 o'clock, so the evening was short. Treves and Harry Legge and Fritz Ponsonby bathed this morning—swimming about round the yacht. My cold is too bad, or I should have been sorely tempted. We are going to have a service presently, not read by Hedworth, as the Bishop of Winchester is on board. The King will be wheeled somewhere in the vicinity. Now the storm has cleared off, I shall go on deck. Charming cabin, not the same as last time—rather smaller but more cosy. I will write to you again this afternoon.

[*To M. V. B.*]　　　　　　H.M. YACHT,
　　　　　　　　　　　　　JULY 27TH, EVENING.

The King came to service on board this morning, wheeled along in his chair. It was very impressive. All the men, and the band, and the Bishop to preach! "Peace, perfect peace" was the first hymn, and I was instantly reminded of you. After luncheon, which followed church, I had a long interview with the King, which he opened by giving me the insignia of the Bath—a private investiture, and the *first* of his coronation honours! also the first since his illness.

Then he sent me ashore to Osborne, and later the Queen came there with Soveral and the Bishop of Winchester. We went all over the house and gardens—and got back about 7. Since then I have been again with the King, and have now said good-bye to him. I propose to leave here fairly early to-morrow morning. The weather was very boisterous until this evening. It was quite difficult to get on board the launch. You would have enjoyed it thoroughly. The Prince of Wales told me yesterday that he has kept a journal for 22 years and never missed a day. He is a chip of his grandmamma. He has kept every family letter ever received.

I have got one of the worst colds I ever remember to have had. *Most* uncomfortable. I am unlucky at Cowes. Last time it was a series of headaches.

The King asked me how you were getting on, and where you were. He was interested about the M.I. He had not been told that the Guards were employed as horse soldiers.

The Queen is very sweet, and made me sit next her at every meal. In spite of a cold I can make her hear fairly well.

[*To M. V. B.*]   ORCHARD LEA,
                                                       JULY 28TH.

I sat next the Prince of Wales at dinner last night. He men- *A Prophecy*
tioned a queer prophecy which he made me promise I would *on Reigns.*
not repeat to the King, who is rather influenced by these old
women's tales. Someone, about 40 years ago, said of the late
Queen that she would have a long and glorious reign, the longest
and most glorious of all the English sovereigns; that she would be
succeeded by *two* kings who would have short reigns, and by a
third whose name would be David, and whose reign would be
as glorious as hers. One of Prince Edward's names is David!

When Lady Waterford was dying (she was a dear thing who *The*
died of cancer about 8 years ago) she sent for the Prince of Wales, *Naming*
and implored him to call his then unborn son David, as she had *of Prince*
some fad about restoring the Jews to the Holy City. To *Edward.*
humour her, he consented, and Prince Edward was given the
names of the four patron saints of England, Scotland, Ireland
and Wales—i.e. George Andrew Patrick David!

I don't think the Prince of Wales is altogether free from
superstition himself, but he is reconciled to a short reign. He
would not, however, for worlds let the King hear the story.
After dinner we went down to the Queen's cabin, and she was *On the*
in one of her ragging moods, and too sweet for words. Her *Queen.*

cleverness has always been underrated—partly because of her deafness. In point of fact she says more original things, and has

more unexpected ideas than any of the family. Prince Charles of Denmark, husband of Princess Maud, is a very nice young fellow. Brave and modest. One of his friends—a middy—had diphtheria, and there was no one to nurse him except the ship's doctor. P. Charles sat up with him for nights, and used to put his finger down the boy's throat to try and loosen the fatal membrane. In the end he saved his life, by his care of him. Plucky, as diphtheria is a horrid and frightening illness.

One source of amusement was the fascination which the Queen exercised over the Bishop of Winchester, when she led him away so far from the paths of virtue, as to make him smoke a cigarette with her. I think she liked him, so this is the second Queen whom he has captivated. When we were at Osborne yesterday, she took him alone up to the room where the Queen died, and they had a little service at the bedside together.

It is this mixture of ragging and real feeling which is so attractive about the Queen. I got back here after luncheon. The morning was beautiful, and all the yachts were shining in the sun. The Princess of Wales and the old Grand-Duchess Mecklenburg came to tea. She is a funny old woman—full of rather spiteful wit—who remembers William IV better than Edward VII. The Princess was gentle and homely in a rather stately way, as she always is. Probably the effect of living with such a *garçon éternel* as the P. of Wales.

My cold is a trifle better, but I am not fit for human society. To-morrow night I sleep in London, and I believe meet K. [Kitchener] at dinner.

[*To M. V. B.*]   1, CHAPEL PLACE,
                                                JULY 29TH.

We had a most curious dinner to-night at Alfred Rothschild's. K. [Kitchener] and Lucas Meyer, the Boer leader, his wife (a very distinguished refined-looking woman), Indians,

Dukes and other swells! It was the sort of thing that could happen nowhere else in the world but in England. Late enemies, not reconciled a couple of months, sitting down amicably in the smartest of London rooms to hear Melba sing. Mrs. Meyer, very well dressed, next to Bobs with K. behind her! and the Duchess of Buccleuch on the other side. Lucas Meyer is as tall as K. and twice as broad. A huge man, rather like W. G. Grace.

I don't know whether you read Kitchener's comments on his generals and others in the final despatch which appeared to-day, but if so, you will have noticed his grim humour.

Funny descriptions of the choleric Tucker, and great appreciation of Birdwood, the Bengal Lancer who rides in his suite, and appeared at both shows on the H.G. Parade.

. . . I forgot to tell you that the Queen spoke enthusiastically of Ellaline Terriss whom she thinks a darling, and very pretty, and likes better than any actress on the stage.

On Saturday, August 9th, the King was crowned and the success of the Coronation, which passed without a hitch, justified all the work which Lord Esher had given to it.

[*From Sir Francis Knollys.*]   BUCKINGHAM PALACE,
                                                    AUGUST 10TH.

MY DEAR ESHER,

The King knows how much of the success of the ceremony in Westminster Abbey yesterday is due to you. He desires me therefore to express his warm thanks to you for all that you have done.

Success of the Coronation.

                              Yours ever,
                              FRANCIS KNOLLYS.

[*To M. V. B.*]   BUCKINGHAM PALACE,
                              AUGUST 11TH.

I am waiting to see the King, so scribble a few lines. Everyone here in raptures about Saturday. The King and Queen especially pleased. The Prince of Wales very grateful for *your*

services. He has asked me to luncheon to-morrow to talk about
it all. The King held an investiture and a council to-day, and
rewarded all sorts of people.

[*To M. V. B.*]   1, CHAPEL PLACE,
                                                  AUGUST 12TH.

The Prince of Wales asked me to send you this present which
he hoped you would like in remembrance of your efficient
kindness to Prince Edward and Prince Albert on the occasion
of the King's coronation. Both the Prince and Princess asked
me to thank you, and to say how well you had managed
everything for the children on that occasion.

The King was perfectly charming to me yesterday. He was
quite affectionate and most complimentary. I have had showers
of compliments. I am pressing Edmund Talbot's claim for a
reward. He has been neglected. Also, the idiots forgot George
Binning, but I have put that straight and he is to get a C.V.O.
That is what Talbot should get. The King walked about and
looked as well and cheerful as possible.

[*To M. V. B.*]   THE ROMAN CAMP,
                                                  AUGUST 13TH.

We arrived all right this morning. Got to Stirling about a
quarter to nine.

. . . I have got a coronation medal. Did I tell you? The
ribbon is very pretty, but the medal is not particularly well
struck. However, it looks quite smart.

[*To M. V. B.*]   THE ROMAN CAMP,
                                                  AUGUST 14TH.

. . . I have to go up to London next Thursday by the night
train, and down to Windsor next morning to receive the *Shah*!
Is it not a horrid nuisance?

[*To M. V. B.*]　　　　　　THE ROMAN CAMP,
　　　　　　　　　　　　　AUGUST 16TH.

... Did I tell you that the Shah is going to shoot a deer in *The*
Windsor Park? Imagine him loosing off a .303 regardless of *Shah of*
everyone and everything. It will be odd if there is not some *Persia.*
catastrophe. However, it will be a distinction to be bagged
by a Shah in the wilds of Windsor Forest.

[*To M. V. B.*]　　　　　　THE ROMAN CAMP,
　　　　　　　　　　　　　AUGUST 22ND.

We had a most glorious day yesterday. Unbroken sunshine
and every hill visible. So hot, even on the sea, that no coat was
possible. We went to Oban—and thence to Port Appin.
Rather a sweet little place—very solitary—and yet an excellent
luncheon in a small highland inn.
... To-day, downpours of rain, thick Scotch mist, and not
much sign of abatement. I have written quantities of letters in
consequence. I have had an offer of £500 for three articles on
the *objets d'art* in Buckingham Palace and Windsor. It is not a
subject I know enough about, and I am doubtful about accepting. What do you think?

[*To M. V. B.*]　　　　　　2, TILNEY STREET,
　　　　　　　　　　　　　AUGUST 24TH.

... As I told Letty [Lind] at luncheon to-day, I never recollect the day when I did not care passionately for *someone*! I
suppose it will come, but life will then be very near an end.

[*To M. V. B.*]　　　　　　THE ROMAN CAMP,
　　　　　　　　　　　　　AUGUST 31ST.

... I have been reading *Sappho*—a novel by Daudet—on *Daudet's*
which the play is founded. Being a genius, the man has suc- *"Sappho."*

ceeded in writing a book containing some very striking things, but the whole tone of the story, the slow corruption of rather a nice youth, by a woman 17 years older than himself, and worn out by riotous living, unable to recognise that *her* amusement is not the first thing, is not true to life. Such a woman would either herself have cared enough for the lad to be willing to make a sacrifice somewhere, or at any rate, among their surroundings there would have been some fresh healthy influence. In *Sappho*, everything and everyone is sordid. I have never come across existence in that form, and I cannot think it is a true picture. Anyhow, it is depressing and rather irritating.

I cannot quite get those verses of which I told you, to my liking. If they are ever finished, I will send them. The strings of the lute are very slack just now.

[*To the Duchess of Sutherland.*]   THE ROMAN CAMP,
SEPTEMBER 1ST.

. . . I have seen no one and heard from no one, except Gladys de Grey, who writes from some place abroad, *en extase* about the coronation, which left her in tears all day, and furious with the behaviour of the women in her box and in the box opposite.

On the Shah. I forgot whether I wrote to you about my trip to Windsor to receive the Shah—who is the worst of frauds. He and his entourage are the commonest of the common and compare most unfavourably with the Indians, even of low caste. All the trouble taken with the creature will be thrown away—as he is a coward, and cannot avoid his fate of slavery to the Russians.

[*To M. V. B.*]   THE ROMAN CAMP,
SEPTEMBER 3RD.

I have been rather ill for two days, but better this afternoon, thanks to a walk in the high south-west wind and driving mist.

Got a brace of grouse and a hare—but it was not the sport, but the actual walking which was fascinating—owing to the wildness of the day. A shepherd was driving sheep down from the high moor, and I sat for a long while watching him. A real highland picture.

[*To M. V. B.*]　　　　The Roman Camp,
　　　　　　　　　September 7th and 8th.

. . . I am slowly preparing my mind for the S. African commission.[1] By the time it is over, there will be very little about the organisation of the Army which I shall not have come across. I hope that we shall be able to lay down a scheme which will really overturn the old red-tape bureaucrats. Much will depend upon our Chairman.

South African Commission.

[*To M. V. B.*]　　　　The Roman Camp,
　　　　　　　　　September 9th.

Such a day. An absolutely cloudless sky. This is quite literal. Not a speck in the azure. Lubnaig was like Como. No movement of the deep blue water, except an occasional ripple, when the lightest of breezes touched the loch.

We sat on the peak just above that on which we have so often lain. All day, from eleven to five. Some highland cattle were being taken from the Hebrides to Falkirk, and the shepherds turned them into the water just opposite. Then the men and the collies lay down to sleep, and the beasts stood passively in the water for a long while—cooling after their hot march. There was no sound except the occasional cry from some bird. The hills are purple with the late blossoming heather—and where they divide over Glenample the pale blue sky seemed to touch them.

[1] He had been appointed a member of the Commission to enquire into the South African War.

[*To M. V. B.*]   THE ROMAN CAMP,
                                   SEPTEMBER 10TH.

. . . I am trying to plan out a series of "groups" for the S.
African enquiry—so that some good result may come of it; but
it is very difficult. I wrote to Arthur Balfour suggesting "Lines-
man" as one of the secretaries. He writes so wonderfully well.

To M. V. B.]   THE ROMAN CAMP,
                                   SEPTEMBER 14TH AND 15TH.

Perhaps I over-write or am too self-indulgent in my letters;
a blunder against which I have so often railed. You ought to
tell me, only you never criticise. It is inconceivable to me that
so much self-inspection should not weary you at times. However, you have always the obvious remedy, which is to skip
freely.

Facts are the most palatable things in letters—not thoughts.
Then, the chance of misunderstanding is reduced to nothing.

. . . After luncheon I retired to the river house and prepared
queries for Kitchener's examination. He is not bound to answer
any of them; but I think we are bound to put them, i.e. questions
to elicit his approval or condemnation of what he found in
S.A. on arrival.

[*To M. V. B.*]   THE ROMAN CAMP,
                                   SEPTEMBER 17TH AND 18TH.

I am thinking about you—and Ellaline and the excitement of
the new play. Personally I am not fond of "first nights!" I only
hope that this was a personal success for the sweet little couple.[1]

---

[1] Ellaline Terriss and Seymour Hicks.

[*To M. V. B.*]   THE ROMAN CAMP,
                                       SEPTEMBER 25TH.

. . . As regards the army criticism—it is all very well—as I *Criticism*
have told Jack Durham, to talk about the Regimental Officer. *of the*
But only two out of every forty regimental officers are any good *Army.*
at all. The rest are *loafers*. How are these two to be discovered?
The staff takes all the competent and ambitious soldiers, as
things are managed at present. Any Commander-in-Chief, or
Military Sec. having to select a man for a responsible post—
naturally turns to the staff. I agree altogether in what he says
about sprigs of nobility. There is favouritism. But even then,
these sprigs—who have had staff experience—are generally
more competent than the *average* officer. Of course nothing
could be more *gallant* than the regimental officer—but gallantry
is not competence. A Commander requires *knowledge* of war—
knowledge of precedent—experience in *business*—all sorts of
things which the Staff teaches; but which are not learnt in
regimental messes.

A young Staff officer with French has heard the General talk
—even that is an education. But what does the young lad learn
from the talk of his C.O. as a rule? The present system is all
wrong no doubt—but until the system is altered the regimental
officers must remain in the background. The Staff and the
Staff College are two totally different things. Staff *College* men
failed in S.A. But all the men who succeeded had been, at
some time or other, staff officers.

There were a few exceptions, but very few. Take the Guards
alone. Polly Carew was the best of the Guards Generals. He has
spent all his life on the Staff. Rawlinson is perhaps the second
best. Ditto. So with the line. Ian Hamilton. Bruce Hamilton.
Both great Staff experience. Until every regimental officer is
forced to go through the staff college and until the army is looked
upon as a profession, and not as a pastime, the regimental officer
will be looked on by commanders of armies as a superior kind
of pawn—but not as one of the active and capable pieces in the
game of war.

[*To M. V. B.*]   BALMORAL CASTLE,
                                   SEPTEMBER 30TH.

On   This side of Scotland is not nearly so attractive as ours. There
Balmoral. is a great deal of wood—fir—planted by the Prince Consort,
which, I think, spoils the contour of the hills. Then, there are
too many *Cairns*—hideous things!

However, the Dee is a fine river. This house has not been
spoilt. It still retains its highland character. All the curtains and
carpets are tartan. The King looks well in his kilt, and is very
happy with a *man* party. He was very jolly at dinner. Bridge
was recommenced, but he goes to bed at 12.30. He also eats
more than is good for him, but not so much as formerly.

I was waked by the pipers walking under my window at 8
this morning. They talk of a deer drive this afternoon, but the
weather is not very propitious.

[*To M. V. B.*]   THE ROMAN CAMP,
                                   OCTOBER IST.

Deer   After writing to you, we had luncheon. The King in his
Drive at Balmoral tartan. Then he changed and we went out deer driv-
Balmoral. ing. Drove a certain way, then walked. The King rode on a
nice chestnut pony. The first drive I did not see a beast of any
kind. The King only got a shot. Missed his stag and shot a
hind! Rather a sadness.

Then we walked over the hill and had another drive. I was
next to McDonnell, then the King and two others, the Adj.-
General and another man further along. The deer this time
came my way. Pom McDonnell wounded a stag, and although
the dogs were loosed after him, ultimately we lost him. I shot
three very well—quite dead! One of them a very heavy beast
with one horn! I am not sure that it was a very popular performance. Long ago I gave up cards and shooting—because at
cards you are always disliked by somebody whether you win or

lose—and shooting, you are disliked if you shoot badly, and people are jealous if you shoot well!

I told you that Pom McDonnell was next me. When the battle of Omdurman was in full swing, the King said to Graham-Murray, "Did you ever hear such a bombardment." "Yes," said he, " it is a Pom-Pom."

I have heard some funny stories of General Tucker. "Poor b——y Tucker" as he called himself!

[*To M. V. B.*]   St. James' Palace,
                                         October 13th.

. . . Tell Seymour [Hicks] that he must come some Sunday to O. Lea with Ella; that we can then go *on the quiet* to the Castle, and inspect the Waterloo Chamber, and make our arrangements. Some Sunday, when for certain *you* are free.

[*To H.M. the King.*]   Orchard Lea,
                                         October 14th.

Lord Esher presents his humble duty, and thinks Your Majesty may like to know that Lord Kitchener gave most interesting evidence to-day before the War Commission. A number of questions had been formulated by the Commissioners, and sent to Lord Kitchener, in reply to which he read a memorandum dealing with the various points raised.

Kitchener before the War Commission.

His remarks were couched in moderate terms, but they amounted to a very careful criticism of the whole Army System, pointing out the defects which experience in South Africa has shown to exist, and suggesting the remedies which in Lord Kitchener's opinion are necessary.

He laid special stress upon training of men, especially in shooting, upon modifications in the firing exercise; upon a complete change in the method of training officers, so as to teach responsibility, and independence of thought and action, not only to officers commanding battalions, but to officers commanding companies and even sections.

He pointed out that his greatest difficulty was in finding officers competent for *staff* work, and that under our present system only a comparatively few officers are trained for the Staff, and even these are not well trained.

He was obviously in favour of practical as opposed to theoretical, i.e. Staff *College* training, and made the excellent suggestion that officers—in time of peace—should not be retained too long on Staff work, in order that a larger number should gain the experience—and officers who have done *well* on the Staff should be sent back to their regiments with brevet rank, as a reward for good *peace* service.

Lord Kitchener also made many practical suggestions for the improvement of transport, and railway management. His evidence was most valuable, and he showed himself once more to be a man of great penetration, decision and organising power.

In reply to a question from Lord Esher he made the astonishing assertion that since returning home he had not been asked by the military authorities to formulate his views upon all these questions, and that this was his first opportunity of doing so. . . .

[*To M. V. B.*]   ROYAL COMMISSION ON THE WAR IN SOUTH
AFRICA, ST. STEPHEN'S HOUSE, VICTORIA
EMBANKMENT, WESTMINSTER, S.W.,
OCTOBER 23RD.

I am going down to-day rather early to Windsor, to lunch with the King—at the Castle. He "motors" down; I suppose he will be back about tea time, and I shall suggest that he sends for you to-night or to-morrow. You shall hear—should he want you—from an Equerry.

We have got Mansfield Clarke before us to-day—the Q.M.G. Such a nice fellow.

[*To H.M. the King.*]   2, TILNEY STREET,
                                          OCTOBER 25TH.

Lord Esher presents his humble duty, and begs to inform   *Sir W.*
Your Majesty that in Col. Sir W. Richardson, K.C.B., who   *Richardson's*
acted as Chief of the Transport and Supplies from September 16,   *Evidence.*
1899, to the date of Lord Roberts' entry into Bloemfontein,
Your Majesty possesses a very capable officer.

The Officer's evidence was most interesting, covering as it did
the early stages of the war, and showing the enormous difficulties with which Your Majesty's forces had to contend. Chief
among these, was the hostility or indifference of every constituted authority at the Cape, so that the Boers obtained
supplies, not only from the Colony, but over-sea, more easily
than the Imperial troops.

The evidence again showed that the War Department had
neglected the lessons of former campaigns, and had failed—
incomprehensibly—to carry into effect the recommendations
of experienced and tried officers, appointed by themselves.

Reports of a Committee, which sat 17 years ago, were laid
before us, recommending certain changes, which experiences
in Bechuanaland and in Egypt, showed to be desirable in the
interest of troops in the field.

Many of the most important had been ignored. To give
Your Majesty an illustration. . . .

[*To M. V. B.*]   2, TILNEY STREET,
                                          OCTOBER 27TH.

A most splendid show this morning.[1] I don't think I ever
saw a finer sight. Nothing could exceed the advance in review
order. Beautiful.

One funny episode, *entre nous*. The King refused to let the
Queen drive round, and she agreed to go up to the window with

---

[1] Birthday Parade.

the old D. of Cambridge. But after the King had started, she drove out of the Palace, and followed—and went all round in the procession! The old Duke in tears upstairs, at being left.

[*To H.M. the King.*]   2, TILNEY STREET,
OCTOBER 29TH.

Sir Evelyn Wood's Evidence.   Lord Esher presents his humble duty and begs to state that Sir Evelyn Wood was examined at considerable length to-day. Your Majesty knows well the very superior intellectual equipment of this officer, and the singular precision of his ideas on all military subjects. Also, how elusive he can be, when face to face with a dilemma.

Sir Evelyn's evidence was of importance, inasmuch as he travelled over most of the whole region of Army organisation, criticising most freely, and stating his views upon all subjects, and the efforts he has made for 30 years to get them carried into effect.

Of course Sir Evelyn found it a matter of some difficulty to explain how it was that having been Q.M.G. and A.G. for a period extending over nearly 10 years, he had been unable to give effect to his ideas. His explanation generally was the help-lessness of the military branch when brought into conflict with the civilian element, i.e. Sec. of State, the Permanent Under Sec., and the Financial Sec. Sometimes when reforms entailed large expenditure this excuse was valid; but there were many questions affecting the comfort of the soldier, recruiting, train-ing of the officers, military organisation, methods of promotion and appointments to commands, upon which the military side of the W.O. could have carried their point, had the distinguished officers been agreed, or had they been firm enough to take the necessary initiative. Sir Evelyn, although he described himself as a "satellite" of Lord Wolseley, spoke with great hopefulness of recent changes, and others in contemplation, brought about by Lord Roberts.

He repudiated all responsibility for the preparations for war in S. Africa. He contended that as Adj.-Gen. he was never consulted either as to the numbers required, nor the officers appointed to command. He told us *privately* that he was the "whipping boy" between Lord Lansdowne and Lord Wolseley.

The gist of his evidence, like that of every other officer hitherto examined, was that for all shortcomings at the W.O. it is Your Majesty's Civil Servants, and not the military Officers, who are to blame.

[*To H.M. the King.*] 2, TILNEY STREET,
OCTOBER 30TH.

Lord Esher presents his humble duty to Your Majesty and begs to state that in the opinion of all the Commissioners, the evidence given by the Adjutant-General[1] to-day was most interesting and valuable. The Adj.-General was restricted to the questions affecting Army Organisation, his evidence on the S. African War being reserved for another occasion. *The Adjutant-General's Evidence.*

When warmed to his subject, the General was most outspoken. Very much of what he said could not be published, but it strongly influenced the Commissioners.

He pointed out the growing cost of the Army System, and the almost limitless expenditure which will have to be incurred if the present system is maintained, and the illusory nature of the statements annually laid before Parliament.

This led up to the only conclusion possible, that the country will have to choose between an enormous expenditure lavished on an imperfect instrument, and some form of compulsory service.

The General gave most interesting accounts of the difficulties of recruiting, and the quality of the soldier, both physical and moral—which all pointed to the same conclusion that under our existing system we are not tapping the right class.

---

[1] Lieutenant-General Sir T. Kelly-Kenny.

The Commissioners were much impressed by the General's firm and clear conviction that the behaviour of Your Majesty's troops in S. Africa—in face of Boers, who almost invariably fought defensive actions—is no real test of their ability to stand against first-class European troops. The General spoke with great freedom, yet in most temperate language. His straightforwardness was in marked contrast to other evidence which has been taken, and which I have reported to Your Majesty.

The Adjutant-General had a long and arduous examination, out of which he emerged with singular credit.

[*To H.M. the King.*]   ORCHARD LEA,
NOVEMBER 1ST.

Lord Esher presents his humble duty to Your Majesty and begs to express his grateful acknowledgment of Your Majesty's letter. The Commissioners rightly gauged the value of Sir Evelyn Wood's evidence, and—from their remarks subsequently—were quite alive to the points to which Your Majesty refers. Had any doubts existed in their minds, the evidence of the Adjutant-General would have dispelled them.

Sir John Ardagh's Evidence.
To-day, we heard Sir John Ardagh, late D.M.I.—and he corroborated what Sir William Nicholson had already told us, as to the full warnings laid before the Government from 1896 onwards as to the preparations of the Boers. He himself had drawn attention to the "preposterously small force" kept in S. Africa during these critical years. In July, 1899, he told the S. of S. that "a serious subject was being trifled with—and that 10,000 men should at once be sent to Natal, and 10,000 to the Cape."

He also stated that as early as 1897 Lord Wolseley had pressed for the mobilisation of one Army Corps.

Sir John Ardagh gave a good deal of interesting evidence as to the formation of a General Staff of the Army corresponding somewhat to the Great General Staff at Berlin; but his proposals were modest, and not unreasonable—involving a very proper increase of expenditure upon the Intelligence Branch, if that Branch is to be made really efficient.

He stated that he had on many occasions suggested widening the scope of the Intelligence Branch and providing for maps of the frontiers of the Empire, but that his proposals had been "scoffed at by the Financial authorities of the W.O. and had never been referred to the Treasury."

Sir John Ardagh struck the Commissioners as a man of great ability, who might have done far more valuable work had he not been hampered by an organisation altogether out of date. By raising the military status of his successor to that of a Lt.-General, an excellent advance has been made, and Sir William Nicholson should succeed where Sir John Ardagh failed.

[*To H.M. the King.*]   2, TILNEY STREET,
     NOVEMBER 18TH.

Lord Esher presents his humble duty to Your Majesty and begs to state that the Royal Commission met again to-day, after an interval of a fortnight, and heard the evidence of Sir Howard Vincent, in connection with the Volunteers in South Africa. *Sir Howard Vincent's Evidence.*

Sir Howard Vincent was very voluble, and took the opportunity of airing many grievances alleged to be felt by the Volunteer Forces, but there were no points to which it is worth while to draw Your Majesty's attention.

Later, Sir Edward Ward was recalled—and the Commissioners for the first time touched upon one of the chief matters of controversy—i.e. the choice of Ladysmith as a *place d'armes*. It has been contended that the defence of Ladysmith was forced upon the C.-in-C. in South Africa by its previous selection as an immense store house for supplies and ordnance. Sir Edward Ward, however, admitted that on his arrival at Durban, there were only two months' provisions for eighteen hundred and seventy men in Ladysmith, but that a month later there were 3 months' provisions for 12,000 men, showing that all the stores, *Sir Edward Ward's Evidence.*

etc. in Ladysmith were poured into that town between October 7, when war was declared, and November 2, when the siege began. The Commissioners have never yet been able to obtain the instructions to Sir George White, before that Officer left for S. Africa, but they have always suspected that these would throw light on the selection of Ladysmith in preference to the line of the Tugela.

Sir Edward Ward was questioned as to changes which admittedly should be made in the organisation of the Supply and Transport Departments—in the event of war—but they could only elicit that these were "under consideration," although there appeared to be no reason why they should not already have been carried out.

[*To M. V. B.*]   WINDSOR CASTLE,
                                    NOVEMBER 22ND.

"*Quality Street*" at *Windsor.*

. . . Everything here this morning in its normal state. Everyone says that the whole thing was a *perfect* success.[1] The Queen was delighted with Ella [Terriss] and all the children. The King thought Seymour [Hicks] and Ella quite *excellent*. He thought the play pretty but lacking in *strength*, but altogether redeemed by the perfection of the acting! Nothing could be more complimentary to Ella and Seymour.

Soveral, who is here, says that no play could possibly have been more suitable, nor better acted. So everyone seems pleased.

[*To H.M. the King.*]   WINDSOR CASTLE,
                                    NOVEMBER 22ND.

General Brabazon's Evidence.

Lord Esher presents his humble duty to Your Majesty, and begs to state that General Brabazon—as the O.C. Imperial

---

[1] *Quality Street*, by J. M. Barrie, given at Windsor Castle.

Yeomanry in S.A.—was examined by the Commission, and gave his evidence in a manner highly characteristic of that gallant officer.

He did not display profound knowledge of the raising, nor of the war services, of that Force; but he electrified the Commission by a recital of personal experiences in hand to hand fighting on the Afghan Frontier and his theories of the use of the Cavalry Arm in war.

The General laid special stress on his lifelong mistrust of the weapons supplied to Cavalry, and of his preference for shock tactics by men armed with a Tomahawk. He drew graphic pictures of a cavalry charge under these conditions, so paralysing to the imagination of the Commissioners that they wholly failed to extricate the General or themselves from the discussion of this engrossing subject.

Lord Chesham gave very manly evidence, indicating dis- *Lord* agreements between the Yeomanry commanders in S. Africa *Chesham's* and the organisers of the Force at home, especially as to the class *Evidence.* of officers selected.

[*To H.M. the King.*] WINDSOR CASTLE,
NOVEMBER 27TH.

Lord Esher presents his humble duty to Your Majesty, and *Lord* begs to state that Lord Wolseley was throughout the day under *Wolseley's* examination. He began by laying before the Commission *Evidence.* copies of memoranda which from time to time, since 1888, he had sent to various Secretaries of State, urging an increase of the Army, and the placing of three full Army Corps upon a proper footing. Thence he passed to the warnings given by him since 1896—in writing—of probable war with the S. African Republic, up to June, 1899, when he strongly urged the mobilisation, on Salisbury Plain, of one Army Corps, properly equipped for service in the field. He then showed that in 1899, although war was imminent, the Government refused, up to September, to take any steps to prepare for a conflict.

All these allegations were supported by documentary evidence in the shape of printed minutes and memoranda.

In dealing with the War Office itself, Lord Wolseley repudiated all responsibility for the choice of Ladysmith, as a strategic post to be held at all costs, and pointed to his telegram to the G.O.C. in S. Africa, warning him against being "shut up" in Ladysmith, and suggesting Colenso and the line of the Tugela as the best for the defence of Maritzburg and Durban.

Lord Wolseley dwelt very strongly upon the fact that during the months preceding the outbreak of hostilities he had never been taken into the confidence of the Cabinet; that their decisions, upon military questions, were taken without hearing what the Commander-in-Chief had to say, except through the mouth of a "third party," meaning the Sec. of State for War.

This procedure he strongly deprecated, as only productive of harm to the country, and he then made two proposals, both of which he advocates.

First, that the Commander-in-Chief should be authorised to lay before Parliament, annually, a certified form that the Defences of the Country (as defined by the Government and by Parliament) are in fit and proper state. If, for example, it is settled that three Army Corps, two for active service abroad and one for home defence, are necessary, and if Parliament have approved of such a proposition, he thinks that on the 31st March each year, the Commander-in-Chief should certify to Parliament that these three Army Corps exist with their full equipment, and could be mobilised in or under a fortnight.

Secondly, and preferably, he suggested that Lord Rosebery's plan should be adopted, and that Your Majesty should be the sole Commander-in-Chief, and that the Sec. of State for War should always be a soldier. He put his arguments for this proposal before the Committee, but was not cross-examined and here his evidence ended for the day.

To-morrow he will be cross-examined upon both propositions, and will further be examined upon the progress of the War, and upon the conditions of the War Department.

Your Majesty will at once realise the serious constitutional difficulties in the way of Lord Wolseley's second proposition; but with regard to the first, although without precedent, it is not so clear that some arrangement could not be devised for placing a check upon the occasionally over-sanguine official statements of the Sec. of St. for War, whoever may happen to be, at the time, Your Majesty's servant holding that high and responsible office.

[*To H.M. the King.*]   WINDSOR CASTLE,
NOVEMBER 29TH.

Lord Esher presents his humble duty to Your Majesty, and begs to state that Lord Wolseley's examination was finished yesterday. There was considerable discussion—the room having been cleared—among the Commissioners, as to whether Lord Wolseley should be asked his opinion upon the strategic movements of Sir Redvers Buller and of Lord Roberts. *Lord Wolseley's Evidence.*

There was a strong divergence of opinion. Lord Elgin and Lord Esher were of opinion that no public advantage is to be gained by eliciting from one military authority, however eminent, a criticism either of the strategy or tactics of another military commander.

Lord Wolseley admitted that he had never interfered with the action of generals in the field. It therefore appeared superfluous to ascertain his view of their strategy.

However, the majority of the Commissioners adopted the contrary opinion; but they limited their questions to asking whether Lord Wolseley thought Sir Redvers Buller was right or wrong in departing from his original plan of advancing straight upon the capital of the Orange State, and whether Lord Roberts was right or wrong in proceeding direct towards Kimberley, rather than adhering to the railway and making straight for Bloemfontein.

Lord Wolseley was evidently reluctant to give an opinion

but, pressed, he stated that in his opinion Sir Redvers Buller was wrong; that he should have adhered to his original plan; advanced upon the Orange Free State; and appointed a subordinate officer to protect the Tugela.

He also said that, in his opinion, Lord Roberts would have done better to make his line of advance that of the railway, thus securing constant supplies for his troops, avoiding the terrible march across to Bloemfontein, and the almost total loss of his cavalry horses.

In his view, Lord Roberts would thus have equally relieved Kimberley and Ladysmith, and captured Cronje. As Your Majesty must see, these views of Lord Wolseley's may or may not be sound, but they are highly controversial, and would admit of endless argument, so that it would not appear that any object has been gained by putting the questions, except to bring Lord Wolseley into direct conflict with Lord Roberts.

Lord Wolseley produced, as Lord Esher had asked him to do yesterday, a form of certificate, which he proposed the C.-in-C. should annually give, as to the preparedness of the country for war; and Lord Esher is inclined to think that this suggestion might take some practical shape. On the other hand, in reply to a question from Lord Esher, as to what would have been likely to occur in 1886 or 1893 when Mr. Gladstone introduced a Home Rule Bill, if a distinguished soldier, say Lord Wolseley himself, had been Sec. of St. for War, he was bound to admit that the War Office would in all probability have found itself without a head, and the Army without a Chief.

Sir Coleridge Grove's Evidence.

Sir Coleridge Grove, an officer possessed of very remarkable intellectual gifts, as Your Majesty knows, then gave evidence as to the selection and education of officers.

. . . He ended by drawing a most interesting and striking comparison between the Administration of the War Dept. and a "business concern"—showing the great difficulties under which the work of the former is carried on, owing to the interference of irresponsible Members of Parliament, and of the caprices of our Party System of Government.

Lord Esher is writing to Your Majesty from the Castle where he has been working all day.

[*To H.M. the King.*]   2, TILNEY STREET,
                                        DECEMBER 3RD.

Lord Esher presents his humble duty and begs to state that the *Sir* evidence taken before the Commission to-day dealt exclusively *Edward* with the subject of naval transport, and was not particularly *Chichester's Evidence.* interesting.

Sir Edward Chichester, who was responsible for landing all stores at Cape Town, is an "old salt" who would have amused Your Majesty. A sailor of the old school. He told us one thing very characteristic of Your Majesty's navy, and the practical way naval men have, in dealing with situations which present to others serious difficulties. There was a mutiny among the Boer prisoners confined at the Cape. Sir E. Chichester selected a not very steady transport, and 400 Boers were sent to sea in a north-easterly gale for a day and a night. They were ill the whole time, and when they got back, and had related their adventure to their companions, the Boer Camp gave no more trouble.

To-day the Commission do not take evidence, but discuss procedure. To-morrow Lord Roberts gives evidence.

Your Majesty—looking dispassionately at the whole question —from Your Majesty's lofty standpoint—is no doubt right about Lord Wolseley's evidence, and Lord Esher is glad that the decision of the Commission was in accordance with Your Majesty's views, although he himself was in the minority.

In reading De Wet's book, Lord Esher observes that upon the point of the advance upon Bloemfontein, De Wet's opinion is that Lord Roberts chose the right route, and that Lord Wolseley's criticism is unsound.

The book is interesting in many ways.

[*To H.M. the King.*]   ORCHARD LEA,
                                        DECEMBER 4TH.

Lord
Roberts'
Evidence.

Lord Esher presents his humble duty, and begs to state that the Commander-in-Chief was examined to-day and gave evidence of a very interesting character, with much directness and simplicity. Lord Roberts described the want of organisation, the lack of material and transport, the scarcity of maps, with which he was confronted on his arrival at the Cape. He exonerated Sir George White from all blame for the retention of Ladysmith, maintaining that that officer had no choice in the matter, although he thinks that the selection of that position, and also of Dundee, was most unfortunate. He expressed surprise that Sir George White should have quitted England without definite instructions, which appears to have been the case.

Lord Roberts praised the quality of the men, including many irregular Corps and the C.I.V.s. He did not speak highly of the Militia, of whose want of training he complained. He holds that this deficiency, both in that Force and the Volunteers, is a fatal drawback; and admitted to Lord Esher's question that unless some remedy is forthcoming, there will remain no option but compulsory service for home defence. He also complained of the lack of officers, but he is not prepared—as yet—to recommend a large *addition* to the regular army; although he was unable to suggest any alternative scheme, to supply this serious want in war.

Lord Roberts complained very earnestly (and made out a strong case) of the change brought about in 1899, when the sphere of action of the Q.M.G. and the A.G. was altered; and he related the efforts he had made to remedy what he thinks is a serious evil in war. But he was overruled by the Secretary of State and by the Cabinet.

It would appear strange that upon a question of purely military organisation, within the Army, involving no expense, the most experienced and eminent soldier of Your Majesty's Empire should have to yield to civilian authority. Lord Esher put to Lord Roberts the question whether, in the event of a breakdown in war occurring, due to a want of trained A.Q.M.G.s in the field, the C.-in-C. would be held by the country to be responsible; and Lord Roberts admitted that this view would undoubtedly be taken, although he has no power to remedy the defect.

Lord Roberts then gave very interesting evidence as to the state of the Artillery, the want of quick-firing guns, the great superiority of the 18 batteries bought from Erhart in Germany, during the progress of the war, and the fact that no quick-firing guns of the new pattern have yet been supplied to the Army.

The impression left upon the Commission cannot fail to have been that the Commander-in-Chief of Your Majesty's Forces, although nominally in a position of great responsibility, is so hampered by the organisation of the War Office, and by the Parliamentary customs which hem that officer within an impassable fence, that his responsibility is an illusion. This would appear to absolve Lord Roberts' predecessor for neglect in the past, and from the burden of the many defects which became apparent to the nation in the winter of 1899. It is also obvious that Lord Roberts himself is morally weakened, in dealing with serious reforms, by the conviction that his responsibility is unreal and that he is absolved by the action of another authority.

This, Lord Esher ventures humbly to suggest, is the gravest question connected with the organisation of Your Majesty's Army.

To-morrow, Lord Roberts commences his evidence upon the operation of the War, and the War Office system as he finds it at the present time.

[*To M. V. B.*]　　　　　　　　2, TILNEY STREET,
　　　　　　　　　　　　　　　　DECEMBER 4TH.

We had Bobs all day, and the little man was excellent. So *Lord* straight. I think we got some useful evidence from him. He *Roberts'* altogether exonerates White. I have the list of generals and *Evidence.*

colonels dismissed for incompetence, it will interest you. To-morrow I will send you De Wet's book. You must read it. Ian Hamilton is *such* a nice fellow. He came with Bobs and lunched with us.

[*To M. V. B.*]   ORCHARD LEA,
                                        DECEMBER 4TH AND 5TH.

On Ellaline Terriss.

. . . Ella [Terriss], almost unique amongst women for perfect womanliness; both outwardly and inwardly the type of which the Gods intended woman to be. Her grace and charm may be equalled possibly, but these combined with that childlike sweetness, and gentle shrewdness, which are so characteristic of her, I never have seen in another of her sex.

[*To M. V. B.*]   SANDRINGHAM,
                                            DECEMBER 6TH.

Just a few lines to catch the early post. A huge party here—including Millie [Duchess of Sutherland], who looked very sweet last night.

. . . She is in very good spirits, although she is to have an operation by Fripp, on the 16th. Everyone here is very nice. The old Duke of Cambridge, feeble on his legs, but quite all there otherwise. The Queen as sweet as usual. Sybil Primrose, Lady Gosford, Lady de Grey, the young Duc d'Albe, Mensdorff —and Strath [Duke of Sutherland]. The latter goes to-day, and Rosebery comes. The King full of interest in the Army.

[*To M. V. B.*]   ORCHARD LEA,
                                        DECEMBER 9TH AND 10TH.

. . . After to-morrow the Commission adjourns until February, so I hope to have more time at my disposal and yours.

There will be a certain amount of city business, but it is nothing like the same tie. As it is, I have not a minute to spare. Our evidence to-day showed rather more ineptitude than usual on the part of the War Office. Their medical arrangements were *The Medical Service.* admittedly not only hopelessly antiquated, but on a *peace* footing only, and not intended to meet any war pressure at all. They are wonderful!

Rosebery complained to me of his great loneliness at Dalmeny. All his family are scattered. Peggy married. Sybil unable to live in the North since her illness. Neil at Oxford. Harry in London. He is to be pitied.

Rosebery has sacrificed too much to ambition—a fatal thing for happiness—unless it really fills a man's life. And this only happens to Napoleonic natures when success is achieved. What a purgatory St. Helena must have been.

[*To H.M. the King.*]   ORCHARD LEA,
                          DECEMBER 10TH.

Lord Esher presents his humble duty, and begs to inform Your Majesty that, Lord Elgin having been called away to Scotland, it became his duty yesterday and to-day, to take the Chair at the S. African War Commission.

We examined Professor Ogston—of Aberdeen University— *The Medical Service.* who, as Your Majesty will remember, was sent out to Africa by Queen Victoria, and reported on the state of the Hospitals to Her Majesty.[1] Professor Ogston has a wide acquaintance with the Army Medical arrangements of Russia and Germany, so that his evidence was most interesting.

He instituted comparisons between those nations and Your Majesty's by no means favourable to us, and he showed how antiquated and behindhand the organisation, knowledge and equipment of the Army Medical Corps, proved to be at the commencement of the campaign.

The Corps—as was subsequently admitted by Surgeon

[1] Apparently an error. See p. 270 (December 1st, 1900).

Colonel Wilson—was not organised at all with a view to *war*. The establishment was a peace establishment, intended to cope with the necessities of peace, but not capable of expansion nor even calculated to fulfil the needs of one Army Corps abroad.

Apparently this is the *one* lesson of the War which the War Office have taken to heart, for the appointment of the Advisory Board—of which Sir Frederick Treves and other eminent civilians are members—has already brought great changes, in the teeth of much bigotry and obstruction.

[*To M. V. B.*]   ORCHARD LEA,
                                        DECEMBER 17TH.

*The
Queen's
Memorial.*

To-day I went to Buckingham Palace, and waited for the King. He came down about 11.30 and we drove together to Brock's studio. It was amusing to drive with him through the streets, and listen to his remarks on shops and private houses which he knew. We spent about three-quarters of an hour with Brock and Aston Webb—the architect—looking at every detail of the fine model of the Queen's memorial. The King has no knowledge of art, but his strong sense enables him to form correct judgments.

Then we drove back. I had a long talk with Mowatt about Army reform—very useful. I can see that the Report of the Commission will give me no end of trouble. I shall have to draft the whole of it. I am sure that otherwise it will be a milk and water affair.

. . . Talking of Grant to-day, the King said, "I suppose Maurice knows him. Is he in his battalion?" Is he?

[*To the Rev. C. D. Williamson.*]   ORCHARD LEA,
                                        DECEMBER 27TH.

I never recollect to have been more overworked than since October. War Commission every day—and then my other business too. This accounts fully for the inevitable neglect of all friendship's duties.

. . . I am negotiating the purchase of Stank Glen and Corrie- *New* chrombie, the beautiful stretch from the far shore of Lubnaig *Scottish Estate.* up to the top of Ben Ledi. It belongs to the Trustees of the Callander Schools, and I made them an offer, which I think they will accept. There are few possessions in Scotland much more beautiful. You have never seen it, but if I buy it, you must come and see next year the lovely glen, very wild and secluded, which runs westward from the loch. As you know, I have rented it for two years, and everyone is devoted to it, for manifold reasons. So I shall be glad to possess it for ever.

[*To M. V. B.*]   2, TILNEY STREET,
                                   FEBRUARY 4TH, 1903.

I feel very seedy to-night, and was not up to much all day. Bored to death by the War Commission. It is not an interest which can be revived. It is like an extinct passion—any attempt to relight the flame is sure to fail! It all—i.e. the commission— seems as flat as possible. Even Treves could not stir interest in me.

[*To M. V. B.*]   2, TILNEY STREET,
                                   FEBRUARY 9TH.

I have just got here—having come up with all the males by the early train. Rather a successful dinner last night. I sat next the Queen, who talked all dinner time and was in great spirits. She is really a very charming woman! It is queer, her determination to have her way. As Princess of Wales she was never, so she says, allowed to do as she chose. "Now, I do as I like" is the sort of attitude. And among her likes is a fixed resolve to go to India and "see the natives." I wonder if she will ever succeed.

Nellie sat next the King, who thinks the *Admirable Crichton* [1] the best play he ever saw. This is most enlightened of him, and shows how really very intelligent he is. After dinner there was no bridge, as it was Sunday and the new Archbishop was there. Not that he would object, for he is very broadminded. [2]

[*To M. V. B.*]   2, TILNEY STREET,
                                   FEBRUARY 10TH.

I had rather a busy day. At Brock's studio for a long while discussing the Queen's memorial and then in the city. . . . Now for Bobs on the Commission. There is not much left to ask him. The subject is pretty well thrashed out.

[*To H.M. the King.*]   2, TILNEY STREET,
                                   FEBRUARY 11TH.

Sir William Butler's Evidence.

Lord Esher presents his humble duty to Your Majesty and begs to say that Sir William Butler was examined to-day.

In view of the accusation made against Sir William Butler in the winter of 1899, a full opportunity was given to that officer to state his case, of which he availed himself. It is clear that he held strong military and political views of the situation then obtaining, which were not in accord with those of Her Majesty's advisers, and Sir William met with the usual fate of those who give unpalatable advice. That much of the advice he gave has since proved correct, is not possibly of advantage to him in certain quarters. There is no doubt that he is among the ablest of Your Majesty's servants, and possesses an intellect capable of grasping large problems, and of dealing with them in a practical manner. His Irish blood may possibly influence his temper and political judgment, but leaves his military capacity untouched. There is an interesting correspondence between him and the

---

[1] By J. M. Barrie.   [2] Dr. Randall Davidson.

W.O. Authorities, dated in the winter of 1901-2, ending with a letter from the present Adjutant-General which altogether exonerates Sir William Butler from any charge against his military honour or action as a soldier. Upon a highly controversial political question—in which as Acting High Commissioner he became involved—his judgment was possibly faulty, and this is all which can reasonably be urged against him. Intellectually he stands (as he does physically) a head and shoulders above the majority of his comrades. His evidence upon the preparations for war, only proved once more that uncertain counsels prevailed throughout the summer of 1899, and that if Sir William was to blame for the strong and clear line of duty which he sketched out for himself, this blame may well attach to others for the vacillating courses which they, no doubt also actuated by a high sense of duty, found themselves constrained to pursue. Under these circumstances, it would appear wise and honourable to sink the quarrel, in view of the great sacrifices made, and the ultimate success of Your Majesty's arms.

[*To H.M. the King.*]   2, TILNEY STREET,
                                         FEBRUARY 12TH.

Lord Esher was asked by Mr. Brodrick to call at the War Office this evening, and he found that it was in reference to Sir William Butler's evidence that Mr. Brodrick wished to see him.

Mr. Brodrick and Sir William Butler.

Being asked what impression he had formed of that officer he stated precisely the same opinion he laid before Your Majesty yesterday.

Mr. Brodrick said that there was a question of this officer being recommended to Your Majesty as Q.M.G. but that his colleagues in the Cabinet were not favourable to the proposal. He, Mr. Brodrick, was not prejudiced against Sir William Butler, but found the decision a difficult one.

Lord Esher ventured to point out, that no political question entered into the duties of that officer, and that in purely military matters no more capable soldier could be found in Your Majesty's forces; and were Lord Esher in Mr. Brodrick's place, he would prefer a highly capable administrator, like Sir William Butler, in the office of Q.M.G., to a less able man, whose amiable qualities might be more assured.

Managed with tact, Lord Esher believes that Sir William Butler would not prove the *mauvais coucheur* which he is represented to be.

Lord Esher ventures humbly to ask Your Majesty not to mention to Mr. Brodrick that he has spoken of this interview; but Lord Esher, as Your Majesty is aware, conceals nothing from his Sovereign.

[*To H.M. the King.*]   2, TILNEY STREET,
FEBRUARY 14TH.

*On the
Defence
Committee.*

Lord Esher believes that the change in the constitution of the Defence Committee is directly due to the questions put by the S.A. War Commission to every witness of importance, as to the work and sphere of action of that Body.

Mr. Balfour's attention was drawn by Lord Esher to the responsibility which must attach to the Defence Committee for the neglect of proper precautions before the war, and to their apparent reluctance or inability to grapple with the military problems of the Empire.

Also, as Your Majesty knows, to the absurd fact that no high military nor naval authority was a Member of, or even present at, the Committee.

Hence, the changes made in the constitution of the Committee.

It now remains to awaken in them, first, a sense of the absolute necessity of settling the *main lines* of Imperial Military policy, and secondly, a full appreciation of the importance of constant and serious deliberation.

Lord Esher understands that the Prime Minister is a Member,

but not the President of the Defence Committee; an arrangement perhaps natural under existing circumstances, but which should not be taken as a precedent.

[*To H.M. the King.*]   2, TILNEY ST.,
                                          FEBRUARY 17TH.

Lord Esher presents his humble duty, and begs to state that Sir *Sir* George White gave his evidence most admirably to-day. His *George* high reputation for a man of perfect honour and unimpeachable *White's* straightforwardness, was unsullied after a long and trying *Evidence.* vindication of his objects and actions both before and during Ladysmith.

Sir George White left England without receiving any definite instructions. He was only two days in Africa before he had to make momentous decisions, which no fair-minded critic could do otherwise than admit were justified both by the state of facts then subsisting, and by subsequent events. So much has been admitted by Lord Roberts himself. Sir George White conclusively proved the great danger of the situation, created by the attitude of 750,000 Zulus on the Natal Frontier, and by the known plan of the rebellious Boers, who were waiting for the evacuation of Ladysmith as the signal for a rising.

He showed that it was impossible for him to neglect the warnings of experienced authorities on the spot. He spoke warmly of General Symons, and the beneficial effect of the battle of Talana, to which he attributes the safety of Ladysmith, by the check it gave to the Boer advance.

He further proved that the charge against him of having failed to assist the advance of General Buller was not due to his inaction, but to the extraordinary changes of plan, communicated to him at the last moment, and the want of information about Sir Redvers' movements. All this was proved by the very remarkable secret heliogram which passed between them, and which was laid before the Commission. His astonishment at receiving an invitation to surrender by the C.-in-C. in S. Africa, was so great as to make him incredulous of the authenticity of the message, which he believed at the time emanated from the Boers. Never did the thought of surrender cross his mind, and he determined—should he be abandoned—to cut his way out, at any sacrifice. This resolution was forced on him by the presence of Indians with him, and the sense of the effect which a surrender of their late C.-in-C. would produce in India.

All this evidence was given with sincerity and modesty and deep feeling, which left Sir George White's reputation, in the estimate of all those who heard him, higher than his previous silence and self-control had left him in the eyes of all unprejudiced men.

To-morrow, Sir R. Buller is called before the Commission.

[*To H.M. the King.*]   2, TILNEY STREET,
FEBRUARY 18TH.

Sir
Redvers
Buller's
Evidence.

Lord Esher presents his humble duty and begs to say that Sir Redvers Buller's evidence was given to-day, from the appointment of that officer to the command in S. Africa until the day previous to the attack on Colenso.

The most noticeable points elicited were, first, the disregard of their chosen commander's request to prepare for war by the Government, and secondly, the remarkable absence of all confidential communication between Sir Redvers and the Ministers before he left England.

No business firm, or indeed any private person, would be likely to send an agent abroad, upon a mission fraught with difficulty, without holding conferences upon the subject-matter of the mission. Yet General Buller attended no meeting of the Cabinet; nor any meeting of the Defence Committee. He never attended an "Army Board" at the War Office. He had no interview with the Prime Minister nor with the Colonial Secretary; and only saw Lord Lansdowne infrequently.

Such a state of things is almost incredible, and no doubt added largely to the General's subsequent difficulties. Sir Redvers laid no great stress upon these facts, which were discovered from cross-examination, nor did he speak with any "animus" of any soldier or Minister. He, however, did not give a very satisfactory explanation of his want of thorough understanding with Sir George White, whom he obviously underrated from the first. He was evidently imbued—like Lord Wolseley—with the erroneous idea that Sir George was responsible for the "Ladysmith entanglement"; and, having lost confidence in him, he did not attempt to act in concert with that officer. Sir Redvers explained his sudden change of plan on the 18th of December, when his movement on Potgieter's was commanded and he determined on a frontal attack on Colenso, by the receipt of the news of Maggersfontein; but this appears to be an inadequate explanation. He also could find no excuse for not attacking at first on his right flank (as he ultimately did with success) except that the nature of the country, covered with bush, was unsuited for raw troops. Considering that he commanded the flower of the Army, this explanation was unconvincing.

Lord Esher, however, is bound to state that Sir Redvers gave his evidence temperately, and with that officer's well-known acumen and knowledge of war.

[*To H.M. the King*.] 2, TILNEY STREET, FEBRUARY 19TH.

Lord Esher presents his humble duty to Your Majesty and begs to state that Sir Redvers Buller's examination was concluded to-day. He explained the nature of his operations, and attributed his repeated failures to two causes. First, the disobedience to orders at Colenso. Secondly, the want of co-operation of the Ladysmith garrison. He gave somewhat lame explanations of his telegrams to the Sec. of State, in which he appeared to despair of relieving Ladysmith, and his heliogram to Sir

Buller's Evidence Continued.

George White suggesting surrender. His object was, so he said, to provoke H.M.G. to send the 5th Div. to Natal rather than to the Modder; and to provoke Sir George White to attempt a sortie southwards to join hands with him.

Lord Esher thought it his duty to press Sir Redvers rather severely upon these two points, and asked him why he could not state his views in plain words instead of attempting to gain his ends by telegraphic stratagem. There was obviously no satisfactory reply to this question.

The examination of a man who has rendered such great service in the past to the State was somewhat painful, and Lord Esher can only say that, on the whole, Sir Redvers did not cut a poor figure, but appeared, what he is, a brave and capable soldier, admirably adapted to hold a high secondary command, but unfitted, by his temperament, to be placed in supreme command of an Army in the field. He gave excellent evidence upon military questions generally, and upon War Office questions.

Lord Esher finally was enabled to understand why Sir Redvers has won the affection of officers who served under him, and of the rank and file.

In spite of his great failings, he is a very human figure. Unpleasing in appearance, with no command of temper, he is nevertheless a man of strong sympathies and generous impulses. There were more instances of this in the course of his examination.

After the somewhat disagreeable passages of arms with Lord Esher, he came up to him in a friendly manner, and upon Lord Esher's asking him *why* he had (assuming the explanation of his telegrams to be the true one) put himself in a position to be hopelessly misunderstood, and never again trusted by his countrymen, he said, "It is my beastly temper. All my life long I have suffered from this. Since old Eton days I have had a formula for myself, 'Remember Dunmore.' It happened in this way. At a football match, the ball came to me, and I had it in my power to 'run down' and secure a goal; but I stopped to have a 'shinning match' with Dunmore, and lost my chance.

Although always present in my mind, I have always failed to remember Dunmore."

Your Majesty's remarkable appreciation, and kindness of heart, will readily understand how disarming so candid a confession necessarily must be upon the mind of a critic; and how completely an apology, offered with a certain rough humour, must often have won back the regard of men upon whom General Buller has trampled.

It was this officer's misfortune that he was selected for a task which he was not qualified, from defects of character rather than of intellect, to fulfil.

It is the misfortune of the State and of Your Majesty's Army, that his services, under conditions when he might still be useful, are, it is to be feared, irretrievably lost.

[*To M. V. B.*]   2, TILNEY STREET,
                                           FEBRUARY 23RD.

We had a levée to-day. The first in Buckingham Palace. I missed the old "setting" of St. James's. The King will revert to the old Palace, when it is fit for use. The King *sat* down after the ambassadors had passed, but the *Corps Diplomatique* was hopelessly muddled up by old Colville, so he was very cross!

I have been very busy all day, with one thing and another, having finally to sit as arbitrator in a row about the Ascot stands.

[*To M. V. B.*]   2, TILNEY STREET,
                                           FEBRUARY 25TH.

I have had rather a less onerous day than usual. This morning *Gatacre's* we had Gatacre before us. *Not* a very impressive personality. *Evidence.* He told us that he had been superseded and sent home for the mishap at Reddesburg. I asked him whether he had had any opportunity of stating his case to Lord Roberts. None. He was "stellenboshed" unheard; nor did he ever get a line from Lord Roberts—nor from K. [Kitchener], under whom he had served with distinction in Egypt—of commiseration or explanation. Not a very kindly proceeding. Kelly Kenny came this afternoon to contradict some evidence of Lord Roberts' as to the command at Paardeberg. He read a curious correspondence with Lord Roberts, which showed that both K. K. and K. were in command at Paardeberg! Three K.s.! A pretty good confusion. Odd people.

Kelly Kenny's Evidence.

. . . The telephone is fixed up in Tilney St. and I have got the books. So I suppose we are now all right. . . .

[*To M. V. B.*]   ORCHARD LEA,
FEBRUARY 27TH.

If all the King's generals were drawn up in a row, in order to select the most capable, the two we saw to-day would be chosen among the first. French[1] was excellent. He is obviously a soldier with not only the instincts of a fighter, but also imbued with common sense, free from fads, and has thought seriously about his profession. Bruce Hamilton is just the sort of man anyone would like to follow in a hazardous enterprise. Perfectly cool, and gentle, yet with most determined eyes; incapable of surprise.

On French.

On Bruce Hamilton.

Both these men gave admirable evidence, and they know exactly what they want! They will not get it, as the Army Corps decentralisation is in reality a farce; and French has no more power under Brodrick's scheme than if he commanded one of the old "districts."

I got down here late last night—could not leave before 8.20 as I had a meeting at B. Palace about the King's household. We have cut down a lot of useless expenditure. I wonder what you think of Kipling's poem in to-day's *Times*. I think some of it is rather rough. He apparently intends to make S. Africa his second literary field of conquest—after India.

[1] Afterwards F.M. Earl of Ypres.

Did you hear that the Italians had placed *in Italian* this inscription on Elizabeth Browning's house in Florence: "Here lived E. B. B., whose poems are a golden thread binding Italy to England." Some such inscription will have been earned by Kipling in India; and if he could do the same for S.A. he would deserve a place in Westminster Abbey.

[*To M. V. B.*]   ORCHARD LEA,
MARCH 2ND.

... what is called "society"? Too much attention is paid to *On* the word, which is really an anachronism now, and rather com- *High* mon! In fact, there is no such thing. Society is dead and died *Society.* with d'Orsay and Lady Blessington. There are people "who give dinners" and people "who give balls." That is all. It is open to you to choose whether you will go or not, as you please. This was not the case when society existed. Then, you could no more refuse than you could now refuse to dine with your Colonel. Either you were "in society"—and in that case you kept its rules, quite simply—or, you were not in society, in which case (if you were anybody out of the ruck) you were generally considered to be some sort of swindler; or to have disgraced yourself.

Now, nobody cares what you do, or who you are; although there are, of course, a lot of country people who come up to London, and imagine that the great city would take an interest in the fact that this man is a country magnate, or that woman a Duchess, whereas it does not care a jot.

There are "interesting people" and there are "rucks." A Duchess may be in either, in these days. So may an out-at-the-elbows author or journalist. The sort of snobism which Thackeray gibbeted has passed away from the great world of London, and you can only find traces of it in country villages, or in Bayswater. Thoughts like these are not worth thinking, and the most attractive people in the world never allow them to cross their minds.

. . . I wonder whether all this will read very pedantically. That is the worst of the feeble medium of the pen. Words that can be spoken without fear of offence, are steel-tipped when written. It is rare that the "irreparable" is spoken; but how often it slips out on paper.

Sometimes, in anger or in argument, or even in jest, the un-forgettable thing is said; but when that is the case one's guardian angels have flown away, and after that nothing very much matters!

[*To M. V. B.*]   ORCHARD LEA,
                                                    MARCH 3RD.

American Literature.   . . . What freshness there is in these stories from the new world.[1] They are a new vein of literature. Chateaubriand and his followers, who wrote about America at the end of the 18th century, merely peopled the continent with the forms of the old. Their characters and ideas and reflections are those of the court of Louis XV passing across a stage painted with virgin forests. These modern American writers describe a new race of men and women, as virgin of soul as the forests through which they move. It is a tribute to the eternal youth of the world that we —living in this old worn-out continent—should be able to appreciate them so fully. In this book which we have recently read, and in the *Virginian*,[2] there are passages containing poetic fervour for what is beautiful in nature hardly surpassed by Keats in *Endymion*, when he was describing the boyhood of the human race.

[*To M. V. B.*]   2, TILNEY STREET,
                                                    MARCH 4TH.

If you find that February has been written instead of this blustering month at the head of my last two letters, alter it in

[1] *The Heart of the Ancient Wood.* By Charles Roberts.
[2] By Owen Wister.

pencil. As you seem to find a pleasure in preserving these written talks, you may as well possess the record correctly.

. . . After an absence, the surest way of taking up threads is to seize them boldly at once; otherwise, there is a risk of entanglement, which may take long to unravel. The *ars amantis* is so difficult and full of delicate shades. Yet the mass of mankind plunge through it, with hobnailed boots, as if they were walking over ploughed fields.

. . . However, to-night I am rather sick and sorry with the world; and possibly my views may be distorted; so you need not pay much attention to them. It is curious what tricks our emotions play with us, and how affection blows like the wind first from one quarter, then from another, for no ostensible reason; but for some hidden and mysterious cause, which neither reason nor science has fathomed. Although I am alone here, there is no solitude—which I crave for at this moment—but the noises of the city are coming up from the streets, with a persistency which galls me.

Perhaps you never have these feelings—and if so, you are fortunate. I wonder if you will ever read those half-plays, half-poems of de Musset's, where he communes with the spirits of the seasons? They are haunting me to-night; and October holds me, although this is spring time.

[*To M. V. B.*]   2, TILNEY STREET,
                                           MARCH 5TH.

I am horrified to find that the ponderous tower of letters lying on this table is for *half* the year 1899. It is incredible that anyone can have written so much, and so monotonously. I remember that I was wont to rally you upon my letters, for not reading them. And although it was with only a half-belief in the truth of the accusation, I now wholly credit it.

. . . To-day was rather spoilt for me by overwhelming illness at times, but it should have been interesting, as this morning I

I—25

visited Lansdowne in his beautiful rooms, hung with splendid portraits by Raeburn of that wonderful group of Scottish writers and liberals who were contemporaries, but not friends, of Scott's. I discussed with Lansdowne two projects which he has much at heart. The first concerns Morocco, and is not really interesting. The second the Bagdad railway, which is now certain to be made under the auspices of England, Germany and France—and will furnish a real over-land route to India. I told you of my interview with the King this evening. He made me sit down, and he talked—as he so often does—with the greatest freedom. His relations with the C.-in-C. are not friendly. Lord Roberts has mismanaged him, and the King chafes under the little man's ignorance of the *English* Army, and his persistence in pushing all his Indian friends into high military posts. The King, in all these Army talks, displays his sound sense and knowledge of the world.

The King and Roberts.

. . . If you write to Ella [Terriss] you might do me the justice to say that I was *not* bored—but tired. Life is so very grey at times, and this greyness is about me now. Perhaps only a phase. Perhaps a moment—God knows.

Anyhow, I should be sorry if that bright little person were for a moment grieved at the thought that my appreciation had waned. It has not, nor could it do so. One might as well try to deprecate the sunlight. Why do poets use the image of strings, speaking of the heart? It is a poor form of viol if that is what they mean.

[*To M. V. B.*]   2, TILNEY STREET,
                                              MARCH IOTH.

. . . I sent the Queen some of these new daffodils with a note congratulating her on her wedding day, which has fulfilled all the highest hopes of the English people. I hope she will be flattered!

I lunched at New Court with the Rothschilds and met two *Modern* smart West-end ladies, Lady Howe and Lady Sarah Wilson, *Feminine* *Manners.* who smoked cigarettes and drank liqueurs after luncheon, like stockbrokers, but thanks to their sex were nevertheless more entertaining. Queer women. What a 20th-century development, and how unlike the manners of Bath in the reign of the third George.

[*To M. V. B.*]   ORCHARD LEA,
                                                   MARCH 11TH.

I hope you enjoyed the King's party.[1] It was a pretty entertainment, from the passing of the guests in review to the supper, which was excellently well done. I wish you had been able to stay for it. The most noticeable thing was the absence of any great beauty among the women. There was no one very striking, either married or otherwise. I escorted Lady Helen Vincent to supper, and I really think she was the belle of the ball. Even the Queen did not look her best last night. The King retired to his bridge, but he reappeared about three, when the whole thing came to an end.

... I am in great hopes that the Commission will have finished its labours, excepting the Report, by the end of the month. You see how Brodrick is anticipating almost every point, as the cross-examination is revealed to him by the officers who pass through the ordeal. It is skilful of him.

[*To H.M. the King.*]   ORCHARD LEA,
                                                   MARCH 11TH.

... Your Majesty will have noticed that Mr. Brodrick in his *Brodrick's* speeches in Parliament has unfolded schemes of reform, based *Reforms.* on the line of cross-examination before the Commission. The

[1] A ball given at Buckingham Palace in celebration of the fortieth anniversary of the King's marriage.

modifications of the Defence Committee, the training and selection of officers, the stress laid on the importance of the War Office Council, the importance of Medical and Educational Advisory Boards, the increase of the Intelligence Branch, all bear witness to the effect of the evidence upon those officers who have been called, and have reported to the Sec. of State the line of examination adopted by the Commission.

It would appear, therefore, that already the appointment by Your Majesty of this Commission has been more than justified.

It is prudent of the Sec. of State to anticipate, as far as he is able, the effect on the public mind of the evidence given, and the obvious direction which suggestions emanating from the Commission cannot fail to take.

Lord Esher hopes that the Report will press for the conversion of the War Office Council into a highly efficient Army Board, on the lines approved by Your Majesty. There are many subsidiary changes, which the evidence will show to be desirable and necessary.

[*To M. V. B.*]   ORCHARD LEA,
                                             MARCH 12TH.

I think that the letter that I enclose—if you can manage to read it—will interest you, and you will gather once more an impression of the charm of friendship with a woman whose mind rings true.

They are very rare—almost as hard to find as the shy intimacies with the wild creatures of the Ancient Wood. I let you read these letters, not only because from you I have no secrets, but also because I hope that some day a friend cast in similar mould will wander down the valley and meet you, as this friend met me—long ago.

Portia, Viola, Rosalind—all the dreams of the poets seem realised here. It makes the world a brighter place to think that the wind has not yet blown them all away, although my sun has passed its meridian.

When I first knew her she came down a garden path, between the roses, a young untamed girl, with untrained mind and reckless spirits—uncertain of the next step on the road of life. Injudicious, dangerous companions about her, with her course undetermined. So far she has steered clear of rocks and sands, and in spite of the manifold storms which have raged about her, has sailed bravely through life. Without undue pride, I think I have helped her a little. This is a pleasant thought.

[*To H.M. the King.*]   ORCHARD LEA,
MARCH 17TH.

Lord Esher presents his humble duty, and begs to state that Admiral Harris and Admiral Lambton gave their evidence to-day. The contrast between the two Services was brought prominently to the attention of the Commission. It can be summed up in the word "professional."

Admiral Harris's and Admiral Lambton's Evidence.

In listening to a sailor, the conviction is forced upon his audience, that he possesses knowledge and experience; whereas although soldiers have wide experience, they rarely possess knowledge of their profession.

Contrast between Army and Navy.

Admiral Lambton spoke, publicly, with great directness; but most of the important things he reserved—very properly—for private conversation, not in the presence of the reporters.

. . . Another very marked point is the responsibility so readily assumed by naval officers in high command. They appear never to shrink from consequences—and consequently their boldness is over and over again justified by results ; such as, first, Admiral Lambton's embarkation of troops at the Mauritius without orders from the Admiralty; and, secondly, that officer's landing of a naval Brigade and his arrival with big guns at Ladysmith in the nick of time. It is doubtful whether any military officer in Your Majesty's Army would have dared to undertake such responsibilities, whereas there is no reason to suppose that many sailors would have shrunk from them.

The totally different training—from early youth—of the two Services accounts for this divergence of character. Officers of both Services are drawn from the same class—and there is no reason why they should exhibit different characteristics. But the Army training cramps the mind and crushes out initiative in men from their boyhood onwards; whereas a naval training, by giving first small responsibilities to young lads, encouraging individual enterprise, constant teaching of duties, gradually increasing in importance, while gradually imposing fresh responsibilities of a heavier kind, creates an independence of mind and judgment, with a fearlessness of consequences, which make Your Majesty's naval officers what they admittedly are, the finest body of men in the world.

Lord Esher can only hope that the evidence taken before the Commission may go some way to convince those who have military education and training at heart, to endeavour to emulate the success of the sister service.

[*To M. V. B.*]   2, TILNEY STREET,
                              ·   MARCH 17TH.

Balfour and Army Reform.

I did not tell you that I had a long talk with the Prime Minister[1] yesterday, about the Army, and found him not at all unfavourably inclined to the scheme which I explained to you. He takes a great deal of interest in the subject, and his mind is so receptive and alert, that it is easy to discuss even the points of detail with him. The more I think over it, the more strongly is the conviction borne in upon me that the wisest thing to do, is to abolish the C.-in-C. altogether, and let the King be the nominal Commander of the Land Forces of the Crown. I shall show you this on paper, and you can criticise the project.

. . . Last night's party was a great success, as those things can be. Ella [Terriss] was preoccupied about the quails and the potatoes, but perfectly sweet withal. I sat between her and

[1] The Rt. Hon. A. J. Balfour.

Barrie, who is a sweet affair. So very appreciative. Frohman is a humourist of a quick and shrewd order; and evidently thinks Ella charming. Mason, the author of *Four Feathers*, was there. I should think a very clever man. Miss Irene [Vanbrugh] was most friendly—and I like her. She spoke very warmly of Margaret [Fraser] whom Dot Boucicault wished to retain in their new piece by Pinero.

[*To H.M. the King.*]   2, TILNEY STREET,
MARCH 18TH.

Lord Esher presents his humble duty and begs to inform Your Majesty that the most interesting evidence taken to-day was that of Colonel Haig[1]—17th Lancers—an officer known to Your Majesty as a most capable cavalry leader. He is evidently a good organiser, and a helpful Staff Officer. Not unnaturally, his views are those which might be expected from a cavalry officer. He holds, with General French, that it would be a mistake to found on the experience of S. Africa a theory hostile to cavalry tactics, as hitherto understood. He regrets the abolition of the lance, and believes in the *arme blanche* as an effective weapon.

... In the summer, this officer goes to India as Inspector-General of Cavalry, a post which he should admirably fill.

In him Your Majesty possesses a very fine type of officer, practical, firm, and thoughtful, thoroughly experienced not only in war, but in military history.

[*To M. V. B.*]   ORCHARD LEA,
MARCH 18TH.

There is nothing much to tell you to-day, except military details, which, I fear, bore you. You know how difficult it is

[1] Afterwards F.M. Earl Haig.

to avoid "shop," and at the present moment I live almost exclusively up to my ears in military organisation.

Direction of the Opera.

It is practically settled that I go on the Direction of the Opera, which may be rather amusing. There was no way out of it, the difficulties of finding anyone who would suit the two sections represented by Gladys de Grey on the one hand, and Harry Higgins on the other, were so great. Before finally accepting I am going to consult the King, as he may have an opinion on the subject. Your account of Letty [Lind] was most pathetic. Few things are more painful to contemplate than a fallen star. There are some beautiful Italian lines about the sadness of remembering, in days of misery, the old days of happiness. They apply equally to the days of glory, when the clouds have gathered darkly about someone who has been admired and loved.

Charles V, the great Emperor, was right when, at the height of his splendour—but conscious of failing powers—he abdicated, and retired into the dark recesses of the Escurial.

[*To M. V. B.*]   ORCHARD LEA,
                                   MARCH 20TH.

. . . I went to the Chamberlain luncheon to-day—and it was rather a pleasant party in its initial stages. I had a talk with Ian Hamilton, who is a most attractive fellow. Several nice women were there too. Then the odious heavy luncheon began. As the King sent for me at half-past three, I left after Turtle soup and Whitebait.

The King was again in one of his good moods. Very practical about some Osborne business, and then I had about an hour with him on the Army. He is more appreciative than you are, and

The Office of Commander-in-Chief.

attaches more importance to my humble views. I think he is ready to agree to abolishing the C.-in-C., and this will be the first reform ever introduced, if we can get the Government to agree. I think the King himself ought to take the title of C.-in-C.

In George IVth's time this was proposed, but the Government of the day would not hear of it. Things have much changed since then. George III had been recently on the throne and there was a strong revolutionary spirit in the air—dating from 1793.

Now, the Imperial idea is accepted—and the King's nominal chiefship of the Army ought to please the Colonials.

[*To M. V. B.*]   ORCHARD LEA,
                                                   MARCH 23RD.

. . . I arranged about the Opera to-day with Harry Higgins, and shall be elected on the Board very soon; it may be rather amusing. What I should like, would be a clear week or ten days, in which to go through all the points of Army changes. Of course, I shall not get this, and it will be hard work fitting it all in, with other things. We examine Lansdowne this week, two whole days.

. . . Doll has embarked on her wild career of Dumas and I *Books and* cannot think that they will do her any harm. The adventures *Morals.* which suggest everything to those who understand, represent very little to those who do not. To her it all seems very heroic and far off. Much as the manners and customs of the Tibetans do to us. Books which do harm, are the worldly, vulgar books—like some of Ouida's—or "problem" hysterical works of passionless spinsters.

Henry IV might have all the mistresses on earth, and it would corrupt no girl's morals. Anyhow, I am sure of this, that had she been forbidden to read them, she would have read them on the sly. Do you agree?

[*To M. V. B.*]   2, TILNEY STREET,
                                                   MARCH 24TH.

We had the evidence of that clever little fellow—Amery[1]—to- *Amery's* day, who writes the his ory of the war for *The Times*. He has *Evidence.*

[1] The Rt. Hon. L. S. Amery.

seen a good deal, and got a great amount of information from officers, but has often naturally been misled as to facts. He is full *Conan* of intelligence. Conan Doyle, who came after him, is like *Doyle.* Jingo, a huge elephantine creature, with blue eyes. Not the least like Sherlock Holmes nor Brigadier Gerard. He was jolly, but not very illuminating.

[*To H.M. the King.*]   2, TILNEY STREET,
                                            MARCH 28TH.

Lansdowne's   Lord Esher presents his humble duty to Your Majesty, and
Evidence.   begs to say that Lord Lansdowne gave evidence yesterday and
to-day before the Commission, evidence marked by a most conscientious desire to conceal no document and no fact in any way material to the questions into which Your Majesty's Commissioners were appointed to enquire.

Upon the main issue, as to the preparations for war during the year 1899, it became abundantly clear that the avoidance of necessary preparations, involving the movement of troops, and expenditure upon a large scale for transport, etc., was a deliberate political act, for which the Cabinet as a whole, and the Cabinet only, can be held responsible.

All the evidence goes to show that information of the fullest kind was in possession of the Government; and that, impressed by the importance of taking no step which might be construed into a hostile act, they deliberately abstained, for reasons explained by them on many occasions, from making preparations for war.

Whether they were justified or not, is a political question, upon which opinions are likely always to be divided.

Lord Lansdowne's evidence proves, beyond a doubt, that his military advisers under-estimated the power and resources of the Boers. Further, it shows the disorganisation of the War Office, and the grave defects of a system under which the Sec.

of State could be left in ignorance of the very serious conditions of our armaments, equipment, etc., disclosed upon the outbreak of the war in October, 1899.

The failure of the Office of Commander-in-Chief becomes clear from Lord Lansdowne's evidence, since under the existing system, that officer is the supreme military adviser of the Sec. of State, and the ultimate channel of information upon all military questions, both concerning the efficiency of the Army, and the condition of our armaments, defences, and military organisation.

For the initial failures of the war, for the enormous cost involved in repairing those failures, for the extravagant expenditure, resulting from hasty purchasing of guns, ammunition, clothing, etc., etc., the Commander-in-Chief, under the present system, is morally responsible. Constitutionally the onus lies on the Sec. of State; but, as Your Majesty knows, the Secretary of State, upon all questions of military detail, is necessarily dependent upon his professional advisers.

Lord Esher need scarcely point out that responsibilities, so onerous and trying, should not be placed upon the shoulders of any one of Your Majesty's subjects.

Under the Constitution, as it has been developed through centuries, the First Minister of the Crown is not solely responsible to Your Majesty for the Government of the country. The responsibility is the collective one of the Cabinet as a whole. It would be unfair to place such a responsibility upon a Minister.

The varied labours of the War Department, the onerous mass of detail, the necessary efficiency of every branch of the service, in order to ensure the safety of the realm, demand a system under which the Sec. of State is not asked to rely—as is now the case under the Order in Council of 1901—upon his "Principal Military Adviser," but upon the collective authority of a Board or Council.

Lord Lansdowne's evidence shows (1) that the Cabinet were responsible (whether right or wrong) for the deliberate neglect to prepare for war; (2) that the late Commander-in-Chief is morally responsible for the condition of our armaments, equipments, etc., etc., in October, 1899.

Lord Esher ventures to submit that all the evidence before the Commission supports the views which he has developed to Your Majesty in his memorandum.

Lord Lansdowne had to admit that if, under the present system, any man in middle life were appointed C.-in-C., his further military employment at the end of five years would be practically impossible. But on this question Lord Esher would like to send Your Majesty some further considerations.

[*To M. V. B.*]   2, TILNEY STREET,
                                   APRIL 3RD.

Imagine last night my having to sit down and play bridge with Cassel, Carl Meyer and another man. *I* played pennies. Two rubbers. Won the first and lost the second, and ended up by winning two shillings! Cassel lost forty-one pounds. I warned them all I was a rotten player; and I certainly was the worst of the four.

[*To M. V. B.*]   ORCHARD LEA,
                                   APRIL 6TH.

The Bagdad Railway.

. . . I seem to have run about a great deal to-day, but saw no one interesting. It looks as though I shall have to accompany Revelstoke and Cassel to Berlin for a few days, some time this month or next, in connection with the Bagdad railway. Do you see that some of the newspapers are attacking it because it is a German project, and wish us to block it—or keep out of it —as we did when the Suez Canal was made?

In that case we had to buy our way in later, at an enormous cost; and it did not prevent the canal being made. Stupid fools!

There is no pacificator like a railway. We ruled the Punjab more by the locomotive than by the sword. Also the Soudan. . . .

[*To M. V. B.*]   ORCHARD LEA,
                                            APRIL 7TH.

. . . It looks as if the Bagdad railway scheme would fall   *The*
through. Lansdowne sent for Cassel this evening, as there is a   *Bagdad*
"question" in the H. of C. about it. My instinct tells me that the   *Railway.*
Government will flinch. They are very timid just now. I don't
much care, although I think there is a lot of money to be made
in it. The Germans will go on just the same and the railway
will ultimately be made, only we shall be out of it. We never
learn by experience.

[*To M. V. B.*]   ORCHARD LEA,
                                            APRIL 8TH.

I have a very civil note from Haig, and from it I gather that
you very likely saw him to-day.

. . . To-day we had long discussions about the Bagdad rail-   *The*
way. The Government are frightened, and run away. In that   *Bagdad*
case Revelstoke and Cassel retire from the scheme, and the   *Railway.*
Germans and the French go on alone. It is a pity.

The Defence Committee are strongly in favour of the line on
strategical grounds. Whether they are right or wrong is one
question. That the line is sure to be made, and under those
circumstances it is well for us to have a joint control, is quite
another thing—and upon this point there can be no doubt. But
the German Emperor is a Bogey just now in certain quarters ;
and the English people, led by a foolish half-informed Press,
are children in foreign politics. They have always been so, and
have often paid dearly.

. . . I went this morning to see how Elgin was getting on   *Progress*
with the Report. It will be a tough job inducing some of these   *of South*
people to agree to any sensible proposals. Their inclination will   *African*
be to have a non-committal report, merely summing up the   *Report.*
evidence. This would be an absurdity, so there will be a hard

fight. During the next few days I must draft some paragraphs for them, in the strongest possible language.

[*From Sir Frederick Ponsonby.*]   GIBRALTAR,
                                                APRIL 12TH.

MY DEAR ESHER,

The Bagdad Railway.   I showed your letter to the King, who asked me to tell you that he hoped that you would not allow "your leg to be pulled" in Berlin. He read an article in the *Spectator* about the Bagdad railway, but the *Spectator's* dislike of Germany is so great that all articles that have any reference to Germany have no value. According to present arrangements we arrive at Malta on the 16th April.

The King at Lisbon.   . . . Our visit to Lisbon seems to have been a great success, but it was rather tiring having functions all and every day. Both at the bull fight and gala opera they gave the King a most enthusiastic reception; the whole audience standing up and cheering for some time while the band played repeatedly God Save the King. A somewhat nasty incident has occurred here. An anarchist well known to the police arrived here armed with a revolver and a long knife. He was promptly put in prison, but there seems some legal difficulty about keeping him there. Of course, until the K. leaves it can be done, but he will have plenty of time to catch us up in Naples if released as soon as we leave. Sir G. White, however, has decided to take advantage of the fact of Gibraltar being a Fortress, and is determined to keep the man locked up until the K. returns home. This is, of course, private, as the whole thing has been kept secret.

                                                Yours ever,
                                                FRITZ PONSONBY.

[*To H.M. the King.*]   ORCHARD LEA,
                                                APRIL 30TH.

Progress of the Report.   Lord Esher presents his humble duty to Your Majesty, and begs to state that the Commission have now sat three days, in private, to consider their Report. It is, up to the present, arranged in three parts. The first deals with the preparations for war, and the Commission have unanimously come to the sad conclusion, that the responsibility for most of the early failures must rest upon the shoulders of the late Commander-in-Chief.

Under the Order in Council defining his duties, there can be no doubt that he was responsible for all plans of defence and offence, for adequate preparations to meet any eventuality in the Field.

The Intelligence Branch was under the Commander-in-Chief, and all its information at his disposal; while the evidence shows that, for some unexplainable reason, he neglected to lay that information before the Secretary of State. This is, so far, the main conclusion in Part I of the Report. The second portion deals with the supplies of men, ammunition, etc., and is in the form of a summary of the evidence.

Although many inferences and suggestions could be drawn, there is very great difficulty in getting the Commissioners to agree; and a marked inclination to shirk difficult questions. This is natural, but should a colourless report be produced, it is obvious that the Commission will very probably be held to have left their principal duty unfulfilled.

The third part was touched upon to-day, and here the divergence of view, upon the organisation of the War Office and of the Army, was very apparent, with again a strong tendency to adopt the line that it was no part of their duty to make recommendations.

Lord Esher holds, as Your Majesty knows, very strongly the opposite opinion, but it will be a hard fight, and possibly a losing battle.

Mr. Brodrick is examined to-morrow, and is the last witness.

Lord Esher ventures to express a hope that Your Majesty is not worn out by the exertion of Your Majesty's very splendid and successful, but most arduous tour.

[*To M. V. B.*]   ORCHARD LEA,
APRIL 30TH.

*The
Report.*

We had a long and difficult day with the Commission. It was a prolonged wrangle over the Report, and there is no chance of an agreement upon the points which I care most about. The majority are timid and do not wish to commit themselves to any proposition which is at all controversial.

There is some risk that the main report will be rather flabby, and little more than a colourless summary of the evidence. I shall print my own ideas in a separate memorandum. There was some temper shown, but not much.

. . . Nellie is not inclined to come to Edinburgh, unless it is certain she will be welcome, and she is probably right. I shall know when the King returns.

It depends upon his general state of mind. I am sure he is rather tired and cross. No wonder, after all the hard work in Rome. It is no gala, that sort of trip. The visit to the Pope, however, is most interesting. It will delight his Catholic subjects.

[*To H.M. the King.*]   ORCHARD LEA,
MAY 2ND.

*Mr.
Brodrick's
Evidence.*

Lord Esher presents his humble duty to Your Majesty, and begs to say that Mr. Brodrick gave his evidence with great frankness, and showed a singular mastery of detail, with really profound knowledge of the Administrative side of the Army. This will not have been unexpected by Your Majesty, who is aware of Mr. Brodrick's assiduity and power of work.

Lord Esher cannot say that the evidence given by the Sec. of State added much to the information already before the Commission, but it decidedly strengthened (although unintentionally) the views of those who think that the organisation of the W.O. requires a drastic alteration.

Mr. Brodrick's abilities are hampered, at every turn, by the conditions under which he administers the War Department.

He is the type of Minister, in Lord Esher's humble opinion, who would be admirably suited to hold a place at the head of a Military Board. His mind is alert and vigorous, and he would be excellently capable of winnowing the wheat from the chaff in a discussion, and summing up an argument.

With a strong Board, there is no reason to suppose that he would not succeed well in administering Your Majesty's Army. But, under existing circumstances, surrounded by high military officials, all pulling in different directions, each man anxious to absorb the authority of his neighbour, the task is hopeless.

This was the impression made by Mr. Brodrick's evidence, although it was very far from his intention to produce it.

Lord Esher begs to say that the Commission has adjourned to May 26th, when the Report will again be considered.

[*To M. V. B.*]　　　　　2, TILNEY STREET,
　　　　　　　　　　　　　　MAY 2ND.

. . . The party at Lansdowne House was a great squash, but the house itself, and the pictures, and the statuary, were all lovely. Every sort of person there. I talked to all the soldiers, but to no one else, except Lady Mar.

No beauties there—Lady Warwick looked better than anyone. I suppose there will be some young ones soon, to vie with this older brigade; but no signs at present.

I have written to the King a full account of Brodrick's evidence. It was very good, but he showed (unintentionally) the weakness of the W.O. A very capable man, rendered incapable by circumstances—by military officials, all with ill-defined duties, all pulling different ways instead of all pulling together.

[*To M. V. B.*]　　　　　2, TILNEY STREET,
　　　　　　　　　　　　　　MAY 5TH.

There is no doubt that Alexander is very skilful in selecting his plays. The house was crammed, and very enthusiastic. " *Old Heidelberg.*"

I—26

Personally I do not think the play itself a very good one;[1] but the idea is fresh, and the character of the old Tutor, and of the girl, charming. The piece of humanity—in the shape of the Tutor—dragged into that weary stiff court, is very telling; and the human relations developed between him and his pupil is the touching note of the play. I think you might perhaps sit through it again some day. I went on to the opera. It was not *very* full, but still was brilliant enough. The orchestra sounded fine, but Lohengrin himself was a mixture of Nero and Louis XIV— and by no means romantic.

[*To M. V. B.*]   2, TILNEY STREET,
                                                    MAY 6TH.

Messager's   The French musical play is very charming.[2] So gay and
"Véronique."   melodious. I think you would enjoy it, and we shall have to go
there some evening. It was well arranged as a first night. All the stalls were taken by Alfred Rothschild, and then invitations issued. So it made a most pleasant party. We all went on afterwards to supper at the Carlton, which had leave to keep open till 12.30. We had supper in the big room, and then went into one of the smaller rooms to hear Paul Rubens and his brother play the piano. Got home at two.

[*To M. V. B.*]   2, TILNEY STREET,
                                                    MAY 7TH.

Fancy the King going to the opera last night at 5.30—in ordinary clothes—then going home to dinner—and returning immediately to remain to the very end. The Queen dined there in the room behind the box. I went twice like the King, and in the interval dined with Lady Warwick. A huge table—round —about thirty people. Everything a mass of La France roses.

---

[1] *Old Heidelberg.*   [2] *Véronique.* By Messager.

Quite lovely. But not many guests at the Ball. Margery Manners[1] was there. Of course, she has all John's fascination.

. . . I am much inclined to creep out of the Edinburgh ceremonials—if I can manage to do so.

[*From Mr. Austen Chamberlain.*]　STOKE COURT,
STOKE POGES, BUCKS,
MAY 10TH.

MY DEAR ESHER,

I am, I need scarcely say, very sorry that you are not able to take the Chairmanship of the Post Office Committee; but I felt I was making a great demand on your time and cannot be surprised at your decision. Many thanks to you for giving it such careful consideration, and for the kind way in which you write.

Yours very truly,
AUSTEN CHAMBERLAIN.

[*To M. V. B.*]　　HOLYROOD PALACE,
MAY 11TH.

So far all has gone well. The King and Queen had a good reception. All the streets lined with Black Watch, who looked very well.　*Edinburgh The Royal Entry.*

Life Guards were much admired. I stood in a dense crowd and heard all the comments. The salute from the Castle sounded fine. We spent all the morning arranging this Palace. Not a very easy matter. I don't know what the shade of Mary thought of it all. The effect to-morrow will be more quaint than splendid. I dine here, but sleep at the Palace Hotel.

[*To M. V. B.*]　　HOLYROOD PALACE,
MAY 12TH.

. . . To-day I was at Holyrood by 9.30 in undress uniform. The King arrived at 11. Then we were all in full dress. Black　*Levée at Holyrood.*

----

[1] Afterwards Marchioness of Anglesey.

Watch mounted guard in the Quadrangle, a beautiful sight. The arrival, in the space before the Palace, with the Highlander and Life Guards, and the brightest sun, was lovely.

Archers of the Guard, in the quaint dress, and bonnets, stationed throughout the Palace. When the King was on the Throne, the colours of the Guard of Archers were on either side of him, with Erroll, Argyll, Montrose, Buccleuch, all the historic hereditary officers, grouped about him. There were addresses and presentations as usual. While the Levée proceeded, I took the Queen over the Queen Mary rooms, and out into the Chapel. Then luncheon, and afterwards the drawing-room. That was quite a pretty sight, but the departure was prettier still—as the procession wound round the road running under the crags, and the crowds of people made a charming picture.

Rosebery was there, looking old—and every sort of Scottish potentate you ever heard of. The Palace really looked splendid —so mediæval—and I don't think that anything could have been better done.

[*To M. V. B.*]   HOLYROOD PALACE,
                                        MAY 13TH.

Review at Everything to-day has been a great success. The review of
Edinburgh. the Archers was curious. A fine body of men, quite unique so far as I know. I don't think any foreign king possesses such a force.

There was a high wind which sent bonnets flying in all directions. We had a huge luncheon, 87 people. The King and Queen sitting under a canopy. Then they went to the Castle, and were received by a sentry on the walls, who challenged in a strong highland brogue. It was all most picturesque.

There was a large number of soldiers about. I dare say 10,000 men. All Scottish regiments. From early morn they began to pass down Prince's St., and you can imagine what a gay sight it was; bands playing, and the old castle hanging over the scene.

. . . To-night I dine at Dalkeith, and leave here to-morrow by the early train. So I shall be in London to dinner. The weather has been superb, and the King could not have been more lucky. I hope this Glasgow trip will be as successful. The Queen has created a vast astonishment by her youthful appearance. She does these things so well, too, is so gracious.

[*To M. V. B.*]   2, TILNEY STREET,
                                        MAY 15TH.

I must conclude my budget of news about the Edinburgh *Dalkeith.* visit, by telling you again about the dinner at Dalkeith. The Buccleuchs lent it to the King, and it was his Palace for the time being. Camps in the Park for the 17th Lancers and the Highlanders. The Duke and Duchess migrated to the Agent's House.

The house, Dalkeith, is not very large, but is fascinating, from its old-world look, and because of the beautiful and interesting things it contains. All dark oak, and fire-places in the 17th-century style put up by Anne—the wife of Monmouth. *His* pictures are too sweet—and there are splendid things—furniture, etc., given by Charles to his beautiful son.

The house and its contents seem to have grown together slowly, like forest trees, and the ensemble is perfect.

The King and Queen came in together, and after dinner we stood and talked until fairly late. The Queen stood the whole time. But he sat down, and beckoned to those he wished to speak to. The Restoration was planned in Dalkeith by Monk, *your* first Colonel of the Coldstream, in the dining-room in which we dined—so we drank to his memory, three Coldstream Officers, the King, Portland, and H. Legge, and I was asked to join in your honour!

At 12 we left and had a long drive home. I returned with old Sir Spencer Ponsonby, who told me many interesting stories about the early days of Queen Victoria's reign. He was present at her coronation. He remembered Conroy—the favourite of the Duchess of Kent. The Queen's household at Kensington used to be called the "Conroyal family." Ponsonby says he was a terrible man, a snob and an intriguer.

[*To H.M. the King.*]   ORCHARD LEA,
                                          MAY 21ST.

Roberts on the War Office.

Lord Esher presents his humble duty and begs to state that two days ago he was asked by Lord Roberts to call at the War Office, to hear the Commander-in-Chief's views upon certain questions upon which the Commission may report. In the course of conversation Lord Esher found it necessary to explain his own view of future War Office organisation, and he thinks Your Majesty may like to know that Lord Roberts seemed interested, and inclined to give the points careful consideration.

But it is certain that before any effective change is made in the administration of the War Department, very strong opposition will be encountered from the Sec. of State and from the Commander-in-Chief.

Esher on the War Office.

Your Majesty will have noticed the inclination so strong in that Department to consider questions of principle from a personal standpoint; and how difficult it is to get the functions of any particular Office carefully considered, apart from the person who happens at the particular moment to be occupying the post.

In framing a scheme for a Secretary of State for War in Council, no thought should be entertained of the particular Officer holding the Adjutant-Generalship, the Ordnance or even the Command of the Army. For these men must inevitably disappear in a few years' time, and their places be taken by men certainly of different temperament, possibly of inferior or superior abilities.

An organisation, to be sound and practical, should work

fairly, whatever the character of the men into whose hands it may temporarily fall. At times the Council of the Viceroy of India contains men of far higher capacity than at other times, yet even when controlled by men of moderate ability, the Government of India works well.

Under the present War Office Organisation, incapacity or weakness, or, on the other hand, overbearing obstinacy, on the part of any of the principal Heads of Branches, dislocates the machinery of war, and may readily produce disaster.

It is, for this reason, so important to obtain collective responsibility, and collective guidance, in the administration of the Army.

Under our Parliamentary system, it is necessary that a Parliamentarian should, as a Member of Your Majesty's Government, stand responsible to Parliament for the acts of the War Department. This practice obtains and works satisfactorily both as regards the Government of India, and the control of the Admiralty. But, the actual authority is vested, in both these cases, in a board or council. No one man, or two men, have supreme authority, except it be, on occasion, the Parliamentarian acting in the *name of the Cabinet*, and of Your Majesty. That is a reserve power, which it is necessary to retain, but which is not usually exercised in either of those Departments of State.

In the War Office, on the other hand, a dual Government prevails—dual government accompanied by jealousy, intrigue and mismanagement; the dual government of the Secretary of State and of the Commander-in-Chief.

Of all forms of administration, dual control is the most impossible to work. In the War Department, it has arisen accidentally, and without design.

The Commander-in-Chief is not a great historic office. It is of modern date. If George III had retained his faculties, it may safely be said that the Duke of York—who was first appointed "Senior General of the Staff," would never have assumed the title of Commander-in-Chief. But even after the death of the Duke of York, the Army was for years without a Commander-

Commander-in-Chief:
History
of the
Office.

in-Chief. That title was never borne by Lord Hill, or by Lord Amhurst, and until the Duke of Wellington closed his political career of office, remained in abeyance.

The analogy between the early years of the 19th century and the present time is not possible, because as Master-General of the Ordnance and Commander-in-Chief, the Duke of Welling-ton was a Minister of the Crown, a position altogether at variance with Your Majesty's ideas, or those of Your People at the present time.

Then came the long rule of the Duke of Cambridge, rule very admirable in many ways, but which would have been altogether impossible but for two conditions, first that a Lady occupied the throne, and secondly that the Duke was a Member of the Royal House.

The Queen's papers show that on many occasions the views of the Queen and those of the Duke of Cambridge came into sharp conflict; and it would be highly undesirable, and in some respects dangerous, if anyone hereafter were to hold the office of Commander-in-Chief, having the long experience and authority of the Duke of Cambridge, together with the much increased power which the Officer holding that post now enjoys. Your Majesty's proper influence, and that of Your responsible Ministers, would inevitably be checked by a man of headstrong temper occupying so unduly powerful a place, and this might lead—if such a man enjoyed the confidence of the Army—to conflicts damaging to the Monarchy and dangerous to the State.

From Lord Rosebery's speeches, from the tendency of certain writings in the Press, from whispers within the War Office itself, a desire appears to obtain, in many quarters, to enhance the authority of the Commander-in-Chief; whereas the fact that Your Majesty is the natural Head of the Army all over the world, and that the "General Officer Commanding the Troops in Great Britain," in a position similar to that now occupied by the Duke of Connaught in Ireland, is the natural and proper position for a senior General of the Army, appointed for five years (and *not* a Duke of Wellington or a Duke of Cambridge) appears to be lost sight of.

It is worth while to remember that the Hartington Commis- *The* sion, consisting of a very able body of men, recommended the *Hartington* abolition of the Commander-in-Chief. Sir Henry Campbell- *Commission.* Bannerman was the only member of the Commission who wished to leave the Administration of the War Office on its present footing.[1]

The recommendation of the Commission was not carried out, because the Queen, very naturally, at the end of her Majesty's long life and reign was unwilling to face the consideration of so great a change.

Furthermore, with a Lady on the Throne, the change was far more difficult to make. But under Your Majesty's rule to place a General Officer—not as Commander-in-Chief *in the field*, but of the whole Army in time of peace—is an anomaly, creating great difficulties in administration, and might become very easily a source not only of inconvenience to Your Majesty but of serious danger to the government of the Army.

Lord Esher has rather laboured this point, which in reality could be developed much more fully if it were not for fear of wearying Your Majesty, because he feels that the creation of an Army Board or Council, if it is to work satisfactorily, involves the abolition of the Office of Commander-in-Chief, as now constituted, and because he feels that the strongest pressure will be brought to bear from many quarters upon Your Majesty, to preserve an Office which in Lord Esher's humble judgment is certain to develop into a source of grave difficulty and danger.

[1] The Commission on National Defence, under the chairmanship of Lord Hartington, made its report in March 1890. The recommendations were drastic, but were much weakened in effect by the lack of unanimity in the Commission, a remarkable number of minority memoranda being appended. The account in the Annual Register for the year is very full and clear.

[*To M. V. B.*]   2, TILNEY STREET,
                                              MAY 22ND.

I saw the King this morning, and talked to him for over an
hour. He was in one of his best moods. Very clear and business-
like. No doubt Brodrick had impressed him by taking the very
unusual line that he was anxious to maintain the Royal
authority, by strengthening the position of the C.-in-C. This
was rather ingenious, for it impressed the King.

He asked me about the Bagdad railway, and said he thought
the Ministers had been weak, and had made a mistake. He
lamented Rosebery's vacillations; and no wonder, as he is alive
to the fact that His Ministers are worn out. Then we passed
to domestic matters.

[*To M. V. B.*]   2, TILNEY STREET,
                                              MAY 28TH.

I could not get away to the station last night to see you off.
The King and Queen did not leave the room until nearly half-
past twelve. It was a prettier court than the last. More pretty
people. The Prince of Wales looked well in a Highland uniform,
and there were lots of Princesses. Mrs. Avory was the beauty,
and she certainly is a very handsome woman. The other
women are furiously jealous already!

. . . I had an interesting short talk with Brodrick at the W.O.
about the two cardinal points of Army reform—and he was
much interested. I see the Duke of Connaught this morning.

[*To M. V. B.*]   WINDSOR CASTLE,
                                              MAY 30TH.

I had, yesterday, a long talk with the Duke of Connaught.
He was most sensible. I developed to him all the views on Army
reform, which you know so well; and as they must have been

startling to him it was remarkable how quickly he grasped their import, and how open minded he showed himself to be.

[*To M. V. B.*]   ORCHARD LEA,
                                              JUNE 2ND.

The ordinary routine began again to-day—but London is a desert. No carriages, not a soul in the streets, and blinds down everywhere.

I got back early, and went to my rooms in the Augusta Tower.[1] No news—I came home, had a hot bath, and lay on *On* the sofa in the Malmaison room, and read the life of Michael *Michael* Angelo. It contains some extraordinary things. His sonnets *Angelo.* and poems, and curious love letters to people he loved.

. . . Through his long life, he never swerved from the simple love of beautiful things, beautiful people and beautiful thoughts. This love of beauty found expression, not only in verses, but in marble and on canvas. In that he was fortunate. The limitations are so great if one possesses only the one medium.

[*To M. V. B.*]   2, TILNEY STREET,
                                              JUNE 9TH.

. . . I had an hour with Brodrick, who was rather frightened *Brodrick* of my proposals. Interested, but too timid to tackle the C.-in-C. *on War* I think I made an impression. He complained of the Adj.-Gen., *Office* and of the other senior officers in the W.O., but he does not *tion.* *Reorganisa-* recognise that the only chance of enforcing loyalty is to get these gentlemen on a Council where they must acquiesce or resign!

Meanwhile there are the most awful rows going on within *Division* the Government; and it looks as if they might break up. *in the* Chamberlain might resign, or Ritchie and the Duke of Devon- *Govern-* *ment.*

---

[1] At Windsor Castle.

shire (who are free traders) might go. A. Balfour saw the King
yesterday, and did not seem very hopeful of being able to keep
his team together.

. . . Nellie and I went to see the "School Girl." It is improv-
ing. Two good new songs in it. And a new girl. American—
quite attractive. That girl with big eyes[1] whom we noticed is
still the prettiest there, I think. However, it is quite a pretty
show!

[*To M. V. B.*]   WINDSOR CASTLE,
                                    EVENING, JUNE 9TH.

I forgot to tell you, that in a box close to our seats at the
theatre last night, was Phyllis Dare, with her family, including
Zena, who is not really so good looking. They were all very
smart.

. . . The War Commission sits to-morrow, and I fancy we
shall continue our sittings on Thursday. However, I hope for
the best. Much will depend on whether I have a very heavy
fight over certain paragraphs of the Report. I have told the
King the views of the Head Master, but have not yet heard from
him. Probably it is a disappointment not being able to go to
Eton[2] as I think he was looking forward to the spree. Possibly
he may propose to go after all.

[*To M. V. B.*]   2, TILNEY STREET,
                                         JUNE 10TH.

I lunched with Millie [Duchess of Sutherland] to-day—and a
long talk afterwards. She came to the Rothschild party to-
night, and looked tired, and not near so well as this morning.
Still, she created quite a sensation, as all people do who go out
very little. All the Royalties were there to-night and stayed very

---

[1] Miss Gladys Cooper.
[2] Owing to a disastrous fire at one of the Houses.

late. It is now a quarter past two. We got through the first part
of our report at the War Commission to-day. No acrimonious
disputes so far. The King told me that he had met the Head
Master when he was driving, and had spoken to him, and that
Warre burst into tears. The Eton visit is definitely postponed.

I had a talk with Mrs. Chamberlain who was in great form. *Chamberlain*
She says Joe will not speak at present for fear of provoking more *and the*
disunion. This *pax* I don't think can be continued, it is hardly *Govern-*
practical. The Duke of Devonshire very nearly left the Govern- *ment.*
ment. They will break up this year. There is very little doubt
of it.

[*To M. V. B.*]   ORCHARD LEA,
                                   JUNE 22ND.

If you had not been with me, all the glories of the ball at *Ball at*
Windsor would have lost their charm.[1] As it is, the whole *Windsor.*
scene, from the entry of the King and Queen, to their departure,
with the really beautiful sight in St. George's Hall, was a perfect
success. I doubt whether any entertainment of the kind, which
was not a state function, but a private party given by a sovereign,
could surpass it in beauty and splendour.

The Windsor uniforms look so well, and add to the decora-
tion very materially. Millie [Duchess of Sutherland], although
she looked tired, made a brave show. Did you not think so?
Very few people looked better. I am not sure that anyone did.
On the whole the Ascot party has gone off well, and there has
been no row. I am sure this is rare in every house where people
live together for a week. No wonder Guy Laking found the
King, and everybody else, rather short in their temper to-day.

[*To M. V. B.*]   2, TILNEY STREET,
                                   JUNE 23RD.

You have no idea how nice the King was yesterday—very
profuse in thanks for nothing I can remember doing. He was

[1] A ball at Windsor Castle, for which nearly 1000 invitations were issued.

much pleased with his ball, but not pleased with the critics! As he truly said, nothing of the kind has been done for 60 years. Everyone worked very hard, and a lapse or two was inevitable. This hardly justifies remarks by people who ought only to have been too thankful to be there.

He asked me to see Cambon and to try and arrange a visit for the President of the Republic to Windsor on the *morning* of the Review. Cambon was delighted, as he had been regretting that the Windsor visit was off. He says the President rises at dawn, so that an early start is quite easy to manage, but *déjeuner* will be wanted at Windsor! *That* may be a difficulty as the King will not be there.

I wish you could have met Loubet. As the Review is in the afternoon—you would have lots of time to get to Aldershot.... The Gala Opera would be the most amusing of the two, because it is such a lovely *spectacle*.

[*To M. V. B.*]   WEST DEAN PARK,
                                                JUNE 28TH.

The journey down was hot—very hot. The King was playing cards in the garden near the house, and played indefatigably from five until after eight.

The house has been practically built by Willie James, and is a great success. Every luxury you can imagine, and yet no appearance of over-smartness. The gardens are shady, and the trees splendid.

After dinner there were three parties of bridge, but the rest sat out without hats or coats until nearly one in the morning. It is rare to be able to do this. Quite late the King came out, and sent for his dog Jack, and we sat another half hour, and went to bed at 1.30.

Evie [James] is such a little dear, that it reconciles me to the visit. Also Molly Sneyd is here. There are no bores. Johnny

Ward, Howe, Soveral, all men I like—so that I shall exist until
to-morrow.

. . . *Such* a fuss is going on about the Loubet arrangements,
the Review particularly.

[*To M. V. B.*]   WEST DEAN PARK,
                                                 JUNE 29TH.

We had a very peaceful Sunday. A motor drive in the afternoon. Rather too much dust—and then a quiet time in the
garden. . . .

The King goes to bed as late as he can, but is up before 8 and
works away until 10—when we breakfast. He never seems to
require rest. Of course, he gets through a great deal of work,
as he *never* leaves over anything until next day. All papers and
letters of the day are dealt with within 24 hours.

He gave a medal last night to Willie James' butler who has
been 21 years in the service of the family and has received the
King four times here. The man was delighted and delivered
the most pompous explanation of the King's motives—as if he
were replying to a vote of thanks!

We leave here by special train at 11.30 and I shall be back in
London by one, where I expect to hear from you where you
are to be found.

We have had a great deal of "rag" about Loubet's visit. The
King inventing absurd speeches for Howe who is in attendance
on the President—and who is not a *first-rate* linguist.

[*To M. V. B.*]   ORCHARD LEA,
                                                 JULY 1ST.

I had no chance to tell you the only bit of news. I saw Aunt
Adele[1] this morning. She goes to-morrow to Devonshire,

---

[1] Miss Gurwood.

summoned to Aunt Zumala's deathbed. Aunt Adele was very sweet and kind to me. A nicer woman never lived, and for that reason she never found a husband! So all her pent-up devotion has been poured out on us. Her sister tried her always very high, but she has shown unwearied kindness and generosity. The final parting, even from one who has often jarred but whose existence is our earliest memory, cannot fail to strain the heart strings.

Aunt Adele is one of the few of whom I would ask a favour, and be sure of a response. There are not many such.

[*To M. V. B.*]   ORCHARD LEA,
                                                            JULY 3RD.

On Shelley's Death—

On the way to Bedford Square, in a shop window, there is a French picture of Shelley's funeral pyre. It is not very accurate, in detail, if Trelawney's account is true, but most pathetic and striking. A grey sea, and the sandy shore of the Gulf of Spezzia. A low pyre is half burnt away, and the smoke drifts seawards. Shelley's face and grave-worn clothes just appear, while Byron and Hunt, in cloaks blown by the wind, stand moodily near the pyre. The soldiers are in the background, and I think the travelling carriage. It is all very vivid and sad. If I remember right, the day was not windy, nor the sea grey. It was so hot that Byron swam out to his yacht, and only Trelawney gathered up the ashes. Do you remember the solitary bird that hovered over the scene? Do you remember also how Shelley's body was recognised? By the *Sophocles* in one pocket and *Keats* in the other. Both volumes were burned with him! Some of his ashes were placed by his wife in the volume of *Adonais*, which was printed in Italy, and which she carried about with her until her death. However, all this is beside the mark—but I should like you to see the picture. It is not well painted, but it is a picture for poetic minds to feast upon. How it came into so dreary a locality, is queer. I cannot imagine why I tell you all this.

. . . Tennyson died with his hand on the open page of *King* —*Compared*
Lear. Shelley with his favourite copy of *Keats* in his pocket. *with*
Tennyson
One sank calmly to sleep in the moonlight. The other equally *and*
calmly beneath the Italian waves. Pleasant deaths, both, and *Byron.*
worthy. Perhaps Byron's ending was the noblest. It sanctified
all his failures. History is such a lying jade. No man has been
more traduced living or dead. Some day perhaps justice will
be done to him.

[*To M. V. B.*]　　　　　　　2, TILNEY STREET,
　　　　　　　　　　　　　　　　JULY 10TH.

After the fatigue of the week, I look forward to the O. Lea *The*
garden to-night. Only you will not be there. The Frenchmen *French*
President
seem to have left profoundly impressed by their reception. *at*
Loubet thought it would be good, but not so spontaneous and *Windsor.*
enthusiastic as it was. They admired the troops and they enjoyed
Windsor. Personally, I liked the trip to Windsor—but I was
too tired to enjoy the Ball. Even your presence did not lighten
the weariness of standing about.

To-morrow the King goes to Eastbourne, to meet Joe at the
Duke of Devonshire's. A curious combination. The King is at
present Chamberlainite! He has asked me for a private copy of
the Report that he may read it during his Irish visit.

. . . On the 22nd there is to be a visit of French senators to
Windsor, about 100 of them—and they are to be entertained.
Will you come and help me, and talk French? After that I
think the functions of the year will be at an end.

[*To H.M. the King.*]　　　　　2, TILNEY STREET,
　　　　　　　　　　　　　　　　JULY 11TH.

Lord Esher presents his humble duty and begs to inform Your *The South*
African
Majesty that the Report of the S.A. War Commission was *Report*
signed by all Your Majesty's Commissioners on Thursday last. *Finished.*

The document has been considerably strengthened in its final stages—and summarises very fairly the mass of evidence. The first part deals with the preparations for the War, and the inevitable conclusion drawn is, Lord Esher regrets to say, not favourable to the late Commander-in-Chief, and not wholly favourable to Your Majesty's Ministers. In language which will not be found indecorous nor discourteous, this conclusion has been made painfully clear. The Commissioners have avoided, properly as Your Majesty will doubtless think, attempting to criticise the military operations. They have stated fairly the facts, and the diverse opinions held by the conflicting military authorities, leaving the final judgment to the reader.

Lord Esher will not conceal from Your Majesty that he would have preferred if upon many questions which have arisen during this enquiry, a clearer judgment had been formed by the Commissioners, but the reluctance to do this was so great that it was not to be overcome.

Under these circumstances he concentrated his efforts to obtain an expression of opinion in favour of a War Office Council properly established by Your Majesty's Order, and to this the Commission has agreed.

The Minority Report.

Still, Lord Esher has found it necessary to write a separate note, appended to the Report, dealing with this question rather fully, together with the question of the position of a Commander-in-Chief in the future, his views upon which are known to Your Majesty. To this note Sir George Goldie and Sir John Jackson have subscribed.

Sir George Goldie has also appended a note upon a most interesting point, that of "compulsory national military education," and has expressed views with which Lord Esher is in cordial agreement.

Value of the Report and Evidence.

The Report and the Evidence will be ready for submission to Your Majesty, and for publication, in about three weeks' time. Lord Esher is strongly of opinion that if the Report of the Hartington Commission had been seriously considered by the

Government, and had been acted upon, thousands of lives, and an expenditure of 100 millions, would have been saved. But Your Majesty well knows that Royal Commissions are, as a rule, the expedient employed by politicians to relegate awkward and difficult questions to the official pigeon hole.

It would require, therefore, a more sanguine temperament than Lord Esher possesses, to hope that this Report will fare better than its predecessor.

Whatever judgment may be pronounced upon the Report, there can be no difference of opinion upon the great value of the evidence taken, most of which will be published.

It will be found to contain a digest of the most varied and highly qualified military opinion upon almost every question which concerns Your Majesty's Army, and cannot fail, if properly studied, to be of the greatest use to those who have the welfare of the soldiers and of the military profession at heart.

If the Members of the Defence Committee, and the officials of the War Office, will take advantage of this evidence, then Your Majesty may rest assured that the labours of the Commission will not have altogether been in vain.

The publication of the Report was not expected to have political consequences of much importance, and in fact the history of Parliaments was almost unaffected by it. There was a storm of indignation in the press; there was even a movement for the impeachment of Lord Lansdowne. Then the wind dropped with equal suddenness.

The Report was quoted at bye-elections, and may have had some effect there; but for the most part it was overshadowed by the new-born Tariff Reform controversy and the resistance to the Education Act. Outside of Parliament and the politics of parties the Report had an immediate consequence in the work of the Esher Committee on War Office reform, which sat, not to enquire but to do the actual work of reorganisation.

END OF VOL. I.

NOTE ON THE INDEX

This index includes a certain number of very broad headings designed to enable a reader to follow a single topic right through the book. They are distinguished typographically, being printed in large capitals.

These are the general heads included:

THE ARMY
BOOKS AND AUTHORS
CAREER
CONSTITUTIONAL ISSUES
THE CROWN
FOREIGN AFFAIRS
THE GOVERNMENT
MEDITATIONS
OFFICE OF WORKS—Official Duties

THE PARTIES
PERSONALITIES
PLAYS AND PLAYERS
POLITICAL THEORY
THE PRESS
THE ROYAL FAMILY
SCOTLAND
SOCIAL EVENTS AND CHANGES

Under CROWN are the official acts of the sovereign in political affairs: the entries under ROYAL FAMILY are of a more personal nature. The entries under GOVERNMENT refer to the concerted official acts of both Parties: those under PARTIES to their internal affairs. Under the heading PERSONALITIES are the fuller estimates of a character, the minor references being arranged under the name of the person in the usual way.

(The letters a, b, etc., refer to the items on each page, whether complete on that page or not.)

INDEX

VICIMUS